The Greenwood Encyclopedia of
Global Medieval
Life and Culture

The Greenwood Encyclopedia of Global Medieval Life and Culture

Volume 2
AFRICA AND THE MIDDLE EAST

Joyce E. Salisbury, General Editor

Victoria B. Tashjian, Africa
James E. Lindsay, North Africa and the Middle East

GREENWOOD PRESS
Westport, Connecticut · London

Library of Congress Cataloging-in-Publication Data

The Greenwood encyclopedia of global Medieval life and culture / Joyce E. Salisbury, general editor.

    p. cm.

  Includes bibliographical references and index.

  ISBN 978–0–313–33801–4 ((set) : alk. paper) — ISBN 978–0–313–33802–1 ((vol. 1) : alk. paper) — ISBN 978–0–313–33803–8 ((vol. 2) : alk. paper) — ISBN 978–0–313–33804–5 ((vol. 3) : alk. paper)

  1. Civilization, Medieval.   I. Salisbury, Joyce E.

CB351.G743   2009

940.1 — dc22   2008036709

British Library Cataloguing in Publication Data is available.

Library of Congress Catalog Card Number: 2008036709

ISBN: 978–0–313–33801–4 (set)
      978–0–313–33802–1 (vol. 1)
      978–0–313–33803–8 (vol. 2)
      978–0–313–33804–5 (vol. 3)

First published in 2009

Greenwood Press, 88 Post Road West, Westport, CT 06881

An imprint of Greenwood Publishing Group, Inc.

www.greenwood.com

Printed in the United States of America

The paper used in this book complies with the Permanent Paper Standard issued by the National Information Standards Organization (Z39.48–1984).

10 9 8 7 6 5 4 3 2 1

The publisher has done its best to make sure the instructions and/or recipes in this book are correct. However, users should apply judgment and experience when preparing recipes, especially parents and teachers working with young people. The publisher accepts no responsibility for the outcome of any recipe included in this volume.

Contents

VOLUME 2

VOLUME 3

Preface for Users of Global Medieval Life and Culture

Two concepts have dominated the twenty-first century: globalization and the information explosion facilitated by the Internet. When we decided to present a new history of the medieval world—also called the Middle Ages—we knew these modern principles could help guide us to new insights into the past. In these volumes, globalization shapes the content that we have chosen to cover, and the electronic age has guided our organization. In addition, the features are carefully considered to make these volumes engaging and pedagogically useful.

Global Content

The medieval age was a European concept. From about the fourteenth century, Europeans defined the 1,000 years from the fall of the Roman Empire to the Renaissance as the "middle," separating the classical world from the "modern" one. Practically from the time of this designation, scholars have argued about whether this periodization makes sense, but scholarly arguments have not substantially changed the designation. Textbooks and curricula have kept the period as a separate entity, and we study the medieval world that extends from about 400 to 1400 C.E. with undiminished fascination.

Scholars of medieval Europe have shown that, during this formative period, many of the ideas and institutions developed that shape our modern world. The rise of democratic institutions, a prosperous middle class, and a vibrant Christianity are just a few of the developments that marked medieval Europe. These are some of the reasons that have kept the field of study vibrant. But what of the world?

Scholarship has disproved the Eurocentric analysis that defined the period of the Middle Ages. Exciting innovations took place all over the world during this pivotal millennium. Religious movements such as the rise of Islam and the spread of Buddhism irrevocably shaped much of the world, innovations in transportation allowed people to settle islands throughout the Pacific, and agricultural improvements stimulated empires in South America.

Furthermore, these societies did not develop in isolation. Most people remember Marco Polo's visit to the China of the Yuan Dynasty, but his voyage was not an exception. People, goods, and ideas spread all across the Eurasian land mass and down into Africa. This encyclopedia traces the global connections that fueled the worldwide developments of the Middle Ages.

To emphasize the global quality of this reference work, we have organized the volumes by regions. Volume 1 covers Europe and the Americas. We begin with Europe because this was the region that first defined the medieval world. At first glance, linking Europe with the Americas (which were not colonized until after the Middle Ages) might seem to join the most disparate of regions. However, we do so to remind us that Vikings crossed the North Atlantic in the Middle Ages to discover this rich new land, which was already inhabited by prosperous indigenous peoples. The organization of this first volume demonstrates that Europe never developed in isolation!

Volume 2 considers the Middle East and Africa. These regions saw the growth of Islam and the vibrant interactions that took place in the diverse continent of Africa. Volume 3 takes on the enormous task of focusing on South Asia, East Asia, and Oceania.

This organization forces us to compromise on some content. Because we are not taking a chronological approach, we must collapse 1,000 years of history in regions that had many diverse developments. We partially address this issue in the Historical Overviews at the beginning of each section. These essays will point readers to the varied historical events of the regions.

However, we gain modern insights through our on Global Ties essays within each section. These essays offer a great contrast with other medieval works because they show the significance of global connections throughout this millennium. Readers will learn that globalization was not invented in the twenty-first century. Indeed, the great developments of the past flourished because people from diverse cultures communicated with each other. Perhaps this was the greatest contribution of the Middle Ages, and this encyclopedia highlights it.

Organization for the Internet Age

The Internet brings an astonishing amount of information to us with a quick search. If we Google Marco Polo, castles, or windmills, we are given an immediate array of information more quickly than we could have imagined a mere decade ago. However, as teachers too readily realize when reading the results of such searches, this is not enough. The very volume of information sometimes makes it hard to see how these disparate elements of the past fit together and how they compare with other elements. We have organized this encyclopedia to address these issues.

Each volume contains two or three regions of the world, and each region includes seven in-depth essays that cover the following topics:

1. Historical Overview
2. Religion
3. Economy
4. The Arts
5. Society
6. Science and Technology
7. Global Ties

These essays provide coherent descriptions of each part of the world. They allow readers readily to compare developments in different regions, so one can really understand how the economy in Africa differed from mercantile patterns in China. In-depth essays like this not only provide clear information but model historical writing. But there is more.

Like other good encyclopedias, we have A–Z entries offering in-depth information on many topics—from the general (food, money, law) to the specific (people, events, and places). All the essays indicate the A–Z entries in bold, much as an online essay might have hyperlinks to more detailed information, so readers can immediately see what topics offer more in-depth information and how each fits in with the larger narrative. In the same way, readers who begin with the A–Z entries know that they can see how their topic fits in a larger picture by consulting the in-depth essays. Finally, this integration of essays with A–Z entries provides an easy way to do crosscultural comparisons. Readers can compare roles of women in Islam and Asia, then see how women fit in the larger context of society by consulting the two larger essays.

This is a reference work that builds on the rapid information accessible online while doing what books do best: offer a thoughtful integration of knowledge. We have enhanced what we hope is a useful organization by adding a number of special features designed to help the readers learn as much as possible about the medieval millennium.

Features

- *Primary Documents*. In this information age it is easy to forget that historians find out about the past primarily by reading the written voices left by the ancients. To keep this recognition of the interpretive nature of the past, we have included primary documents for all regions of the world. These short works are designed to engage readers by bringing the past to life, and all have head notes and cross-references to help readers put the documents in context.
- *Chronologies*. The chronologies will help readers quickly identify key events in a particular region during the medieval period.
- *Maps*. History and geography are inextricably linked, and no more so than in a global encyclopedia. The maps throughout the text will help readers locate the medieval world in space as well as time.
- *Illustrations*. All the illustrations are chosen to be historical evidence not ornamentation. All are drawn from medieval sources to show the Middle Ages as the people at the time saw themselves. The captions encourage readers to analyze the content of the images.
- *Complete Index*. The key to gathering information in the twenty-first century is the ability to rapidly locate topics of interest. We have recognized this with the A–Z entries linked to the essays and the extensive cross-referencing. However, nothing can replace a good index, so we have made sure there is a complete and cumulative index that links the information among the volumes.
- *Bibliographies*. Each of the long essays contains a list of recommended readings. These readings will not only offer more information to those interested in following up on the topic but also will serve as further information for the A–Z entries highlighted within the essays. This approach furthers our desire to integrate the information we are presenting.
- *Appendixes*. The appendixes provide basic factual information, such as important regional dynasties or time period designations.

The Greenwood Encyclopedia of Global Medieval Life and Culture has been a satisfying project to present. In over 30 years of research and study of the Middle Ages, we have never lost the thrill of exploring a culture that's so different from our own, yet was formative in creating who we have become. Furthermore, we are delighted to present this age in its global context, because then as now (indeed throughout history) globalization has shaped the growth of culture. In this information age, it is good to remember that we have always lived linked together on spaceship earth. We all hope readers will share our enthusiasm for this millennium.

AFRICA

Victoria B. Tashjian

Chronology

c. 9th–10th centuries	Igbo-Ukwu cast metal sculptures produced in Igboland, to the east of the lower Niger River
	Berbers adopt Islam
9th–11th centuries	The city of Jenné-jeno, which emerged in the Inland Niger Delta around 200 B.C.E., at its apogee
c. 10th century	Kanem emerges in the lands lying north and east of Lake Chad
	Al-Azhar University founded in Cairo
969	Cairo founded by the Fatimids
Late 1st millennium	Yoruba states emerge in the lands lying west of the lower Niger River
Early 2nd millennium	State of Benin emerges in the lands lying west of the lower Niger River and becomes an empire in midfifteenth century
	Tuareg Berbers found Timbuktu on the desert–sahel border above the Niger Bend
11th century	First identification of Takrur, an early West African state located along the Senegal River, in writings by Muslim visitors
	Mapungubwe emerges on the Zimbabwe Plateau
11th–12th centuries	Almoravid Movement expands its control from its place of origin in the western Sahara to the North African Maghrib and Muslim Spain
c. 11th–15th centuries	Yoruba cast metal and terra-cotta sculptures produced
c. 11th–16th centuries	Construction of Benin earthworks
1068	Al-Bakri writes history of the western Sudan
12th–13th centuries	Zagwe dynasty's rock-hewn churches carved out of living rock at Lalibela
	Almohad Movement supplants the Almoravids
1137	Zagwe dynasty emerges in the Ethiopian Highlands
13th century	Zimbabwe emerges on the Zimbabwe Plateau
13th–14th centuries	Stone wall enclosures constructed at Great Zimbabwe
c. 1200–1500	Swahili city-states at their peak
c. 1203	The Soso sack Kumbi Saleh, hastening the decline of Ghana
c. 1205	Birth of Sundjata, founder and first ruler of the West African empire Mali
c. 1235	Mali emerges under the leadership of Sundjata following the defeat of the Soso at the Battle of Kirina
1255	Death of Sundjata
1270	Solomonid dynasty emerges in the Ethiopian Highlands
14th century	Kongo kingdom emerges in Central Africa
	First Luba kingdom emerges in Central Africa
	Construction of Sankoré Mosque and University, Timbuktu
	Kilwa rises to prominence as the wealthiest Swahili city

	Construction of Husuni Kibwa (a palace), Kilwa
14th–15th centuries	Construction of the Great Mosque, Kilwa
14th–16th centuries	The Beta Israel of the Ethiopian Highlands embrace an "Isra-elite" identity
1312–1337	Reign of Mansa Musa of Mali
1324–1325	Mansa Musa's pilgrimage to Mecca
1331	The great medieval traveler Ibn Battuta visits East Africa's Swahili coast
1352–1353	Ibn Battuta visits Mali
1375	Catalan Atlas, famed European map of Africa, created by Abraham Cresques
c. 15th century	Emergence of Mutapa and Torwa states, successors to Zimbabwe
	Walled Hausa city-states appear in the grasslands of to-day's northern Nigeria and southern Niger
c. 1400	First Akan state, Bono, appears in the savannah-forest fringe of West Africa
	Saifawa rulers of Kanem move their capital to Bornu, in the lands to the south and west of Lake Chad
1433	Tuarag Berbers seize Timbuktu from Mali
1464–1492	Reign of Sonni Ali, who transforms Songhai into a powerful empire
1468	Sonni Ali takes Timbuktu from the Tuareg Berbers
1473	Sonni Ali conquers Jenné-jeno
c. 1490	Massacre of Jews of the Saharan oasis of Tuat
1492	Jews expelled from Spain, increasing Jewish populations in North Africa and some Saharan oases
1493–1528	Reign of Askiya Muhammad of Songhai, founder of the Askiya dynasty
1591	Sultan of Morocco sends across the Sahara troops that de-feat Songhai

Timeline of Sub-Saharan African Medieval States

Aksum	1st century C.E.-long decline begins 7th century
Ghana	c. 4th–13th centuries
Christian Nubia	6th–15th centuries
Swahili City-States	c. 9th–16th centuries
Songhai	c. 9th century–1591
Kanem-Bornu	c. 10th–19th centuries

Yoruba States	late 1st millennium on
Takrur	?–13th century
Mapungubwe	11th–13th centuries
Zagwe dynasty	12th century–1270
Benin	early 2nd millennium–19th century
Mali	c. 1235–15th century
Zimbabwe	13th–15th centuries
Solomonid dynasty (Ethiopia)	1270–1974
Kongo	14th–18th centuries
Luba	14th–19th centuries
Hausa City-States	c. 15th–19th centuries

Trans-Saharan Trade

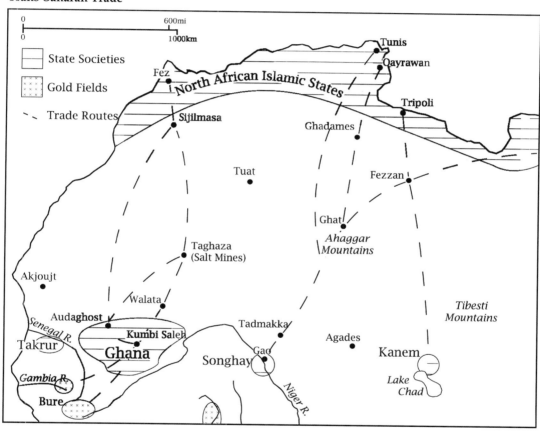

Mali Empire

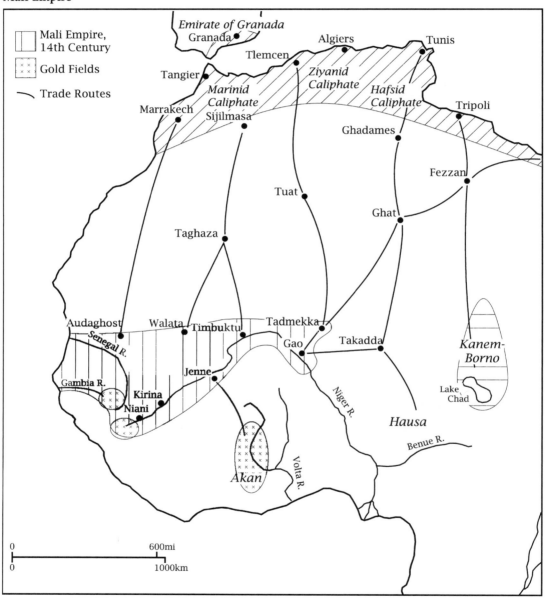

Mali Empire, 14th Century

Gold Fields

Trade Routes

Emirate of Granada
Granada
Algiers
Tunis
Tlemcen
Tangier
Ziyanid Caliphate
Marinid Caliphate
Hafsid Caliphate
Tripoli
Marrakech
Sijilmasa
Ghadames
Fezzan
Tuat
Ghat
Taghaza
Audaghost
Walata
Timbuktu
Tadmekka
Takadda
Kanem-Borno
Senegal R.
Gao
Gambia R.
Jenne
Kirina
Niani
Niger R.
Hausa
Lake Chad
Akan
Volta R.
Benue R.

0   600mi
0   1000km

Rise and Fall of Songhay

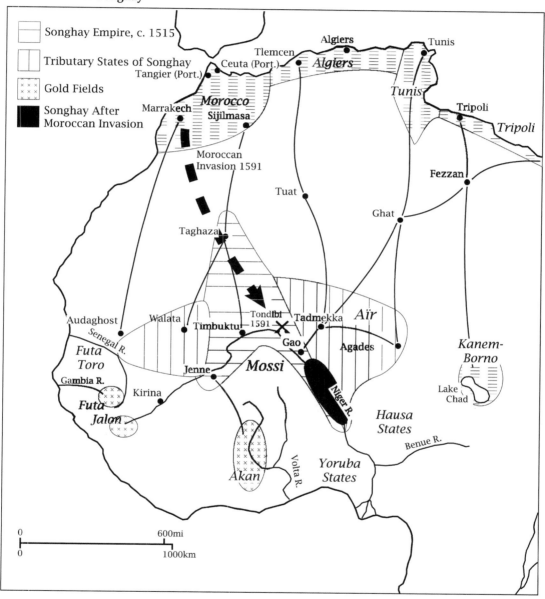

Songhay Empire, c. 1515

Tributary States of Songhay

Gold Fields

Songhay After Moroccan Invasion

Algiers

Tunis

Tlemcen
Ceuta (Port.)
Tangier (Port.)

Algiers

Tunis

Tripoli

Tripoli

Marrakech

Morocco
Sijilmasa

Moroccan
Invasion 1591

Fezzan

Tuat

Ghat

Taghaza

Audaghost

Walata

Senegal R.

Tondibi
1591
Timbuktu

Tadmekka

Aïr

Futa
Toro

Gambia R.

Kirina

Jenne

Gao

Agades

Kanem-
Borno

Futa
Jalon

Mossi

Niger R.

Lake
Chad

Hausa
States

Akan

Volta R.

Yoruba
States

Benue R.

0   600mi

0   1000km

Swahili States

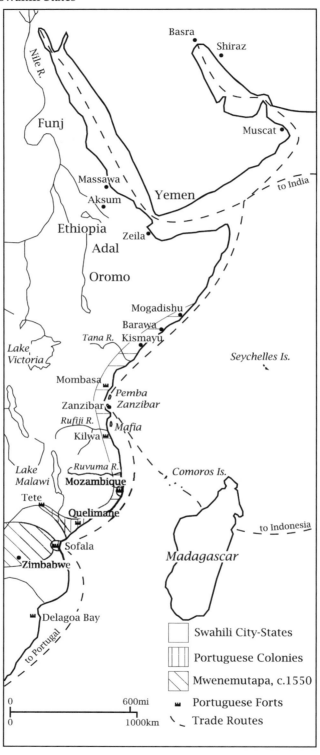

Overview and Topical Essays

1. HISTORICAL OVERVIEW

This essay first explores the problems inherent in applying the framework of the medieval period to Africa. An overview of key events in African history during the centuries from 400 to 1400 C.E. follows. An introduction to the physical geography of this large continent, highlighting its great diversity, comes next and includes discussion of ecological zones, major mountains and rivers, environmental change, key weather systems, and disease. The following section addressing methodology considers the range of sources consulted by the interdisciplinary scholars of the African past, assesses their strengths and limitations, and concludes with a discussion of the scope and organization of this work. This essay and those that follow it demonstrate that there is much we know about Africa in the medieval centuries, and that the picture which emerges is of a vibrant continent whose inhabitants engineered ongoing and constantly evolving innovations in social institutions, religion, governance, technology, productive activities, artistic expression, and commerce, in the process engaging in extensive interactions with others on the continent and outside its borders.

Was There a Medieval Period in Africa?

This may seem an odd question to pose for an encyclopedia of global medieval life and culture. However, the idea of a medieval era derives from the history of a different continent, Europe, whose scholars have long identified the period from approximately 400 to 1450 C.E. as a time that can be differentiated in meaningful ways from what came before and after. Historians of Europe distinguish the medieval period from the earlier Classical Age by the fall of the Western Roman Empire in the fifth century C.E. On the other end of the spectrum, the medieval period segues into the modern age in the fifteenth century (many would add a bit earlier for Italy) as a result of two things. First, the intellectual movement known as the Renaissance led to new ways of understanding and portraying the human condition and the natural world as a result of scientific, cultural, and artistic developments including a passionate reembrace of the intellectual achievements of the now-distant Classical Age, whose surviving texts—a number of which had, in a neat example of global interconnections, been kept alive by Arab intellectuals—began to be studied again and interpreted anew. Renaissance thinkers, known as humanists, valued reason over faith, the secular over the religious, and championed the rights of the individual. Second, the age of European global exploration, ushered in by advances in maritime and navigational technologies—some once again reintroduced to Europe from the Arab world—first mastered among Europeans by fifteenth-century Portuguese mariners, opened the world's oceans and from thence their bordering lands to European exploration and, eventually, commerce and in many cases conquest, events that profoundly changed the shape and trajectory of the history of the modern age not only for Europeans, but for people around the globe.

Are these demarcators in any way relevant to Africa? To take the onset of what has been labeled "medieval" for Europe, it is the case that since the Roman Empire acquired territories all along the North African coast after conquering and destroying the prominent Phoenician-founded city of Carthage in 146 B.C.E., and also controlled lands far up the Nile into **Egypt**, Roman affairs do impinge upon the history of at least this portion of Africa. But on the other hand, the fall of the Western Roman Empire that concluded Europe's Classical Age is not what ushered in epoch-making changes even for the very limited portions of the African continent affected by Roman overrule. Instead, it was the arrival in North Africa of Muslim Arabs in seventh- and eighth-century waves of conquest that marked the onset of a new era in this region.

There is more substantial overlap between Europe and Africa when the end date of European medievalism is considered. It is the case that the onset of the European age of exploration that was in part responsible for drawing the medieval period to a close ushered in new developments for Africa. Indeed, the earliest Portuguese voyages of Atlantic exploration were made in a southerly direction, down the western coastline of Africa, with stops off the coasts of what are today Senegal, Sierra Leone, and **Ghana** during the 1440s to 1470s. Exploration continued, with Bartolomeu Dias rounding the Cape of Good Hope at the southern tip of Africa in 1488 followed by the famed navigator Vasco de Gama, who continued up East Africa's Indian Ocean seaboard in 1497 to 1498.

The arrival of Europeans on Africa's coastlines had profound ramifications for the continent. Africans and Europeans developed extensive new trade relations in which Africans exported **gold**, ivory, and a host of raw goods destined for transformation into manufactured goods in Europe's burgeoning factories, while Europeans exported guns, cloth, metal wares, and a variety of other manufactured goods to African consumers. This new Atlantic-based trade affected Africa deeply, providing new markets and greatly increased demand for Africa's commodities, creating new commercial venues for enterprising individuals who seized with alacrity and often great business acumen the new opportunities stemming from trade with Europeans, redirecting long-distance trade, for example to the Atlantic coasts at the expense of older trans-Saharan routes, greatly increasing the amount of iron available to Africans, and undermining the production of certain African commodities such as cloth that were replaced by less costly European imports. The slave trade, which eventually (and postmedievally) followed, changed life irrevocably for those who lost their freedom, and in too many cases their very lives, to the brutal institution of chattel slavery in the Americas. It must be remarked that the values of the Renaissance, the second event held to mark the end of the medieval period in Europe, were not taken by many Europeans to apply to Africa and Africans, as can be seen in the fact that the slave trade and colonial conquest that followed were marked by a crude and all-consuming racism that denied African people, at least in the minds of most "modern" Europeans, their humanity.

Yet when considering these changes it is important to remember that with very few exceptions Europeans did not venture into the interior of sub-Saharan Africa until 400 years after the age of exploration began but were instead limited to Africa's coastlines as a result of tropical diseases for which Europeans lacked immunity and African military resistance. For the first four centuries of what has been termed "postmedieval" for Europe, then, a majority of Africans had no direct contact with Europeans, and the impact Europeans had on the continent was highly uneven.

If the notion of a medieval Africa thus has some limited meaning but is also deeply, perhaps fatally, flawed, how else have the continent's chroniclers periodized its history? Historians of Africa, like historians of Europe with their delineations of classical, medieval, and modern ages, have sometimes utilized a very broad tripartite understanding of the continent's history, dividing Africa's past into precolonial, colonial, and postcolonial eras. However, this approach has fallen out of favor today, collapsing as it does the entire long, complex human history of a vast continent up to the nineteenth century into one unwieldy whole that in no way does justice to the complexities and diversities of Africa's past; privileging the brief period of European conquest in a problematically Eurocentric fashion; and ignoring the many continuities that bound precolonial to colonial Africa, and link the postcolonial era to what preceded it.

No standard way of periodizing African history of the past 3,000 years has followed: A perusal of textbooks shows that authors choose approaches to covering the African past as varied as moving from region to region, state to state, and ethnicity to ethnicity. Alternately, some break this part of the continent's history down into chunks that are centuries or even millennia long, with great variation between authors in the points at which one era ends and another begins. Others highlight innovations in production and technology; for example, a very common demarcator of a new era in African history is the transition to an iron age, a development associated with a host of society-shaking outcomes.

Thus there are correspondences as well as disjunctures, legitimations as well as illogicalities, associated with applying to Africa or indeed to any non-European part of the world the notion of a "medieval" period defined by events central to European history. Nevertheless, there is tremendous value in studying what was occurring in Africa during the vibrant centuries from 400 to 1400. This remains a history unfortunately all too often unknown outside the relatively small group of Africanist specialists, a history that it is hoped will be made at least in broad outline accessible to nonspecialists through this section of this encyclopedia.

Historical Overview of Medieval Africa

Medieval Africa was a dynamic place, and one key event driving its dynamism was the continent's entrance into the Iron Age. Although ironworking in Africa predated the medieval period by some 1,400 years—there is a growing body of evidence dating smelting sites as far back as 1000 B.C.E. and corroborating the spread of ironworking technologies throughout virtually the entire continent by around 200 C.E—it is the case that the influence of ironworking on the lives of most of the continent's inhabitants continued to intensify in scope well into the medieval centuries. For example, the southern half of the continent, where ironworking became widespread early in the Common Era, experienced a constellation of essentially contemporaneous developments that unfolded for this area over the first millennium c.e. These developments included not only ironworking but also the introduction of fixed **agriculture** with a focus upon grain cultivation, intensified herding of cattle and other **domesticated animals**, the production of pottery marked by great similarity of style over a very wide range of this territory, life in settled village communities, and the linguistic dominance of Bantu languages (*see* **Bantu Expansions**). The previous Stone Age preeminence of nomadic hunting and gathering was thus done away with, though many continued to practice this older foraging episodically alongside the new cultivating and herding.

Ironworking—and the medieval expansion of copper working, particularly in the Copper Belt of what is today the Congo and Zambia, and gold mining in East and West Africa—affected many aspects of human life throughout the continent. For example, iron tools such as hoes, scythes, machetes, axes, and knives made farming far more productive than it had previously been, resulting in notable increases in harvests and the generation of significant surplus wealth. This in turn allowed for much greater occupational specialization in medieval Africa because all no longer had to produce their own **food** supplies, and growing numbers of individuals focused their energies on activities such as craft production, political or religious leadership, trade, and even **warfare**.

The generation of more and surplus goods, which occurred as a result of the Iron Age, also affected trade very deeply. Local and regional trade networks cutting across broad swathes of the continent intensified in the medieval centuries, in no small part because places with rich deposits of iron or copper ores traded them to regions lacking these now critically important resources. The finished products of smelting and smithing, particularly from **regions** noted for a high quality of work, further stimulated trade on the continent. Regional trade also involved the exchange of goods produced in neighboring but ecologically distinct zones, which most bountifully produced different commodities, as for example in the trades linking the desert, sahelian, sudanic, and forest zones of West Africa (*see* **Ecological Zones**). At times and in certain places trading was dominated by particular ethnic groups, whereas in other instances involvement in the occupation of long-distance trading came to confer a sort of ethnic identity, as with the West African traders who came to be know as the Juula/Dyula.

The medieval centuries witnessed Africa's greater involvement in intercontinental trade too. This was concentrated in the two major trading networks, trans-Saharan and Indian Ocean, which linked Africa with Europe, the Middle East, and Asia. External demand for gold and ivory helped to drive this long-distance trade. Trade through the Red Sea further connected Africans with the Mediterranean Basin. Intercontinental connections also led to the introduction into Africa of new religions, most notably **Christianity** and **Islam**, as well as a continuing Jewish presence in the **Ethiopian Highlands** and North Africa (*see* **Judaism**). Pilgrimages to Jerusalem and Mecca made by, respectively, Africa's Christian and Muslim faithful further cemented intercontinental links. In a different kind of reinforcing cycle of change, one of the offshoots of these intercontinental interactions was the introduction of new food crops. The banana and plantain from Asia further heightened the growing productivity of African agriculture as these became staple starchy crops in many parts of the continent; Africa in turn introduced the cultivation of sorghum and cowpeas to Asia.

A history of continuous interactions between closely neighboring and more distant peoples on and off the continent was thus a constant in the medieval centuries and resulted in ongoing and reciprocal flows of technological information and occupational knowledge as well as the sharing and borrowing of varied cultural norms, practices, and beliefs. The ripple effects of such contacts reached far beyond those individuals in direct association with outsiders as goods and ideas spread via intra-African trading networks. These interactions led also to a norm of multilingualism, and the development of regional lingua francas such as **Hausa** in West Africa and **Swahili** in East Africa. In short, continuous cultural sharing over short distances and vast expanses, which led to a continuous process of innovation and evolution, is the hallmark of African societies during the medieval centuries, rather than the stagnation and isolation so often and so erroneously assumed of Africa.

The developments just discussed led in turn to the heightened social complexity, which is another hallmark of medieval Africa. These centuries were characterized for much of the continent, though not all of it, by greatly increased social stratification. For example, some managed to monopolize a disproportionate share of the continent's greatly increasing wealth, and the copper and gold jewelry that were among the products of metalworking became one of the ways of distinguishing the elites who arose in this heightened social stratification, as numerous sites such as Great Zimbabwe and Igbo-Ukwu demonstrate (*see* **Igbo** and **Zimbabwe Plateau**). Other manifestations of this expanded social complexity included the emergence across the continent of large states and empires, which privileged centralized systems of governance. It is also the case, however, that many on the continent experiencing these far-reaching changes eschewed centralized governments in favor of the diffuse political authority of acephalous societies (*see* "Society" section), a form of organizing society that could and did reflect as much social complexity as centralized authority. Yet other examples of social complexity include the great artistry and technical sophistication of medieval artworks and monumental architecture, and much-expanded urbanization. Well-known African cities of today that date back to the medieval period include **Cairo** and Fez in North Africa, **Jenné-jeno** and **Timbuktu** in West Africa, Mogadishu in the Horn of Africa, and Mombasa and Zanzibar Stone Town on the East African coast. Cities important and widely known in their medieval day, which have not survived to the present, include, to mention just a few, **Kilwa**, Kumbi Saleh, **Sijilmasa**, and Adulis. Many of these medieval cities had populations in the tens of thousands, while mighty Cairo reached a half million or more inhabitants.

Physical Geography: A Continent of Diversity

The African continent is notable for its size and diversity. Slightly more than three times the area of the United States at just under 11.7 million square miles, and nearly 5,000 miles north to south and east to west at its broadest length and width, all of the United States, India, Australia, and Brazil could be comfortably accommodated within its borders. Its mass is often surprising to those who grew up with Mercator projection maps of the world, which artificially inflate areas further from the equator making Africa, which lies across this line, appear artificially small.

In terms of geography and environment, Africa, which is located mostly with the tropics, contains within its borders many different climate zones. Along portions of the equator, which runs across the continent roughly equidistant from its northern and southernmost points, rainforest predominates and the continent receives its heaviest rainfall averaging 80 inches and more per year. With movement north and south from the equator comes a steady decrease in rainfall and a concomitant change in environment, with savannah and savannah-woodland bands followed, as one continues moving further away from the equator, by sahel and then desert zones—the mighty Sahara in the north and the Namib and Kalahari deserts in the south. Finally, with an increase in rainfall once again, Mediterranean strips are found along portions of North Africa's Mediterranean and South Africa's Atlantic coastlines.

Places of high elevation include the Ahaggar, Tibesti, and Atlas Mountains and the Ethiopian Massif in the northern half of the continent, the Drakensberg Mountains in South Africa, and mountains including the continent's highest peak, Mount Kilimanjaro at 19,340 feet, found alongside the Rift Valley, a massive rupture in the earth's crust, which runs from far south of the Great Lakes (Table 6) region of East Africa through the Ethiopian Highlands, with their many peaks and gorges (Table 7), before continuing as the Red Sea. Great **rivers** such as the Nile in the Northeast, the Niger in West Africa, the Congo in Central Africa, and the Limpopo and Zambezi in southern Africa form major watersheds; the Nile and the Niger are also noted for their floodplains that are inundated on a predictable, annual basis as these mighty rivers overflow their banks, depositing silt and enriching nutrients and thus creating some of the richest agricultural land on the continent .

Table 6. The Great Lakes of East Africa Today

Lake	Surface Area in Sq Mi	Greatest Depth in Feet	Details
Victoria	26,560	280	Largest lake in Africa in surface area; second largest freshwater lake in world in surface area.
Tanganyika	12,700	4,820	Second largest lake in Africa in surface area; deepest lake in Africa; second deepest freshwater lake in world; second largest freshwater lake in world by volume.
Nyasa	11,500	2,320	Third largest lake in Africa in surface area.
Kivu	10,040	1,575	
Turkana	2,500	360	
Albert	2,050	190	

Note: Lake Chad, formerly an inland sea, has shrunk precipitously over recent centuries and would have been among the largest lakes in Africa, and in the world, in the medieval period.

The African environment has not been unchanging over the medieval centuries, and variations in it have affected how people live their lives—as well as being caused by how people have lived their lives. During the medieval period, people in Africa engaged in activities as varied as hunting and gathering, fixed agriculture, herding, and metalworking that could and did affect the environment very directly. For instance, the medieval expansions of fixed agriculture and iron smelting led to clearing of forests to create farmland and to fell and burn trees to make the charcoal that fired iron-smelting furnaces, activities that significantly expanded the portions of the continent composed of grasslands. Greater reliance on cattle herding—an activity advantaged by the expansion of grasslands—sometimes led to overgrazing and consequent environmental degradation. It is believed that Great Zimbabwe, a powerful state whose economic base included cattle herding, declined in part because of such overgrazing. Elsewhere, West Africa has experienced long-term wetter and drier phases, with a wetter phase from 700 to 1100, while the subsequent four centuries were far drier. Some connect the twelfth-century decline of Ancient Ghana to the pernicious effects on agricultural production of this decreased precipitation, though whether this was truly a causal factor remains debated.

Vitally important annual weather systems affect rainfall and thus human life in Africa. Two prominent examples are the Intertropical Convergence Zone (ITCZ) and the monsoon. The ITCZ is a region of low pressure created where the Northeastern and Southeastern trade winds meet, resulting in a front that produces heavy rainfall on some 200 days annually. Over the course of the year the ITCZ moves north and south, driving annual patterns of rainy and dry seasons across broad stretches of the continent. These seasons in turn shape the annual cycles of agriculture and herding. For example, many West Africans practice transhumance, moving herds to the drier north in the rainy season and the better-watered south in the dry, thereby ensuring an ongoing food supply for their cattle by protecting the pasturage in both locations from overgrazing. The monsoon winds that affect the lands on both sides of the Indian Ocean, East Africa as well as South Asia, is critically important to eastern and southern Africans, bringing rain annually to the southeastern coast and creating winds in the Indian Ocean that change direction semiannually, blowing from Africa to Asia for one-half of the year and from Asia to Africa for the other half, facilitating maritime travel and thus the Indian Ocean trade so vital to the history of East Africa.

Table 7. African Mountains and Mountain Ranges

Higher Mountains	*Height in feet*
Kilimanjaro	19,340
Mount Kenya	17,058
Mount Meru	14,979
Mount Toubkal	13,665
Mount Cameroon	13,435

Major Mountain Ranges	*Their Highest Elevations in Feet*
Ethiopian Massif	> 14,000
Atlas Mountains	> 13,000
Drakensburg Mountains	> 11,000
Tibesti Mountains	> 11,000
Marra Mountains/Jebel Marra	just under 10,000
Ahaggar Mountains	just under 10,000

Another natural phenomenon that has shaped human life and society is **disease**. A host of tropical illnesses, some of them caused by parasites carried by insects that thrive in the more humid parts of the continent, played important roles in the lives of medieval Africans. For example, they affected where people lived, with avoidance of malarial regions or places where the river blindness carried by black flies was prevalent. Disease also affected the range of productive activities engaged in by people: A parasite carried by the tsetse fly caused the illness known as trypanosomiasis or sleeping sickness. It affected cattle and horses as well as humans, making broad swathes of the medieval continent unsuitable for either of these domesticated animals with the result that cattle herding and the use of ox- or horse-drawn plows and carts were impossibilities for many Africans, and exacting a heavy price in human deaths too. Diseases such as malaria and guinea worm, endemic to many parts of the continent, took their toll by limiting the productivity of people weakened, often chronically, by these illnesses. Plague has also been a factor in African history; the Black Death, which decimated medieval Europe, did not leave Africa unscathed, and is estimated to have resulted in the deaths of four-tenths of Egyptians in the midfourteenth century. Dysenteries and intestinal parasites also affected many. The climate change discussed above could affect some of these diseases, for example by pushing the regions hospitable to the humidity-loving tsetse fly further south during the dry phase of late medieval West Africa. More positively, the host of diseases found on the continent led to deep local knowledge of herbal pharmacopeias as remedies or palliatives for many of these illnesses.

Sources, Methodology, and Organization

There have long existed institutionalized ways of keeping history on the African continent, different though they have often been from Western forms. Upon turning to history as it is practiced in the Western academic tradition, however, the field of African history is still in its infancy. It is the case that until surprisingly recently—the middle of the twentieth century—it was routinely assumed that Africa had no history, had undergone none of the evolutions in politics that were then taken to be the legitimate stuff of historical inquiry, and this conviction left the African past unexplored by scholars from the Western historical tradition. Stasis, the antithesis of history, was assumed for an entire continent's human population. This is literally true. For example, British histories of the imperial age penned by eminent scholars repeatedly asserted that nothing had happened, no change had occurred, in Africa's past that was worthy of attention. Resulting from a combination of the virulent racism that has permeated this "modern" age as well as the challenges posed to the dominant methodologies of the Western historical tradition by a very finite set of written sources for most of the premodern African past, this lack of attention, which lasted until the field of African studies emerged in the second half of the twentieth century, means that many aspects of African history are still either hazily understood or the subjects of vigorous dispute. This also, however, makes the field of African history richly vital and interesting to engage.

As a result of the scholarship of the last 50 years there is much that is known about medieval Africa; there is also much about the continent that remains unclear, some of which doubtless never will be known. The study of medieval Africa is a study bounded by the sources that are available to students of the continent's past. Documents written by Africans do exist for select portions of the medieval continent such as parts of North Africa and the

Ethiopian Highlands, but a majority of medieval Africans lived in oral cultures and thus did not leave behind written records of their times. However, an additional source of written documents is found in the words penned by literate visitors, such as the great and peripatetic medieval Muslim travelers **Ibn Battuta** and al Masudi who visited places including the West African Sudan and East Africa's Swahili coast. These sources have their limitations: Most of these visitors, drawn by involvement or interest in long-distance trade or simply the ease of traveling via its established trade routes, focused their remarks first upon this sector of the economy and second upon political organization and elites, leaving the history of everything else virtually unremarked upon. Their emphases skew our knowledge base toward intercontinental trade (with a notable overemphasis upon Arab/Muslin agency) and societies with centralized governments, which remain the best-investigated parts of medieval Africa. Furthermore, as outsiders their observations could be alternately astute and obtuse. On the positive side they were unaffected by the norms of the societies they were observing, leaving them free to "see" what might be invisible to those who took the shape of their own societies for granted. Yet they were also hampered by lack of knowledge and context for the places they toured, at times misunderstanding what they witnessed. Thus it is always illuminating to have recourse to documents produced by Africans themselves, and with the arrival of Islam on the continent in the seventh century came, for some, literacy and the Arabic script. Nonetheless, for vast swathes of medieval Africa historians have recourse to no written records at all.

Other sources are, however, available to those who attempt to understand Africa's past, and African history is distinctive in the Western academic tradition for the broad range of sources its interdisciplinary scholars routinely consult. Archaeology, the interpretation of artifacts excavated in their original contexts to construct an understanding of the past and its trajectories of change, has proved extraordinarily important to knowledge of the medieval centuries given the relative paucity of written materials. Much of what is known about iron technologies and metalworking more generally, for example, as well as farming, herding, pottery, and other productive activities, comes from archaeology, as does evidence of the great reach of local, regional, long-distance, and intercontinental trade and the growing understandings of urbanization, state formation, social stratification, architectural achievements, religious history, and much, much more.

There are, however, limitations to what can be learned from the tangible remains of a place and time that are the focus of archaeology. For example, though an artifact and its context shed much light on many aspects of a culture, they cannot deeply reveal the mentalities or the thought processes of the people who lived then and there. And the focus has most often been upon elites, leaving the lives of commoners far less fully understood. Additionally, with the exception of long-ago Ancient Egypt, Africa has been a poor stepchild in the field of archaeology, with relatively little money spent upon digs on the continent. In part this reflects the presumption, until recently so widespread, that little worthy of investigation had happened. It also reflects the newness of the field of African studies, the high costs of conducting digs there, and the difficulty of locating sites in certain environments such as the rainforests of West and Central Africa, with their imposing and often impenetrable blankets of vegetation. It remains the case that archaeologists have barely scratched the surface of the continent, with most places of archaeological promise as yet unexcavated.

Oral traditions, through which people in oral cultures keep their histories alive through the faculties of human memory and public recitation, remain a critically important source of information about Africa's past. In acephalous societies oral traditions were in essence community property, to be related by any who could tell a history intended for public performance compellingly and well. In other societies, particularly some states and empires with centralized governments, serving as an oral historian was the purview of a professional class, such as the griots of West Africa. These oral traditions typically focused upon political events such as the emergence of new states, the doings of rulers, and their genealogies. In regards to their accuracy, long suspect as unverifiable by the dominant Western historical profession, it has been found through the use of outside corroborating sources, such as written traditions where they are available or archaeology, that core events of oral traditions are often—though far from uniformly—accurate. They can also be used for entrée into the social mores and mentalities of a particular time and place. On the other hand, it is also the case that the chronology of events in oral traditions is often inaccurate, with anachronisms occurring with regularity. Bias, for example toward the perspective of the rulers of the society creating the oral tradition or recounting it long after the fact—who may be seeking through history to legitimize their own contemporary political authority—is routine. Clearly this is not a concern unique to oral traditions, as any critical examination of written sources and histories quickly reveals. The performative aspect of oral traditions has also received much consideration in recent years, with recognition of the need to consider the creative impulses of individuals, the performative norms of their societies, and the performer's own subjectivity. In short, the imperative to consider oral traditions critically rather than taking them at face value, the need to interrogate them as a careful historian would any other source, is now the norm in African history, which has led the way in developing methodologies for judiciously using these oral texts.

Art forms such as the continent's extraordinarily rich history of sculpture and rock art provide additional windows into the African past, shedding light upon social stratification, medieval preoccupations such as disease, subsistence activities, technological developments, and in-migrations of new peoples. The question of how to interpret extant works of art from long ago remains central, and Africanist art historians often work in concert with archaeologists who can analyze the context in which a particular artwork was found. Yet a majority of the artistic production of medieval Africans has not survived for contemporary consideration, made as it was out of perishable media such as wood, gourds, textiles, and animal skins. The natural sciences have also contributed extensively to our understanding of the African past, for example through identifying and charting significant environmental change that as discussed above affects human history, using botany to substantiate and understand technological developments in agriculture such as the domestication and ennoblement of crops, and demonstrating linkages (or the lack thereof) between members of different human societies via genetics. Historical linguistics has also shed light upon the evolution and movement of languages on the continent.

These richly varied sources of information, when mined to piece together knowledge of the African past, are used by historians in mutually reinforcing ways, and this interdisciplinarity is another of the methodological contributions of the field of African history. For example, oral traditions can be used to identify fruitful sites for archaeological digs, and the findings from such excavations can then be used to test the oral traditions, either upholding or refuting the claims of these oral texts. Likewise, the accurate chronologies of events that can result from carefully conducted archaeological excavations can compensate for the errors in chronology that are one of oral tradition's shortcomings. Used in concert with one another, the many types of sources that currently inform the study of the African past are expanding knowledge of medieval Africa far beyond the focus on states, empires, and long-distance trade that until recently received the lion's share of attention. This methodology also has the potential to reshape and invigorate historical inquiry in other parts of the world, though this interdisciplinarity created and utilized by Africanists holds promise as yet too little fulfilled outside of Africa.

Further Reading

Ehret, Christopher. *The Civilizations of Africa: A History to 1800*. Charlottesville: University Press of Virginia, 2002.

Hull, Richard W. *African Cities and Towns before the European Conquest*. New York: W.W. Norton & Company, 1976.

Philips, John Edward, ed. *Writing African History*. Rochester, NY: University of Rochester Press, 2005.

Stahl, Ann Brower. *African Archaeology: A Critical Introduction*. Oxford, UK: Blackwell Publishing, 2005.

2. RELIGION

The three largest religious traditions found in medieval Africa were **African traditional religions**, **Islam**, and **Christianity**. In addition to these three dominant faiths, medieval communities of Jews existed across North Africa and at some Saharan oases, and immigrants belonging to other religious traditions, such as Hinduism, Zoroastrianism, and Manichaeanism, arrived on the continent from time to time as well (*see* **Judaism**). The majority of medieval Africans, however, practiced African traditional religions. Because of a lack of sources—there are no sacred scriptures leaving a written record of these faiths, and the intangible nature of religious thought means it is not clearly reflected even in the surviving religious artifacts unearthed in archaeological digs—we have little specific information about medieval African traditional religions outside of the indirect evidence of a continuation among early Christian and Muslim converts of earlier religious practices, and some very brief references to religious practices recorded by medieval visitors to Africa. However, the elements of African traditional religions discussed below existed in many places in the early modern period, as attested to by literate visitors of that time, making it a near-certainty that they existed at least in the late medieval years too. Unfortunately, though, the specifics of African traditional religions' beliefs and practices in the medieval centuries, and their variations from place to place, are generally unknowable today, as are the trajectories of change in those years. Thus the discussion of African traditional religions below is problematically ahistorical. Extensive documentation does exist for Islam, which became well established in Africa during the medieval centuries, and for the

Christian communities also found in the medieval period, in large part because of the traditions of literacy attending these two religions with their holy books and scriptures, and extensive literatures of religious treatises and texts. The religions that depended upon literacy for their transmission strongly influenced the **education** in Africa.

African Traditional Religions

The religious traditions indigenous to the African continent reach backwards at least into the medieval period and continue to be practiced by many into the present. Although the specifics of any one African traditional religion vary from ethnicity to ethnicity, there are broad similarities found in these religions across much of the continent such as beliefs in numerous gods, goddesses, and spirits, as well as unseen powers and the ability of human beings to wield special powers. There is also much overlap across African traditional religions in the forms of religious observance, which highlight prayer, sacrifice, and offerings, conducted either personally or with the assistance of a religious leader, and performed either individually or in community-wide acts. The existence of religious specialists such as priests, priestesses, spirit mediums, healers, diviners, seers, and prophets are another commonality. Finally, across Africa there are parallels between African traditional religions regarding beliefs about the causes of misfortune for either individuals or communities, and how best to either prevent problems or treat them once they arise. Alongside all of these broad similarities, there are also variations in African traditional religions from culture to culture and place to place; it has not been the case that one unvarying African traditional religion has existed for the entire continent. For example, divination has been practiced in very different ways in different settings, with variety in the materials cast and how the results are read. African traditional religions have followed very different historical trajectories in different parts of the continent too. Sacred spaces have differed from place to place, as has the range of recognized deities. Although such differences have existed, on occasion gods, goddesses, spirits, or oracles have developed such strong reputations that they have been taken up by a host of neighboring peoples as word of the divinity's power and prowess spread, creating regionally recognized divinities. In short, the similarities that link various African traditional religions are numerous and profound, and this essay focuses upon the commonalities that can be found across them.

African traditional religions are polytheistic, and in their belief in a multitude of gods and goddesses stand in contrast to the monotheistic traditions of Islam and Christianity also found in medieval Africa. Deities found in African traditional religions commonly have included creator, earth, sky, weather, water, and heaven gods or goddesses, with the creator god, when one existed, often privileged as the supreme deity. African traditional religions include another category of divinities known in English translation as spirits. An important example is ancestral spirits. African traditional religions teach that after death, a person who has led a good life and left still-living descendents behind becomes an ancestral spirit, living in a realm close by though not visible to the world of its living descendents who are yet walking the earth. Thus, the now-living and their ancestral spirits coexist in connected worlds that allow for interaction between the two. It is further believed that ancestral spirits, like all spirits, have the ability to affect either positively or negatively the lives of their descendents, in whom they continue to hold a lively interest because of their family bond. It is appropriate and right—and prudent—for the living to pay homage to their ancestors, for example by making offerings of **food**, drink, or sacrifice, and making reference to them in the course of carrying out certain family activities such as prayer or infants' naming ceremonies. The living thus remembers with honor and respect those who preceded them.

Ancestral spirits, recognized for their wisdom, may also be applied to for support or advice about any troubles or pending decision, with consultation occurring either directly or through the assistance of a religious specialist such as a diviner. Although ancestral spirits are respected they may also be feared, because they do have the ability to intervene problematically in their descendents' lives. Ancestral spirits who are forgotten or unduly ignored may seek to revenge themselves on their neglectful descendents by causing problems such as infertility, ill health, crop failure, or any sort of trouble. Ancestral spirits continue to exist for as long as living people have specific memory of them, typically for four to five generations. They then move into a more nebulous world of unnamed spirits. The belief in ancestral spirits has often been misidentified by outsiders as ancestor worship, although that wording is a misnomer; the ancestors are venerated as those who went before, without whom the living would not exist, but are not worshipped or prayed to.

In addition to the ancestors, African traditional religions share a belief in large numbers of spirits that can reside in all kinds of naturally occurring bodies including streams, **rivers**, lakes, trees, groves, caves, rocks, hills, mountains, and certain animals, as well as in shrines and temples. All of the gods, goddesses, and spirits of African traditional religions can affect the lives of people for good or ill. They may be approached in an attempt to ensure their support by people who hope to receive favorable outcomes for all kinds of things, ranging from such intangibles as peace of mind and spiritual strength to highly specific desires such as for children, wealth, health, success in battle, a good harvest, or any of the range of things that can be wanted by human beings.

Complementary to the range of recognized divinities in African traditional religions is the wide range of religious specialists. These include priests and priestesses, men and women with deep religious knowledge who are often dedicated to the service of a particular god, goddess, oracle, or spirit, and engage in activities as diverse as leading prayers or making offerings or sacrifices to the deities they serve, diagnosing and treating illness, making protective or healing charms and medicines, leading community-wide religious observances, and responding to allegations of witchcraft or sorcery. Diviners, skilled in the art of divination, can communicate with spirits by interpreting cast stones, bones, nuts, shells, or other objects. They address all sorts of questions or problems, spiritual and secular, profound or mundane, present or future oriented, brought to them by clients. Spirit mediums, as the name implies, serve as the medium or link between a particular divinity and the secular world of the living. When not possessed, a medium is a regular person, fully immersed in the normal, nondivine world of living people. But a medium has the capacity to be possessed by a spirit, a state often entered into in the context of dance and drumming. While possessed the medium transmits the word of the spirit to the human community, thereby creating a link between the secular and the divine. Their utterances, made while in an altered, trance-like state and often not remembered once the possession ceases, are frequently translated or interpreted by another religious leader.

Healers, who may be male or female, address physical illness and more metaphysical woes such as misfortune. They possess significant knowledge of an extensive African pharmacoepia drawn from the local flora and fauna and create medicines to treat a broad range of **diseases**. Some also set broken bones and provided treatments for sprains and strains through the careful manipulation of limbs. They also incorporate spiritually based techniques into their treatments, in keeping with the widespread belief that illness, though it might be treated with a medicine or manipulation, often has a deeply significant spiritual component that when properly considered can help to answer the question of why one person gets sick rather than another, or identify the root cause of any of the many illnesses believed caused by supernatural machinations. For example, healers might identify offended relatives or neighbors and treat instances of witchcraft or sorcery perpetuated by these aggrieved individuals. Or they might identify offended spirits or gods to whom redress has to be made through prayer, offerings, or sacrifice before an illness or woe such as infertility will abate. Healers might also address community-wide problems deemed to have a religiously based origin such as epidemic, drought, famine, or warfare. As is clear from this roster of religious leaders, women and men serve as religious specialists though, at least in more recent centuries, women have usually been the spirit mediums whereas divination has been the province of men. It is also important to note that religious leaders can have expertise in more than one area; they did not have to specialize in only one of the aspects of religious leadership covered here.

African traditional religions share a belief in the existence of special or unseen powers. Outsiders have often labeled these convictions "magic" or "superstition," though these terms are problematic insofar as they connote irrational and fear-laden thinking. In fact, such negative implications do not accord at all with the highly developed African religious cosmologies in which beliefs in unseen powers form a critically important element. Followers of African traditional religions believe that in addition to deities and spirits, some people can harness special powers, have the ability to control unseen forces that exist in the world, that they can then employ against others for either good or ill. Those people who make use of these forces only to harm have become known, in English translation, as witches (female) and sorcerers (male) practicing witchcraft or sorcery. The belief in these powers is intimately connected to notions of causation in African traditional religions; if things go wrong in a person's life—if pregnancy cannot be achieved or sustained, if a child dies, if one's life activities fail, if illness or epidemic strikes, if one suffers any of the host of causes of human dissatisfaction, deep unhappiness, or despair—the cause will not be understood simply as bad luck. Instead, the assumption is that someone is wielding special powers against the aggrieved person. The person causing the harm might do so because of jealousy or anger toward the target. It is therefore unsurprising that the person believed responsible for another's woes is most often a relative, neighbor, or coworker, someone with whom the person transgressed against lives in close contact, and with whom there may in fact exist a history of stresses or strains.

There are specific steps to be taken when people believe special powers are being wielded against them. A common response is consultation with a religious specialist such as a priest or priestess who has a reputation for skill in identifying the person causing the harm, and devising ways to neutralize these actions and even prevent their future occurrence. It might be necessary to identify or find any charm or medicine made by the person harnessing special powers that is actually causing the harm, so it can be destroyed or its power otherwise nullified. Or, the specialist might recommend certain ritual actions to eradicate the threat, or make a protective charm or medicine for his or her client, often a small container or pouch containing any of a variety of spiritually charged objects such as plant or animal matter, or earth, believed to confer a protective power when made by a skilled religious practitioner. These objects might then be worn by the person seeking assistance, or placed in his or her home, or on property thought to be at risk, to block the efficacy of the other person's malevolent powers. On other occasions there is public identification of the individual believed to be wielding harmful powers, who is then put through trials to ascertain guilt or innocence. A finding of guilt often leads to that person's exile or death to safeguard individuals and the community from their destructive actions.

In sum, when life's unhappinesses, troubles, great sorrows, and unpredictabilities strike, followers of African traditional religions may seek explanation and relief through these beliefs in unseen powers. A functionalist explanation of this understanding of misfortune typically focuses upon its usefulness in creating a structure through which to make sense of and rationalize the otherwise inexplicable, and give remedies that allow people to assert some sense of control over painful life events. It is also important to keep in mind, as T.O. Ranger and Benjamin Ray point out, that African traditional religions express a worldview and set of ideas that stress relationships—among people, between the living and the ancestors, between people and the natural world that they inhabit, and between the natural world and the world of the divine—and the construction and maintenance of these relationships in appropriate ways as necessities for the harmonious unfolding of human affairs.

Positive applications of special powers include the actions of religious practitioners who use their understanding of and command over unseen powers to protect people against those who utilize such powers to harm. Individuals approach them for charms or medicines not only in the face of witchcraft and sorcery, but also to help them achieve any desired life end and protect them from any harm. African healers, who historically have combined understandings of physiology, psychology, and the medicinal properties of numerous plants with spiritually based methods of healing, are another category of individuals who use special powers as well as secular knowledge to help. Rainmakers represent a third category of positive users of special powers, in this case to bring the waters so necessary to the survival of individuals and communities dependent upon harvests and grazing lands. Those who can foretell the future, such as seers, priests or priestesses of oracles, and diviners, also assist positively by helping people understand and plan for what lies ahead.

The practices of African traditional religions, its forms of religious observance, are woven throughout daily life and form part and parcel of it: It is a truism that the religions are not separable from lived human activity. Indeed, because of the link between the supernatural and notions of causation, much of the human experience is closely linked to spirituality according to African traditional religions. Hence it is not surprising that religious observances are scattered throughout daily life. For example, prayer, conducted often daily by an individual, the head of a family, or a religious leader, on behalf of an individual, a family, or an entire community, and directed toward any of the divinities of African traditional religions, might request desired things or outcomes, give thanks when desired events occur, or give praise. Likewise, people frequently turn to religious specialists such as healers, seers, diviners, mediums, prophets, priestesses, or priests for advice, insights, and remedies. Community-wide observances such as harvest festivals, which celebrate the new crop, are yet another type of religious practice, and such festivals often occur on an annual cycle closely tied to subsistence activities such as farming and herding. Prayers and ritual observances also accompany important activities like iron smelting, forging, fishing, and hunting. Families regularly recognize and honor the spirits of their departed ancestors, and it is also quite common to have family shrines, which serve divinities associated with a lineage. Individuals might also have a particularly close relationship with a divinity if their parents sought the assistance of a god, goddess, or spirit in conception, bringing a pregnancy to term, or keeping an infant or young child alive, and the surviving child might then have an association to that deity throughout his or her life. Offerings made to a divinity form another important and frequent category of religious observation. These typically consist of food or drink, the latter known as libation, which might take the form of water, milk, or alcohol, often poured upon the ground in recognition and appreciation of the spirit receiving it, and as an act of hospitality toward that spirit and a symbolic rendering of the relationship between the divinity and the person making the offering. Finally, sacrifice exists as a kind of offering in which the living being so proffered to a divinity is killed in recognition of the fact that all life flows from the divine, and so as not to approach a divinity empty-handed when making application to it.

Christianity

At times Christianity had a very significant presence in parts of northern and northeastern medieval Africa. It initially came to Alexandria shortly after the time of Christ, during the first or second century C.E. and rapidly became established as the majority religion in **Egypt**. By the end of the fifth century it is estimated that some that 90 percent of Egyptians practiced the faith through Egypt's **Coptic Church**. Early Egyptian Christianity was marked by a strong embrace of monasticism, the appeal of which may in part be connected to parallels in the religion of Ancient Egypt that favored austere living for its priestly class, and in part to the development of monasticism as a new form of asceticism that arose as persecutions waned. The Coptic Church also stood out for its allegiance to what supporters of the Chalcedonian Creed called Monophysitism, a doctrine that asserts that Christ had only one nature—divine—rather than the two natures, divine and human, embraced at the Council of Chalcedon in 451 that declared Monophysitism heretical.

Further west, in the Maghrib, Christianity also gained a firm hold among the predominantly **Berber** population of this part of North Africa, who had turned to Christianity in significant numbers by 400 C.E. Initially, this development was resisted by the Romans, who then controlled the North African littoral, and in 180 C.E. twelve Maghrib Christians were the first known to be martyred for their faith. They were followed by many more martyrs until the legalization of Christianity by the Romans in 313. An important aspect of Christianity in the Maghrib was the emergence there of the Donatist Church, which took a hard line against readmitting Christians who reluctantly renounced their faith under the Roman persecutions led by Diocletian in 303. Donatism also provided opportunities for Maghrib Berbers to retain elements of their earlier religious traditions in its melding of Christianity and local practices and beliefs. These positions set Donatists at continuing odds with the Roman Church, which eventually labeled Donatism heretical. The doctrinal controversies sparked by Monophysitism and Donatism notwithstanding, the early Christian communities of North Africa are also notable for their roster of prominent Christian intellectuals from Egypt and the Maghrib, a list that includes Augustine, Origen, Tertullian, and Cyprian.

In the early fourth century, under the influence of Coptic Christians from Egypt or the Levant, Christianity spread to the kingdom of **Aksum** in the **Ethiopian Highlands** during the rule of King Ezana, who converted around 340. Christianity continued to flourish in Ethiopia under the Zagwe and Solomonid **dynasties** that succeeded Aksum, and **Ethiopian Christianity** was closely linked to the Coptic Church throughout the medieval period, sharing its Monophysite beliefs and receiving bishops from that church too.

The final foothold of Christianity in medieval Africa, **Nubia**, received the religion as Egyptian traders brought the faith with them in the fifth and sixth centuries as they moved south down the Nile into northeastern Africa's interior and to the three Nubian kingdoms of Nobatia, Makuria, and Alwa. Egyptian Christians were joined in Nubia in the sixth century by Byzantine missions, at which point Christianity became quickly and firmly established throughout Nubian society. Christian Nubia flourished for almost a millennium and like the Ethiopian Church initially had close ties to the Coptic Church from which it in part sprang, with the Coptic Church appointing Nubia's bishops. Archaeological excavations conducted at the cathedral at Faras, the capital city of Nobatia, have yielded an incredibly rich heritage of Nubian Christian artwork, including exquisite depictions of Nubian bishops and biblical and nativity scenes.

Christianity appealed to these diverse populations of Africans for a variety of reasons. For Egyptians and North Africans of the Maghrib who were suffering under oppressive Roman rule, one appeal of Christianity lay in its promise of a better life in the hereafter. In Aksum, linked through Red Sea trade to growing Christian populations in the Mediterranean, it was politic to adopt the Christianity of valuable trading partners, a motive that also operated in Nubia. The fact that African Christians typically molded the religion in accordance with their own cultural norms and religious antecedents further hastened its acceptance.

Although Christianity initially flourished in these parts of Africa, the religion faced a profound challenge from the east as Muslim Arabs swept out of the Arabian Peninsula into northern Africa in a series of invasions during the seventh and eighth centuries. Christianity survived in Egypt, where the Coptic Church remains to the present day, but the Muslim conquest led to a radical decline in the Egyptian Christian population to what has been estimated at less than 10 percent of the total Egyptian population by the end of the medieval period, a process hastened through conversions sparked by practices such as taxing non-Muslims and excluding them from various offices. Except in isolated pockets Christianity did not survive Muslim incursions in the Maghrib, though its Berber practitioners there put up spirited and initially successful military defenses. Christian Nubia's renowned archers repelled Arab Muslim forces, which attacked in the seventh century. The early victories did not hold, however, and the twelfth through fourteenth centuries witnessed a gradual evolution in Nubia as ever-expanding numbers of Muslim immigrants profoundly changed its religious makeup, until by the end of the fifteenth century, Christianity was virtually exterminated there. Only in Ethiopia did Christianity flourish uninterrupted, and indeed the Ethiopian Church remains vital to the present day in a tradition unbroken since the arrival of Christianity in this region nearly seventeen centuries ago.

Islam

Islam, founded by the Prophet Mohammed in the Arabian Peninsula early in the seventh century C.E., spread immediately into North Africa. Between 639 and 711, Arab Muslims conquered the North African coast from Egypt to Morocco and introduced their religion in these regions in the process of this conquest. Here and elsewhere on the continent where Islam spread some converted to avoid enslavement and taxes levied by the conquerors on unbelievers, or to share the religion of the newly dominant Muslim political class. Others wanted to share the religious identity of merchants in Muslim-dominated trading networks of intercontinental reach and great economic importance. Yet others embraced Islam due to an appreciation of its religious teachings and practices, and the social and political norms and mores that formed the Muslim cultural order that attended the religion. And still others saw a potent source of special powers in aspects of the new religion, particularly its script.

In Egypt Islam gradually replaced Christianity as the majority religion, and Arabs replaced the Byzantines as the ruling class by 642. Berbers in the Maghrib accepted Islam only after the initial decades of successful military resistance to the unwelcome Arab conquerors failed in the early years of the eighth century, and most came to embrace Islam over the next 200 years. However, their resistance to Arab overrule continued even after conversion, with many Berbers drawn to the Kharijite branch of the faith, which stressed a radical egalitarianism very attractive in light of the Arab political and cultural dominance that attended their North African conquest.

From North Africa Islam spread south with trans-Saharan trade, first to the nomadic Berbers of the Sahara who began converting in the ninth and tenth centuries. Sanhaja Berber Muslims of the western Sahara dominated the Almoravid Movement of the eleventh century, which ushered in a turn to an extremely rigid and puritanical form of Sunni Islam in this part of the continent. Almoravids then achieved military conquests as far afield as Morocco and Andalusia in southern Spain, before falling in Africa to a new Muslim power, the Almohads, and in Spain to the Christian Reconquista (*see* **Almoravid and Almohad Movements**). During the tenth to twelfth centuries Islam moved yet further south from the desert to the West African sahel and Sudan that lay below the Sahara and were also involved in trans-Saharan trade. Conversion in these regions typically began with the rulers of states such as Gao, **Takrur,** and **Kanem-Bornu**, whose leaders accepted Islam in the late tenth and eleventh centuries no doubt recognizing the political and commercial acumen of conversion. The same process unfolded in the important medieval West African empire of **Mali**, whose rulers first embraced Islam after which the religion made inroads into the general population. **Mansa Musa**, a famous thirteenth-century ruler of Mali, is noted for the very lavishly conducted *hajj*, or religious pilgrimage, he made to Mecca, the holiest site of Islam, in 1324 A.D. His fantastic expenditures of gold in **Cairo** brought the attention of Europeans to his kingdom, which was for the first time identified as the specific source of the West African **gold**, which medieval Europeans used to strike their coins. Mansa Musa also began the development of the Malian city of **Timbuktu** into a center of medieval Islamic scholarship and learning, which in its heyday attracted Muslim scholars from far afield.

Islam also traveled from its birthplace in the Arabian Peninsula to East Africa, brought there by Muslim merchants via the maritime trade routes running from Arabia south through the Red Sea, into the Indian Ocean, and down the East African coast. Islam appears to have arrived as early as the eighth century C.E., though it did not become widely embraced by coastal East Africans until the eleventh century. The **Swahili** culture that was at its peak from around 1200 to 1500 was characterized in part by its embrace of Islam, but the religion did not move from the coast into the East African interior during the medieval centuries. The Red Sea also facilitated the movement of Muslims across its relatively narrow waters from Arabia into the Horn of Africa and as far west as Nubia which lay along the Middle Nile, while simultaneously Muslim teachers and merchants came to Nubia from Egypt.

The rapid spread of Islam across North Africa, into the Sahara and West Africa, along the Nile, and down East Africa's coast, is striking. One factor underlying its successful transmission was the relative ease with which the basic obligations of the faith, the Five Pillars of Islam—five practices incumbent upon all Muslims—could be met even by converts not yet fully conversant with the tradition. Another factor aiding its spread was the ability of new converts to combine Islam with a continuation of certain pre-Islamic religious practices. For example, the belief in spirits intrinsic to African traditional religions found an easy home in the *jinns* or spirits of Islam. The use of amulets containing passages written in the Arabic script, which were believed by many to be powerful charms, further connected the new religion to the ones that preceded it. Frequently the social and political orders dictated by Islam were adopted selectively too, making conversion less culturally disruptive than would otherwise have been the case. These sorts of religious blendings were engaged in by most converts, and the continuation of older religious and social traditions no doubt eased the transition from one religion to another.

The African traditional religions practiced by a majority of medieval Africans addressed a world richly populated by gods, goddesses, spirits, and unseen forces, all of which had the ability to affect for good or ill the lives of the living. Through their cosmologies, religious practices, and religious specialists, African traditional religions focused upon the construction and maintenance of relationships among people, between people and the divine, and between people and the natural world. These religions provided explanations, understandings, treatments and preventions for the adversities and misfortunes that are intrinsic to the human condition. Medieval Africa was also home to significant numbers of Christians and Muslims. The inroads Christianity initially made in northern and northeastern Africa were eventually muted by Islam. This left only the Egyptian Coptic Church and the Ethiopian Church to continue as representatives of Christianity in Africa throughout the medieval period, as Islam became dominant in North Africa and the Sahara and on the East African coast and developed a significant presence in West and northeastern Africa. In the case of Christianity and Islam, the introduction of a new faith caused social and cultural as well as religious change. Yet simultaneously, Africans remade both faiths in profound ways by blending old religious traditions with the new. This process is reflected in the widely used nomenclature of African Christianity and African Islam, labels that distinguish their practice on the African continent and speak to the very active rather than passive responses to these imported faiths, which characterized their reception by Africans.

Further Reading

Chadwick, Henry. *The Church in Ancient Society: From Galilee to Gregory the Great*. Oxford, UK: Oxford University Press, 2002.

Karp, Ivan. "African Systems of Thought," In *Africa*. 3rd ed. Edited by Phyllis M. Martin and Patrick O'Meara. Bloomington: Indiana University Press, 1995, pp. 211–222.

Mbiti, John S. *Introduction to African Religion*. 2nd ed. Portsmouth, NH: Heinemann, 1991.

Ranger, T.O. "African Traditional Religion," in *The Study of Religion, Traditional and New Religion*. Edited by Stewart Sutherland and Peter Clarke. London: Routledge, 1991.

Ray, Benjamin C. *African Religions: Symbol, Ritual, and Community*. Englewood Cliffs, NJ: Prentice-Hall, 1976. See "Introduction: Perspectives on African Religions."

Robinson, David. *Muslim Societies in African History*. Cambridge, UK: Cambridge University Press, 2004.

Tilley, Maureen. *The Bible in Christian North Africa: The Donatist World*. Minneapolis, MN: Fortress Press, 1997.

3. ECONOMY

In the medieval centuries, people across the vast African continent engaged in a broad range of economic activities. Small Stone Age communities practicing hunting and gathering continued to exist in parts of southern and Central Africa, whereas societies utilizing fixed **agriculture**, herding, and iron smelting formed the majority of the medieval African population. In the medieval period craft production, engaged in within the household and also practiced on a larger scale, played an important role in producing a wide range of items people used in their daily lives. Systems of exchange including barter and local, regional, and long-distance trade were additional critical features of African economic life during these centuries. This mix of economic activities, in addition to the hunting, fishing, and foraging of earlier millennia, which continued to be practiced at least sporadically by many in medieval Africa, produced surplus wealth in the continent, allowing growing numbers of individuals to avoid subsistence activities in favor of specialized occupations (*see* **Hunting and Gathering**). This specialization also supported the emergence of the large states found across Africa in the medieval centuries.

Agriculture, Herding, and Iron Technology

Fixed agriculture developed many millennia before the medieval period in some parts of Africa, though in other places on the continent it was not practiced until just before the medieval era began. The transition from foraging for naturally occurring edible plants to the intentional farming of food crops represents a major change in how human populations support themselves. Farming opens up the possibility of surplus production of foodstuffs and the consequent ability of some members of society to specialize in nonsubsistence occupations. It also allows for settled life, and thus an increase in personal possessions. Population generally increases too, as a result of the greater security of food supply and the greater ease in raising children, which is associated with settled life. Exchanges of goods with neighboring peoples follow the creation of surpluses too. All these developments, as well as a need for heightened social organization to regularize access to farmland and the organization of cooperative labor, are in turn linked to the development of more complex political entities.

The earliest archaeological evidence for farming in Africa dates to 7000 B.C.E. in the Western Desert of **Egypt**, located near what is today the border of Egypt and the Sudan. Cultivation along the Nile River Valley followed by around 5000 B.C.E. Archaeological evidence for farming dating to 5000 B.C.E. has been found in the Saharan region too, which was at that time well watered and fertile rather than the desert it is today. Although until recently most scholars believed farming in Africa to be an import from western Asia, more and more scholars are exploring the possibility that farming techniques diffused from the Western Desert to the Nile River Valley, and a minority even argue that perhaps the knowledge was transmitted from the Saharan region to the Nile. Although there no longer exists a consensus on what was until recently a widely held belief that agriculture in Africa arose in the Nile River Valley based on transmission from Asia, and from there traveled down the Nile and thence to points west and south, it can be stated that agriculture was firmly established in portions of the northern half of the continent by 5000 B.C.E., whether it developed at one or more locations indigenously, diffused from western Asia, or resulted from a combination of these two sources. Farming spread throughout the entire continent by the first centuries C.E.

The earliest crops grown in northeastern Africa were the cereals wheat and barley, most likely domesticated in western Asia and brought to Africa. These crops cannot be cultivated in the tropical and subtropical parts of the continent, so the cultivation of other grains and cereals indigenous to Africa developed in the grasslands of the West African Sudan and in the **Ethiopian Highlands**. These starchy staples included pearl and finger millet, sorghum, African rice, ensete, and teff; non**food** crops including cotton and indigo were cultivated too. In the vegeculture of the forest regions of West Africa, where cereals and grains are not easily grown, Africans farmed yams, melons, fluted pumpkins, gourds, cowpeas and the crops of the oil palm, raffia palm, and kola nut trees. Across the continent Africans planted and harvested many vegetables too. Before and during the medieval centuries, African agriculture was enriched further by the diffusion of crops from Asia including cocoyam, coconuts, sugar cane, citrus fruits, Asian rice, and perhaps the banana and plantain too. Strains of crops domesticated by Africans including sorghum and cowpeas, and the kapok and baobab trees, were diffused from Africa to western and South Asia too.

By the medieval period, then, the planting and harvesting of crops was well established across the continent. The dominant form of farming practiced in Africa was hoe agriculture because the presence across broad swathes of Africa of the tsetse fly, whose bite transmitted trypanosomiasis to cattle, made it impossible in many places to use draft animals to do the heavy work of plowing. The fact that people in some areas where cattle thrived used them as a form of currency, as a way of holding wealth, as they did in parts of southern and eastern Africa, also mediated against using these animals for the more prosaic work of plowing. In addition to relying on hoe agriculture, frequently African cultivators practiced shifting plot agriculture wherein farming sites were used intensively until the soil fertility was depleted, at which time the land was either left to lie fallow and regenerate, or was simply abandoned permanently in favor of a new plot. In other instances, though, land was cultivated continuously due either to its high natural fertility or the use of fertilizers. Sometimes Africans utilized additional farming techniques such as the construction of irrigation channels or hillside terracing. Cultivation occurred at Saharan oases too, made possible through the construction of underground irrigation channels to provide the necessary water and dependent on an underclass of workers who undertook the heavy labor needed in this system of farming.

If more recent gendered patterns of production held true for the medieval era too, women played a key role in producing food crops in Africa, in large part due to widespread beliefs that **women** were responsible for providing the bulk of the food for their children, their husbands, and themselves. While women did the sowing, weeding, harvesting, processing, and storing of food crops in the majority of the continent, typically men bore responsibility for clearing new plots of land, a recurring need in many places given the dominance of shifting plot agriculture. Farming was gendered entirely male among a small minority of African societies, including the **Hausa** and **Yoruba** of what is today Nigeria, and mixed-sex farming occurred in some locations also, including the West African sahel.

Like agriculture, the origins of **domesticated animals** in Africa are a matter of some dispute. Many argue that domestication came to Africa from western Asia, whereas others assert that it was an indigenous development. In any event cattle raising may have been established in Egypt's Western Desert by 7000 B.C.E., whereas widely accepted evidence of cattle rearing exists from around 5000 B.C.E. for the Nile River Valley, the North African coast in what is today Libya, and the central Sahara. Cattle herding spread more slowly in the southern half of Africa and reached the southernmost portions of the continent only by the early centuries of the Common Era. Cattle, whether indigenous or imported in origin, sheep and goats indigenous to Asia, camels from the Arabian Peninsula, donkeys very probably domesticated from the African Wild Ass, and poultry were the main domesticated animals, though in forest and some savannah regions of Africa cattle, horses, donkeys, and camels could not survive the trypanosomiasis transmitted by the bite of the tsetse fly. After the spread of fixed agriculture, the benefits of interweaving herding and farming were quickly recognized by some African cultivators, with farmers who raised cattle using manure to fertilize their fields while feeding their animals the roughage that remained following harvests.

By the medieval period, then, animal husbandry like farming held a prominent position in the African economy across the continent. Unlike farming, herding livestock was the work of males, often boys or young men, while women bore responsibility for milking and churning butter. Migration to fresh pastures and sources of water, often following a seasonal cycle of movement, was common among herders. Although it was the ideal of pastoralists to be able to live entirely from their animals, who were valued for their meat, milk, blood and hides, it was typically impossible to sustain life solely from this source. In reality, activities such as hunting, fishing, foraging, and exchanges with local farmers generally supplemented animal husbandry. Indeed, hunting and gathering activities continued in the medieval period, not only among the remaining peoples for whom this remained the primary subsistence activity. These practices were also engaged in at least occasionally by farmers and herders: For many, they remained important sources of foodstuffs, either routinely or during times of crisis in herding or agriculture.

Knowledge of how to smelt iron emerged in a number of places in West and East Africa in the first millennium B.C.E. and then spread across Africa between approximately 1000 B.C.E. and 400 C.E. The expansion of ironworking skills was facilitated by the broad availability of iron ore across much of the African continent. Once again, it is a matter of some debate whether iron-smelting technologies arose independently in Africa or were transferred to the continent from western Asia. In any event, iron smelting spread across virtually the entire continent by 400 C.E., so at the beginning of the medieval period the Iron Age already encompassed all the peoples of Africa with the exception of some hunting and gathering societies which remained in the Stone Age. The production of metal tools and weapons allowed for a great expansion in agriculture using iron hoes and axes, and more effective hunting and greater military capabilities using iron-tipped spears and arrows and metal knives. Metallurgy also had profound effects upon African art, notably with the eventual production of striking cast metal bronze and brass sculptures produced at Igbo-Ukwu and Ife (see **Igbo**).

It is important to note that for the African continent as a whole in the medieval period the production of iron remained less than the demand, some argue to such an extent that in places it served as a brake on economic development. Indeed, after Europeans began sailing to the continent in the fifteenth century, iron emerged as one of the most important African imports, revealing a hunger for additional supplies of this metal. However, it is also important to recognize that the scale of iron production varied widely in medieval Africa, ranging from small-scale smelting targeted only to local consumption, to large-scale smelting involving from hundreds to thousands of furnaces at one location. Additionally, a second significant brake on economic expansion lay in the relatively low population density of Africa: People to work land and other resources, not the resources themselves, generally limited the amount of production that occurred in medieval Africa.

Smelters, who transformed ore into usable metal, often held a special place in medieval African life. Although African cultures are far too varied to generalize accurately about the role of metallurgists, and though the distinction is critical between smelters who created metal and smiths or forgers who simply worked it, in some cultures smelters, who often closely guarded knowledge of their craft, were respected for their generative ability to create much-desired iron, while people feared them for what seemed the occult powers of creation they thus possessed. Other cultures drew positive links between ironworking and political leadership. And some cultures saw smelting as just an occupation. In certain societies any man (it was an occupation gendered male) could become a smith, while in others the profession was open only to members of particular families. In addition to ironworking, mining and smithing of **gold**, tin, lead, and copper existed in medieval Africa and formed activities agricultural peoples might engage in seasonally when the demands of farming were at a low ebb.

Craft Production and Domestic Work

In the medieval period craft production led to the creation of all kinds of items used in daily life. Sometimes artisans produced just for their households, whereas at other times they worked on a far larger scale with exchange of the resulting goods the end result. The many aspects of cloth making could include collecting and processing raffia or bark and/or growing cotton, producing thread, weaving, tailoring and often decorating the cloth through dye, stamped designs, embroidery or some other technique, and significant cloth industries grew up in a number of locations. Salt production also occurred on a larger as well as smaller scale, for example in the Niger Delta where the Niger meets the Atlantic, where salt collected after evaporating ocean waters was traded for agricultural products with the people of the coastal hinterland. Gold smithing was another craft commonly done for exchange rather than self-use.

Particular crafts were gendered male or female and though in many cases these genderings were constant across the continent, in others they varied from society to society. Women tended to dominate pottery, salt processing, beer-brewing, weaving of mats and baskets, broom making and spinning, whereas leather and woodworking, palm wine tapping, the construction of homes, smelting, and smithing were typically the purview of men. Cloth weaving might be gendered male or female; usually though not exclusively male weavers produced for exchange while women weavers produced for their households. Some crafts were restricted only to certain families, while others could be engaged in by anyone. In the latter case, apprenticeship to a specialist was typically how one learned the skill.

Women across the African continent bore responsibility for most domestic work, which included cooking, fetching water and firewood or other fuels, laundry, child care, nursing the sick, and providing a variety of personal services to husbands. Largely because of their constant responsibility for the ongoing work involved in the never-ending, indeed daily, demands of food cultivation and household work, on average women in medieval Africa worked several hours a day longer than men, even when men's responsibilities for hunting, fishing, and military work are factored in. The notable exception to this pattern was hunting and gathering societies, in which a hierarchy based on gender did not exist and where the number of hours spent daily in subsistence activities was far lower than in agricultural and pastoral communities; hunting and gathering societies have considerably more leisure time available to their members than is available to people who practice other ways of sustaining life.

Regional and Long-Distance Trade

Medieval Africa was notable for its extensive trade networks, which not only criss-crossed many parts of the continent but linked Africa and the outside world through intercontinental trade. Significant trading partners of Africa included Europe, the Middle East, and Asia. Indeed, Africa played a key role in the economy of the medieval world, for example, as a primary source of gold for Europe. Two commercial networks critically important to Africa and other continents in this time period were trans-Saharan and Indian Ocean trade.

Throughout the medieval period, trans-Saharan trade plied the inhospitable and dangerous Sahara desert, connecting West Africa, located south of the Sahara, and North Africa, to the desert's north, while also funneling African exports to a much broader world via the Mediterranean. Trans-Saharan trade was based most fundamentally upon a gold-for-salt transaction in which gold from sub-Saharan West Africa was traded north, while salt from the Sahara went south. This vast trading network connected the communities and peoples of sub-Saharan West Africa with the peoples of the great Sahara desert and North Africa. In the medieval period, the most important West African export, gold, was mined primarily at the Bambuk and Bure goldfields, located, respectively, between the headwaters of the Senegal and Falémé rivers and near the headwaters of the mighty Niger River. In the late medieval period, the **Akan** goldfields located in the forest region of what is today **Ghana** also began to send their output north into trans-Saharan trade. In addition to gold, other significant West African exports included ivory, captives destined for slavery, agricultural products, ostrich feathers, animal pelts, and kola nuts. In return for these products from the savannah and forest regions of West Africa, salt produced in the Sahara at places such as Taghaza and Bilma was traded south. Other Saharan exports included copper ore from Agades and Azelik in the central desert's Aïr region and Akjoujt in the western Sahara, among other sites, and dates cultivated at desert oases. North African exports sent south in exchange for the goods of West Africa included a variety of what can be thought of as luxury goods, such as fine cloths, either whole or sewn into garments; precious stones; metal wares; horses, used for civilian and military purposes in the grasslands of West Africa; and books, which were in high demand among the growing literate, Muslim population in West African cities such as **Timbuktu**, which from the 1300s began to emerge as a center of Islamic learning under the patronage of **Mansa Musa**, ruler of the empire of **Mali**.

Transportation took a variety of forms along the reaches of the trans-Saharan trade network. In the West African savannah, people transported goods across the grasslands by head loads (human porterage) or donkeys and along the Niger River by boat. People of the Sahara, such as the Tuareg and Sanhaja **Berbers**, made the dangerous desert crossing in camel caravans of as many as thousands of animals that moved commodities north and south across the sands. Camels, well-suited to desert travel due to their ability to travel for 10 days between water sources, and the spreading of their hooves in a "snowshoe" effect that keeps them from bogging down in the sand, allowed for the reinvigoration of trans-Saharan trade after the widespread adoption of their use in the Saharan region in the early centuries of the Common Era. Oases such as Awdaghust also played key roles in making the crossing possible. The length of the desert journey varied considerably depending on whether the routes traversed the desert in a fairly straight north-south axis of 2- to 3-months' duration, as they would do going from West African goldfields to the North African city of Fez, or veered far east, as was the case with caravans headed to the highly significant North African city of **Cairo**.

Interest in the goods exported from West Africa via trans-Saharan trade lay not only in the Sahara and North Africa. From the Arab-controlled cities of the North African littoral, where gold was in demand to mint the coins of Islamic states, West Africa's exports traveled the long-established maritime trade networks of the Mediterranean, thereby making their way north into Europe, where Africa's gold undergirded the medieval European turn to a gold-based currency, recognized at a later date in the elephant mint mark of the famous Golden Guinea of King Charles II, and also east into western Asia, where African gold was again in high demand. Before the Americas emerged as a new, less costly source of the precious metal in the modern era, West Africa served as the main supplier of gold to Europe and the Islamic world, producing fully two-thirds of their supply of this valued commodity.

The second intercontinental trade route of great importance in the medieval period traversed an ocean not of sand, but of water. Indian Ocean trade created a world of commerce and cultural exchange linking the peoples of Egypt, the Horn of Africa, and the East African coast with trading partners in the Arabian Peninsula, Persia, South Asia, Indonesia, and the southern ports of China. Indeed, the Indian Ocean world is now increasingly understood as a medieval and even premedieval locus of activity and exchange parallel to what has much longer been recognized as the Atlantic World, which emerged following the age of Atlantic maritime exploration in the modern era.

Deeply involved in Indian Ocean trade was a portion of the East African coastline affected by the annual monsoon winds, which drove this maritime network by facilitating the ocean crossing. This approximately 1,000-mile length of coast stretched from Mogadishu in the north to Cape Delgado in what is today Mozambique in the south. A new people, the **Swahili**, emerged along this coastline late in the first millennium C.E. and created a spectacular and opulent culture that derived a significant share of its wealth from the role of Swahili merchants, who acted as intermediaries buying and selling goods central to Indian Ocean commerce. In its heyday that lasted from approximately 1200 to 1500, some fifty Swahili towns, the most prominent of which was **Kilwa**, and several hundred settlements in total, dotted the shoreline, peninsulas, and off-shore islands of this stretch of the East African coast.

Swahili merchants facilitated the movement of goods from the East African interior and the East African coast into Indian Ocean trade. Prominent among these commodities was gold that was mined in the interior to the southwest of the coast on the **Zimbabwe Plateau**, located between the Zambezi and Limpopo rivers. The movement and sale of this gold was controlled by Zimbabwe, which directed it from the plateau east to the coastal town of Sofala, from where it was moved north along the coast to Kilwa and other Swahili towns. Other commodities included ivory from the elephant herds of the inland grasslands of East Africa, in demand in India and China to make a variety of luxury goods eagerly consumed by their elites as well as bangles worn by women of all social strata; enslaved peoples from Ethiopia and the interlacustrine region surrounding the Great Lakes of East Africa, sold into slavery in western Asia where they labored in backbreaking work such as draining swamps and mining salt in what is today southern Iraq; and rock crystal, which traveled to the Mediterranean world via the Red Sea. Products of animals such as leopard skins and rhinoceros horns, the latter in demand in parts of Asia for their purported qualities as an aphrodisiac, formed another category of East African exports. Swahili merchants also traded East African coastal products including iron, tortoise shell, spices including cloves produced primarily on the offshore island of Zanzibar, and mangrove poles, the last in high demand for constructing buildings in the sandy, unforested desert lands surrounding the Persian Gulf.

Via the Red Sea, medieval Africans from Egypt and Ethiopia also contributed commodities to Indian Ocean trade. Egyptians exported linen and cotton cloth, a variety of iron tools and weapons, and agricultural goods including wheat and wine produced in the rich agricultural lands around the Nile, whereas the people of the Ethiopian Highlands exported the aromatics frankincense and myrrh as well as gold, ivory, captives, and other goods. In return for its exports, Africans imported from India items including silk and cotton textiles and small glass beads. Africans also imported China's celebrated fine porcelain, which wealthy Swahili merchants displayed in wall niches in their elaborate stone homes as a sign of their prosperity, and incorporated into their pillar tombs. Beads and other imports from Asia attesting to the broad reach of Indian Ocean trade have been found not only in coastal locations, but far into the eastern and southern African interiors in what are today Zimbabwe, Botswana, and the Transvaal.

The monsoon winds of the Indian Ocean, which blow in a northeastern direction from East Africa to the Persian Gulf and India between April and October, and reverse direction to blow southwesterly from India and the Persian Gulf to East Africa between November and March, made it relatively easy to transport goods by dhow across this sea. Knowledge of how to beat against the prevailing wind in a series of tacks came to East African sailors at least 2,000 years ago, most likely from sailors further east, further facilitating ocean-based trade off of East Africa many centuries before the development of African–European commerce via the Atlantic emerged following fifteenth-century maritime innovations in Europe.

Adding to the broad geographic scope of Indian Ocean trade was the utilization of other waterways, including the Red Sea and Persian Gulf, which incorporated Egypt, Ethiopia, the Mediterranean world, Arabia, and Persia into this network, in addition to the Indian Ocean links to India, Indonesia, and southern China. The earliest surviving written record of this trading network dates to around 100 C.E., when *The Periplus of the Erythraen Sea*, a mariner's account written in Greek and published in Alexandria, left a detailed record of the route, terrain, market towns, peoples, trading relationships, and merchandise that made up the Red Sea and East African portions of Indian Ocean trade. Given the scope and regularity of trade described in this document, it is clear that the trading network was already very well established and thus of considerable age at that point in time, if smaller in scale than in subsequent centuries. For Indian Ocean trade grew quite dramatically from around the ninth and tenth centuries, an expansion attributed first to East Africa's connection to the larger Islamic world that occurred at that time and served as an economic stimulus to the East African economy, and second to rising demand for African ivory, gold, and rock crystal in the Mediterranean world.

Like trans-Saharan trade, Indian Ocean trade was thus intercontinental in scope and of considerable significance to the medieval economies of the parts of the world involved in it. East African ivory was very important for ceremonial, ritual, and display purposes in India and China; the slave trade that took so many East Africans to western Asia flourished for centuries, well into the modern era; East Africa was a significant purveyor of gold not only to western Asia but, through Red Sea links, to the Mediterranean world. Rock crystal followed the same route and was in demand in Mediterranean workshops until it was replaced by the use of clear glass in the eleventh century.

In addition to archaeology and **oral traditions**, information about trans-Saharan and Indian Ocean trade comes from literate travelers. Arabs, who moved from the Arabian Peninsula to the North African coast in waves of conquest in the decades following the emergence of Islam in the seventh century, as well as culturally Arabized North Africans, traveled south deep into the West African interior via the camel caravans plying the trade routes of the Sahara, and elements of what they witnessed were recorded. For example, the tenth- and eleventh-century writers Ibn Hawqal and **al-Bakri** described the wealth, size and grandeur of **Sijilmasa**, a northern oasis city very important in trans-Saharan trade. Others followed trade routes to eastern Africa. Al-Masudi, who visited the just-emerging Swahili coast in 922 to 926, described the towns of this coastline in a piece most memorably titled, "The Meadows of Gold and the Mines of Gems." **Ibn Battuta**, a particularly well-traveled Arabized Berber born in North Africa in 1304, traversed trans-Saharan and Indian Ocean networks as well as venturing to what are today Crimea, the Balkans, and southern Russia; Turkey, Iraq, Iran, Jordan, and Arabia; India, Malaya, Indonesia, and China; and southern Spain. In 1331, this world traveler described the preeminent Swahili town of Kilwa as "one of the most beautiful and well-constructed towns in the world" (Freeman-Grenville, p. 31).

Although many Africanist scholars have focused upon long-distance and intercontinental trade as most important engines driving the creation and accumulation of wealth and the rise of states in medieval Africa, more recently historians and archaeologists have turned greater attention to the role of local and regional exchange occurring within the African continent through markets and other systems of exchange such as barter. For example, scholars of West Africa have established that vibrant trade in the area around the inland Niger Delta was a hallmark of the early medieval period and began even earlier, in the last centuries of the first millennium B.C.E., and led to the founding of towns and many kinds of heightened social complexity in these centuries. This local and regional trade, driven by the creation of surpluses and the fact that different places within Africa produced different goods, is increasingly recognized as an important motor of economic activity and growth leading to social change. In short, within and between societies, in medieval Africa many goods changed hands through a wide variety of systems of exchange, in total doubtless much larger in economic scope and impact than the long-distance trade that has so often gained greater attention.

In the medieval centuries Africa had a multifaceted economy that included foraging, hunting, farming, herding, metal production and metalworking, crafts, and domestic work. Most Africans partook in a number of these activities as they worked to support themselves and their dependents. Medieval Africans also engaged in local, regional, long-distance, and intercontinental systems of exchange through which they transferred surplus goods to other peoples in return for desired items. These exchanges not only linked Africans of different communities, but also connected Africans and peoples of Europe, the Middle East, and Asia through far-reaching intercontinental trading networks of great importance to global medieval economies. *See also* Documents 1 and 2.

Further Reading

Bovill, E.W. *The Golden Trade of the Moors*. Princeton, NJ: Marcus Weiner Publishers, 1995.

Fage, J.D., ed. *The Cambridge History of Africa: Volume 2, From c. 500 BC to AD 1050*. Cambridge, UK: Cambridge University Press, 1978.

Freeman-Grenville, G.S.P. *The East African Coast: Select Documents from the First to the Earlier Nineteenth Century*. Oxford, UK: Clarendon Press, 1962.

Hamdun, Said, and Noel Q. King, eds. *Ibn Battuta in Black Africa*. Princeton, NJ: Marcus Weiner Publishers, 1995.

Levtzion, Nehemia, and Jay Spaulding, eds. *Medieval West Africa: Views from Arab Scholars and Merchants*. Princeton, NJ: Marcus Weiner Publishers, 2002.

Middleton, John. *The World of the Swahili: An African Mercantile Civilization*. New Haven, CT: Yale University Press, 1992.

Oliver, Roland, ed. *The Cambridge History of Africa: Volume 3, From c. 1050 to c. 1600*. Cambridge, UK: Cambridge University Press, 1978.

Phillipson, David W. *African Archaeology*. 3rd ed. Cambridge, UK: Cambridge University Press, 2005.

Web Site

Mali Interactive, Rice University: http://www.ruf.rice.edu/~anth/arch/maliinteractive/index.html.

4. THE ARTS

The study and understanding of medieval African artworks is complicated by a number of challenging factors. First, much of the corpus of medieval African art is unavailable today because virtually all objects made from wood, textiles, plant fibers, gourds, and animal skins, media that were widely used in the production of medieval African arts yet are highly susceptible to decomposition, have not survived to the present. Written descriptions of medieval poetry, and performing and musical arts, are similarly rarely available. What have survived are examples of medieval architecture, beads, rock art, pottery, paintings, and sculpture from various parts of the continent. Although the body of surviving artwork is relatively small compared to what was originally produced, these artifacts attest to the artistry and technical skills of medieval African artists.

Another challenge to the understanding of medieval African art derives from the fact that works of art are best understood and appreciated when the viewer is familiar with their cultural and historical contexts, because art records and reflects a society's values, mores and points of tension, as well as its aesthetics. But the deep understanding of medieval African art forms that would come from context is limited by the very circumscribed knowledge that exists of many of the cultures that produced them: For many of the surviving examples of medieval African art, these contexts are understood either incompletely or not at all. Further archaeological work on the African continent will help to expand knowledge of the contexts in which medieval African artworks were produced, and indeed today archaeologists and art historians routinely draw upon one another's work to enrich the analysis and understanding of this art.

An additional challenge comes from the fact that Western art historians have accepted African art as a legitimate field of artistic achievement and hence inquiry only since the 1950s, and consequently African arts (Table 8) of all time periods have only been studied by them for half a century. This lack of recognition of Africa artistry outside of the continent resulted in large part from the fact that Africans and their arts have been all too routinely stigmatized as primitive or tribal, traditional or unchanging, closed to innovation and hence uninfluenced by other traditions—racist misconceptions that have been successfully challenged only in the last 50 years.

Table 8. Highlights of Medieval African Art and Architecture

	Place of Artwork Production	Approximate Dates of Production
Rock art, paintings and engravings	Continent-wide	c. 27,000 B.C.–present
Aksum stelae and palaces	Aksum	c. 4th–7th centuries
Ethiopian and Nubian Ecclesiastical art	Ethiopian Highlands and Nubia	c. 5th century on
Lydenburg heads	Southern Africa	c. 6th–7th centuries
Igbo-Ukwu cast metal sculptures	Igbo-Ukwu, Igboland	9th–10th centuries
Terra-cotta sculptures	Inland Niger Delta	c. 900–1400
Yoruba cast metal and terra-cotta Sculptures	Ife	c. 1000–1500
Benin bronzes	Benin	c. 1000–19th century
Rock-hewn churches	Lalibela, Ethiopian Highlands	12th–13th centuries
Coral-stone houses	Swahili Coast	c. 1200–1500
Stone wall enclosures	Great Zimbabwe	13th–14th centuries
Sankoré Mosque	Timbuktu	14th century
Husuni Kubwa (palace)	Kilwa, Swahili Coast	14th century
Great Mosque	Kilwa, Swahili Coast	14th–15th centuries

Finally, Western criteria for judging artistic achievement, which have tended to privilege objects understood to be created for aesthetic enjoyment rather than practical use and, until the advent of photography, naturalism—the most realistic or true-to-life portrayal—has led to the further devaluing of African arts that most commonly though not uniformly tend to the abstract or stylized rather than strictly representational, and often serve purposes other than solely ornamental—though this did not mean that their aesthetic qualities were not highly valued in the societies that produced them.

In sum, knowledge of medieval African art is bounded by the limited artifacts that survive, by dominant Western definitions of *art* that have too often excluded, devalued, or stigmatized African art forms, and by limited knowledge of the cultures that produced it and thus incomplete understandings of the meaning and aesthetic appeal of African arts to the artists, patrons, and consumers who produced, underwrote, utilized, and appreciated them in the medieval era. These challenges notwithstanding, in the last 50 years scholars of the African arts have greatly deepened their knowledge of medieval African rock art, jewelry, sculpture, architecture, painting, and pottery.

Sculpture

Africa is recognized for an extraordinarily rich tradition of sculpture. Two stunning and well-known collections of medieval African sculpture come from what is today Nigeria in West Africa. The earlier of the two are the Igbo-Ukwu sculptures, some of which were first unearthed in the late 1930s by a farmer named Isaiah Anozie as he dug a cistern behind his home in the village of Igbo-Ukwu, located near the eastern bank of the lower Niger River (*see* **Igbo**). Formal excavations at this and two neighboring sites were carried out by the archaeologist Thurstan Shaw between 1959 and 1964. Igbo-Ukwu yielded magnificent bronze sculptures radiocarbon dated to the ninth and tenth centuries C.E. and made by the lost-wax casting technique. The cast sculptures recovered at Igbo-Ukwu include basins, pots, bowls, and other vessels, two cast in the unusual shape of forest snails, with an extraordinarily rich profusion of delicately worked details covering the surface of the objects. Abstract designs include spirals, lines, dots, filigree, and concentric circles, though equally finely worked representations of animals and insects include frogs, flies, locusts, beetles, snakes, and leopards. The delicacy and extraordinary detail of these objects attest to the exquisite artistry and technical skills of the individuals who achieved these results through the lost wax process. Ceramic vessels of great artisanship that likewise display extensive and detailed surface decoration, different in style from that of the cast vessels, were also excavated from these sites, as well as objects made from hammered copper and iron.

Many of the artworks from Igbo-Ukwu were recovered from one burial chamber, obviously that of a very powerful and wealthy man, who appears to have been interred sitting erect with his feet on an elephant tusk, a common symbol of authority in West Africa. Other regalia associated with rulers found at this burial site include statues of leopards and elephants, a fly whisk, staffs, bells, and a fan holder. This site also contained over one-hundred thousand glass beads, many imported from outside the continent, whose immense profusion attested to the prosperity of this individual, hammered copper ornaments, and a hollow, cast bronze stand, striking for the delicacy with which it portrays on its openwork panels two human figures surrounded by twining vines and snakes. These cast bronze objects recovered at Igbo-Ukwu demonstrate the extraordinary artistry achieved by ninth- and tenth-century West Africans.

The second great Nigerian example of cast metal medieval sculpture comes from the city of Ife, also known as Ile-Ife, historically the spiritual and political center of the **Yoruba**. These sculptures initially came to the attention of the Western world in 1910 through the actions of Leo Frobenius, a German ethnologist who, in keeping with the racism of his time, thought these beautiful and striking naturalistic sculptures of life-size human heads could not have been produced by Africans. He attributed them, variously and on the basis of no evidence, to the classical Greco-Roman tradition and even the lost city of Atlantis, whereas others posited an Egyptian or South Asian provenance; these invented attributions have since been thoroughly discredited. Interest in this artistic tradition heightened with the accidental unearthing of more artifacts, first in 1938 in the course of excavating house foundations at the Wunmonije Compound that abutted the medieval palace of the *oni*, or king, of Ife, and then in 1957 through the actions of workers building near an important gate in the medieval city wall. The cast sculptures thus unearthed date to 1000 to 1400, the Pavement Period of Ife history, so called because of the practice of paving gateways, shrines, and some courtyards and verandahs of the royal palace and private houses with mosaics constructed from potsherds and white stones. The Ife sculptures dating to the Pavement Period were produced through the lost-wax casting technique also practiced at Igbo-Ukwu. They were made primarily of brass but occasionally of pure and almost-pure copper. Archaeological digs conducted by Frank Willet, Ekpo Eyo, and Peter Garlake in the 1950s through the 1970s followed in an attempt to provide an archaeologically reconstructed context for these accidentally uncovered artworks.

In contrast to the vessels of cast metal discovered at Igbo-Ukwu, the focus of the Ife sculptures is the human face and form. Fewer than thirty cast metal pieces have been recovered, a majority of which depict life-size heads that in their calm beauty and composure most likely depict the ideal *oni* or king, rather than actual individual rulers. These brasses are studded with lines of holes located along the hairline and jaw as well as around the mouth. It is conjectured that crowns and veils made from strings of beads were attached to the sculpted heads via these holes, because Yoruba rulers avoid showing their faces and mouths publicly. They might also have served as attachments for recreations of facial hair. Some of these heads are covered with vertical striations, which don't resemble actual Yoruba scarification designs and according to Garlake might be either aesthetic devices or representations of the shadows, which would have resulted from a veil's strands of beads (*Early Art and Architecture*, 125, 136). The remaining cast metal sculptures include smaller-than-life-size heads, the complete figure of a standing *oni*, the joined figures of two royals, staff and mace heads, a vessel, and one final and most unusual metal sculpture from Ife: a copper mask that was not unearthed but has been kept continuously at the *oni*'s palace. The great difficulty of casting copper, combined with the perfect execution of this graceful and beautiful mask, speaks to the immense technical skills of Ife artists.

In contradistinction to a common African sculptural preference for stylized depictions of people, the Ife cast metal full-size heads stand out for a significant degree of facial naturalism—in fact it was in part this characteristic that led Frobenius to think they could not have been West African—combined however with the nonrepresentational elements of small, almond-shaped eyes, simplified ears, and stylized lips—what Frank Willett labels the "idealized naturalism" characteristic of this Ife art (*African Art*, 72). The Ife heads are noted for capturing a serene beauty that not only articulates the kingly ideal, but also has drawn many who know nothing of their cultural context to these artworks for their deep and abiding innate appeal.

In addition to the brasses, Ife artists produced large numbers of terra-cotta pieces. These include naturalistic full-size heads, exquisitely executed, which are similar to the brass heads in style. Other Ife terra-cotta faces, however, are deeply stylized and bear strictly limited resemblance to actual human form. Terra-cotta renderings of full-size figures have also been excavated. The surviving full-size sculptures made of brass and terra-cotta follow the typical African sculptural convention of a disproportionately large head. Terra-cotta animals and pots have also been found.

Current interpretations of the uses or symbolic meanings of the full-size cast metal Ife heads focus upon their striking uniformity of style, which makes it probable that they were produced quite rapidly by a small group of artists working cooperatively. Suzanne Preston Blier has proposed that the sixteen heads related to coronation ceremonies legitimizing the kingship of the sixteen Yoruba rulers most closely connected to Ife. Peter Garlake has focused upon the great personal character, inner power, and divine authority of Yoruba monarchs, ideals that are reflected literally and figuratively by the form and beauty of these heads. Rowland Abiodun connects these sculptures to the complex and multifaceted Yoruba concept of *ase*, which in part can be understood as the vital force or energy of a living thing. In regards to political leadership, *ase*, which also connotes power, authority and control, is conferred upon a new ruler verbally at his or her installation. In the visual arts, he adds, heads are the most important symbols of *ase*, because it resides in this part of a person, and representations of heads can, if well executed, transmit *ase* as potently as words. Thus sculpted heads are well-chosen symbolic as well as literal representations of Yoruba political authority and beliefs.

Another very rich example of medieval African sculpture exists in the thousands of terra-cotta forms, which have been found in the Middle Niger region of West Africa. The Middle Niger stretches across the Inland Niger Delta, a large flood plain of the Niger River with very fertile soil and rich agricultural harvests that has created an environment highly conducive to human settlement. It contains sites of early urbanization, trade, and cultural achievement in West Africa stretching back even before the medieval period. The majority of Middle Niger sculptures have been removed through looting and subsequent sale in international art markets rather than controlled excavations, making their contexts lost forever. But happily, and in contrast to the Ife finds, some Middle Niger sculptures have been unearthed in the course of carefully structured archaeological digs, most notably excavations conducted by Roderick and Susan McIntosh over some 30 years at the Middle Niger site named **Jenné-jeno**. The Middle Niger figurines whose provenance is clear have radiocarbon datings of 900 to 1400. The figures, typically 4 to 10 inches in height, most commonly depict individuals who are kneeling or sitting, with arms placed either on knees or raised and crossed with hands on shoulders. Individuals on horseback, people exhibiting disfigurement and disease, and animals are also well-represented subjects. Like numerous African sculptural traditions, many of the figurines exhibit a stylized rather than strictly representational depiction, in this case with ovoid and upturned heads characterized by prominent, bulging eyes, and a jutting jaw. Substantial detail is often paid to body decoration in the forms of jewelry and scarification. In regards to the context in which these artworks were created, based on the urbanization and social differentiation that intensified at Jenné-jeno from around 500, the McIntoshes hypothesized that these developments led to increasingly complex categories of social identity and concomitant desires to emphasize group solidarity, and that each group's identity may have been maintained in part through art forms such as these extraordinarily numerous terra-cotta sculptures.

Many examples of surviving medieval sculpture are also found in southern Africa. Among these are the Lydenburg heads, hollow terra-cotta sculptures decorated with hatching and incisions which may represent scarification, dating to the sixth or seventh century C.E. and found in the early 1960s in what is today South Africa. The Lydenburg heads fit into a broader southern African tradition of Early Iron Age terra-cotta sculpture, frequently small human or animal figurines, though these ceramic works were more often solid rather than hollow like the heads. Another important sculptural find from southern Africa is a small statue of a rhinoceros constructed from gold sheeting, originally affixed to a wooden core. This sculpture was found at a burial site at Mapungubwe, a hilltop polity dating from the eleventh century C.E. located on the **Zimbabwe Plateau**. Its artists produced a variety of objects from gold sheeting fastened to wood and also worked gold into wire, tacks, and jewelry such as beads and bangles. A final southern African example are the well-known if little understood soft greenish soapstone carvings of birds perched atop pillars found at Great Zimbabwe.

Although the sculptures discussed above are among the best-known examples from medieval Africa, other sculptures from throughout the medieval period and produced in a range of media including rock, ivory, terra-cotta, and metal have been found widely across sub-Saharan Africa. Doubtless new finds will continue to be made that will enable future scholars of African art to more fully comprehend medieval African sculpture.

Generalizations about African arts are always problematic given the immense cultural and artistic variation found on this large continent, so exceptions to all of the following statements can certainly be found. Nonetheless, some stylistic conventions and aesthetic preferences do emerge from a study of sub-Saharan African sculpture. For example, the most common subject is a single person. Although depictions of individuals dominate, a person on horseback, a mother (or far more rarely father) and child pair, and twins are not unusual sculptural subjects. Individuals with physical anomalies or diseases such as hydrocephaly, elephantiasis, and boils form another common motif, reflecting environmental challenges Africans have had to face. Animals are frequently depicted too. It is certain that masks formed another significant sculptural genre in medieval Africa, given the clearly deeply rooted tradition of masking that is richly documented in the accounts of European visitors to Africa's coastlines from the early modern period and descriptions of masked dancers made by some medieval visitors. But because masks would typically have been carved from wood to lighten them and thus make them more easily worn, medievally produced masks have not survived to the present with rare exceptions such as the copper face mask from Ife and, some conjecture, the hollow Lydenburg heads, which might have served as masks though their weight makes this questionable.

Other aesthetic and stylistic conventions are common in medieval African sculpture. For example, sculptures typically present people in the prime of young adulthood, even if the actual age of the individual being depicted was far older or younger. There is also a preference for facial expressions of serenity and calm. A body to head ratio of 3–4:1 dominates African sculptural traditions, in contrast to the usual adult human body to head ratio of approximately 5:1, which the Western sculptural tradition often extends in the opposite direction from African sculpture to an artificially elongated ratio of 6–8:1. These differing Western and African preferences, combined with the nineteenth- and twentieth-century Western tendency to dismiss Africans and their artistic traditions as primitive, led early Western collectors and students of African art to misidentify the preferred African ratio as an indication of imprecision, childishness, or incorrectness in this art form, rather than as the deliberately chosen stylistic convention it actually represents. Finally, African sculpture shows a strong though certainly not uniform preference for abstraction over realism.

Thus sculptures most commonly depict individuals according to the stylizations of a given cultural/artistic tradition (though with variation from artist to artist within a given genre reflecting personal aesthetic and style) in preference to creating as realistic as possible a replication of an individual's actual features or a given animal's precise form.

Architecture

As with other African art forms, relatively little of medieval architecture remains today due to the perishability of common building materials such as wood, mud, clay, and thatch. The architectural traditions that have survived are mainly either far more durable stone constructions, or mosques and churches that have been maintained carefully over the centuries because of their religious significance. Examples of the latter will be covered in the next section. Two other notable architectural traditions from medieval Africa are found in a pair of places whose economies were intertwined in their joint contributions to the intercontinental Indian Ocean trading network, yet whose cultures, including architectural styles, influenced each other very little: Zimbabwe and the **Swahili** coast.

Great Zimbabwe, located on the Zimbabwe Plateau in the East African interior, is noted for its magnificent and awe-inspiring massive stonewall enclosures. Constructed from the thirteenth through fourteenth centuries A.D., these majestic walls, still deeply impressive today, were built of blocks of the local granite found in the surrounding hills. The earliest walls at Great Zimbabwe were constructed from slabs, which had split away from the bedrock naturally as a result of daily changes in temperature, whereas thereafter workers built fires on the granite slopes and then doused them with water to cause additional slabs to break free. Each wall, which is actually formed of two parallel walls with granite slab fill in between them, is composed of blocks fitted together without mortar with great care in a series of courses, which retain their stability to the present day. As much as 20 feet thick at their base, the walls taper as they rise to heights of over 30 feet. Abutting walls simply adjoin one another rather than being bonded together. Inside the large enclosures formed by these walls, which have perimeters reaching 800 feet, were raised platforms, a striking conical stone tower in shape resembling a granary, the carved soapstone birds mentioned above, and narrow passageways with high walls through which people had to walk single file, giving a sense of solitude, privacy, and grandeur to the sites. Increased sophistication of style and mastery of technique developed over the approximately two centuries of construction, with a change from irregular to regular courses, square to round and buttressed doorways, and greater use of decorative motifs such as chevrons, herringbone patterns and strips worked into the upper levels of later walls as the masonry skills of the workers became increasingly refined.

Great Zimbabwe today incorporates three main ruins, all closely linked in their location on a hilltop and its valley below: the Hill Complex, the Great Enclosure, and the Valley Complex. In regards to purpose, the walls of Great Zimbabwe could not have served a defensive function given their numerous open entryways and lack of defensive fortifications. The Great Enclosure appears to have surrounded the royal palace of the rulers of Great Zimbabwe, and walls also encompassed sites of religious importance. Additionally and probably most important, all of the walls served a prestige function by virtue of their imposing size and the ability of the state to command labor they so clearly represented. In addition to Great Zimbabwe, stonewall enclosures are found at numerous sites on the Zimbabwe Plateau and even beyond it, indicating that this architectural tradition expanded far beyond Great Zimbabwe itself. As the most powerful of the Zimbabwe plateau polities, though, it is unsurprising that Zimbabwe's walls reached a more colossal size and impressive style than those of its neighbors in East Africa.

Much as Frobenius asserted a Western provenance for the Ife brasses, the first Europeans to see the mighty walls of Great Zimbabwe assumed they must have been constructed by non-Africans, variously and spuriously identified on the basis of no evidence whatsoever as Phoenician or Arab, even including King Solomon and the Queen of Sheba. Also sadly similar is the fact that early excavations in Great Zimbabwe had a focal point not of archaeological exploration and preservation, but in the case of Great Zimbabwe looting for gold. Thus far less is known of Great Zimbabwe than would be the case if controlled digs had been conducted before the site was so deeply disturbed. Nonetheless, archaeologists working subsequently at Great Zimbabwe have found a clear African provenance for these walls with confirmed African habitation of the site dating back to the early medieval years.

Contemporaneous with Great Zimbabwe is the rise of a highly distinctive form of architecture found on East Africa's Swahili coast. Here, between 1200 and 1500, wealthy East African merchants who made their fortunes as intermediaries buying and selling goods in the trans-continental Indian Ocean trading network (see "Economy" section) developed a unique style of opulent home construction. Swahili merchants built their lavish homes from coral. When quarried from the reefs located just off the East African shoreline and kept underwater, this building material is soft and easily shaped into decorative elements of the houses, like door jambs, which upon removal from the water and exposure to air harden into a very durable construction material. Already hardened coral gathered on shore was typically shaped into basic building blocks with which to form the four outer walls of these rectangular homes. The coral blocks were joined together with mortar and plastered dazzling white with lime, whereas short rafters made from mangrove poles were used as ceiling and roof supports. Due to their sturdy walls and high ceilings, the interior rooms of these houses tended to remain pleasantly cool no matter the temperature outside. Constructed on a north-south axis around a central courtyard, the houses also possessed systems of internal sanitation in the form of dry pit toilets, stored water in cisterns, and the tallest reached three stories in height. As testament to the wealth and financial stability of the merchants who owned them, elaborately carved niches and recesses were built into the interior walls of these homes for the display of valuables such as imported Chinese porcelain wares or a copy of the Qur'an, and many interior surfaces were not only plastered white but richly carved and decorated.

Swahili stone house architecture put a very high premium upon privacy in domestic space, due in part to the upper-class practice of secluding women from the gaze of outsiders in keeping with the tenets of their Islamic faith, and in part to the implied purity and thus family respectability associated with privacy. Therefore, movement farther and farther into the interior of a Swahili home also represented movement into places of greater and greater seclusion and purity. Immediately inside the intricately carved wooden doors leading from the street into the northern side of a Swahili home was located first a porch and then the interior courtyard, in which Swahili merchants welcomed visitors and conducted business with Middle Eastern and South Asian trading partners. Only rarely would anyone other than a family member or very close friend be allowed beyond the porch and courtyard into the inner reaches of the home. Indeed, the inner doorway that led from the courtyard to the interior rooms on the southern side of the house was purposely unaligned with the house's exterior door so that a casual visitor could never see accidentally into the home's true interior. Behind the courtyard, at the southern end of the house, lay one or more inner galleries, each raised a step above the one preceding it, where much of the daily life of a family such as eating, socializing, and sleeping took place. Long and narrow, the shape of the inner galleries was limited by the unavoidably short length of the mangrove pole rafters to a typical width of approximately 9 feet, and a length, which stretched as long as the east-west extent spanned by the house's side walls. Beyond these inner galleries, continuing the spectrum of most public to most private space, lay the private bedroom of the wife and husband of the house. Behind this bedroom, and hence most secluded, was a bathroom used by the inhabitants of this room, and the chamber in which took place the most intimate activities of women such as childbirth and preparation of bodies for burial. In their comfort, size, beauty and symbolic meanings, these homes reflected the riches, sophistication, material comfort, and beliefs of their owners.

Other Art Forms and Global Influences

In Africa, rock art is a continent-wide phenomenon though the most numerous finds are concentrated in southern Africa and what is today the Sahara Desert. Rock art had its origins long before the medieval period. Although difficult to fix in time, the earliest dated rock art is believed to have been produced in what is today Namibia some 27,000 years ago. Saharan rock art appears to be a much more recent phenomenon dating back some 8,000 to 10,000 years. In any event, it is an art form that has had a continuous history, as medieval examples indicating the introduction of camel or cattle, and modern subjects depicting nineteenth-century colonial officials and soldiers and twentieth-century airplanes, attest. Common subjects of medieval rock art include wild and domesticated animals; depictions of people engaged in hunting, farming, pastoralism, warfare, and other activities; handprints; and abstract designs incorporating ovals, dots, spirals, concentric lines, and more. Techniques of rock art include painting and engraving. Common locations for paintings are cave walls and ceilings and rock overhangs, which would have protected artists and their creations from the elements, whereas the more enduring engravings or petroglyphs are more often found in exposed locations. Styles of rock art range from naturalistic to idealized to abstract.

Another form of art that existed in medieval Africa, modification of the surface of the human body, yet again utilized a perishable medium so that today it can be observed only indirectly, through depictions of scarification, raised keloid scarring, cicatrices, and the like in surviving medieval statuary from traditions as diverse as the Middle Niger terra-cottas, Igbo-Ukwu and Ife sculptures, and the Lydenburg heads. Body art in the form of elaborate styles of hair arrangement are also documented, as is body ornamentation using beads. Decorated gourds are represented in surviving sculptures too but like most domestic art forms have not survived first-hand. Medieval textiles, which have been preserved to the present only in extraordinarily rare instances, have been cursorily described for some parts of medieval Africa such as **Ghana** and **Mali** through the writings of visitors to the continent, but for the most part information about what was undoubtedly a very important medieval medium for artistic expression is absent.

Significant outside influences on medieval African art include the arrival of **Christianity** in the first century and **Islam** in the seventh. For example, a stunning example of ecclesiastical architecture is found in the highly unusual rock-cut churches of medieval **Ethiopian Christianity**. Built in extremely arduous acts of deep piety in the mountainous **Ethiopian Highlands** beginning in the twelfth or thirteenth centuries under the royal patronage of kings of Zagwe, these eleven churches were actually carved from living rock, working from the surface downward, according to tradition in an attempt to create a "New Jerusalem" as a response to the Islamic warrior Saladin's conquest of Jerusalem in 1187. They incorporate domes, pillars, archways, basilicas, naves, sacristies, windows, aisles, galleries, and many finely worked decorative details, among other things, and clearly draw on extraordinary skills of architectural planning and masonry since the finished structure had to be planned in complete detail before any carving of the rock began, and the method did not allow for significant error in the subtraction of the bedrock. As new finds of churches and tombs continue to be made, it appears that these eleven churches at Lalibela actually draw upon an older, pre-Christian regional tradition of rock-cut edifices such as the stelae of **Aksum**. In addition to these rock-cut churches, Ethiopia and Christian **Nubia** to its northwest developed traditions of ecclesiastical painting such as wall murals, frescoes, and illuminated manuscripts that seem to draw upon Byzantine conventions such as frontal poses, very large eyes, and little attempt to create the appearance of depth, as well as local traditions such as the use of regionally dominant color palettes and the replacement in Nativity scenes of the wise men's usual camels with horses by the artists of equine-loving Nubia. Among the subjects of these paintings are portraits of Nubian bishops and well-known Biblical scenes.

A prominent Islamic influence upon the arts of medieval Africa is found in mosque architecture. Modifications in keeping with local aesthetics, building materials, environmentally imposed needs, and patterns of religious observance are characteristic of mosques across the continent, though the precise forms these regional variations take differ from place to place. For example, with the notable exception of the expansive Great Mosque of **Kilwa**, wealthiest and most prominent of the Swahili cities, mosques along the Swahili coast were typically small places of worship serving very localized neighborhoods, their size in part dictated by the tightly knit ward-based identity of Swahili towns. In savannah regions of West Africa, medieval mosques constructed of the dominant local building material, mud brick, were and are characterized by the bristling appearance of large wooden beams that jut out horizontally up and down their exterior walls to create a permanent scaffolding, an adaptation that allows for easy repair of the walls that frequently incur damage during the rainy season. Calligraphy is another important Muslim contribution, valued for its use in creating copies of the Qur'an and because of the widespread tradition of decorating artworks produced in the Islamic world with writing such as verses from the Qur'an and other religious texts, or benedictions.

Medieval African art stands out for the exquisite technical virtuosity displayed by its creators in media as varied as clay, ivory, wood, rock, and metal sculpture; jewelry and beadwork; rock paintings and engravings; domestic arts; body decoration; textiles; regalia; pottery; painting; and architecture. The scope of artistry and aesthetics demonstrated in these art forms, which range from naturalistic to stylized to abstract, also stands out—indeed, it was the stylization and abstraction of many African arts that underlay the early-twentieth-century modernist movement of Picasso and other Western artists who were inspired in new nonrepresentational directions by their exposure to African artworks. Although varied regional styles and aesthetic preferences certainly existed in medieval Africa, as they do today, the African art of that time also reveals a history of adaptability and innovation, for example the incorporation of new art forms in response to the introduction of Christianity and Islam. Other global influences on the arts came from medieval trans-continental trade, which led to African importation of artifacts including Chinese porcelain and South Asian and Italian beads. Although in this still-new field an understanding of the meanings attached to medieval African art forms by those who produced and consumed them is anything but complete, it is clear that African art works reflected not only local aesthetics, and the individualized vision of a given artist, but also the beliefs, concerns, social structures, and cosmologies of their communities.

Further Reading

Abiodun, Rowland. "Understanding Yoruba Art and Aesthetics: The Concept of Ase." *African Arts*, 27:3 (1994): 68–78, 102–103.

Blier, Suzanne Preston. "Kings, Crowns, and Rights of Succession: Obalufon Arts at Ife and Other Yoruba Centers." *The Art Bulletin*, 67:3 (Sept. 1985): 383–401.

Garlake, Peter. *Early Art and Architecture of Africa*. Oxford, UK: Oxford University Press, 2002.

Gillon, Werner. *A Short History of African Art*. New York: Facts on File, 1984.

McIntosh, R.J., and S.K. McIntosh. "Middle Niger Culture," in *The Dictionary of African Art*. London: Macmillan Publishers, 1996.

Sieber, Roy, and Roslyn Adele Walker. *African Art in the Cycle of Life*. Washington, DC: Smithsonian Institution Press, 1987.

Turner, Jane, ed. "Africa." in *The Dictionary of Art*. Vol. 1. London: Macmillan Publishers, 1996.

Willett, Frank. *African Art*. New York: Thames and Hudson, 1971.

Web Sites

Indianapolis Museum of Art's award-winning web site "Cycles: African Life through Art: http://www.ima.museum/cycles/index.html.

National Museum of African Art web site: http://africa.si.edu.

5. SOCIETY

This essay covers two critically important aspects of medieval African societies. First, a section on social organization addresses kinship, descent, and marriage.

Although it is often assumed that ethnicity must have played a critical role in the social framework of medieval Africa, in reality ethnicity—though not unimportant—was a very fluid concept, for instance affected by place/environmental zone of residence, occupation, or intermarriage, and consequently it was often overshadowed by very localized kinship identities. Thus this essay focuses on kinship rather than ethnicity. Significant social stratification existed in medieval Africa too, so this first section also explores the varied sources of social hierarchies. Second, a section addressing political structures looks at the broad division of medieval African societies into, first, places with centralized political authority, some of which were culturally homogenous states and others of which were heterogeneous empires that included conquered peoples; and, second, those places, typically referred to as either stateless or acephalous societies, in which political power was diffused throughout a broad range of community members. This second section also addresses legitimations of political authority. Effects of gender are noted throughout the essay. The social complexity attested to by this essay clearly reflects the increase in surplus wealth that characterized medieval Africa and existed as a result of the greater productivity of fixed agriculture, herding, ironworking, and the resulting local, regional, long-distance, and sometimes intercontinental trade in surplus goods also characteristic of the medieval centuries.

Social Organization

Kinship played the most fundamental role in social identification and was the basic building block of most medieval African societies. Kinship typically defined who was and was not family, where one lived, with whom one lived, and who was a legitimate marriage partner. Kinship also determined access to some key forms of political authority, for example via membership in royal clans, and at times imposed a broad range of rights and obligations upon family members, such as with whom or for whom one worked. Although kinship provided a deep sense of belonging, place, and security for individuals, it also introduced strains and tensions between family members who had to live, share resources, and in certain circumstances work together in occasionally stiflingly close interaction, and in ways which typically privileged some family members over others, notably men over women and elders over those junior in age. In short, kinship shaped, mediated, and controlled most key aspects of a person's day-to-day life for good and ill.

In regards to how kinship was structured, most African societies were divided into a number of large descent groups, or clans, all of those members were considered to belong to one extended family by virtue of shared descent from a common ancestor. Because in a large society a single clan might encompass literally tens or hundreds of thousands of individuals, this demarcation was often unwieldy in practice. Therefore clans were typically broken down into a number of distinct sub-units that typically were limited to all of the descendents of a common ancestor to a fourth, fifth, or sixth generation, known in English translation as lineages and sublineages. Generally it was in these smaller, more meaningful subdivisions of a clan that kinship matters played out for any given individual.

Numerous methods of tracing descent—of determining who was considered a bona fide member of a particular descent group, be it clan, lineage, or sublineage—existed in medieval Africa. Most common on the African continent then (as now) was unilineal descent, in which family membership and identity were derived either from one's father or mother but never from both parents. Patrilineal descent traced family membership through the paternal line and created patriclans and patrilineages, whereas matrilineal descent traced family membership through the maternal line resulting in matriclans and matrilineages. In sum, in patrilineal societies children belonged to their fathers' families, whereas in matrilineal societies children belonged to their mothers'. Over the course of the medieval centuries a number of societies moved from matrilineal to patrilineal descent, making matrilineality a distinctly minority practice as it remains today. An even smaller minority of medieval African societies practiced bilateral descent—also known as dual, double, or cognatic descent—wherein a child possessed membership in the families of both parents. Examples of well-known medieval societies practicing the more common unilineal descent include the matrilineal Soninke rulers of **Ghana** and the patrilineal Malinke rulers of **Mali**.

Although membership in a particular descent group created an individual's most important and fundamental social place, marriage, a near-universal expectation for adults in medieval African societies, was also a key social institution. The vast majority of African societies practiced exogamy, the requirement that an individual marry someone from outside of his or her clan or lineage, which broadened the network of social connections for both families. This was critically important in African societies because wealth in people was most valuable: The continent's low population density meant that people and their labor power, not other productive resources like land, set the limits of productivity. Because marriage was an affair affecting more than individuals, typically both families were actively involved in choosing a spouse, approving a potential spouse, and formalizing the union. Exceptions to the general rule of exogamy were found primarily in certain occupational castes. For example, Mande smiths and griots formed closed castes; only individuals born into smithing or griot families, which practiced endogamy or marriage within the extended caste group, could take up these occupations.

For the majority of Africans practicing exogamous marriage, for women from patrilineal societies, which typically practiced virilocal residence, marriage meant movement away from the security of family to the status of a stranger (outsider) in her husband's village, often with relatively low status until she gave birth to a son. In matrilineal societies, however, married wives and husbands commonly resided separately, each remaining in his or her own lineage home, in the practice known as duolocal residence. In matrilineal societies wives and husbands also typically remained financially independent of each other and kept their resources separate rather than melding them in one conjugal pot, and though this was true also of some patrilineal societies such as the **Yoruba**, in others it was not. **Women** also bore greater responsibility for raising children in matrilineal societies—often with the assistance yet also under the ultimate authority of male members of their matrilineage—than did women in patrilineal societies where the children belonged to their father's family.

Many medieval African societies practiced polygyny, allowing men to marry more than one woman simultaneously. Only wealthy or otherwise successful men were likely to attract second, third, and subsequent wives, though the practice was broadly appealing to men insofar as the conjugal unit of wife, husband, and children most commonly formed the productive unit, with the result that the more wives, the more a man benefited from their labor power. Institutionalized practices to minimize the inherent potential for conflict among cowives (women married simultaneously to the same man) could include regular rotations for sex and cooking; sharing the burden of domestic work such as child care and the production of **food** for the family; and the imperative — often, however, honored in the breech — that cowives be treated equally in all respects. In patrilineal societies, family compounds generally contained a separate house for each wife as well as one for the husband, giving privacy, autonomy, and an independent home to each woman and her children, while in matrilineal societies the practice of duolocal residence achieved the same result. Nonetheless, clearly in a polygynous marriage the husband represented the scarce resource, and it is thus not surprising that the word for co-wife in more than one African language translated as "the jealous one." Significant differentials in age of first marriage, with men marrying much later than women, to some extent ameliorated the scarcity of marriageable women polygyny created for some men, but contributed also to intergenerational tensions between older and younger men. The privileged access older men in a family typically had to family resources also gave them in edge in marriage, not least in the many southern African societies which required men's families to pay bride wealth to women's families as part of the process of marrying.

The near-universality of marriage was connected to the social imperative to bear children, in order both to continue the lineage and produce the descendents who would honor the family's ancestral spirits. The death of a lineage, and thus of individuals who could keep alive the memory of those members of the family who had preceded them, was among the worst of all possible fates. Children also provided valuable assistance in work such as farming, cattle herding, and domestic labor and served as a form of social security for old age. The prevalence of tropical **disease**s such as malaria, yellow fever, and sleeping sickness, as well as dysenteries, parasites, and the plague, which were endemic to broad stretches of the continent and caused very high rates of infant and childhood mortality, made successful childbearing and rearing all the more important and valued.

In short, marriage was a centrally important social institution. It was most commonly through marriage that women in matrilineal societies and men in patrilineal societies continued their lineages (exceptions included when individuals such as immigrants and slaves were incorporated into a descent group even though their descent from the common founding ancestor was putative rather than literally true). Yet like kinship, marriage had the capacity to create a variety of profound tensions. For most individuals, the dominant exogamous form of marriage caused a strong pull between lineage and conjugal ties and obligations. Between men and women, the access to women's productive and reproductive labor and capacities that marriage gave men could cause strains. Polygyny, which sanctioned nonmonogamy for men, often while requiring monogamy of women, created an additional source of stress. Polygyny also had the potential to create tensions between individual women who lived as cowives, whereas among men the greater access to marriageable women held by older men could create intergenerational conflict.

The profound social importance of kinship in medieval Africa, which existed side-by-side with the concomitant reality of people traveling frequently to conduct regional and long-distance trade, created the social category of strangers (outsiders or nonkin): people far removed from the safety and security of their own families. One solution, explored with great elegance and detail by George Brooks, was the creation of a longstanding, many-centuries-old West African tradition of offering hospitality and security of person and property to strangers. The epic of **Sundjata**, an orally transmitted history recounting the thirteenth-century emergence of the mighty West African empire of Mali, gives evidence of this tradition of hospitality in its descriptions of the food and shelter freely offered by so many to the young prince Sundjata and his mother and sisters as they wandered in exile before his eventual triumphal return home. A similar tradition was described by the great medieval traveler **Ibn Battuta** for East Africa's Indian Ocean coast; he wrote of the regularized hospitality afforded visiting merchants by their **Swahili** hosts. The frequent travels of African peoples also created conduits for the cross-cultural sharing and dissemination of ideas for which the medieval period is noted. For example traveling merchants played a key role in the spread of **Islam**, and the Mande-created Sande and Poro secret societies became important and influential across a broad swathe of West African societies as a result of traveling to trade.

Although kinship and marriage constituted the basic pillars of the social order, medieval African peoples also lived with a number of widely utilized social hierarchies derived from other loci for social identity. These differed in detail, importance, and even existence from place to place on the continent and over time; what follows is a very broad overview of some of the most common delineators of social authority, power, and prestige. To begin, medieval Africans typically practiced gerontocracy, or the privileging of older over younger members of a society. Deference to elders was expected, and elder members of a family generally wielded great authority over those junior to them in age. Changes in status from childhood, to marriageable, to parent, and to elder were often marked by explicit rites of passage, which could involve education and, particularly for the earlier transitions, some physical manifestation of the changed status through bodily modifications such as circumcision, scarring, or tattooing. Second, although the degree to which precolonial African societies were patriarchal is a matter of considerable dispute, and undoubtedly there were broad divergences from place to place and also within given societies, it is generally agreed that a hierarchy of sex often privileged men over women, giving males preferential access to social authority and economic resources. An interesting exception existed in hunting and gathering societies, which were and are recognized for a far greater egalitarianism regarding gender than that found in any other type of society. Achievement was a third important indicator of success, and those who acquired renown via trading, hunting, farming, fighting, wrestling, childbearing, religious authority, or wealth benefited in social standing as a result of their prowess. A reputation for insight, wisdom, and common sense, and the ability to speak well, also added to one's standing. Finally, personal power could be derived through membership in one or more of the many corporate bodies such as age grades, women's collectives, and secret societies available to many medieval Africans.

Political Structures

Both highly centralized forms of political governance and the much more diffuse rule characteristic of what are known as stateless or acephalous (literally, without a head; in this context, without a governing head) societies existed in medieval Africa. Beginning with the former, among the best-known examples of centralized medieval African states are the great and fabulously wealthy West African Sudanic empires of Ghana and Mali. Recent scholarship indicates that these storied empires followed upon a far older, premedieval tradition of urbanism and interregional commerce in Sudanic West Africa attested to by archaeological sites such as the Inland Niger Delta community of **Jenné-jeno**, which emerged around 200 B.C.E. Political developments here, as elsewhere on the continent, depended in part upon the creation of agricultural surpluses, which were relatively easily achieved in the fertile grasslands of the West African Sudan and reached their apogee in the extremely rich soils of the Inland Niger Delta. The refinement of iron technologies and agricultural innovations such as the ennoblement of crops assisted in the creation of larger harvests too. This generation of surplus wealth made possible occupational specialization, including the emergence of a political class, as some individuals could concentrate on affairs other than subsistence activities.

Ghana, which had emerged by 400 and lasted into the early thirteenth century, encompassed portions of the West African sahel and northern sudanic belt that was located to the sahel's south. In addition to income derived from agriculture, tribute demanded from conquered neighbors, and trade within West Africa, Ghana gained significant wealth from the trans-Saharan trade that famously exported the **gold** of sudanic West Africa, mined to Ghana's south, across the Sahara to the North African coast and Europe beyond, in return for Saharan salt, copper, and dates and a variety of luxury goods imported from North Africa and Europe. Located astride the trade routes that brought gold from its south and salt from its north, Ghana prospered from the taxes and tariffs it imposed on the trade goods passing through its territory, fees merchants paid willingly in return for the safe passage of their immensely valuable caravans of goods through the great security of the empire's territory. Ghana was ruled by a king, chosen from among the men of the royal family of the Soninke who founded the empire. The king's power was legitimated in part through his fabulous personal wealth—the king was said to keep for his own pocket all nuggets of gold, leaving only gold dust to others—demonstrated on ceremonial occasions by public appearances bedecked in extravagant gold jewelry and rich gold-colored fabrics. Similar if less lavish forms of ornamentation were extended also to members of his court, who carried ceremonial staffs made of gold. Even the royal dogs and horses were collared and tethered with gold. Ghana flourished for many centuries until gradually declining over the eleventh and twelfth centuries as a result of an eastward shift in trans-Saharan trade routes, the onset of a dry period that negatively affected agriculture and iron smelting, and revolts by tribute-paying vassal states.

A second great medieval West African empire, Mali, emerged in the early thirteenth century out of the political instability that followed Ghana's eventual collapse. Under the leadership of Sundjata, the still-hallowed first king of Mali whose achievements have been celebrated in a continuously transmitted **oral tradition** for nearly 800 years, the Malinke clans united to defeat their bitter enemy and conqueror the Soso, who served briefly as the dominant power in sudanic West Africa following Ghana's decline. In subsequent decades the Malinke rapidly extended their political hegemony over a massive swathe of West Africa, so that by the midthirteenth century the empire stretched from the Atlantic Ocean in the west, past the Niger Bend in the east, into the southern fringes of the Sahara Desert to the north, and the northern fringes of the forest zone to the south. Fortuitously situated as it was, Mali gained its great wealth from a combination of **agriculture**, which flourished in the Sudan in general and most notably in the Inland Niger Delta that lay within the lands of the empire; fishing in the waters of the Niger; tribute demanded from conquered peoples who had been forcibly incorporated into the empire; regional trade within West Africa, often from **ecological zone** to ecological zone as people exchanged the products of the forest, sudanic, sahelian, and desert zones for the goods of the other regions; and trans-Saharan trade.

Mali lasted for two centuries, until it crumbled in the midfifteenth century as a result of struggles over succession to the position of mansa, or ruler of the empire, as well as revolts by tribute-paying states. Other important medieval West Africa states with centralized governments flourished at **Songhai**, at **Takrur** in the Senegal River valley, at **Kanem-Bornu**, located in the lands surrounding Lake Chad, at **Benin** and in the **Hausa** and Yoruba city-states, all located in what is today Nigeria, and in the emerging **Akan** polities centered in what is today Ghana.

On the other side of the continent the medieval centuries witnessed striking political developments in East and southern Africa, parts of the continent in places interconnected through their common involvement in Indian Ocean trade. The wealthy and sophisticated Swahili culture had emerged by the end of the first millennium C.E. and reached its peak along East Africa's Indian Ocean coastline during the thirteenth to fifteenth centuries (Table 9). It derived an important piece of the material base for its wealth from its merchants and their critical position as intermediaries in Indian Ocean trade, exporting goods including gold and ivory from the adjacent East African interior and importing goods from Indian Ocean trading partners including Arabs, Persians, South Asians, and Chinese. The Swahili were noted for the opulent coral-stone architecture of the elegant homes their well-to-do merchants constructed in the city-states scattered along the East African coastline from Mogadishu to Mozambique. The city-states remained politically independent of one another, each with its own ruler.

Table 9. Urbanization in Medieval Africa:
Population Estimates, Select Cities

City	Date	Population Estimate
Jenné-jeno cluster settlement	Fifth to eleventh centuries	10,000–20,000
Kilwa	Fourteenth century	12,000–20,000
Mombasa	Fourteenth century	> 15,000
Sijilmasa/the Tafilalt Oasis	Fourteen century	30,000
Great Zimbabwe	Fourteenth century	18,000

Source: Ronald Messier. *Archaeological Survey of Sijilmasa.* Murfreesboro: Middle Tennessee State University, 1988.

Meanwhile, the southern African interior to the southwest of the Swahili coast saw the emergence of a series of states on the **Zimbabwe Plateau**. The first of these hilltop polities, Mapungubwe, dated to the eleventh to thirteenth centuries C.E. whereas the largest and best-known, Zimbabwe, flourished from the thirteen into the fifteenth centuries. These states had economies focused upon cattle rearing and agriculture as well as controlling the flow of ivory and gold to the East African coastal port towns of, respectively, Chibuene and Sofala, from where the goods traveled north to **Kilwa** and other Swahili towns and thence into Indian Ocean commerce. Although knowledge of the politics of Mapungubwe, Zimbabwe, and the other related states found on the Zimbabwe Plateau is limited, they stand out for evidence of social stratification and their construction of massive, finely constructed stone walls and enclosures, many of which still exist today, which presuppose states with the power and resources to mobilize the extensive labor necessary for their construction.

In the northeastern portion of the continent, the medieval **Ethiopian Highlands** witnessed first the continuance of the premedieval state of **Aksum**, noted for its cities, monumental architecture, currency, and highly valued exports including frankincense and myrrh, and subsequently the midtwelfth century emergence of the Zagwe dynasty, which was supplanted in 1270 by the Solomonid dynasty. The shape of these Christian states was affected by the rise and fall of Red Sea trade, which commercially linked the Highlands with the Middle East and the Mediterranean world. This trade flourished in the early medieval centuries and at that time served as an important generator of wealth for Aksum, which partook in this trade through its Red Sea port city of Adulis. Red Sea trade dropped off precipitously in the seventh and eighth centuries as the Persian Gulf gained in ascendancy as a locus for maritime trade. Aksum weakened following the loss of this important source of wealth, and the history of the Ethiopian Highlands is poorly understood until the Zagwe and Solomonid Dynasties appear in the historical record. They thrived by creating feudal states with lords supported by the agricultural output of the peasantry, a form of governance that continued even after Red Sea trade rebounded in the ninth and following centuries, from which time it was dominated by Muslims. In Central Africa the important **Kongo** and **Luba** states emerged around 1400, just before the medieval era drew to a close.

North Africa lay under Roman control at the beginning of the medieval period but experienced near-total Islamicization and in places cultural Arabization following the seventh and eighth century waves of conquest by Muslims from the Arabian Peninsula. **Egypt** then experienced rule by a succession of Islamic **dynasties**, from the Umayyads through the Abbasids, Fatimids, Ayyubids, and Mamluks. West of Egypt the Maghrib, where Arab control and cultural hegemony were more tenuous, saw two successive medieval **Berber** polities, the Almoravid and Almohad empires, in the eleventh, twelfth, and thirteenth centuries (*see* **Almoravid and Almohad Movements**). Medieval North Africa flourished economically due to its role in trans-Saharan trade and experienced significant urbanization, with a definite Islamic architectural influence, in its many trading cities, which formed the northern entrepôt of the numerous trade routes that criss-crossed the Sahara. Literacy in the Arabic language and script came also, and **Cairo** developed into a medieval center for Islamic scholarship and learning renowned throughout the Muslim world due to the reputation of al-Azhar University, established in the late tenth century by the Fatimids and regarded as one of the intellectual seats of the Islamic world. Up the Nile from Egypt into the African interior lay the long-lasting Christian states of **Nubia**, whose existence neatly overlapped with the medieval centuries.

A number of questions faced all societies with centralized and hierarchical governance, though they might be answered differently by different peoples. For example, all states needed to legitimize political authority. As in the case of Ghana discussed above, the personal wealth of the ruler could serve this function; wealth in cattle, which served as a form of currency in parts of southern Africa, often legitimized chiefly rule there. Another common route to acceptance lay in royal clans or lineages, whose members were widely viewed as the legitimate rulers from whose ranks all leaders should be chosen. In other places the institution of divine or sacred kingship, in which the king was believed to be the literal embodiment of the state, granted full and supernaturally sanctioned legitimacy to that leader — it also meant that regicide, or killing the king, could follow the development of any physical frailty on his part, because his ill health was understood to indicate a potentially fatal weakness in the body politic as well.

Beyond legitimization, states needed mechanisms for ensuring compliance with social rules. Consequently medieval centralized governments formalized systems of justice, often in the shape of a series of courts in which to resolve disputes and transgressions of the society's rules, culminating in the king's court as the ultimate locus of appeal. In regards to gender, in some of the medieval states, such as the Yoruba city-states, women as well as men could ascend to positions of high-ranking political authority. In others, however, ultimate formal political authority rested solely in male hands. Finally, it is important to note that medieval African states and empires often held rather loose control over their outlying provinces, with the strong hand of government felt most keenly and regularly only at the state or empire's core.

Medieval Africa's large states and empires, which possessed formal governmental structures, significant numbers of specialized political and administrative positions, and hierarchies of authority with ultimate political authority vested in a chief or king, have generally attracted the greatest attention in contemporary written histories of medieval Africa, as they did also in literate medieval visitors' written accounts. Indeed, a much richer body of evidence exists for them, skewing the record further in their direction. What may well have been a majority of medieval Africans, however, lived instead in what are typically referred to as stateless or acephalous societies, communities that chose not to create a centralized government with a ruling class and one individual at the apex of political authority. Instead, stateless societies diffused political authority throughout members of the community, empowering many to be actively involved in corporate, consensus-oriented decision making. In these acephalous societies, when a decision was to be made affecting the well-being and direction of the community as a whole, such as going to war or communally addressing a plague or famine, community members gathered, shared their individual perspectives, and finally decided jointly upon a course of action to be followed by all. Since villages were typically conterminous with one or several lineages, this form of decision making was often lineage based.

Acephalous societies are often referred to as democratic, and in their inclusiveness of many in the political process they were so. As in all democracies, however, the question arose of who was enfranchised. Some of the social hier-archies mentioned previously in this essay came into play here. For example, as hinted at in medieval sources and if postmedieval practices are a guide to the past, many societies empowered only men to take part in these communal discussions and deliberations. Others allowed women to voice their opinions, either individually or through a spokeswoman who alone was to represent all of the community's women, but their expressed opinions often counted less in the subsequent deliberations. And women might be invited to participate only if the issue at hand was narrowly considered to be of relevance to the women in the community. Even when one or more women could speak, often they were not allowed to take part in the ultimate decision making, which followed the voicing of opinions.

The hierarchy of age also figured prominently in acephalous societies, with the voices of older men known as elders, often defined as greater than 30 to 40 years of age, typically bearing far greater influence than those of younger males. Again, patterns varied. In some places all adult men could speak, but only el-ders made the ultimate decisions, whereas in other communities it was the el-ders alone who conducted political discussions and made final decisions. Some societies, most notably in East Africa, created a series of age sets, with all males born in a certain span of years belonging to one. In some of these societies, when a given age set was composed of young men they fulfilled the most physically demanding tasks, serving as warriors protecting the community or clearing new plots of land for farming, whereas an age set containing elders monopolized political authority and the control of social resources. And ev-erywhere, the very old and frail reverted to a lesser status than the elders.

In a final hierarchy, in acephalous societies the voices of those most widely respected as sage, thoughtful, careful thinkers, and skilled orators, received far greater attention and thus weight in the decision-making process. In short, in-sight trumped age, with the result that a particularly insightful younger per-son's words received greater consideration than those of an unrespected elder.

Although centralized forms of government are often perceived by those who live within them as superior ways of organizing societies, in fact acephalous societies functioned smoothly and with the benefit of broad community input, albeit through very different mechanisms than existed in state societies. These societies could reach levels of social complexity, reflected for example in population, urbanization, and social differentiation, parallel to those of states with centralized and hierarchical governance. Indeed, acephalous societies often proved to be more durable and stable than governmentally centralized states and empires; in short, they were not the simple entities they have so often been assumed to be.

Medieval African societies gave people identity and place primarily through their systems of kinship. It was through kin ties that individuals gained their most fundamental social identities and access to social, economic, and political resources. Additionally, marriage and parenting formed near-universal adult experiences. Social hierarchies based on age, sex, achievement, religious au-thority, wisdom, oratorical skills, political authority, wealth, and membership in age sets, voluntary organizations, and secret societies further identified an individual's standing in the social order: It is clear that well-developed mecha-nisms of social stratification were hallmarks of medieval African societies. Large and complex political states and empires with centralized forms of government existed across the continent, though many—probably a majority—of medieval Africans eschewed such hierarchical political organization in favor of the broadly diffused governance of acephalous societies which vested authority in a range of adult members of the society. The material bases for most medieval African societies included agriculture, herding, metalworking, and other productive activities and, as the examples explored above indicate, involvement in local, regional, long-distance, and sometimes intercontinental networks of trade, which linked African peoples and polities in reciprocal exchanges of surplus goods not only with one another, but with peoples of Europe, the Middle East, and Asia. In sum, significant social complexity reflected in sophisticated systems of kinship, marriage, and social stratification, social institutions such as age grades and voluntary associations, centralized states and corporate governance, urbanization with cities whose populations regularly reached into the tens of thousands and in the case of Cairo a half million or more, and trading networks of varied scope were all hallmarks of medieval African society.

Further Reading

Brooks, George E. *Landlords and Strangers: Ecology, Society, and Trade in Western Africa, 1000–1630*. Boulder, CO: Westview Press, 1993.

Ehret, Christopher. *The Civilizations of Africa: A History to 1800*. Charlottesville: University Press of Virginia, 2002.

Horton, Mark, and John Middleton. *The Swahili: The Social Landscape of a Mercantile Society*. Oxford, UK: Blackwell Publishers, 2000.

McIntosh, Roderick J., and Susan Keech McIntosh. "Early Urban Configurations on the Middle Niger: Clustered Cities and Landscapes of Power," in *The Social Construction of Ancient Cities*. Edited by Monica L. Smith. Washington, DC: Smithsonian Institution Press, 2003, pp. 103–120.

Stahl, Ann Brower. *African Archaeology: A Critical Introduction*. Oxford, UK: Blackwell Publishing, 2005.

6. SCIENCE AND TECHNOLOGY

This essay is disproportionately weighted toward metallurgy because evidence of this particular medieval African technology has most often survived in the archaeological record, which is a primary source of information for the medieval centuries. Although references to an African "Iron Age" that was fully established by the early centuries of the Common Era sometimes imply that the development of iron technologies ushered in an entirely new stage in African history, in fact the use of nonmetal implements made out of stone and wood, and previous subsistence activities such as foraging and hunting, continued to play an important role in African societies long after the advent of iron. Thus, the ability to smelt iron is best understood as a development, which, though giving Africans access to innovative and highly productive new tools, nonetheless coexisted with the ongoing use of older, still valuable ways of manipulating the environment and supporting human life.

Although medieval Africans practiced systems of medicine and used mathematics, unfortunately information about these activities has rarely been preserved making it impossible to explore these sciences in any depth. More thoroughly documented scientific and technological achievements in medieval

Africa include the manufacturing of cloth, pottery, and salt; the development and large-scale production of currencies; innovations in farming and animal husbandry; new modes of transportation; and architectural accomplishments. Indeed, a complex of society-altering changes dating to the immediately pre-medieval and early medieval centuries in Africa affected the continent profoundly throughout the medieval centuries. These developments included the rapid expansion across Africa of iron working, grain or cereal farming, and cattle herding, and increased networks of local, regional, long-distance, and intercontinental trade based on surpluses of the goods produced as a result of these activities.

Metallurgy

The archaeological evidence for metalworking in Africa demonstrates that in addition to very early copper smelting in Upper **Nubia** dating to around the third millennium B.C.E., copper was also smelted in two West African locations, Azelik and Akjoujt in what are today, respectively, Niger and Mauritania, beginning around the tenth to fifth centuries B.C.E. Along with the early production of copper at these discrete North and West African sites, knowledge of how to smelt iron—turn iron ore into usable metal—appeared in widely dispersed African locations as far back as 1000 B.C.E. and then spread across virtually the entire African continent by around 400 C.E., making the adoption of this technology an accomplishment of the millennium and a half preceding the medieval era, though its steadily intensifying effects were felt throughout the medieval centuries. Copper mining in parts of Africa beyond those identified above, in the Copper Belt located in what are today the Congo and Zambia, began on a small scale in the early medieval period and reached massive extents by the end of this era. In addition to copper and iron, metals worked on the medieval African continent included **gold**, tin, lead, the copper alloys brass and bronze, and the iron alloy carbon steel. As Childs and Herbert demonstrated, the technology of metal production can best be understood through consideration of its major stages of mining, smelting, and shaping, and the following explorations of these processes draw in part upon their work.

Mining

Iron ore is found widely across much of the African continent, copper ore less so as it is located at a few sites in West Africa and in far larger concentrations in southern and Central Africa. Iron and copper ores have been mined in different ways depending on their presentation. Both ores were often deposited superficially, in which case they could be dug out from these surface or near-surface locations easily through either small shallow pits or the large-scale removals of soil known as opencast mining, which could cover many acres of ground. In other places, however, these ores existed in less easily accessible veins that could only be excavated via shafts dug deep into the earth. Ores could also be found in river sands and bogs. Once recovered, these ores were typically broken down into smaller, more manageable pieces, washed, and then smelted. Alluvial or quartz reef deposits of gold are found in numerous places in West Africa including the Bambuk, Bure, and **Akan** goldfields, as well as on the **Zimbabwe Plateau** and in southern Africa. Medieval Africans typically collected alluvial gold by panning the sand and gravel of auriferous streams and rivers, and the soil of auriferous earth, a technique most productively practiced early in the rainy season when the newly disturbed materials of the riverbed and surface soil more easily yielded their grains of gold, and the moisture reflecting the sun could even make these tiny particles visible to the naked eye. Auriferous zones sometimes though far more rarely yielded nuggets of gold in addition to these small flecks. Gold reefs were worked through mining via open trenches or shafts from which the gold-bearing soil or ore was extracted and removed, the ore subsequently processed by pulverization and then panning, and the soil simply panned to separate out the gold. Large pits were sometimes excavated as far down as the water table in West African goldfields as well. Medieval miners became highly skilled at identifying likely underground sites of gold, copper, and iron ores, as each was associated with telltale signs such as particular vegetation and streaks of color in the surface soils that lay above the ores themselves.

Smelting

Iron, whose wares most profoundly affected daily life in medieval Africa, almost never exists in a pure state naturally. Instead, it occurs in the form of iron ore, rock that contains iron and other minerals. Iron smelting is the process whereby iron ore is heated to extremely high temperatures so that the iron separates from the other materials, creating iron on the one hand and liquid slag composed of the waste rock and noniron minerals on the other. The liquid slag is drained off, leaving the iron behind. The slag heaps that are the refuse created by this process often lead archaeologists to medieval and premedieval African smelting sites, which are very important to understanding the development of ironworking in Africa because the iron implements produced have often rusted away.

Medieval Africans practiced what is known as bloomery smelting, where the temperatures are not raised high enough to actually melt the iron. Instead in this process the iron separates from the now-liquefied slag, creating what is known as a bloom, or mass, of iron. To practice bloomery smelting successfully, iron ore must be heated in a furnace to very high temperatures of 1,100 to 1,300 degrees Celsius. Achieving this temperature requires the introduction of oxygen into the furnace. Smelting also requires the introduction of carbon, typically through a carbon-based fuel source, which causes a chemical reaction that reduces the iron oxide to iron metal by removing oxygen from it. Finally, use of a flux such as lime or old slag, which could help to purify the ore and increase the liquidity of the slag, might be included. In short, smelting is a technically complex process because of the need to achieve a very high temperature, introduce an air flow, provide a source of carbon, and possibly use a flux. Further, the precise needs for these requirements vary depending on the grade of the iron ore itself, which differed widely from source to source of ore in Africa, requiring skilled assessments and adjustments before and during the smelting process to end up with iron rather than an unsuccessful attempt at smelting.

Medieval African peoples devised a variety of ways to achieve the very exacting conditions required for successful bloomery smelting. Iron smelting occurred in either bowl or shaft furnaces constructed from clay. A steady flow of oxygen-rich air was achieved in shaft furnaces via either the labor-intensive use of bellows, which introduced air flows into furnaces through clay pipes known as tuyeres that were inserted into the furnace wall, or reliance upon a draft that pulled air in at the bottom of the furnace from where it rose as it grew warmer. Charcoal produced from hardwoods, which burned slowly while producing great heat, served as the main fuel and also introduced the carbon necessary to achieve chemical reduction. In fact, the quantities of charcoal required to produce iron in Africa over the past 2,500 or so years have affected the African environment profoundly: In the medieval period as iron production soared, charcoal manufacturing led to significant deforestation in large stretches of what are now grasslands in West Africa, and west of Lake Victoria in Central and East Africa. Doubtless the deforestation also resulted from the greater ease of creating farmland from forest following the production of iron tools.

Although it is very hard, indeed typically impossible, to know medieval African cosmologies because of the paucity of relevant sources, it is possible to conjecture about how they conceptualized and thought of ironworking: Eugenia Herbert has demonstrated a long-standing and widespread understanding of smelting as a generative process analogous to sexual intercourse and childbirth. These beliefs were reflected in constructions of smelting furnaces, which resembled women's bodies; and in the language used in reference to smelting and its production of an iron bloom, which drew analogies between this process and the stages of human reproduction such as intercourse, labor, and delivery. Much of the evidence for this gynecomorphism postdates the medieval period, however, and it is not known how far back in time such beliefs extended.

Today experts disagree about whether Africans invented the technology of iron smelting themselves, or received this knowledge from outside the continent in a diffusion of metalworking technologies. Proponents of the diffusion argument such as Mauny and Tylecote have pointed out that in western Asia, where iron smelting appears to have been first achieved, the Iron Age was preceded by a Copper Age, facilitated by the fact that copper sometimes occurs in pure form that does not require smelting but gives experience in metalworking; its smelting is also far more easily achieved than that of iron. However, most of Africa experienced no Copper Age as an antecedent to its Iron Age, and this absence has led many scholars to deduce that iron smelting must have been introduced to Africa via outside sources that experienced the stages of metalworking that are believed to have been followed in all parts of the world that independently developed ironworking technologies. On the other hand, as proponents of innovation within Africa such as Schmidt/Avery and Trigger asserted, evidence that iron smelting in Africa may be autochthonous is growing with the identification of more and more radiocarbon-dated sites showing the smelting of iron in Africa throughout much of the first millennium B.C. before this knowledge could have diffused from places such as Phoenician or Roman North Africa or Meroë. These early sites of ironworking are widely spread over the continent from West to East Africa, making it unlikely that the technology spread neatly and chronologically south and west from Anatolia in western Asia in the ways that have been theorized. Additionally, African smelting shows striking divergences in technique from western Asian smelting. Although the question of diffusion from outside the continent, local innovation inside the continent, or a combination of the two remains open and debated, it is no longer routinely assumed that knowledge of how to smelt iron definitively came from outside Africa. The dominant position today is that it is a truly open question unanswerable on the basis of currently available evidence.

Shaping

In the case of iron still unacceptably adulterated after smelting, smithing had to begin with extensive hammering to remove impurities prior to the creation of the desired end products. But for the most part smithing or forging iron involves first heating the metal to be shaped until it is malleable, second forming it into desired objects via hammering, and third rapidly cooling the object in water, which strengthens and hardens the metal, a three-step process repeated many times until the final shape is satisfactory. Softer metals such as copper and gold might be subjected to smithing but could also be worked through other techniques such as hammering without heating, granulation, plating with thin sheets of hammered metal, filigree, and drawing or pulling to create wire. Lost-wax casting of various metals, not including iron, was also practiced in parts of medieval West Africa.

Metalwares produced in medieval Africa included farming implements such as hoes, scythes, and axes that not only facilitated actual cultivation but allowed for far greater ease in clearing farmland, no small gain given the prominence on the continent of shifting plot agriculture requiring the constant creation of new farming plots from difficult-to-clear virgin or long-fallow land. Weapons such as arrow and spearheads allowed for greater effectiveness on the battlefield and also in hunting; fishhooks similarly allowed for greater ease in catching this category of game. Metal currencies formed in medieval Africa included coins minted at the island of **Kilwa** on East Africa's **Swahili** coast, coins struck in first Roman and then Islamic North Africa, the **Berbers**' famous and intercontinentally circulated golden dinar, and the copper cross-shaped currency developed in Central Africa. Jewelry formed another significant category of medieval worked metal objects, and there is rich evidence of it from all across the continent, north to south and west to east. Jewelry sometimes served as a way of storing wealth, as was the case with the striking golden earrings, which could reach vast size and were the repository for wealth for many women in the medieval West African Sudan. Gold ornamentation also served to symbolize the riches and prestige of the kings of the medieval sudanic empires of **Ghana** and **Mali**, who were bedecked in magnificent and lavish gold jewelry on state occasions. Although exceptions to this pattern occurred frequently, more often iron was used to make tools and weapons while other, softer, metals such as gold and copper were used for ornamentation and coinage.

In some parts of Africa the occupation of smith became limited to particular castes, as among the Malinke of medieval West Africa where smithing became a family occupation passed down from father to son, whereas in other places it remained broadly available to any man willing to serve an apprenticeship with a master smith. Smiths might also be the miners and/or smelters of their societies, or these various parts of the metalworking process might be the province of different sets of specialists. In recent centuries smithing, like smelting, has been ubiquitously gendered male, although there is evidence that slave women sometimes smelted in medieval West Africa; mining, however, could be and was conducted by women, men, and children alike as attested by skeletons of victims of mining accidents found in medieval mine shafts throughout the continent.

Farming

Knowledge of agriculture developed in parts of Africa long before the medieval period, as farming was firmly established in parts of the northern half of the continent by around 5000 B.C.E. It then spread across the southern half of Africa by the first centuries C.E. The utilization of iron technology across the continent, which occurred between approximately 1000 B.C.E. and 400 C.E., dovetailed propitiously with the expansion of mixed farming in Central, East ,and southern Africa because iron-bladed hoes, axes, scythes, knives, and other tools proved extremely useful in making the demanding work of farming less arduous.

Medieval African farmers consciously chose those farming technologies best suited to their particular environments. For example, in many parts of this often-arid continent close attention had to be paid to ensuring a consistent source of water, which was accomplished by techniques such as constructing irrigation channels, devising ways to raise precious water from sources located below the earth's surface, and manually watering crops. Similarly, in steeply hilled areas farmers terraced the land to avoid soil erosion and create level ground where crops could be more easily cultivated. And in virtually all of Africa—Ethiopia is the striking exception—medieval farmers chose to practice hoe rather than plow agriculture, in large part because the bite of the tsetse fly, which is endemic in many parts of the continent, transmits the deadly **disease** trypanosomiasis to cattle making it impossible to rely upon these draft animals to draw heavy plows.

In regards to cultivation, again African agriculturalists paid close attention to the techniques best suited to their environment. In rain forest regions, for example, where soil fertility is quickly exhausted due to the very rapid decomposition of organic material in the heat and humidity, which characterize this tropical climate zone, farmers practiced shifting plot agriculture. This method of farming involves the intensive use of one plot of land until its fertility is exhausted, at which point it is either abandoned permanently or left to lay fallow for the many years needed to reestablish vital nutrients in the soil while the farmer works a different plot. However, more fertile land could be and was worked continuously. Further, farmers who lived in regions conducive to herding cattle and cultivating crops quickly recognized the value of fertilizing their fields with cow manure, whereas farmers who practiced shifting plot **agriculture** knew the fertilizing properties of the ash that resulted from burning the vegetation cleared off of new plots of farmland. Farmers also made it a point to grow a variety of crops that had their greatest demands for work at different times of the growing season, so as to space out the need for the labor involved in their production and permit more extensive farming.

Farmers also selected the crops best suited to their particular climate. In the forest regions where grain and cereal farming is not easily practiced they turned to vegeculture, cultivating yams, melons, cowpeas, gourds, and fluted pumpkins. They also gathered the output of the oil palm, raffia palm, and kola nut trees that grow naturally in the forest zone and that farmers intentionally left standing when they cleared all other trees from plots of new farmland. Farmers in the grasslands of the savannah belts and in the **Ethiopian Highlands**, where cereals and grains flourished, focused upon a variety of these crops, a majority of which were domesticated in Africa because the wheat and barley that probably came to Africa from western Asia could not survive in the tropical and subtropical portions of the continent. Commonly cultivated cereal and grain species included African rice, sorghum, teff, ensete, and pearl and finger millet. Farmers in all parts of the continent planted vegetables too, and where these flourished also cultivated nonfood crops such as cotton and indigo for use in cloth making and dying. Farmers also took up with alacrity useful crops diffused to Africa from Asia such as citrus fruits, coconuts, sugar cane, and what became starchy dietary staples of Asian rice and cocoyams. As the variety of crops enumerated above implies, African farmers recognized the great value of diversified cultivation, so that even if some plantings failed due to crop-specific blights or infestations, others were likely to survive and famine could be avoided.

Herding

Like farming, raising cattle became well established in the northern half of Africa by 5000 B.C.E., long before the medieval period, and there is evidence for it dating back to around 2000 B.C.E. in parts of East Africa too. Throughout the continent, animal domestication grew in extent and significance over the course of the medieval centuries (*see* **Domesticated Animals**). Domesticated cattle, whether indigenous or imported in origin, became a very important animal in medieval Africa, particularly the savannahs of southern, eastern, and West Africa, utilized for their milk and blood and much less commonly for their meat and hides. Cattle also became a major way of storing wealth in the southern half of the continent. The clearing of forests and brushlands in medieval Africa, which resulted from producing charcoal to fire iron-smelting furnaces and creating new plots of arable land, also decreased the tsetse fly–infested portions of the continent because this insect flourished in forest and more well-watered grassland regions, allowing for more widespread raising of cattle. Analogous to farmers choosing the most productive cultivation methods, herders consciously developed methods of cattle rearing best suited to their environments. In the grasslands of Africa, for example, herders practiced open-range grazing of cattle and devised annual patterns of migration in which they moved their cattle from place to place to take continuous advantage of seasonal changes in the availability of fresh pasturage and sources of water, and to allow their cattle to benefit from the varied nutrients and trace minerals of different pastureland.

In another parallel with farmers, African herders had long recognized the advantages conferred by rearing animals that came to Africa from outside the continent, such as sheep and goats indigenous to Asia; a new and hardy type of cattle, the humped Zebu, from South Asia; and camels from the Arabian Peninsula. Camel raising was first taken up some 3,000 years ago in the Horn of Africa, and much like the later cattle keepers of southern Africa people in the Horn utilized their herds for milk and as a way of storing wealth, as had the peoples of Arabia from where the camel came. Romans in North Africa utilized camels in the first centuries C.E., and immediately they were adopted by the Berbers of the vast Sahara Desert on the eve of the medieval centuries. Camels revolutionized medieval Berber life, as the Berbers with great skill created a viable desert life in which the camel played key roles as a beast of burden, moving trade goods north and south across the desert, and as a means of transportation in the desert environment, a role for which they were perfectly suited given their ability to travel 10 days between water sources and the way in which the two pads of each foot flatten as camels walk, allowing them to expend less energy in their travels than horses or humans because they remain on the surface of desert sands.

Craft Production and Manufacturing

Large-scale cloth production has a long history in many parts of Africa and can be assumed to have been practiced during the medieval period given its documented existence in the early modern years, though it is not possible to verify the scale of production because the textile industry does not leave much evidence in the archaeological record. Examples of African textiles do, however, appear in medieval artworks such as sculptures, and it is clear that medieval Africa produced significant quantities of cloth made from raffia, bark, and cotton, the last of which was produced in **Egypt** by the tenth century C.E. and in many other parts of the continent shortly thereafter. Stages of cloth making included cultivating or gathering the fibers that are its basic element, making thread, weaving, decorating cloth by dying, embroidery and stamped designs, among other techniques, and tailoring. Salt-making industries also existed in many parts of the continent, from medieval Saharan mining of rock salt and production of rock crystal from underground reservoirs of brine, to the seaside evaporation of ocean waters to isolate its salt crystals practiced along coastlines in West and East Africa. These salt manufacturers produced far more than required for local consumption to trade the surplus for desired commodities through local, regional, long-distance, and intercontinental commercial networks. Pottery, which is well preserved in the archaeological record, was also widely produced across medieval Africa, often with striking similarities of style over large areas that sometimes exhibited dramatic stylistic changes over very short periods of time. Other crafts mastered by medieval African artisans include wood carving, leatherworking, grass weaving, and the metalworking discussed above.

Architecture and Mathematics

Sophisticated and exquisitely constructed public and private buildings, elaborate and extensive city walls, and massive monuments are all elements of Africa's medieval architectural traditions. The evidence is skewed toward buildings constructed from stone because other widely used medieval building materials such as mud, clay, thatch, wood, and leaves have not survived. In East Africa, Swahili merchants built lavish and opulent multistory homes from coral stone. Swahili houses attest to attention to ease and comfort, exemplified by bathrooms with pit toilets, systems of indoor plumbing, concern with airflow and other cooling techniques, and beautiful decorative detail. Medieval monumental architecture, found at sites across the length and breadth of the continent, speaks to desires to showcase the wealth, power, and authority of leaders and states. The massive and awe-inspiring stonewall enclosures constructed at Great Zimbabwe attest to not only the prestige of its rulers, but also the great skills of its stonemasons. Another architectural achievement are the stelae of **Aksum**, long, thin pillars carved out of single pieces of granite set upright, which reached heights of nearly 110 feet and weighed over 500 tons. Their surfaces were finely carved to represent facades of multistory houses, and the tallest known stelae represented 13 floors; they had to pose huge challenges to quarry, move, shape, and erect. Aksumites also constructed huge, multistory palaces and private residences containing scores of rooms, which exhibited an unusual architecture, built as they were upon large stone bases that increased their majesty and height. The Ethiopian Highlands were also the setting for the very unusual medieval Christian rock-cut churches, hewn from living rock and illustrative of exquisite skills of architectural planning and masonry with their elaborate incorporation of windows, galleries, aisles, basilicas, naves, sacristies, domes, pillars, archways and finely worked decorative details, all carved into the bedrock. **Islam** brought to Africa traditions of mosque architecture, then modified by local aesthetic preferences, building materials, and environmental concerns. A prominent example from the West African savannah is **Timbuktu**'s Sankoré Mosque, which dates from the early fourteenth century. It illustrates one common form of sudanic mosque architecture with its tapering, pyramid-shaped minaret and thick mud-brick walls with protruding wooden beams, which served as a permanent scaffolding to allow for easy repair of damages to the walls caused by the annual rains.

These medieval African architectural achievements indicate a keen awareness of mathematical and engineering principles, though today it is not known specifically how Africans of this era conceptualized of, articulated, and transmitted this knowledge. But it is certain that these architectural accomplishments could not have occurred without knowledge and understanding of geometry, principles of weight-bearing, systems of precise measurement, and appreciation for the unique characteristics of the arch and barrel-vaulting. Similarly, the wide use of currencies ranging from animals, to cowrie shells imported from the Indian Ocean, Aksumite and Swahili coins, ivory disks, and the copper cross currency of Central Africa, among many other monetary systems, as well as systems of taxation documented for empire of Ghana, among other places, presuppose numeracy (numerical literacy). Likewise, the widespread use of geometrically complex patterns in African games, textiles, architecture, house painting, and other art forms speaks to knowledge of mathematical principles. The evidence Claudia Zaslavsky has marshaled about how Africans have thought mathematically, which reaches as far back as the early modern period, allows for speculative extrapolation back into the medieval period because these traditions certainly drew upon older African mathematical knowledge. For example, Zaslavsky's deeply fascinating research shows that in different parts of the continent Africans have used bases ranging from 5, the most common, to 10 and 20, and have a long and complex history of denoting numbers through hand gestures as well as spoken number words. Long-ago African peoples involved in large-scale and lucrative trade developed number words into the millions, a necessity when utilizing what eventually became low-value cowry shell currency, and African traders have long showed great dexterity at making complex mental calculations extremely rapidly. Furthermore, African music and games, which again reach back into the medieval period, have generally depended upon knowledge of highly complex numerical patterns. Finally, the medieval incorporation of significant parts of Africa into the Islamic world led to familiarity with the mathematical knowledge of the Islamic intellectual tradition.

Iron smelting and other metalworking techniques form the most prominent and influential medieval African technologies. This metallurgy influenced life in medieval Africa in profound ways: Metalworking technologies underlay more efficient agriculture, more effective hunting and fighting, new systems of **currency**, and new forms of bodily adornment; and in the southern half of the continent mutually reinforcing interconnections between iron smelting, cereal and grain agriculture, and cattle herding stimulated new and more complex forms of social organization in the medieval centuries. All of these interrelated activities, which often produced surpluses, also stimulated local and regional trade within the continent, for example with the emergence of southern African trade networks spanning the continent from the Atlantic to the Indian Ocean and northern networks linking West and North Africa across the Sahara, as well as external, intercontinental trade routes reaching across the Mediterranean Sea and Indian Ocean. Subsistence activities including foraging, hunting, farming, animal husbandry, and craft production continued to be of importance in the African Iron Age that had been established across the continent by the earliest medieval centuries. African agriculturalists and herders continued to tailor their techniques to the specifics of their local environments while also welcoming new inputs from outside the continent, an indication of their openness to innovation. Achievements in architecture in places as diverse as Great Zimbabwe, the Ethiopian Highlands, the Swahili coast, and the cities of the West African Sudan also stand out, whereas architecture, currencies, artworks, and musical traditions incorporating complex, multilayered polyrhythms all speak to medieval mathematical knowledge.

Further Reading

Childs, S. Terry, and Eugenia W. Herbert. "Metallurgy and its Consequences," in *African Archaeology*. Edited by Ann Brower Stahl. Oxford, UK: Blackwell Publishing, 2005: pp. 276–300.

Falola, Toyin, ed. *Africa, Volume 2: African Cultures and Societies Before 1885*. Durham, NC: Durham Academic Press, 2000.

Garrard, Timothy F. *Gold of Africa*. Munich: Prestel, 1989.

Herbert, Eugenia W. *Iron, Gender, and Power: Rituals of Transformation in African Societies*. Bloomington: Indiana University Press, 1993.

Mauny, R. "Essai sur l'histoire des métaux en Afrique occidentale." *Bulletin de l'Institut Français d'Afrique Noire* 14: 545–595.

Phillipson, David W. *African Archaeology*. 2nd ed. Cambridge, UK: Cambridge University Press, 1993.

Schmidt, Peter R., and Donald Avery. "More Evidence for an Advanced Prehistoric Iron Technology in Africa." *Journal of Field Archaeology* 10:4 (1983): 421–434.

Trigger, B.G. "The Myth of Meroe and the African Iron Age." *African Historical Studies* 2:1 (1969): 23–50.

Tylecote, R.F. "The Origin of Iron Smelting in Africa." *West African Journal of Archaeology* 5 (1975): 1–9.

Zaslavsky, Claudia. *Africa Counts: Number and Pattern in African Cultures*. 3rd ed. Chicago: Lawrence Hill Books, 1999.

7. GLOBAL TIES

In sharp contrast to common stereotypes of isolation, Africa held far-reaching ties to other regions of the world during the medieval period. A few of these interconnections resulted from foreigners extending their political dominion over portions of North Africa, and at least one from Africans asserting political control over outsiders. The majority, however, were forged through intercontinental commerce. Religion provided another significant basis for connections between Africa and other parts of the world. In sum, all of these ties led to exchanges of goods, technologies, foodstuffs, domesticated animals, information, and religion between Africa, the Middle East, Europe, and parts of southern and southeastern Asia including what are today India, Indonesia, and China. These intercontinental ties, as well as events internal to Africa, made the medieval centuries ones of vibrancy and innovation. They also illustrate that expansions and migrations of peoples over longer as well as shorter distances are a prominent feature of world history, for medieval Africa as for other places and times.

Global Ties and Conquest, Expansion, and Migration

African connections to other peoples of the Mediterranean have existed for many millennia. North Africa, which forms the southern side of the Mediterranean Basin and whose inhabitants are thus of the Mediterranean themselves, was in close contact with the Greco-Roman world long before the medieval centuries, for example through the ties of trade that existed between Ancient Egypt and Ancient Greece. The Greek historian Herodotus reflected the very high regard in which Greeks held Egyptians in his characterization of them as very civilized and devoutly religious people from whose culture Ancient Greece received many things. Africans also traded extensively with the subsequent Mediterranean power of Ancient Rome that, by colonizing lands along the entire length of the North African coast and well up the Nile into **Egypt** like Ancient Greece before it, also linked Africa politically to the broader Mediterranean world. The consequent control of North Africa and Egypt by the Byzantine or Eastern Roman Empire, centered in Constantinople in what is today Turkey, continued this involvement into the early medieval centuries. Peoples of the **Ethiopian Highlands** located further south in the Horn of Africa were also closely involved with the Mediterranean world: The Ethiopian kingdom of **Aksum** that flourished well into the medieval centuries had close commercial ties through the Red Sea to the Greeks and later Romans, reflected for example in the use of Greek inscriptions on some Aksumite coins and monuments. This trade via the Red Sea also connected people of the East African coast south of the Horn of Africa to the medieval Mediterranean Basin.

Connections to the Middle East also predated the medieval period and were notably strengthened during it. For example, from the first millennium B.C.E. and even earlier Phoenicians spread their maritime empire from their homeland in the Levant throughout much of the Mediterranean world, conducting trade with and creating settlements in North Africa premedievally and channeling the goods of the African interior into the Mediterranean Basin. Their city of Carthage, founded around the ninth century B.C.E. in what is today Tunisia, held a place of distinction unmatched in Phoenician affairs and was a mighty power in its day. Another important African–Middle Eastern tie resulted from interactions between the Ethiopian Highlands and the Arabian Peninsula that were facilitated by their proximity to one another, divided as they are only by the relatively narrow (though not always easily traversed) waters of the Red Sea. The Ethiopian Highlands received immigrants from Saba in the southwestern Arabian Peninsula as long ago as the first millennium B.C.E., resulting in a lasting linguistic influence in this region seen for example in the languages of first Ge'ez and subsequently Amharic, both of which descended from the southern Arabian Semitic Sabaean. In most cultural aspects, however, the people of the Highlands followed internal dynamics. These Ethiopian–Arabian interactions continued in the medieval years, with the powerful state of Aksum making military incursions into southern Arabia in the sixth century C.E.

Most prominently of all when it comes to medieval African–Middle Eastern interconnections, North Africa became significantly incorporated into the Muslim religious world and the Arab cultural world through the seventh- and eighth-century waves of conquest that followed the movement of Muslim Arabs out of the Arabian Peninsula and across North Africa from Egypt in the east to the Atlantic in the west between 639 and 711 A.D. following the emergence of **Islam** in the early seventh century. Influences on northern Africa resulting from these incursions included the development of an Arab ethnic identity and an Islamic religious identity though these varied in profundity from place to place in North Africa, and the introduction of shari'a or Islamic law and Arab/Islamic statecraft, Arab artistic and architectural traditions, and the Arabic language, script, and literature. African Muslims themselves then had a profound influence on the Iberian Peninsula of southwestern Europe; the Almoravid Movement of the eleventh to twelfth centuries arose among **Berbers** from the southwestern Sahara who then conquered what are today southern Spain and Portugal (*see* **Almoravid and Almohad Movements**).

Finally, movements of people occasioned by Indian Ocean commerce, which linked the lands of East and northeastern Africa, the Middle East, and South and Southeast Asia, brought premedieval and medieval trading partners from Arabia, Persia, India, Indonesia, and China to the East African coast. Some, mainly Arabs and Persians, intermarried with local residents. This mixing and intermingling resulted in the medieval emergence of the **Swahili** culture, whose city-states dotted East Africa's Indian Ocean shoreline from Mogadishu to Mozambique. Another Indian Ocean migration, this one from Southeast Asia and most likely via outrigger canoe, brought Indonesian immigrants to a then-uninhabited Madagascar—the large island separated from southeastern Africa by the Mozambique Channel—through one or more strikingly long ocean voyages early in the first millennium C.E., where they were joined shortly thereafter by East Africans. In consequence the Malagasy language of Madagascar is the westernmost member of the Austronesian language group, spoken also in Southeast Asia as well as in the Pacific Islands of Melanesia, Micronesia, and Polynesia such as Fiji, the Marshall Islands, and Samoa.

Intercontinental Trade and Global Connections

As the previous section implies many of medieval Africa's links with other parts of the world resulted from intercontinental trade, and in fact this was the most significant cause of connections between Africans and people outside the continent's borders. This commerce occurred throughout the medieval centuries via the trans-Saharan and Indian Ocean trading networks, two vast systems of exchange that linked Africa and places in the Middle East including Arabia and Persia, in Asia including India, Indonesia, and China, and in Europe, all in highly profitable economic interactions. These ties led to two-way transfers not only of the surplus goods exchanged through these trading networks, but also of a far broader range of information, ideas, and technologies including food crops, domesticated animals, intellectual traditions, and religions.

Over the course of the entire medieval period, through a regularized exchange of their surplus goods trans-Saharan trade served to connect West Africa, which lies to the desert's south, with both the Sahara itself and North Africa, which is located to the desert's north. Through the trade routes of the Mediterranean trans-Saharan trade also, however, channeled African exports much farther afield, to Europe and the Middle East. West African **gold**, ivory, captives, agricultural goods, and animal products such as pelts and ostrich feathers thereby made their way outside of the continent. Indeed, West Africa was the primary supplier of gold to Europe and the Islamic world during these medieval centuries, making possible medieval Europe's gold-based currencies, a debt later acknowledged in the elephant-shaped mint mark found on the famous Golden Guinea of King Charles II that indicated the African provenance of the coin's gold. In fact, it is estimated that Africa served as the source of an astounding two-thirds of the gold supply of Europe and the Islamic world at this time, before the discovery of additional and less expensive sources of this precious metal in the Americas in the modern age of exploration that was yet to come. African gold became the fabled subject of European legends, many fantastical in nature. Getting directly to the source of this West African gold and thereby cutting out the Muslim intermediaries in North Africa on whom they were unhappily dependent eventually emerged as a medieval Christian European preoccupation, one not satisfied however until the modern era and its age of maritime exploration.

The second great medieval intercontinental commercial network in which Africa was involved was the Indian Ocean trading system, which created a world of commerce and cultural exchange connecting East and northeastern Africa, Arabia, Persia, South Asia, Indonesia, and the ports of southern China through trade which occurred not only on the Indian Ocean but also via the feeder waterways of the Persian Gulf and the Red Sea, the last of which also involved the Mediterranean world in this exchange. The Swahili of the East African coast, the powerful state of Aksum in the Ethiopian Highlands with its great Red Sea port city of Adulis, and Egyptians all took part in this trade and collectively exported to their Asian, Middle Eastern, and Mediterranean counterparts highly valued commodities including ivory, gold, iron, rock crystal, the aromatics frankincense and myrrh, obsidian, mangrove poles, cotton and linen fabrics, agricultural goods including coffee and spices, animal products including rhinoceros horns, leopard skins, tortoiseshells, and the musk of the civet cat that was used in perfume, and captives who were forced to work as slaves in the Middle East in occupations ranging from hard physical labor draining swamps in what is today southern Iraq to soldiering to concubinage.

The trade goods Africa received in exchange for its exports into Indian Ocean and trans-Saharan trade demonstrate the very long reach into medieval

Africa of this intercontinental trade, as attested to by numerous archaeological finds. For example, though direct East African involvement in Indian Ocean trade occurred only through the Swahili cities that were located right on the coast—on its shoreline, promontories, and offshore islands—goods imported through this trade network have been found far inland. Caches of many thousands of the small glass beads that were one of India's prominent exports to Africa, and other trade goods such as cowry shells, Persian ceramics, and the fine Chinese porcelain that was another highly prized import, have been unearthed at sites including the ruins of the medieval states of Mapungubwe and Great Zimbabwe, located on the **Zimbabwe plateau** in the southeastern African interior, as well as even further west and south of the East African seacoast at locations in what are today Botswana and the South African Transvaal. A parallel body of evidence can be found on the other side of the continent, where Hellenistic or Roman beads dating to just before or after the beginning of the Common Era have been unearthed at **Jenné-jeno** in the Inland Niger Delta, attesting to the ability of goods from Roman North Africa to make their way, via many intervening trading networks, to the West African Sudan at this early date. Likewise, more than one-hundred thousand imported beads, most likely of either Venetian or Indian provenance, were discovered during the archaeological excavation of the burial site of an obviously wealthy and powerful man at the eighth to tenth centuries site of Igbo-Ukwu in what is today Nigeria (*see* **Igbo**). If Venetian in origin, these beads would have come to North Africa from Europe, and then traveled to West Africa via trans-Saharan trade. If Indian, they would have arrived in East Africa from South Asia through Indian Ocean trade and then been carried clear across the continent to West Africa. As well as demonstrating the great reach of intercontinental trade, these finds demonstrate the extensive intra-African trade networks of the medieval centuries that transported imports from other continents, as well as Africa's own commodities, throughout broad stretches of the continent.

The extent and value of trade between Africa and other parts of the globe, and within the continent's borders, drew numerous visitors, many of them great travelers of their day who had traversed broad swathes of their known world of Europe, Asia, and Africa. Around 100 C.E., a Greek-speaking mariner from Alexandria penned the Periplus of the Erythraen Sea, the earliest extant written account of the Indian Ocean commercial system that described in significant detail the routes, ports, peoples, and goods of the East African, Ethiopian Highlands, and Egyptian components of Indian Ocean trade. Following the seventh-century spread of Arab culture and Islamic faith many Arabs with birthplaces as varied as Spain, North Africa, Persia, and Baghdad traveled widely in East and West Africa. Some wrote extensive descriptions of their journeys, thus leaving the world first-hand accounts of geography, trade, and medieval African polities and places including Ancient **Ghana**, Ancient **Mali**, and the Swahili coast. Prominent among these Arab travelers and chroniclers were Ibn Hawqal, Ibn Khaldun, **al-Bakri**, al-Biruni, and al-Masudi. A Chinese fleet visited East Africa in the early fifteenth century, whereas the Portuguese first glimpsed the Swahili coast nearly a century later.

In like fashion medieval Africans journeyed outside their continent, very famously in the *hajj* or religious pilgrimage made in 1324 by **Mansa Musa**, the great leader of the mighty and fabulously wealthy West African empire of Ancient Mali that then controlled the flow of gold into trans-Saharan trade.

No doubt motivated by a desire for secular glory as well as by deep piety, he took with him a very large entourage including thousands of servants, assistants, and dignitaries and also many thousands of pounds of gold. En route from his home in the western Sudan to Mecca in the Arabian Peninsula, a journey of many thousands of miles that included the arduous and dangerous Saharan crossing, he stopped at **Cairo** in North Africa where he put so much gold into local circulation that he depressed the price of this precious metal. This act captured the attention of Europeans, who for the first time learned of the specific empire that exported the West African gold to which they so eagerly sought unmediated access. This knowledge then began to appear on European maps such as the famous Catalan Atlas of 1375, which portrayed the king of Mali sitting on his throne, holding aloft in one hand an orb of gold, and approached by several camel-riding **Berbers**, the individuals responsible for bringing the gold Europe so fervently desired across the treacherous Sahara to the Mediterranean world. Another African, **Ibn Battuta**, a Berber born in Morocco in 1304, proved to be one of the great world travelers of his day. A partial listing of his travels includes visits to what are today Iraq, Iran, Syria, and Yemen in the Middle East; China, India, and Indonesia in Asia; the Byzantine Empire's Constantinople; and the Balkans, southern Russia, and Spain in Europe. He also journeyed to Ancient Mali in West Africa and the Swahili coast in East Africa. His wonderfully detailed and very positive descriptions of East Africa—he characterized the Swahili cities as places of wealth, beauty, hospitality, and sophistication—are all the more meaningful given his broad basis for comparison.

Ties of Religion

The three great monotheistic traditions of **Judaism, Christianity** and Islam were no strangers to the medieval African continent. Judaism has had a long presence in North African cities, Saharan oases, and the Ethiopian Highlands, dating most anciently in North Africa to Biblical times. Like the Christian presence in medieval Africa, these Jewish populations often resulted from linkages created by trade. These could lead to intercontinental ties through what were often ongoing interactions between the branch of a Jewish or Christian trading family which had relocated to Africa, and the branches of the family that had remained at home or settled elsewhere. However, persecution played a role in some Jewish migrations: A significant new Jewish influx into North Africa followed the Roman destruction of the Second Temple in Jerusalem in 70 C.E. Judaism continued as a minority religious presence in all of the above-named regions throughout the medieval centuries, with new inflows of people occurring from time to time. For example, self-identification as Jews by the contemporary Lemba of southern Africa, an identity supported by their **oral traditions** and recent genetic analysis, admits for the probability that another movement of Jews to Africa, this one from what is today Yemen in the southern Arabian Peninsula, occurred around 1000. In addition to asserting Jewish origins, Lemba oral traditions indicate that they originally came from a village named "Senna" and that a flood precipitated their departure. The failure of a dam in Senna in Yemen in the appropriate timeframe is documented, as is the correspondence between the genetic signatures of Lemba men and the *cohanim*, or

Jewish priests. Sporadic medieval Spanish persecutions of Jews, as well as the medieval Reconquista that at its conclusion expelled Spain's Jewish population, similarly increased Jewish communities in North African cities and Saharan oases, particularly toward the end of the medieval period. Harassment occurred in Africa as well as outside it: The community of medieval Jews in the Ethiopian Highlands eventually found itself alienated from the Christian Solomonid dynasty that came to power in 1270 and relegated Ethiopian Jews to a lower social status, actively persecuting them periodically too. It was the descendents of this Beta Israel community (or Falasha as they are often called, though that term is considered pejorative today) who were airlifted to the modern state of Israel in Operation Moses during 1984 and 1985.

Christianity traveled the relatively short distance from its homeland in the eastern Mediterranean to North Africa in the first or second century C.E., so its presence on the continent is almost as old as the religion itself. Initially established in Egypt, the new faith flourished in cities such as Alexandria before becoming widely established throughout rural as well as urban portions of Egypt during the first millennium of the Common Era. From Egypt Christianity moved west along the North African coast, where it was taken up by many among the Maghrib's Berber population by 400 C.E. Quite quickly Christianity was also embraced in the Ethiopian Highlands, first by King Ezana of Aksum who converted in the fourth century after contact with Christians merchants who traveled down the Red Sea and were soon succeeded by Syrian monks seeking more converts. Christianity in **Nubia** followed shortly thereafter, from the middle of the first millennium C.E.

Much as Christianity moved very quickly from its place of birth to Africa, Islam spread across all of North Africa immediately after its founding in the Arabian Peninsula in the early seventh century. From there Islam spread south, carried by merchants of trans-Saharan trade accompanying camel caravans into the desert and the grasslands beyond. The Berbers of the Sahara converted first, from the ninth and tenth centuries, with Islam reaching the West African sahel and Sudan during the tenth to twelfth centuries. Islam also moved from the Arabian Peninsula to East Africa, here too progressing along well-established trade routes. Although signs of Islamic identity can be discerned in the archaeological record of East African coastal communities as early as the eighth century, the new religion was not broadly embraced there until the eleventh. Finally, Islam also spread from Arabia across the Red Sea to the Horn of Africa, and from there traveled further west to Nubia along the Middle Nile. Nubians also received Islam from Egyptian scholars and merchants who traveled south up the Nile to Nubia's more interior location.

Islam and Christianity champion pilgrimage, though with greatly differing degrees of obligation: Although a Christian pilgrimage to Jerusalem remains a matter of individual choice, Islam enjoins all Muslims who can afford it and are physically able to accomplish what is for many in the far-flung regions of Islam a long and arduous journey to travel at least once in their lives to Mecca in the Arabian Peninsula. Many African Christians and Muslims made these journeys, with the result that these pilgrimages created continuous linkages between Africans and their coreligionists from other parts of the world. In the case of the Muslim *hajj*, this could have effects far beyond connecting African Muslims to the larger Islamic world. For example, the Almoravid Movement, which swept across portions of West and North Africa and then conquered the southern Iberian Peninsula, followed the eleventh century *hajj* taken by Yahya bin Ibrahim, a Berber from the southwestern Sahara. This experience inspired him to seek to introduce a more rigorous and puritanical version of Sunni Islam among his people, an effort eventually resulting in the far more broadly reaching outcomes of the Almoravid Movement. Others, such as Mansa Musa whose *hajj* brought knowledge of Ancient Mali to Europe, returned from Mecca determined to create top-notch centers of Islamic scholarship at home. Mansa Musa's vision came to eventual fruition with the emergence of the Malian city of **Timbuktu** as a world-renowned center of Islamic scholarship and learning. All of the new, flowering centers of Islamic scholarship, such as al-Azhar University in Cairo that was regarded as one of the intellectual seats of the Islamic world, created additional and very potent sources of intercontinental communication, drawing scholars as they did from around the Muslim world and giving medieval Africans educated in these institutions access to the full range of knowledge of the Muslim intellectual tradition, as well as adding new strands to it. Turning to Christianity, in addition to pilgrimages the Crusades created linkages when Christian Nubians met with European crusaders in Constantinople in 1204 and attacked Islamic rule in Egypt in support of their European coreligionists. Some believe this history is reflected in the statue of St. Maurice erected in the Cathedral of Magdeburg in Germany in the thirteenth century, shortly after the Sixth Crusade. In this depiction St. Maurice appears as a Nubian crusader dressed in chain mail, in the analysis of the historian Basil Davidson a testament to the African contribution to this episode of Christian history.

Religion, art, and intercontinental influences coincided time and again in medieval Africa. For example, the rock-hewn churches of Lalibela in the Ethiopian Highlands that were sculpted from the twelfth and thirteenth centuries, according to tradition in an attempt to create a "New Jerusalem" following Saladin's capture of Jerusalem in 1187, were clearly inspired by that city's centrality to the Christian faith. The artistic traditions of medieval Nubian and **Ethiopian Christianity** drew in part from Byzantine conventions, for example in their privileging of frontal poses and very large eyes, whereas the artwork of many Muslim parts of Africa quickly came to incorporate the calligraphy so central to Islamic artistry. Arab influences on mosque architecture could also be seen across medieval Africa. Yet it is also the case that indigenizing of these imported traditions was common, indeed the norm. For example, mosque architecture in late medieval sudanic West Africa was hugely influenced by local architectural conventions, which varied from place to place across this vast region and led to a fascinating range of mosque styles. Likewise, Ethiopian ecclesiastical art utilized regionally dominant color palettes in preference to those of the Byzantines, and the Nubians, who loved well their equine steeds, were wont to replace the three wise men's camels with horses in their Nativity scenes.

Although the three great monotheistic traditions of Christianity, Islam, and Judaism are the most prominent examples of intercontinental linkages created through religion, other faiths made their way to medieval Africa with other travelers of that time. For example, visitors and immigrants practicing Hinduism, Buddhism, Zoroastrianism, and Manichaeanism came to medieval Africa from time to time too, though these traditions made no significant inroads into the African communities to which they came.

Transfers of Ideas and Technologies

The movements of people and patterns of trade discussed above also resulted in transfers of information, many of which can be broadly thought of as forms of technology. New foodstuffs made their way to Africa in the medieval and even premedieval centuries, some of which revolutionized food production on the continent. From Asia came citrus fruits, coconuts, sugar cane, Asian rice, cocoyam, plantains, and bananas. The last two flourished in many parts of Africa, including its rainforests that form an inhospitable climate for growing cereals and grains, adding vital new sources of starch to the African diet, becoming staples of the **food** supply, and underlying modest increases in the medieval rate of population growth. Western Asia may have contributed domesticated wheat and barley, though these had a limited impact on the continent because they could be grown only outside the tropical and subtropical **regions**, which dominate in Africa. In a reverse flow, African crops disseminated to Asia included sorghum, cowpeas, and the kapok and baobab trees. Intercontinental exchanges of foodstuffs continued in the modern era with the creation of an Atlantic world and its Columbian Exchange, which brought foods cultivated in Africa such as okra, bananas, and citrus fruit, as well as the guinea fowl, to the Americas, whereas the latter introduced foods including corn, cassava, and tomatoes to the African continent.

Animals domesticated by Africans include the guinea fowl and, most likely, the domestic cat beloved by Ancient Egyptians as well as many millions of people throughout the world today. The African Wild Ass, subsequent to its domestication by Africans, became the probable ancestor of the domestic donkey, which has since disseminated very widely around the globe from its African point of origin. Many domesticated animals also came to Africa from elsewhere, some medievally and some earlier. India contributed the humped zebu cow, widely raised in Africa to the present, whereas from other parts of Asia came sheep, goats, and the chicken. The Arabian Peninsula contributed the camel, which was taken up many millennia ago by people in the Horn of Africa with their longstanding ties to Arabia. In keeping with Arabian practices and also much like later, medieval cattle keepers of eastern and southern Africa, people in the Horn eschewed killing their camels for meat, preferring to use their herds for milk and as a way of storing wealth. The peoples of North Africa and the Sahara gained access to the camel only at a significantly later date: Romans first brought the camel to North Africa in the early centuries of the Common Era that was then quickly taken up by Berbers. This development revolutionized Berber life by allowing them to practice nomadic pastoralism in the Sahara. This evolution in turn changed life radically for so many others on and off the continent, because it was a necessary precursor to the expansion of trans-Saharan trade, which depended upon utilizing the animal as a beast of burden in the camel caravans that moved trade goods north and south across the desert.

Although less fundamentally revolutionary than the transfers of domesticated plants and animals just discussed, the interactions of peoples that resulted from the medieval interconnections between Africa and other parts of the globe led to many other shared ideas and customs. These included the introduction to Africa of new systems of coinage, which joined indigenous currencies such as gold dust in the West African Sudan and the copper cross **currency** of Central Africa. For example, the currency of Aksum seems to have been derived from that of the Byzantines. In a reverse flow, the gold coins known as dinars produced by the Berber Almoravids in North Africa and Spain, but most copiously at the oasis town of **Sijilmasa** in the northern Sahara, had a very wide range and were in demand in the Middle East, and in Europe before that continent began its own widespread minting of gold coins. Large caches of Almoravid dinars have been found at archaeological sites as far away from Sijilmasa as France and Jordan. Traditions of hospitality could also result from intercontinental interactions: The use of betel leaves and areca nuts to welcome visitors, which occurred at times on the medieval East African coast, is a clear illustration of this region's ties to South Asia, from where this tradition came. In turn, West Africans exported to parts of the Muslim world their rainforests' caffeinated kola nut, which acts as a mild stimulant and is offered to visitors by many peoples in the West African forest and Sudan.

It is clear that deeply rooted, continuous, and highly meaningful interactions connected Africans and peoples in Europe, the Middle East, and South and Southeast Asia throughout the medieval centuries. Typically stimulated by intercontinental trade through trans-Saharan and Indian Ocean commercial networks that served to redistribute the surplus goods of all of these world regions, these interconnections led to transfers not only of commodities but also of religions, food crops, domesticated animals, and a host of shared ideas and ways between Africans and Arabians, Persians, South Asians, Indonesians, the people of southern Chinese ports, and Europeans. These interactions enriched the lives of all of these peoples materially, spiritually, technologically, intellectually, and culturally. For Africa, they added new and vibrant strands to the many developments internal to the medieval continent, while creating avenues for medieval Africans to contribute to these other parts of the world their own ideas, cosmologies, technologies, and commodities.

Further Reading

Dunn, Ross. E. *The Adventures of Ibn Battuta: A Muslim Traveler of the Fourteenth Century.* Berkeley: University of California Press, 2004.

Gilbert, Erik, and Jonathan T. Reynolds. *Africa in World History: From Prehistory to the Present.* Upper Saddle River, NJ: Pearson Education, Inc., 2004.

Hunwick, John O. *Jews of a Saharan Oasis: The Elimination of the Tamantit Community.* Princeton, NJ: Markus Wiener Publishers, 2006.

Levtzion, Nehemia. *Medieval West Africa: Views from Arab Scholars and Merchants.* Princeton, NJ: Markus Wiener Publishers, 2002.

Robinson, David. *Muslim Societies in African History.* Cambridge, UK: Cambridge University Press, 2004.

Short Entries: People, Ideas, Events, and Terms

Abdallah ibn Yasin (d. 1059)

The spiritual leader of the eleventh-century Almoravid Movement, the Muslim scholar Abdallah ibn Yasin was recruited in 1039 to 1040 by the Sanhaja **Berber** chief Yahya ibn Ibrahim to come from North Africa to the western Sahara to instruct his people, a subset of the Sanhaja Berber known as the Juddala, in a more fully orthodox practice of **Islam** (*see* **Almoravid and Almohad Movements**).

Abdallah, whose Berber mother came from the southern Sahara herself, rose to this challenge that took him to the far fringes of the Muslim world where an only partial, and unorthodox to boot, embrace of Islam was the norm. However, after arriving he angered the Juddala with his very strict and rigid dictates, and they rose up in rebellion against his teachings. Consequently for several years Abdallah made a retreat, or *hijra*—an Islamic practice emulating the Prophet Muhammad's own *hijra* of 622 when he withdrew from Mecca to Medina—from which he returned with the support of the Lamtuna Sanhaja. With this the Almoravid Movement accelerated, and by the late eleventh century had through military conquest created a vast, Berber-controlled empire reaching from Andalusia in southern Spain across the Mediterranean and all the way through the Sahara to its southern edge. Abdallah died in 1059 in the fighting that attended the Almoravid Movement's conquests.

Further Reading

Hiskett, Mervyn. *The Development of Islam in West Africa*. London: Longman Group Limited, 1984.

Levtzion, Nehemiah. *Ancient Ghana and Mali*. London: Methuen & Co. Ltd., 1973.

Abu Bakr ibn 'Umar (d. 1087)

A member of the ruling family of the Lamtuna, a subset of the Sanhaja **Berber** of the western Sahara who were the earliest supporters and subsequent leaders of the eleventh-century Almoravid Movement, after his brother's death Abu Bakr ibn 'Umar played a key role as a military and political leader of this Movement that promulgated adherence to a more austere and orthodox **Islam** in the western Sahara and created a vast, Berber-led empire stretching from the southern Sahara all the way north across the Mediterranean into southern

Spain (*see* **Almoravid and Almohad Movements**). Following the emergence of the Almoravids in the mideleventh century, Abu Bakr quickly rose to the fore as one of the Movement's military leaders.

After the Almoravids conquered important settlements in the Sahara that were central to trans-Saharan trade in the western desert and thus a source of great wealth, they moved further north and under Abu Bakr's leadership conquered Morocco. After doing battle in North Africa, Abu Bakr returned south to the desert where he successfully put down other Berber challenges to the Lamtuna ascendancy. After serving as the political leader of the Almoravids following the death in 1059 of the Movement's founder and spiritual leader, **Abdallah ibn Yasin**, Abu Bakr died in 1087 as the empire reached its greatest territorial and political strength. He was succeeded as ruler by his cousin, Yusuf ibn Tashfin, who had extended Almoravid control throughout much of the Maghrib and even into Muslim Spain shortly before Abu Bakr's death.

Further Reading
Hiskett, Mervyn. *The Development of Islam in West Africa*. London: Longman Group Limited, 1984.
Levtzion, Nehemiah. *Ancient Ghana and Mali*. London: Methuen & Co. Ltd., 1973.

African Traditional Religions

African traditional religions vary from ethnicity to ethnicity so subsuming them under one label is somewhat problematic, but because of commonalities between them generalizations can be made. African traditional religions are polytheistic, with a belief in multiple gods and goddesses, and spirits who can inhabit a wide range of natural features such as rocks, individual trees, sacred groves, caves, hills, mountains, lakes, and **rivers**. Often these religions contain a creator god, who is recognized as the supreme deity, as well as gods or goddesses of the earth, sky, waters, heavens, and weather.

Ancestral spirits play a prominent role in these traditions too and stem from beliefs about the afterlife: After death, a person who has lived a virtuous life becomes an ancestral spirit and continues to observe and influence the lives of its descendents still living upon the earth. The descendents do not worship ancestral spirits but are expected to remember them and honor them, for example, by making offerings of food and drink and invoking their names and memories of them on certain occasions such as the naming of a new child. A wide range of forms of religious leadership exist, with specialists serving as diviners, seers, spirit mediums, healers, prophets, oracles, and priestesses or priests attached to any one of the host of divinities. Religious observances include prayer, sacrifice, and offerings.

African tradition religions also embody a belief in the ability of deities and spirits as well as some people to wield unseen or special powers, through which they can affect the lives of others for good or ill, depending on whether the person harnessing this mysterious power is a benevolent or malevolent individual. A variety of protective mechanisms such as charms, amulets, and medicines, which can shield or guard against these special powers, can be made by religious specialists. In the medieval period (and to the present) most African converts to **Islam** and **Christianity** were unwilling to entirely abandon their former beliefs and instead practiced religious syncretism, blending elements of African religious traditions, most notably beliefs in ancestral and other spirits, the protective forces of amulets and medicines, and special powers, with their new faiths.

Further Reading

Mbiti, John S. *Introduction to African Religions.* 2nd ed. Portsmouth, NH: Heinemann, 1991.
Ray, Benjamin C. *African Religions: Symbol, Ritual, and Community.* Englewood Cliffs, NJ: Prentice Hall, 1976.

Agriculture

In some parts of the continent Africans have farmed for thousands of years, dating to many millennia before the medieval period began, whereas in other places farming was adopted only on the eve of the medieval centuries. In the Western Desert of Egypt fixed agriculture dates as far back as 7000 B.C.E. and possibly far earlier, whereas by 5000 B.C.E. it was practiced in the Nile River Valley and what is today the Sahara, which was then a well-watered and fertile place. People were farming in the **Ethiopian Highlands** and in the forest zone of West Africa by 3000 B.C.E., if not very considerably earlier.

By the opening centuries of the Common Era farming had spread throughout the southern half of the continent from these areas of early cultivating and was practiced in virtually all of Africa. The embrace of ironworking, which moved across Africa between around 1000 B.C.E. and 400 C.E., led to an increase in the productivity, and thus the allure of farming by contributing far more efficient tools such as iron hoes, scythes, and knives. In keeping with the scholarship on the origins in Africa of animal domestication and ironworking, controversy and lack of consensus exist over whether farming was independently developed by Africans or transmitted to them by peoples from western Asia (*see* **Domesticated Animals**). Indeed both possibilities, indigenous innovation and diffusion from outside, may have occurred. However farming came to exist in Africa, it is indisputably the case that the majority of crops grown by early African farmers were African domesticates—types of plants indigenous to Africa that African cultivators transformed from their natural, wild incarnations into crops modified through seed selection for desired traits.

In the vast grassland **regions** of Africa the most important crops included the cereal grasses sorghum and pearl millet. In the well-watered Inland Niger Delta, which lay in the grasslands of West Africa, African rice flourished, and eventually its cultivation spread to the lands lying to the interior of the western African coastline from today's Senegal to Liberia. In the densely vegetated and heavily watered climate of the rainforests lying along the equator, whose challenging environment did not allow farmers to cultivate grains, the earliest crop to be grown was the yam, eventually followed by melons, fluted pumpkins, gourds, and cowpeas. The output of the naturally occurring oil palm, raffia, and kola nut forest trees were exploited as well, and these highly valued trees were left standing when land was cleared for farming. The Ethiopian Highlands, whose elevation creates unique microclimates, saw the domestication of teff and noog, crops cultivated nowhere else on the continent (or in the world), as well as coffee, qat, and finger millet.

Moving beyond African domesticates, even the arid Sahara supported agriculture at its medieval oases, whose sources of water were harnessed via systems of irrigation to raise crops including date palms, grapes, and a variety of other fruits. Dates, in significant demand in the lands to the desert's south, were traded for the cereals and grains of the West African savannah that were equally desired by the desert peoples, an exchange that helped drive medieval trade between the Sahara and sub-Saharan West Africa. Other crops cultivated in medieval Africa whose origins lay outside the continent included wheat and barley from western Asia, which because of their need for a more temperate climate could be grown only in portions of North Africa, the Ethiopian Highlands, and the Nile River Valley, and a large number of Asian foodstuffs including citrus fruits, coconuts, sugar cane, Asian rice, cocoyams, and possibly plantains and bananas. The last flourished in rainforest environments and revolutionized forest agriculture because bananas require less labor to grow and process than yams and are simultaneously nutritionally superior. Across the continent, medieval African farmers also grew vegetables and chose to cultivate a diversified range of crops to minimize the risks of the periodic crop failure that is inherent in farming, and to increase the size of their harvests by taking advantage of the fact that different crops required the highest inputs of labor at different points in the growing season. They also identified and cultivated crops that would add to their diets sources of nutritionally necessary fat, important given limited medieval access to dietary fat acquired from animals.

In the forests people turned to the oil palm tree and in the West African savannah shea nuts filled this requirement, while Ethiopians utilized noog. Farming methods varied depending on the local environment: In the tropical rainforests where soil had low fertility, people practiced shifting plot agriculture, clearing land, using it for several years until the soil's fertility was exhausted, and then moving on to a new or long-fallow plot. With the exception of Ethiopian Highland farmers, African agriculturalists practiced hoe rather than plow agriculture: The trypanosomiasis or sleeping sickness that proved fatal to horses and cattle made it impossible to use plows pulled by draft animals in many portions of the continent. Irrigation and terracing created additional arable land in more arid or very hilly locations, whereas those parts of Africa possessing reliable sources of water and a more level topography could be cultivated continuously even without such labor-intensive improvements. In addition to furnishing new ways to provide food for people's daily diets, the development of farming in Africa had profound social ramifications. Farming required people to make the switch to sedentism rather than continuing the life of constant movement characteristic of foragers practicing hunting and gathering, and the combination of sedentary life and agriculture in turn promoted higher rates of population growth and population density. The creation of surpluses, common with agricultural production especially in tandem with herding, as well as the need to organize access to the resources of land and labor made increasingly valuable by farming, resulted in growing social complexity, with the emergence, in parts of medieval Africa, of heightened class distinctions and increased numbers of societies choosing centralized forms of government and forming larger states or empires. Simultaneously, however, large numbers of medieval African farming peoples continued to prefer and very successfully practice "stateless" forms of political organization, characterized by political authority broadly diffused across the members of their societies.

Finally, it is important to recognize that medieval African cultivators typically engaged in multiple productive activities rather than practicing only farming. Many raised domesticated animals, most commonly cattle, sheep, goats, donkeys, and fowl. Many also continued to practice at least episodically the earlier subsistence activity of foraging, or collecting naturally occurring edible plants and hunting wild game. Trading surplus goods in local, regional, and long-distance trading networks was another common activity for medieval African farmers, though mutually beneficial systems of local exchange bound together farmers and herders, and farmers and foragers, in many parts of the continent.

Further Reading

Clark, J. Desmond, and Steven A. Brandt, eds. *From Hunters to Farmers: The Causes and Consequences of Food Production in Africa*. Berkeley: University of California Press, 1984.

Shaw, Thurstan, Paul Sinclair, Bassey Andah, and Alex Okpoko, eds. *The Archaeology of Africa: Food, Metals, and Towns*. London: Routledge, 1993.

Akan

The Akan-speaking peoples of West Africa originated on the savannah–forest fringe just south of the Black Volta in what is today the modern state of **Ghana**. Their history has been shaped in part by their proximity to the Akan goldfield, which lay in the forest region to their south. Although their early history is still imperfectly understood, from the first half of the second millennium C.E. the Akan were trading **gold** and kola nuts as well as other commodities north to **Jenné-jeno** in the Inland Niger Delta, from where these commodities entered trans-Saharan trade. As a result of this burgeoning trade the market town of Begho, with an Akan quarter, was founded on the forest–savannah border in the very early centuries of the second millenium. This development was followed around 1400 by the appearance of the early Akan state of Bono.

Akan gold became increasingly important as the older West African goldfields at Bambuk and Bure became less productive in the late medieval period, which led the itinerant Dyula traders of the savannah region to seek larger quantities of Akan gold from the fourteenth century. Shortly thereafter, in the fifteenth century, the Akan moved south into the rainforests of what are today Ghana. Their ability to live and farm in the challenging tropical forest environment was facilitated by their trade with a new party who avidly sought their gold, the Portuguese who arrived on the Atlantic coastline even further to their south in the 1470s. The Akan agreed to redirect the export of a significant portion of their gold to the Portuguese in return for guns, cloth, and enslaved Africans the Portuguese purchased from the polities of **Kongo** and sometimes **Benin**. The Akan used this slave population, as well as slaves they procured in northern markets in exchange for gold, to do the backbreaking work of creating clearings in the forest where farming could take place, and also some of the more dangerous forms of gold mining.

The Akan benefited from new and highly productive food crops introduced through the Atlantic exchange, such as corn and cassava, which together transformed forest agriculture and accelerated population growth. Clearly possessing a highly stratified society, postmedievally the Akan continued to create states in the forest and in the coastal region to the forest's south, the most powerful and best known of which was Asante. The Akan provide yet another medieval example of the indigenous development of significant networks of regional and long-distance trade exchanging the goods of varied **ecological zones**, which then intersected with external markets, in this case trans-Saharan and Atlantic, that provided additional opportunities for economic and social growth and complexity.

Further Reading

Anquandah, James. *Rediscovering Ghana's Past*. New York: Longman, 1982.
Effah-Gyamfi, Kwaku. *Bono Manso: An Archaeological Investigation into Early Akan Urbanism*. Calgary, Canada: University of Calgary Press, 1985.
Wilks, Ivor. "A Medieval Trade Route from the Niger to the Gulf of Guinea." *Journal of African History* 3 (2) (1962): 337–341.

Aksum

Aksum emerged in the northern half of the **Ethiopian Highlands** in the first century C.E. and flourished for centuries until it entered its long decline in the seventh century. It was a sizeable African empire of its day, stretching from the former Meroë on the Nile in the west to the Red Sea in the east, which it sometimes leapfrogged to conquer southwestern Arabian polities. It also reached from as far as the current Eritrea in the north to beyond Lake Tana and the Blue Nile in the south. The material base for Aksum's success lay in Red Sea trade, which provided connections to highly lucrative Mediterranean and Indian Ocean commerce. Aksum gained additional wealth from herding and agriculture, activities of long standing in this region, and also taxed the trade passing through Adulis as well as demanding tribute such as cattle from conquered peoples. With its prosperity Aksum became a place of great sophistication and material achievement. Urban centers flourished, including the capitol city of Aksum and the Red Sea port of Adulis through which the empire's international trade flowed. Literacy had come to the Highlands from South Arabia before Aksum's emergence, and a tradition of writing in the local Highland language of Ge'ez continued throughout the empire's reign. Aksum also minted its own coins, and early inscriptions in Greek and South Arabian Sabaean as well as Ge'ez stand today as testament to the international nature of this long-ago state. Another illustration of interconnections with people far as well as near can be found in the adoption of **Christianity** by the fourth-century King Ezana after its introduction by Christians from either Egypt or the Levant, who were in turn followed by sixth-century Syrian monks seeking converts, events that led to the flowering of Christianity in this region and the emergence of the Ethiopian Orthodox Church. Elements of **Judaism** were introduced very early in the Common Era too, apparently before Christianity came to Ethiopia.

Aksum is also renowned for its monumental architecture, most particularly its massive and striking stelae—tall, intricately carved stone monuments—which still draw tourists to Ethiopia today. Less well known are its rock-hewn churches, which presaged those of the Zagwe dynasty (*see* **Dynasties**). When Red Sea trade declined following the seventh-century redirection of shipping to the Persian Gulf so did Aksum, though a simultaneous change in climate, which negatively affected agriculture appears to have harmed the state too. The period between the onset of its decline and the twelfth-century emergence of the next major Ethiopian state, the Zagwe dynasty, remains imperfectly understood in Africanist scholarship today, though it is clear that feudalism replaced international commerce in these centuries and the locus of Aksum's power shifted south. *See also* Document 2.

Further Reading

Munro-Hay, Stuart. *Aksum: An African Civilization of Late Antiquity.* Edinburgh, Scotland: Edinburgh University Press, 1992.

Al-Bakri (d. 1094)

Al-Bakri, a Muslim of Arab background, was born at an unknown date and lived his entire life in Spain until his death in 1094. Although he never left Spain, by speaking with and utilizing the reports of those who had traveled to sub-Saharan West Africa he was able to author a critically important work on medieval West African history, variously translated as *The Book of Highways and Kingdoms* or *The Book of Routes and Realms*, which he wrote in 1068. It stands out as one of the earliest efforts to write a synthetic history of the western Sudan and addresses, among other things, the polities of **Ghana** and **Takrur**, the important Saharan oases of **Sijilmasa** and Awdaghust, the Almoravid Movement, and regional and long-distance trade involving West Africa and the Sahara (*see* **Almoravid and Almohad Movements**).

Al-Bakri's description of Ghana provides one of the earliest written accounts of that empire and sheds interesting light on its court, its military, indigenous religious traditions, the relationship between the people of Ghana and the Muslims who visited it largely as a result of trans-Saharan trade, the state's taxation of trade and control of **gold**, and other significant matters (*see* **African Traditional Religions**).

Further Reading

Bovill, Edward William. *The Golden Trade of the Moors: West African Kingdoms in the Fourteenth Century.* Oxford, UK: Oxford University Press, 1958.

Levtzion, Nehemiah, ed., and J.F.P. Hopkins, trans. *Corpus of Early Arabic Sources for West African History.* Cambridge, UK: Cambridge University Press, 1981.

Almoravid and Almohad Movements

The Almoravid and Almohad Movements were Muslim social movements of the eleventh through thirteenth centuries arising, respectively, in the western Sahara and North African Maghrib that sought religious and sociopolitical reform. In both cases achieving rapid political control over large swathes of territory, they proved ephemeral and each fell quite rapidly after initial spectacular success. These movements arose among different clans of the **Berber**s, the inhabitants of the Maghrib and Sahara at the time of the Arab incursions of the seventh and early eighth centuries. Although many North African Berbers embraced **Islam** in the initial centuries of Arab contact, the new faith only more gradually made inroads among the nomadic Berbers in the vast Sahara Desert to the south, who began taking up select elements of Islam in the ninth and tenth centuries while practicing a religious syncretism also inclusive of many elements of their previous religion (*see* **African Traditional Religions**).

This syncretism, and the lax practice of Islam which was part of it, came to be viewed as unacceptable by Yahya ibn Ibrahim, an eleventh-century chief of the Sanhaja Berber who lived in the southwestern Sahara. He sought to introduce greater Islamic religious orthodoxy to his people in what quickly mushroomed into a far broader set of events known collectively as the Almoravid Movement. Yahya ibn Ibrahim's impetus toward religious reform followed his 1035–36 *hajj*, or pilgrimage to Mecca required at least once in a lifetime of all pious Muslims able to undertake the journey. Inspired by the experiences and knowledge he gained during his pilgrimage and associated travels, Yahya ibn Ibrahim stopped at Qayrawan in North Africa on his way home from Mecca, seeking an Islamic scholar willing to leave the more cosmopolitan North African coast to instruct the desert Sanhaja in the finer points of Islam. The Berber scholar **Abdallah ibn Yasin** agreed to take on this task, moved to the western Sahara, and began preaching a very rigid Islam based upon the Malikite legal school and emphasizing strict adherence to shari'a (e.g., Islamic law). Faced with dissent due to his harsh and unyielding dictates, Abdallah ibn Yasin withdrew for several years only to return and this time gain widespread support among the Lamtuna branch of the Sanhaja in the 1040s.

As the strength of his movement grew, the Almoravids, as his followers were now known, turned to military actions and by midcentury conquered important Saharan settlements including **Sijilmasa** on the northern desert fringe and Audaghast in the south, which led to a lucrative Almoravid control of trans-Saharan trade in the western Sahara. Even further to the south, under the leadership of the Lamtuna chief **Abu Bakr ibn 'Umar**, the Almoravids extended their territory from the Sahara into the West African savannah below, influencing the mighty empire of **Ghana**, whose rulers converted to Islam at this time. On the other end of their expanding empire, by the mid-1080s the Almoravids also controlled the North African Maghrib from Morocco's Atlantic coast to Algiers, from where they leaped the Mediterranean to seize Muslim Spain. The creation of this large empire, however, provided one reason for its very rapid downfall, because controlling this vast territory stretching from southern Spain right through the Sahara proved impossible. The rigid, legalistic Islam the movement imposed was widely resented too. And thus by 1150 the Almoravids were supplanted by the rising Almohad Movement led by sedentary Masmuda Berbers from the Atlas Mountains, which at its peak controlled the entire Maghrib as well as southern Spain.

The Almohads preached a far more tolerant form of Islam with a particular emphasis upon not legalism but more approachable Sufi mysticism. Also overstretched territorially, a mere century later the Almohad empire in its turn fell to various powers including Christians in the Spanish Reconquista and nomadic Berbers from south of the Maghrib, resulting in the end of Almohad rule by the midthirteenth century.

Further Reading

Abun-Nasr, Jamil M. *A History of the Maghrib in the Islamic Period*. 3rd ed. Cambridge, UK: Cambridge University Press, 1993.

Hiskett, Mervyn. *The Development of Islam in West Africa*. London: Longman Group Limited, 1984.

Levtzion, Nehemiah. *Ancient Ghana and Mali*. London: Methuen & Co. Ltd., 1973.

Askiya Muhammad (c. 1442–1538)

Askiya Muhammad (r. 1493–1528) founded the Askiya dynasty of **Songhai**, the largest-ever West African empire, after seizing power in 1493 from the son and successor to the great **Sonni Ali** (r. 1464–1492) who had transformed Songhai from a state to an empire in the 1460s. Askiya Muhammad further expanded the already-large empire, using a sizeable and greatly feared cavalry to enforce Songhai overrule over a huge swathe of West Africa.

He extended Songhai control far north into the Sahara to Taghaza, which was a critically important source of desert salt, and far south into the savannah well beyond **Jenné-jeno**, which gave Songhai control of the all-important export routes for **gold**. With authority over these two highly valuable commodities, which drove trade between the Sahara and West Africa, Songhai was perfectly situated to benefit from the profits generated by this trans-Saharan trade, which expanded at this time, and its taxation. Askiya Muhammad also stands out for his administrative innovations. He took firmer central control over many provinces of the empire by appointing individuals from his inner circle as their governors rather than allowing internal governance by local rulers as had been the norm.

A deeply pious Muslim, Askiya Muhammad is also noted for mending relationships between the empire and the Muslim scholars of **Timbuktu** and Walata, which had become frayed in the time of Sonni Ali. In fact, because of his religiosity and sensitivity to their interests and concerns, these scholars eagerly supported his successful challenge to Sonni Ali's son and successor. In what he labeled a jihad, Askiya Muhammad further persecuted the Mossi, who had previously been pushed back by Sonni Ali, using the novel and explicitly religious justification that they were infidels. He also made the *hajj*, or religious pilgrimage to Mecca, shortly after ascending to power, and during it persuaded the caliph of **Egypt** to name him caliph, or commander of the faithful, of all Muslims in the western Sudan.

It was also under the rule and patronage of the Askiyas that Timbuktu rose to its greatest prominence as a center of Islamic scholarship. The Askiya dynasty's alignment with the Muslim notables of its empire solved one problem, but caused another—when Morocco sent an invading force to conquer Songhai in 1591, the lack of internal cohesion, which resulted in part from the disjuncture between the Islamized ruling elite and the non-Muslim commoners, contributed to the difficulty of successfully repelling the invasion.

Further Reading

Bovill, Edward William. *The Golden Trade of the Moors: West African Kingdoms in the Fourteenth Century*. Oxford, UK: Oxford University Press, 1958.

Hunwick, John O., ed. and trans. *Timbuktu and the Songhay Empire: Al-Sa'dis Ta'rikh Al-Sudan Down to 1613 and Other Contemporary Documents*. Leiden, The Netherlands: Brill, 1999.

Bantu Expansions

A key case study when considering the movements and migrations of peoples, cultures, and languages that were hallmarks of medieval Africa is found in the Bantu expansions. One question that has long occupied historians of

Africa's more distant past is how virtually the entire southern half of the continent came to speak Bantu languages during the period from approximately 3000 B.C.E. to the early centuries of the Common Era. Previous generations of scholars envisioned literal migrations of conquering Bantu peoples, sweeping southward and in an easterly and then southern direction from their ancestral homeland where Nigeria and Cameroon nowadays meet.

More recently, this perspective has been replaced with the theory that though there was an early movement of Bantu peoples from their homeland south into the equatorial rainforests of what is today the Congo basin in Central Africa that began some 5,000 years ago, the dominance of Bantu languages throughout virtually all of central, eastern, and southern Africa is best attributed to the further slow, steady spread of Bantu languages, rather than of Bantu people engaged in conquest, through ever-enlarging zones of intercultural contact. Thus the earlier understanding of "Bantu migrations" of human beings has been replaced with the idea of "Bantu expansions" that were certainly linguistic and cultural in nature but did not involve a wholesale displacement of earlier central, eastern, and southern African populations engulfed by waves of Bantu immigrants.

Still a matter of considerable dispute is whether these Bantu expansions are also responsible for the appearance, in most of central, southern, and eastern Africa by the early centuries of the Common Era, of a broad range of linked phenomena that included ironworking technologies and agricultural innovations. Whatever their genesis, the spread of these trends across the entire southern half of Africa by about 300 C.E., as the medieval era was about to unfold, led to increased populations, sedentism, and heightened social complexity characterized by far more marked social hierarchies, urbanization, and centralized political authority.

Further Reading

Ehret, Christopher. *An African Classical Age: Eastern and Southern Africa in World History, 1000 B.C. to A.D. 400*. Charlottesville: University Press of Virginia, 1998.

Vansina, Jan. *Paths in the Rainforests: Towards a History of Political Tradition in Equatorial Africa*. Madison: University of Wisconsin Press, 1990.

Benin

The state of Benin was established by Edo-speaking peoples early in the second millennium C.E. in the tropical forests of what is today southwestern Nigeria, in the lands to the west of the lower Niger River. It expanded into an empire in the midfifteenth century under the leadership of its *oba* or King Ewuare, and at its greatest extent wielded authority over what is today most of Nigeria to the south and west of the confluence of the Niger and Benue rivers. At its height it incorporated some of the **Yoruba** city-states and the western **Igbo** into its territory.

Benin history asserts that its founder, Oranmiyan, descended from Oduduwa, the founding ancestor of the Yoruba, though linguistically it appears an unlikely connection. The claim does, however, indicate the desirability of asserting a connection to the Yoruba who have played such a prominent role in this part of the West African tropical forest zone. Benin City, the empire's capital, is noteworthy for its massive earthen walls that were constructed by first excavating a ditch, from which was then erected a huge earthen bank. Including

Oba King between two warriors with lances and shield. Bronze plaque from wall or pillar of royal palace of the Oba, Benin, Nigeria, West Africa. The Art Archive/Antenna Gallery Dakar Senegal/Gianni Dagli Orti.

the depth of the ditch, the tallest of these earthworks reached some 50 feet in height. In addition to the walls surrounding Benin City, earthworks were also constructed around other Benin towns with the result that in a region of approximately 2,500 square miles, an astonishing total of just under 10,000 linear miles of earthen walls were built. It has been estimated that their construction required 150 million hours of labor, a statistic bearing striking testament to the power of the state to command and control human and financial resources. Some have conjectured that these massive earthworks protected valuable farmland from outsiders, an argument that has its roots in the fact that clearing tropical forest land for agriculture requires a staggering investment of human labor given the many tons of vegetation per acre that must be removed before farming can commence.

The oldest of these earthworks have been dated to the late first millennium, though a majority were probably constructed closer to the middle of the second millennium. Like the Yoruba with whom they claim a close connection and share significant elements of their culture, Benin is renowned for its tradition of brass sculptures created through lost-wax casting. This method involves making the original sculpture in wax, encasing that wax in clay, and then pouring into this clay mold molten metal, which melts and replaces the wax. When the clay mold is broken away, a brass sculpture remains. The Benin royals patronized the arts, and one specialty of its court sculptors was producing brass plaques depicting significant events in Benin history, which were then mounted on the palace walls. Sadly, when the British sacked Benin City in 1897, many of these Benin Bronzes as they are known, though brass was the usual medium of composition, became part of the loot of conquest. To the present, a number of them remain in the collection of the British Museum in London.

Further Reading

Eboreime, O.J., and Barbara Plakensteiner. *Benin: Kings and Rituals*. Ghent, Belgium: Snoeck, 2007.

Ezra, Kate. *Royal Art of Benin: The Perls Collection in the Metropolitan Museum of Art*. New York: Harry N. Abrams, Inc., 1992.

Berbers

The Berbers are the original inhabitants of the North African Maghrib whose precise origins have been lost to history. In antiquity they were known as Libyans and Numidians among other names; they called themselves the Imazighen. Premedievally, as conditions grew increasingly arid, some Berbers moved south into the Sahara's northern fringes and then deep into the Sahara proper, making them a people of the desert as well as the Maghrib. This process accelerated in the first centuries C.E. with the introduction into North Africa and then the Sahara of the camel, which revolutionized life and movement in the desert.

Medieval Berbers living in the Maghrib were generally sedentary and practiced herding and agriculture, whereas those in the Sahara lived a largely nomadic existence and raised camels, controlled the movement of trade goods across the Sahara by camel caravan, produced dates and cereals with the assistance of servile labor at oases where they constructed underground irrigation channels, and at times raided one another and the settled communities of the desert fringe in the north and south, though they also developed mutually beneficial cooperative relationships with these more sedentary neighbors and sometimes even settled among them.

Socially, the Berber were divided into a large number of subgroups, prominent among them the Sanhaja of the western Sahara, the Tuareg of the central Sahara, and the Masmuda of the Atlas Mountains; these subgroups were then divided again into smaller lineage-based clans. Outsiders have often been struck by Saharan Berber men's practice of veiling their faces below the eyes, and the indigo-colored cloth used for this purpose by the Tuareg has led some to call them the "Blue Men" though this is a problematically exoticizing label. Early medieval Berbers of the North African Maghrib adopted **Christianity** in large numbers by 400 C.E., with a particular affinity for Donatism, while a much smaller proportion embraced **Judaism**. The medieval history of the Berbers was then deeply affected by the seventh- and eighth-century Arab conquest of North Africa, and the subsequent eleventh-century large-scale immigration into North Africa's Maghrib of the Banu Hilal and Banu Sulaym, nomadic pastoralists from Arabia, events which led to the near-total Islamicization of the Berbers of first North Africa and subsequently the Sahara, though in an assertion of independence early Berber Muslims typically embraced the unorthodox and egalitarian Kharijite branch of the faith.

Berbers often resisted cultural Arabization, however, retaining much of their own culture and language (though of necessity Berber men in particular often learned Arabic too), relocating further south away from Arabs at times, and asserting their political independence whenever possible. For example, Berbers created two notable medieval empires of the eleventh to thirteenth centuries through their **Almoravid and Almohad Movements**, whose territory stretched from the North African Maghrib across the Mediterranean to include al-Andalus or Muslim Spain and, in the case of the Almoravids, south right through the Sahara to the desert edge below.

Further Reading

Abun-Nasr, Jamil M. *A History of the Maghrib in the Islamic Period*. 3rd ed. Cambridge, UK: Cambridge University Press, 1993.

Brett, Michael, and Elizabeth Fentresss. *The Berbers: The Peoples of Africa*. Oxford, UK: Blackwell Publishers Ltd., 1996.

Cairo

Founded as their capital city by the Fatimids in 969 after they gained control of **Egypt**, Cairo quickly became one of the world's preeminent cities. The Fatimids situated Cairo at the base of the vast Nile Delta, near the older settlement of al-Fustat, which had been founded by the first Arabs to invade Egypt as a garrison safely inland, where it would be free from the predations of the Byzantine Empire's formidable navy. In the economic renaissance of Egypt, which attended Fatimid rule, Cairo became a cosmopolitan center of commerce attracting merchants from Europe, the Middle East, and Asia as well as portions of Africa ranging from the Horn and East Africa to the West African sudanic belt, the Sahara, and the Maghrib.

The Fatimids devoted a portion of their substantial resources to the creation of Cairene architectural treasures including twin palaces located on either side of one of the city's main avenues, and the al-Azhar and al-Hakim mosques. The Fatimids also established Al-Azhar University, still operating today, which quickly ascended to the pinnacle of medieval Islamic scholarship and drew Muslim scholars from far and wide, including Ibn Khaldun, one of the most prominent intellectuals of the fourteenth century. Constructed as protective fortifications, Fatimid Cairo's walls and eight gates, two on each side of the city, still stand out for their beauty and design. The succeeding Ayyubid dynasty added to Cairo's rich architectural legacy with its expansion of the city walls and construction of the Citadel overlooking the city from the east. The Mamluk dynasty that followed likewise served as a patron of architecture, underwriting the construction of dozens of mosques of great beauty, which are noted for their innovative construction and uses of minarets (*see* **Dynasties**).

Cairo's overall fortunes were in decline by the late medieval centuries as Europe's ascendancy began and diverted highly profitable trade away from the city. Cairo also suffered catastrophic population loss in the Black Death, which struck North Africa savagely in the fourteenth century, and it lost many people more in the recurrences of plague, which occurred with tragic regularity right into the nineteenth century (*see* **Disease**). Cairo has endured through these challenges, however, and as a vibrant metropolis today is among the world's twenty most populous cities, with over 17 million residents.

Further Reading

Abu-Lughod, Janet. *Cairo: 1001 Years of the City Victorious*. Princeton, NJ: Princeton University Press, 1971.

Doris Behrens-Abouseif. *Cairo of the Mamluks: A History of Architecture and Its Culture*. London: I.B. Tauris, 2008.

Sanders, Paula. *Ritual, Politics, and the City in Fatimid Cairo*. Albany: SUNY Press, 1994.

Yeomans, Richard. *The Art and Architecture of Islamic Cairo*. Reading, U.K.: Garnet Publishing Ltd., 2006.

Christianity

Although many Christians today erroneously consider it a "Western" religion, Christianity quickly spread from its home in the eastern Mediterranean south to North Africa where the great and cosmopolitan city of Alexandria emerged as one of the most important centers of early Christianity. Christianity was initially embraced in the first century C.E. by Jews in Alexandria, rapidly spreading from there to Alexandrian Greeks and then throughout all of **Egypt** over the next two to three centuries. Christianity also moved from Egypt west along the North African Maghrib, where it was adopted by many of this region's **Berbers** by 400. In the fourth century, Christianity was adopted by King Ezana of **Aksum** in the **Ethiopian Highlands**, and after its embrace by ruling elites it gradually spread into the general population under the influence of proselytizing Syrian missionaries of the fifth century.

Nubians along the Middle Nile were the next to convert, which they did at the hands of Egyptian traders and Byzantine missionaries in the fifth and sixth centuries, and Christianity flourished there for almost 1,000 years (*see* **Nubia**). Christianity did not move beyond these regions of Africa until the European missionary activities of the nineteenth and twentieth centuries. As an early home to Christianity and with Alexandria one of its leading centers, Christian scholars from the region such as Augustine, Cyprian, Origen, and Tertullian contributed profoundly to early Christian thinking. The centrality of North Africa to early Christianity also meant that the region was deeply involved in many of the doctrinal disputes, which helped to shape the emerging faith, including the debates over Gnosticism, Arianism, Donatism, and Monophysitism. Some of the beliefs the Roman Church labeled heretical, such as Donatism and Monophysitism, found ready homes in North Africa, in the first instance among the Berbers of the Maghrib and in the second instance in the Coptic, Ethiopian, and Nubian Churches.

Finally, the early presence of Christians in North Africa meant that martyrdom following persecutions by pre-Christian Roman emperors affected the emerging faith. For example, many Berber Christians supported Donatism, which rejected accepting back into Christianity any who had even reluctantly renounced it in the face of Roman persecution. This history of persecution is also related to a key aspect of Egyptian Christianity, monasticism, which arose in the third century in part as a way to escape tortures and killings by withdrawal into the desert. This North African element of early Christianity influenced the religion globally, with an eventual embrace of monasticism throughout the Christian world. Additionally, African ecclesiastical arts add a rich strand to the world's corpus of Christian art. Although sadly much of it has been lost to time in the ruins of former churches and monasteries that did not survive the Muslim incursions, its contributions range from the stunning murals of the Nubian Cathedral of Faras and many Egyptian churches and monasteries, which drew upon Byzantine as well as Nubian and Coptic conventions, to the triptychs, monasteries, and rock-hewn churches of Ethiopia.

In conclusion, though these early African churches profoundly influenced the course and history of Christianity not all of them have survived to the present. In the Maghrib, Berber Christianity did not live through the Muslim incursions of the seventh and eighth centuries except in isolated pockets, which were then targeted at a later date by the Almohads (*see* **Almoravid and**

Almohad Movements). Nubian Christianity lasted for nearly a millennium, only to be pushed completely aside by the late fifteenth century as a result of in-migrations of Muslims who came to numerically overwhelm the Christian populations. The Coptic and Ethiopian Orthodox churches have survived to the present, though the **Coptic Church** includes only 10 percent or so of Egyptians today, whereas the Ethiopian Church has maintained its dominance in its historical area of prominence. *See also* **Ethiopian Christianity**.

Further Reading

Chadwick, Henry. *The Church in Ancient Society: From Galilee to Gregory the Great.* Oxford, UK: Oxford University Press, 2002.

Isichei, Elizabeth. *The History of Christianity in Africa: From Antiquity to the Present.* London: Society for Promoting Christian Knowledge, 1995.

Tilly, Maureen A. *The Bible in Christian North Africa: The Donatist World.* Minneapolis, MN: Augsberg Fortress Publishers, 1997.

Coptic Church

Christianity was adopted by some residents of **Egypt** in the new religion's first century. It was embraced initially by members of the significant Jewish population of cosmopolitan, urbane, multiethnic Alexandria, from where it spread over the next several centuries throughout culturally Egyptian populations, and village and rural areas. Christianity in Egypt developed into the Coptic Church. One notable aspect of Coptic Christianity is its strong and early emphasis upon monasticism with its life of poverty, prayer, and a rejection of worldly pleasures, a practice adopted by Egyptian Christians in significant numbers from the third century. They also formulated the two strands of monasticism, anchorite and cenobite, and from Copt's monasticism eventually spread afar to all of Christendom.

Coptic monks who retreated from society to a life of contemplation and spirituality became known as the Desert Fathers, though in fact many women chose this path too. It is thought that one motive for retreat into monasticism might have been its resonance with earlier ascetic practices of the indigenous Egyptian religion, whereas another was the escape it offered from the severe Roman persecutions faced periodically by early Christians. Indeed, the savage persecutions, tortures, and killings that reached their apogee during the reign of Diocletian, who became

Crucifixion of Christ with Saint John. Coptic icon, byzantine influence, 14th century. The Art Archive/Church of Saint Barbara, Cairo/Gianni Dagli Orti.

Roman Emperor in 284 C.E., are also reflected in the fact that in the Coptic calendar, year one is year 284 of the Gregorian calendar in commemoration of how Copts to this day remember the year of Diocletian's accession as the "Year of the Martyrs." Another striking feature of the Coptic Church is its embrace of Monophysitism, the belief that Christ had only one nature, divine, rather than the divine and human natures asserted by the Roman Church. The schism that resulted from this early medieval doctrinal controversy places the Coptic Church in the Oriental Orthodox branch of Christianity, which also includes the Armenian, Ethiopian, Indian, and Syrian Churches.

So successful was the Coptic Church in Egypt that it is estimated that some 90 percent of the population had embraced Christianity by the fifth century. Following the seventh-century Muslim invasion and conquest of Egypt, however, Coptic Christianity faced new challenges. Although Copts initially welcomed these newcomers as a positive alternative to overrule by the Byzantines with whom they were involved in such bitter doctrinal disputes, and though Muslims in Egypt initially had a formal policy of accepting the legitimacy of other religions, they simultaneously imposed onerous poll and property taxes on non-Muslims. And though Muslim governments of Egypt relied heavily upon Coptic administrators initially, from the eighth century on the treatment of Copts generally worsened, though with occasional periods of relief and greater acceptance, until eventually Copts were forbidden to hold administrative positions as well as facing many other expressions of marginalization. In short, over time a number of factors led many Copts to choose conversion to **Islam**, and by the eighth to tenth centuries it is estimated that only 20 percent of Egyptians remained Christian, with a further reduction to around 10 percent by the fourteenth century. Approximately 10 percent of Egyptians remain Copts today. *See also* **Ethiopian Christianity**.

Further Reading

Cannuyer, Christian. *Coptic Egypt: The Christians of the Nile*. New York: Harry N. Abrams, Inc., 2001.

Goehring, James E. *Ascetics, Society and the Desert: Studies in Early Egyptian Monasticism*. Harrisburg, PA: Trinity Press International, 1999.

Currency

Many forms of currency crafted from a wide variety of media existed in medieval Africa. One type familiar to the contemporary world, coins, were first minted at **Aksum**, a state in the **Ethiopian Highlands** involved in long-distance trade, which began striking coins made of bronze, silver, and **gold** just premedievally, in the third century C.E., and continued their production into the seventh century. As well as facilitating the state's extensive commercial transactions, today these coins serve as a valuable source of information about Aksum because inscriptions identify over twenty rulers and illustrations demonstrate Aksum's early embrace of **Christianity** with the fourth-century change from pre-Christian religious symbols including a crescent and disk to the Christian cross. Gold coins named dinars were minted in large quantities for centuries at **Sijilmasa**, an important city in trans-Saharan trade located in the northwestern Sahara, as well as in North African locations including Fez and Marrakesh and in Muslim Spain.

Dinars played an immensely important role medievally not only in Africa but also in Europe and the Middle East, where caches of them have been recovered in modern archaeological digs. Almoravid dinars were of the highest repute due to their purity and exceptional craft (*see* **Almoravid and Almohad Movements**). Dinars made in all of these locations were struck from gold imported from the vast auriferous deposits of West Africa, as were a majority of the explosion of late medieval European gold coins that couldn't have been created without West Africa's precious metal. The **Swahili** of the East African coast were the third medieval African people to strike coins, collections of which dating from the tenth through fourteenth centuries have been found at Pemba, **Kilwa**, and other Swahili sites. At least one of the Kilwa coins made its way far into the interior to Great Zimbabwe, an important Swahili trading partner, where it was recovered in an archaeological dig (**Zimbabwe Plateau**). These examples speak to the production and circulation of African coins—and medieval Africans used coinage imported from intercontinental trading partners too—but far more medieval Africans utilized noncoin currencies. These alternatives ranged from cattle in East and southern Africa; to cowry shells imported from the East African coast in West and Central Africa; to cloth, and crosses fashioned from copper, in Central Africa; and salt, ivory disks, beads, gold dust, and copper, brass, and iron bars and implements in a wide variety of other locations. All of these forms of currency—which are actually ways of representing value, storing wealth, indicating social prestige, and mediating exchange—testify to the economic and social complexities of medieval Africa.

Further Reading

Messier, Ronald A. "The Almoravids: West African Gold and the Gold Currency of the Mediterranean Basin." *Journal of the Economic and Social History of the Orient* 17:1 (March 1974): 31–47.

Stiansen, Endre, and Jane I. Guyer. *Credit, Currencies and Culture: African Financial Institutions in Historical Perspective*. Stockholm: Nordic Africa Institute, 1999.

Disease

Diseases endemic to parts of the African continent have affected Africans in ways ranging from patterns of land settlement to the practicability of various subsistence and occupational activities. Diseases that have had particularly large impacts on Africans include the following. Malaria, which is caused by a parasite transmitted by the female Anopheles mosquito, exists in most tropical portions of Africa in the particularly virulent Plasmodium falciparum strain and was a major killer of people, particularly children, medievally as it is today. Other strains of malaria are chronic, life-long conditions, so that the fevers and extreme lassitude, which are among malaria's effects, exact a high and repeated cost in sickness and inability to work. Sleeping sickness or trypanosomiasis, caused by a parasite transmitted by the tsetse fly, leads to neurological disorders and often death in people and some animals such as cattle, horses, and dogs. It limits cattle and horses to those drier parts of the continent where the tsetse fly cannot live and causes widespread illness among the people who live in the more humid areas where the fly and sleeping sickness flourish. It may have existed only in West Africa medievally, spreading elsewhere in the continent in succeeding centuries.

River blindness or onchocerciasis, transmitted by the black fly, is another devastating disease; as its common name implies, it is found in river bottoms that are home to the black fly and causes skin disorders and sometimes blindness in those who contract it (*see* **Rivers**). Schistosomiasis or bilharzia, contracted through contact with water containing the disease-causing parasites, has debilitating effects including moderate to severe bladder, bowel, and kidney diseases. Guinea worm disease or dracunculiasis, caused by an intestinal parasite found in parts of the continent, is spread by drinking water contaminated with its larvae. After growing to lengths as great as 3 feet, the worms burrow slowly out of the host's body over a period of weeks or months, typically emerging from the lower extremities and causing months of pain and physical incapacitation as well as the risk of secondary infections and permanent joint damage. Other diseases with profound effects upon medieval Africans include many parasitic diseases such as leishmaniasis, transmitted by sand flies, a variety of viral diseases including Lassa fever and yellow fever, and a host of diarrheal illnesses.

Plague carried by rats' fleas made its way to medieval Africa too, with devastating outbreaks leading to widespread death and famine in **Egypt** and the North African Maghrib in the fourteenth and fifteenth centuries; it occurred regularly in medieval East Africa too. In addition to causing high rates of mortality, disproportionately though not solely infant and childhood mortality, disease caused a significant reduction in medieval people's productivity due to the many physical disabilities it induced. The effects on animals of some of these illnesses likewise limited productivity, for example by removing from swathes of the continent animal dung as a crop fertilizer and the use of draft animals in agriculture, transportation, and warfare. Further, people often chose not to live in areas associated with high levels of river blindness or malaria, with the effect that some fertile and potentially highly productive lands became essentially off limits to human populations.

The geographic range of some diseases varied considerably over the medieval centuries due to climate change and human activities that led to expansions and contractions of the lands in which these diseases flourished. For example, the drying of West Africa during the late medieval twelfth through fifteenth centuries was associated with a southern shift of the tsetse fly zone, while the growth of farming in the early medieval centuries was associated with a rise in rates of malaria. Annual changes in climate and annual cycles of human activities also affected medieval disease patterns, for instance with peaks of malaria in grasslands during the rainy seasons that created the pools of standing water needed for reproduction of the mosquitoes responsible for its spread, and lower rates of the disease during dry seasons.

Further Reading

Akhtar, Rais, ed. *Health and Disease in Tropical Africa: Geographical and Medical Viewpoints*. London: Harwood Academic Publishers, 1987.

Hartwig, Gerald W., and K. David Patterson, eds. *Disease in African History: An Introductory Survey and Case Studies*. Durham, NC: Duke University Press, 1978.

Packard, Randall M. *The Making of a Tropical Disease: A Short History of Malaria*. Baltimore: Johns Hopkins University Press, 2007.

Domesticated Animals

Extensive utilization of domesticated animals has a deep history in Africa far predating the medieval centuries. Africans were certainly raising cattle as long ago as 5000 B.C.E. in the central portion of what is today the arid Sahara, which was then a green and well-watered place, and in North Africa and the Nile River Valley. Cattle have also been raised in parts of East Africa since around 2000 B.C.E. or slightly later. It is probable, though not substantiated to everyone's satisfaction, that Africans were also raising cattle as early as 7000 B.C.E. in the Western Desert of **Egypt**. It is still an open question whether Africans domesticated their own wild cattle independently, as growing numbers of scholars believe, as well as raising cows first domesticated in Asia that were then introduced to northeastern Africa, but they have indisputably herded domesticated cattle for 7,000 years if not considerably longer.

The spread of cattle throughout most of eastern and southern Africa has been a more recent development, concluding only in the first few centuries of the Common Era right before the medieval period began. In concert with the early Common Era embrace in these parts of Africa of ironworking technologies, these near-simultaneous developments ushered in a new way of life in medieval eastern and southern Africa characterized by intensified farming and herding that benefited from the utilization of far more efficient iron tools. Camels, critically important to herders in the driest parts of the continent given their ability to flourish in desert environments, were initially introduced to the Horn of Africa from Arabia around 3,000 years ago and from there spread south to what is today northern Kenya and north to Egypt and then, in the earliest centuries of the Common Era, from North Africa into the Sahara, where their use by the Berbers revolutionized desert life and trans-Saharan trade.

Although Africans from the Horn rarely used their camels as beasts of burden, Africans of the Sahara relied upon the camel to transport goods in and across the desert in caravans that could contain literally thousands of camels, with profound ramifications not only for Africa, but also for the peoples of the continents with whom Africans traded. Sheep and goats, which came from western Asia to northeastern Africa, where they were widely raised by 3000 B.C.E., are additional important domesticated animals, which were used across the continent by the time the medieval era began. The fat-tailed sheep was valued for its wool and the thick, viscous oil contained in its tail, which could weigh up to 12 pounds and provided an important medieval source of fat for the human diet. Chickens, first domesticated in Asia, made their way to Egypt and East Africa via the Indian Ocean by the beginning of the Common Era and spread across the continent over the next 1,000 years, where typically they were raised by women and valued for their eggs and, less frequently, their meat. Guinea fowl are a known African domesticate also raised by medieval Africans.

Horses, which were familiar to Ancient Egyptians over 3,000 years ago, were utilized extensively only in very select portions of the continent medievally, mainly North Africa and to a much more limited degree the West African sahel and northern savannah, due to their extreme susceptibility to trypanosomiasis. The far tougher donkey, very commonly used in the northern but not southern half of medieval Africa as a beast of burden and for human transportation, is very likely an African domesticate dating to around 4000 B.C. and derived from the African Wild Ass. Dogs, cats, and pigs rounded out the list of medieval African domesticates.

A number of important factors affected livestock rearing in medieval Africa. First, because cattle, camels, donkeys, and horses are all susceptible to the often-fatal trypanosomiasis or sleeping sickness transmitted by the tsetse fly, for the most part they could not be utilized in the portions of the continent where this insect thrived, with the result that much of West and Central Africa as well as a significant chunk of the East African interior and a smaller stretch of its coastline were essentially off-limits to these breeds of livestock (*see* **Disease**). The most prominent exception lay in the N'Dama breed of cattle, which has significant resistance to trypanosomiasis and therefore could survive in the forests and savannahs of West Africa where it was raised. It is also important to note that human activities had profound effects on the medieval African environment and increased the portions of the continent inhospitable to the tsetse fly, which requires brush and moisture: clearing land for farming, and harvesting trees to make the charcoal used to smelt iron, increased the proportion of the continent composed of tsetse-free grasslands that could be used to raise cattle. Second, herders of camel and cattle in medieval Africa usually practiced transhumance, movement of the herds from place to place, often in an annual cycle driven by the alternating rainy and dry seasons, to gain access to successively fresh grazing grounds and water sources and avoid overgrazing in any one location. Third, though the meat of cattle and camels was eaten at times, medieval Africans far more commonly consumed the milk and in some cases the blood of these animals, thereby preserving their herds. Fourth, certain domesticated animals served as very important ways of holding, increasing (through natural reproduction), and circulating stored wealth for some medieval Africans: Camels were used for this purpose in the Horn and the Sahara, whereas cattle filled this role in significant portions of eastern and southern Africa. Finally, it must be kept in mind that the term *pastoralism*, which is often used generically in reference to herding in Africa, actually refers to a way of life in which the majority of a people's food supply comes from their domesticated animals.

In reality, most livestock in medieval Africa was raised by people practicing a mixed economy involving farming and animal husbandry, as well as other activities such as craft production, trading, and foraging. Research has shown that even those medieval Africans who did focus their productive activities near-exclusively upon herding, and whose cultural ethos stressed the centrality of these animals to their social identity—in short, true pastoralists—typically lived in mutually beneficial symbiosis with settled agriculturalists. The pastoralists sold or traded milk, meat, and soil-enriching manure from their herds for grains, grazing rights, and crafts produced by their sedentary neighbors. In sum, medieval Africans raised a broad range of domesticated animals, which they utilized as sources of food, sources of transportation, and methods of storing, increasing, and circulating wealth.

Further Reading

Clark, J. Desmond and Steven A. Brandt, eds. *From Hunters to Farmers: The Causes and Consequences of Food Production in Africa*. Berkeley: University of California Press, 1984.

Shaw, Thurstan, Paul Sinclair, Bassey Andah, and Alex Okpoko, eds. *The Archaeology of Africa: Food, Metals, and Towns*. London: Routledge, 1993.

Dynasties

North Africa was ruled by a number of Islamic dynasties over all but the earliest of the medieval centuries. Some of these controlled **Egypt** and the Maghrib, whereas others ruled only a portion of North Africa. The most significant of these dynasties are mentioned here, though many others of lesser renown have been omitted. Shortly after the emergence of Islam in the early seventh century, and following the Arab conquest of Egypt in 639 to 641 by early believers, the first Muslim dynasty, the Umayyads (661–750), extended the Arab presence all the way across North Africa to the Atlantic, though they did not effect meaningful control of the Maghrib as they did Egypt. Ruling as the still-new religion was being shaped in fundamental ways, they are important for establishing the precedent that conversion to **Islam** must be voluntary to be meaningful, and thus, contrary to much popular opinion, forced conversion was neither their practice nor that of succeeding Muslim dynasties. Rather, a process of gradual assimilation led to conversion.

The Umayyad's successors, the Abbasids (750–1258), ruling from their capital in Baghdad, controlled North African lands from Egypt to Tunisia until near the end of the first millennium. Their Shi'ite rivals, the Fatimids (909–1171), emerged as a Syrian-originated, **Berber**-supported challenge from Tunisia, from where the Fatimids drove east to Egypt that they took from the Abbasids in 969, in that year also founding their capital at **Cairo**. Their control of the Maghrib, however, faded away with their move east. Their two-centuries-long reign over Egypt was noted for its religious tolerance and for the prosperity, which followed the successful Fatimid reorienting of trade from the more distant Persian Gulf to the Red Sea which abuts Egypt.

The Fatimids were supplanted by the Ayyubids (1169–1250), founded by the legendary Kurdish general Salah al-Din al-Ayyubi (Saladin in the West), who the Fatimid rulers perhaps unwisely called on for assistance when Egypt was threatened by European Crusaders. Salah al-Din successfully repulsed that threat but then took over Egypt himself. In their turn, the Ayyubid dynasty's army of Mamluk slave soldiers of Turkish, Kurdish, and Circassian origin took power into their own hands in their eponymous Mamluk dynasty (1250–1517), which maintained power in Egypt until the Ottomans supplanted them as the Middle Ages drew to a close. Additional Islamic Maghrib polities included the **Almoravid and Almohad** dynasties of the eleventh to thirteenth centuries, whereas important dynasties ruling Morocco alone included the Idrisis in the eighth to tenth centuries, the Marinids in the thirteenth to fifteenth centuries, and the Sa'dids at the end of the medieval period. Most of the empires mentioned above controlled land far beyond the borders of Africa, so their overrule helped to incorporate medieval North Africa into the broader Muslim world.

Moving beyond North Africa, powerful Christian dynasties spread their rule from the medieval **Ethiopian Highlands**. **Aksum**, which emerged very early in the Common Era and was a large and dominant empire for centuries, was succeeded by the short-lived Zagwe dynasty, which came to power in the eleventh century when the Cushitic Agaw who were its rulers took control from the fading Aksumites. Zagwe's successor, the Solomonid dynasty led by the Amhara, seized power from the last Zagwe king in 1270 and then ruled Ethiopia in one form or another until the overthrow of Haile Selassie in 1974. The Solomonid leaders legitimated their authority by claiming descent from King Solomon of Jerusalem and the Queen of Sheba, an assertion best understood allegorically rather than literally. This legitimizing story of the Solomids, recorded in the *Kebra Negast* or Glory of Kings, tells how the Ethiopian Queen Sheba, hearing of Solomon's wisdom, traveled to Jerusalem to learn from him.

She returned to Ethiopia carrying his child, and their son, Menelik, in his turn eventually journeyed to Jerusalem to meet his father. It is said that either Menelik or one of his party stole the Ark of the Covenant and brought it back to Ethiopia, where the Ethiopian Church claims to be in possession of it to this day.

With these events Ethiopians believe that Ethiopia became the New Zion, Ethiopians God's chosen people, and the Solominids Ethiopia's anointed rulers. One important aspect of the Zagwe and Solomonid dynasties is their identity as Christian empires with state sponsorship of religion, accompanied by their use of conversion to assimilate conquered peoples. Many other important polities of medieval Africa that are not typically labeled dynasties could also be considered in this entry, because in them power passed from member to member of a ruling family—a common practice given the existence in many African societies of royal families through which succession occurred. *See also* **Christianity** and **Judaism**.

Further Reading

Abun-Nasr, Jamil M. *A History of the Maghrib in the Islamic Period.* 3rd ed. Cambridge, UK: Cambridge University Press, 1993.

Marcus, Harold G. *A History of Ethiopia.* Updated ed. Berkeley: University of California Press, 2002.

Petry, Carl F., ed. *The Cambridge History of Egypt.* Volume 1: *Islamic Egypt, 640–1517.* Cambridge, UK: Cambridge University Press, 1998.

Ecological Zones

A simplified map of Africa's ecological zones reveals a general mirroring of environments with movement north and south from the equator, which cuts through the middle of the continent. Along the equator itself, in Africa as in many other parts of the world, tropical rainforests predominate. Moving north and south, the next zone encountered is the Sudan or savannah. Further movement north and south leads to the sahel or semidesert, and movement north and south yet again to desert. Finally, along portions of the northern and southern extremities of the continent lie temperate Mediterranean climate zones. Temperate highlands, where the climate is affected by altitude, are found in the **Ethiopian Highlands** and on South Africa's highveld. Although Africa is often stereotyped as mostly "jungle," in fact the dominant landscapes are Sudan and desert, with rainforest occupying less than 10 percent of the continent's landmass.

Africa's rainforests are characterized by very high annual rainfall ranging from 55 to over 300 inches per year, and extremely lush and dense vegetation. The rainforests of Africa have posed a challenge, though not an insurmountable one, to people seeking to live in this environment given the difficulty of clearing land for cultivation or herding. Over the medieval centuries people living in them practiced foraging and, in places, farming of select crops well suited to the rainforest environment such as yams and oil palms. The well-watered Sudan, which spreads over large swathes of Africa, has formed a relatively hospitable environment for human habitation, and the **agriculture** and herding activities that had expanded across the entire continent by the early medieval centuries have flourished in these grassland and woodland savannahs. The sudanic pattern of alternating rainy and dry seasons does present certain challenges for these activities even in this relatively welcoming climate zone, in comparison to parts of the globe in which rainfall is spread more evenly across the year, but these challenges were met successfully by medieval populations. The semidesert or *sahel*—the word is Arabic for shore, in this case the shore of a figurative ocean of sand—receives significantly less rainfall than the Sudan, well under 20 inches per year on average, making this a steppeland **region** in which agriculture is practiced but with less than optimal outcomes, and in which hardier goats and sheep are raised more successfully than cattle (*see* **Domesticated Animals**).

Africa's deserts include the mighty *Sahara* (desert in Arabic), the world's largest at approximately the size of the 48 contiguous states of the United States. It extends over 1,000 miles north to south, reaching from just below North Africa's coastal plain to around the latitude of West Africa's Niger Bend. It also stretches a vast 2,000 miles west to east, from the Atlantic to the Red Sea. Africa's other desert, the much smaller Namib, lies in the southwestern part of the continent where it runs right along the Atlantic shore. This coastal desert gains incrementally in rainfall with movement east and simultaneously up with the rise of the Great Escarpment to the interior plateau. The Kalahari to the Namib's east, which is sometimes referred to as a desert, is more properly identified as steppeland like the sahel abutting the Sahara. Africa's northern desert, the Sahara, has served as a barrier to and conduit for travel, trade, and communication: It constituted an impenetrable barrier between North and sub-Saharan Africa from the time it emerged as an impassable desert in the first millennium B.C.E. until the introduction of the camel reopened it to human passage in the first centuries C.E.

The portions of Africa constituting any of these climate types have shifted over the medieval centuries, with the Sahara and its accompanying sahelian zone, for example, expanding and contracting over time. Likewise, the sudanic regions have shifted with fluctuations in patterns of rainfall as well as climate changes introduced by medieval human activities such as logging, charcoal production, farming, and herding. *See also* **Rivers**.

Further Reading

Adams, William M. et al., eds. *The Physical Geography of Africa*. Oxford, UK: Oxford University Press, 1999.

Aryeetey-Attoh, Samuel. *The Geography of Sub-Saharan Africa*. 2nd ed. Englewood Cliffs, NJ: Prentice Hall, 2002.

Cole, Roy, and H.J. De Blij. *Survey of Subsaharan Africa: A Regional Geography*. Oxford, UK: Oxford University Press, 2007.

Education

Medieval African societies that embraced **Christianity** and **Islam** also took up and typically in significant ways indigenized these religions' traditions of literacy and formal education. Centers of learning were generally associated with monasteries or mosques.

Normal education occurred in Christian monasteries. This began in the desert monasteries of Egypt premedievally, in the earliest centuries of Christianity, whereas education in the monasteries of Ethiopia, though dating from middle of the first millennium C.E., reached its apogee from the twelfth century on in the time of the Zagwe and Solomonid **dynasties**.

In Muslim Africa, formal education ranged at the introductory level from Qur'anic schools in which children learned the Qur'an—the Muslim Holy Book—through rote memorization and recitation, to renowned medieval universities that produced and attracted some of the most highly regarded scholars of the medieval world. These universities offered instruction in subjects ranging from theology and textual exegesis to law, medicine, mathematics, geography, astronomy, history, literature, poetry, grammar, logic, and rhetoric. The most noted of these medieval African centers of Islamic scholarship were Al-Qayrawiyyin in Fez, Al-Azhar in Cairo, Az-Zaytun in Tunis, and Sankoré in **Timbuktu**. Al-Qayrawiyyin and Al-Azhar, founded in the ninth and tenth centuries, respectively, are generally recognized as the oldest continuously operating universities in the world. Because Islamic scholars often moved from institution to institution across the Islamic world, through these highly regarded universities Africa constituted a vital part of the medieval Islamic intellectual tradition.

In addition to these seats of learning and scholarship, in the medieval centuries private libraries with extensive collections of valuable and rare holdings were established by a number of wealthy West African Muslim families of a scholarly bent; some of them can still be found intact in West African locations today including Chinguetti in contemporary Mauritania and Timbuktu. Beyond the medieval systems of formal education situated in monasteries and mosques, though documentation does not exist for medieval African societies practicing oral rather than written traditions, it is a near-certainty that in them knowledge was also routinely disseminated to adults-in-the-making through many avenues, including rites of passage marking the transition to adulthood. These rites typically have involved educating adolescents about a given society's values—its beliefs regarding social norms and expectations, duties and responsibilities, right behavior, gender roles, and marriage/childrearing.

Practical knowledge about particular crafts and occupations such as healing or spiritual leadership would have been passed on through formal apprenticeships too. The widely held expectation that children would have a productive role in society, helping in daily life activities such as farming, herding, child care, cooking, trading, and the like, also meant that education in these arenas occurred routinely as children matured. The transmission of political history and cultural knowledge through oral traditions, and of religious teachings and cosmological beliefs through religious practices, existed as additional widely practiced forms of education during the medieval centuries.

Further Reading

Dodge, Bayard. *Al-Azhar, a Millennium of Muslim Learning*. Washington, DC: Middle East Institute, 1961.

Hunwick, John O., ed. and trans. *Timbuktu and the Songhay Empire: Al-Sa'di's Ta'rikh Al-Sudan Down to 1613 and Other Contemporary Documents*. Leiden, The Netherlands: Brill, 1999.

Saad, Elias N. *Social History of Timbuktu: The Role of Muslim Notables and Scholars 1400–1900*. Cambridge, UK: Cambridge University Press, 1983.

Egypt

Medieval Egypt was deeply cosmopolitan, reflective of its location in the southeastern corner of the Mediterranean, which gave it ready connections to peoples of Europe and the Middle East as well as the African interior. Red Sea trade further linked Egypt to the Horn of Africa and the continent's eastern shoreline, and also to Asians drawn into these interconnected commercial networks through Indian Ocean trade. This worldliness was reflected, among other things, in the religious diversity of medieval Egypt, which had moved just premedievally from practicing the still-extant religious traditions of Pharaonic Egypt to a widespread adoption of **Christianity** brought from the Levant and then, after the arrival of Muslim Arabs in the seventh century, to a gradual embrace of **Islam**.

Egypt's numerous medieval visitors, many of whom stayed permanently as a result of the opportunities offered, adhered to a wide variety of additional religious traditions, and this led, for example, to significant Jewish populations in Alexandria and other cities (*see* **Judaism**). Politically, medieval Egypt moved from Byzantine overrule to governance by a succession of Islamic **dynasties** of various Middle Eastern and African provenances from the seventh century on, some headquartered in the great city of **Cairo** which was founded in 969. Economically, Egypt flourished during most of the medieval centuries due in part to the extraordinarily profitable trade of great geographic reach, which flowed through its lands. Agricultural production in the rich farmlands of the vast Nile Valley added to its wealth (*see* **Agriculture**). Tensions did exist in medieval Egypt between cities and rural areas, for its rulers tended to exploit the countryside's farmers mercilessly. In the last centuries of the medieval era Egypt faced twin challenges—it was devastated by the fourteenth-century Black Death that killed an estimated 25 percent to 35 percent of the population and recurred regularly thereafter, and it also faced profound economic decline as Europe's star rose and the merchants of that ascending continent siphoned trade away from the formerly mighty Egypt (*see* **Disease**). *See also* Document 3.

Further Reading

Cannuyer, Christian. *Coptic Egypt: The Christians of the Nile.* New York: Harry N. Abrams, Inc., 2001.

Petry, Carl F., ed. *The Cambridge History of Egypt.* Volume 1: *Islamic Egypt, 640–1517.* Cambridge, UK: Cambridge University Press, 1998.

Ethiopian Christianity

Inevitably, the medieval trade that flowed from the Mediterranean through the Red Sea to the Indian Ocean and linked people from all of these regions resulted in the exchange of ideas as well as goods. Thus it is not surprising that shortly after its emergence **Christianity** made its way to the **Ethiopian Highlands**. Ezana, a fourth-century king of the Ethiopian Highland state of **Aksum**, adopted Christianity after being introduced to it by Christians from **Egypt** or the Levant. Influenced by Coptic beliefs, the Ethiopian Church, also known as the Ethiopian Orthodox Church, embraced what outsiders call Monophysitism and Ethiopian Christians label non-Chalcedonianism, a doctrine that asserts that Christ had only one nature, divine, rather than divine and human natures, which set it as well as other Oriental Orthodox Churches (Armenian, Coptic, Indian, and Syrian) at odds with the Roman Church that labeled this belief heretical. The **Coptic Church** from which it sprang also appointed the Ethiopian Church's bishops, a right it retained through the midtwentieth century.

Two angels with swords. Parchment with magic text, 14th century Ethiopian. The Art Archive/Coptic Museum Cairo/Gianni Dagli Orti.

Another important element of Ethiopian Christianity is monasticism, introduced in the fifth century by monks from Syria known as the Nine Saints. They came to proselytize and helped to spread the new faith widely, far beyond Aksum's ruling elite. They also sparked translating the Bible into Ge'ez, spoken in the Northern Highlands medievally. Although no longer a living language, Ge'ez remains the Ethiopian Church's liturgical language. Another important aspect of Ethiopian Christianity, and one that also stemmed from the circulation of people and ideas discussed above, is **Judaism**'s early influence upon it, seen in practices such as a Saturday Sabbath, circumcision of boys on the eighth day following birth, Old Testament food proscriptions, Hebrew loan-words for explicitly religious concepts, and the like.

The new religion gradually came to be embraced by more and more Ethiopians, a process hastened early on by the Syrian monks and throughout the medieval period by the polities of Aksum and its successor states, the Zagwe and Solomonid dynasties of the eleventh and subsequent centuries, which all used Christianity as one legitimization of their secular authority. Aksumite leaders put the cross on their coins; the rulers of Zagwe sponsored the creation of elaborate rock-hewn churches at Lalibela to create a "New Jerusalem" following Saladin's conquest of Jerusalem in 1187; and the Solomonid rulers claimed descent from King Solomon and the Queen of Sheba, asserted that Ethiopians were God's chosen people who had in their possession the Ark of the Covenant, and declared Ethiopia the new Zion. The Zagwe and Solomonid dynasties used conversion to Christianity to assimilate conquered peoples into their empires, sponsoring monasteries in new locations as Ethiopian political control spread and using their monks as proselytizers.

As the Church grew it accepted a variety of pre-Christian practices important to converts such as using amulets as protective charms, in the religious syncretism that has been a common feature of the spread in Africa of Islam as well as Christianity. The relative isolation of Ethiopian Christianity meant it developed following an internal logic and trajectory, so that it is in many ways distinct from the forms of Christianity practiced elsewhere, with for example a very strong emphasis upon frequent fasting. The Ethiopian Orthodox Church remains central to Ethiopian society and identity down to the present, though in the contemporary state of Ethiopia, whose southern half embraced **Islam** rather than Christianity medievally, members of the Ethiopian Church and Muslims constitute roughly equal percentages of the population. *See also* **Dynasties** and Document 6.

Further Reading

Heldman, Marilyn Eiseman. *African Zion: The Sacred Art of Ethiopia*. New Haven, CT: Yale University Press, 1993.

Tamrat, Taddesse. *Church and State in Ethiopia: 1270-1527*. Oxford, UK: Oxford University Press, 1972.

Ethiopian Highlands

Ethiopia, located in the Horn of Africa, has a medieval history in some ways distinctive from and in other ways very much in keeping with dominant strands of medieval African history. A portion of the region, the Ethiopian Highlands, stands out for its rugged terrain and the altitude, which gives its higher elevations a temperate climate, located though it is within the tropics. As early agriculturalists, Ethiopians domesticated a number of crops suited to Highland cultivation, which are grown nowhere else, and alone in tropical Africa embraced the use of the plow. Ethiopia's early history is partially entwined with that of South Arabia, from which it is separated only by the narrow Red Sea. Migrations from Arabia by the first millennium B.C.E. brought to Ethiopia the Sabaean language and its consonant-based system of writing, preserved in inscriptions on coins and stone monuments, although this was soon modified by Ethiopians who refined its script and wrote in the local language of Ge'ez. Furthermore, the significant Jewish influence that came to Ethiopia early in the early Common Era and has affected elements of Ethiopian culture and identity ever since was most likely introduced from South Arabian Jewish communities (*see* **Judaism**).

Political interconnections also existed, and in the sixth century C.E. Aksumites briefly ruled a portion of South Arabia. Turning to the medieval Ethiopian economy, in addition to **agriculture** and herding Ethiopia was enriched in many medieval centuries from involvement in Red Sea trading networks, and through them commerce with the Mediterranean and Indian Ocean worlds. The city of Adulis, located on the Red Sea, played a critical role as the port through which were funneled many Ethiopian exports including gold, ivory, captives, rhinoceros horns, civet musk, and the aromatics frankincense and myrrh. Ethiopia was home to the medieval polities of **Aksum** and, after a period of retrenchment in the last centuries of the first millennium due to a decline in Red Sea trade, the Zagwe and Solomonid **dynasties**. Stunning ecclesiastical architecture that reached its apogee in the rock-hewn churches of Lalibela are among the artistic achievements of the Zagwe dynasty, though these structures are rooted in a far older Ethiopian tradition of sculpture that was previously expressed in the stelae, church, and domestic architecture of Aksum. Finally, **Christianity** held a prominent position in medieval Ethiopia. In the fourth century King Ezana of Aksum embraced Christianity, and though Muslim and Beta Israel populations also existed in medieval Ethiopia the Ethiopian Orthodox Church has played a fundamental role in Ethiopian society, politics, and identity ever since. *See also* **Ethiopian Christianity** and Document 6.

Further Reading

Marcus, Harold G. *A History of Ethiopia*. Updated ed. Berkeley: University of California Press, 2002.

Tamrat, Taddesse. *Church and State in Ethiopia: 1270-1527*. Oxford, UK: Oxford University Press, 1972.

Food

Although foraging—collecting naturally occurring edible plant materials and hunting wild game—was still practiced at least episodically by many medieval Africans, Africa is frequently described as a continent of cultivators, and this was true for the medieval period as it remains today. Foodstuffs farmed on the continent medievally varied considerably depending on the local climate and ecology. In the rainforest zones of West and Central Africa yams and oil palm were early primary crops, the former serving as a main starchy source of carbohydrates while the latter added needed fat to the diet. Another crop eventually grown in the forest zone was the very prolific banana, which requires far more modest labor inputs than yam production and proved to be an extremely important carbohydrate source in this region where the high humidity and rainfall makes it difficult if not impossible to cultivate grains.

Africa's savannahs were the continent's primary site of cereal production, dominantly sorghum and millet. In the more well-watered parts of the savannah such as the lands surrounding the Inland Niger Delta farmers also produced African rice (*Oryza glaberrima*). Other savannah crops included groundnuts, the grain fonio, and melons. Finally, in the varied climates of Ethiopia with its mix of highlands and lowlands farmers produced some unique crops including teff and finger millet, both grains; noog, which produces a seed very high in oil; and enset, also known as false banana, whose pith is consumed. In addition to these specifically Ethiopian domesticates, imported cereals such as wheat and barley, cultivable in Africa only in Ethiopia and portions of the Nile River Valley, were farmed too. Farmers in all parts of the continent grew a variety of fruits and vegetables. In addition to crops domesticated in Africa, which includes most of those listed above, in the medieval period Africans cultivated Asian crops, which had made their way across the Indian Ocean in conjunction with its maritime trade, such as citrus fruits, mangos, and Asian rice (*Oryza sativa*).

These intercontinental contributions continued in the Atlantic Age, when many crops from the Americas such as maize, potatoes, tomatoes, and hot peppers came to play critical roles in the agriculture and cuisine of Africa. For farming in most of Africa seasonality was a meaningful reality, because the pattern on much of the continent of alternating rainy and dry seasons meant that cultivated food, plentiful following the harvest, was typically in very short supply by the time the next year's rainy season commenced. A greater reliance on foraging was often a necessity during particularly extensive dry seasons. Beyond agriculture, medieval Africans gained animal protein from hunting wild game including birds, antelope, elephants, monkeys, and a variety of rodents; fishing, and preserving through smoking or salting portions of the catch not immediately consumed; collecting forest snails, a large species of land snail, and some insects including locusts; and raising domesticated animals including goats, sheep, fowl, cattle, and camels, though not all of these species could be raised in all parts of the continent.

Africans also produced a variety of alcoholic beverages including beer brewed by fermenting grains, palm wine made by tapping and fermenting the sap of certain varieties of palm trees, and mead made from fermented honey. Finally, medieval Africans produced consumables that are sometimes considered broadly medicinal rather than strictly foodstuffs. Included in this category are the mild stimulants coffee and qat, both grown in the **Ethiopian Highlands**, and kola, which was harvested from naturally occurring kola trees in West African rainforests. A variety of herbal medicines were also part of medieval Africans' utilization of the continent's flora. *See also* **Agriculture**, **Ecological Zones**, **Hunting and Gathering**, and **Regions**.

Further Reading

Clark, J. Desmond, and Steven A. Brandt, eds. *From Hunters to Farmers: The Causes and Consequences of Food Production in Africa*. Berkeley: University of California Press, 1984.
Shaw, Thurstan, et al., eds. *The Archaeology of Africa: Food, Metals, and Towns*. London: Routledge, 1993.

Ghana

Ghana, one of the great medieval empires of West Africa, emerged in the sahel along the Sahara's southern edge and at its height encompassed lands stretching from the Senegal River in the west to the Niger River in the east, to the important oasis town of Awdaghust in the north and well into the savannah in the south, territory that today lies in **Mali** and Mauritania. The origins of Ghana, or Wagadu as it was known by its own people, *Ghana* being the title of their kings and the name appended to the empire by medieval authors writing in Arabic, are not clearly understood. It appeared some time around the fourth century C.E., arising out of an already-established West African tradition of social complexity involving urbanism, ironworking, social stratification, and long-distance trade across ecological zones, a pattern demonstrated for example at Jenné-jeno in the Inland Niger Delta from around 250 B.C.E.

It is probable that people living along the desert edge also recognized the benefits of joining together to fend off raids made by the nomadic desert dwellers to their north, who periodically swept down upon sedentary villagers. Whatever the specifics of its rise, clearly Ghana predated the flowering of trans-Saharan trade and the arrival in this part of Africa of **Islam**, factors that earlier generations of Africanist historians erroneously believed to be responsible for its emergence. Ghana did, however, gain an additional and critically important source of wealth when trans-Saharan trade flourished. Its location on the border of the Sahara and sahel, as well as its position in between the source of West African **gold**—at this time Bambuk, located between the upper Senegal and Falémé **rivers**—and the Saharan rock salt for which that gold was exchanged, allowed it to profit hugely by taxing the trade that passed through its lands on the only trans-Saharan trade route through which West Africa then exported its gold.

Ruled by the Soninke, one of a number of West African Mande language-speaking peoples, the empire held loose control over the other peoples of its realm who were allowed a high degree of autonomy in exchange for payments of tribute and recognition of Soninke sovereignty. To further ensure compliance, the Soninke also required the rulers of those they conquered to leave sons at the royal court, which glittered with public displays of the gold that underlay its prosperity. Ghana's military, which included a cavalry very difficult for those without horses to combat, could muster up two-hundred thousand fighters according to the historian al-Bakri. Ghana's capital city of Kumbi Saleh had a separate quarter for the Muslims who came from the Sahara and North Africa to trade, a number of whom were also hired by Ghana's kings to serve as interpreters, ministers, diviners, makers of protective amulets, and the like, and the empire exhibited a very high level of tolerance for this religious diversity. Ghana flourished until the **Berber**-led Almoravid Movement, which began in the eleventh century, successfully challenged its control of the southern end of trans-Saharan trade (*see* **Almoravid and Almohad Movements**). The Almoravids wrested Awdaghust from Ghana and that, coupled with a subsequent shift east beyond Ghana's lands of trans-Saharan trade routes, as well as the onset of a drier climate less conducive to agriculture and herding, resulted in Ghana's slow decline and eventual disappearance by the thirteenth century. *See also* Document 4.

Further Reading

Bovill, Edward William. *The Golden Trade of the Moors: West African Kingdoms in the Fourteenth Century*. Oxford, UK: Oxford University Press, 1958.

Levtzion, Nehemiah. *Ancient Ghana and Mali*. New York: Africana Publishing Company, 1973.

Gold

Gold played a critical role in medieval Africa in part as a very valuable export highly desired by the continent's trading partners. Trans-Saharan trade, which linked West and North Africa before extending to Europe and the Middle East; Indian Ocean trade, which connected East Africa with Arabia, India, Indonesia, and southern Chinese ports; and Red Sea trade connecting the Horn of Africa and **Egypt** with Arabia, the Mediterranean world and India were all wide-ranging commercial networks in which gold played a prominent role. It has been estimated that fully two-thirds of the gold circulating in Europe medievally came from African deposits, and that Africa supplied more gold to the late medieval international economy than any other parts of the world.

The main sources of this African gold were the Bambuk and Bure goldfields of West Africa that fed trans-Saharan trade, the former located between the upper Senegal and Falémé **rivers** and the latter along the Upper Niger, and deposits in the southern African interior that fed Indian Ocean trade and were located northwest of Great Zimbabwe between the Limpopo and Zambezi rivers on the **Zimbabwe Plateau**. The **Akan** goldfields of the West African forest zone began to be intensively exploited only as the medieval centuries were drawing to a close, when the Bambuk and Bure goldfields were nearing exhaustion. (Much more recently, since their discovery in the late nineteenth century, the vast gold reefs of South Africa have been intensively mined too.)

In addition to meeting a seemingly insatiable external demand for gold, which enriched many African polities, medieval Africans themselves made use of the metal for a variety of purposes. Due to a paucity of sources of salt in the savannah, West Africans traded their gold for much-needed salt from the Sahara which they used to satisfy their nutritional needs for this essential mineral and as a medicine for their animals; they also used it to cure hides and preserve meat. Rulers of the great sudanic empires Ghana and **Mali** utilized it for display purposes justifying their authority, on ceremonial appearances draping their bodies in gold ornamentation ranging from bracelets, rings, and necklaces to gold-encrusted sandals and headwear. Members of their retinues carried ceremonial objects of solid or plated gold, and even royal animals such as horses and dogs shared in the display with gold leashes, collars, tethers, and the like. Gold nuggets were the exclusive property of the king of Ghana, whereas gold dust served as **currency**, which could be possessed by anyone.

Gold and gold-plated objects have also been uncovered from archaeological excavations of the medieval polities of Mapungubwe and Great Zimbabwe, located, respectively, in the Limpopo Valley and on the Zimbabwe Plateau. **Women** of the medieval West African Sudan often held their personal wealth in the form of gold jewelry, such as nose-rings and earrings of stylized design. Goldsmiths made their living working the precious metal, whereas others benefited from collecting it in unmodified form through mining or panning auriferous soil.

Further Reading

Bovill, Edward William. *The Golden Trade of the Moors: West African Kingdoms in the Fourteenth Century*. Oxford, UK: Oxford University Press, 1958.

Garrard, Timothy F. *Gold of Africa: Jewellery and Ornaments from Ghana, Cote d'Ivoire, Mali and Senegal*. New York: Prestel Publishing, 1989.

Hausa

Hausa-speaking peoples emerged in the grasslands of what are today northern Nigeria and southern Niger, in the region to the west of Lake Chad and well to the north of the confluence of the Niger and Benue rivers. This placed them between the medieval West African states of first **Mali** and then **Songhai** to their west, and Bornu to their east, and some have postulated that they acted as a buffer between these powerful empires (*see* **Kanem-Bornu**). At times the Hausa fell loosely under the orbit of Songhai. Hausa origins remain murky and not clearly understood though it is known that ironworking populations of unknown identity existed in this region in the first millennium C.E.

A distinctly Hausa culture was apparent by the eleventh century. In the fifteenth century, the Hausa developed a series of independent city-states, each based on a walled capital city ruled by a Muslim sarki or king. Among the most prominent of these cities were Kano, Katsina, Gobir, and Zazzau (Zaria). An overarching state encompassing all of the Hausa polities never developed, and instead the city-states existed as rivals, engaging repeatedly in warfare fueled by their cavalries. The Hausa had a mixed economy in which agriculture, large-scale craft production, and trade all played significant roles. Their location in the grasslands allowed for extensive farming of crops including millet, groundnuts, and beans as well as numerous vegetables. A significant cloth industry developed at Kano, whereas other cities emphasized metalworking, leatherworking, and glassmaking.

The Hausa also played a prominent role in long distance trade within West Africa, where they did business with Songhai, Bornu, the **Akan**, and points beyond through a network of specialist traders who created stranger's quarters from which to conduct their trade in numerous locations outside of Hausaland. To facilitate their many commercial transactions, these traders also developed a shell currency using cowries from the East African coastline first imported to North Africa by Arab merchants and then sent south across the Sahara to Hausaland. The Hausa also traded across the Sahara to North Africa, and in regards to trans-Saharan trade they benefited from the general shift east to the central Sudan of West African–Saharan commerce that occurred in the sixteenth century. Imports included the horses, which fed their warfare and facilitated their large-scale enslavement of peoples lying to their south, some of whom they retained as agricultural workers and others of whom they sold north into trans-Saharan trade.

Islam came to Hausaland no later than the fourteenth century, though in keeping with the experiences of other West African states the urban elites were the first to convert, with a mass embrace of Islam occurring only with the early-nineteenth-century Fulani jihad. At the conclusion of the medieval period the Hausa city-states were reaching their apogee, which lasted from the sixteenth to the eighteenth centuries.

Further Reading

Adamu, Mahdi. *The Hausa Factor in West African History*. Oxford, UK: Oxford University Press, 1979.

Barkindo, Bawuro M., ed. *Studies in the History of Kano*. Ibadan, Nigeria: Heinemann, 1983.

Hunting and Gathering

Following the emergence of fixed **agriculture**, Africa became what is often referred to as a continent of farmers. At an earlier stage of human society, however, before the ascendancy of herding and farming, people gained sustenance through hunting and gathering. This practice of hunting wild animals and gathering naturally occurring sources of plant and insect food, also known as foraging, continued to play a vital if steadily decreasing role in the lives of Africans over the course of the medieval centuries. Many medieval Africans practiced foraging episodically as a useful and practical supplement to other methods of subsistence, whereas ever smaller numbers maintained hunting and gathering as their primary mode of sustenance.

Foraging people typically organized themselves into small bands of 12 to no more than 50 to 100 individuals who worked cooperatively and practiced egalitarian, corporate decision making while eschewing political leadership vested in select individuals. Highly mobile to take advantage of **food** and water sources in varied locations, foragers owned few material possessions and limited their childbearing so they could travel lightly. Although the relative material poverty of foragers often appeared unappealing to sedentary peoples who owned many more possessions, in fact the nomadic foragers had the great benefit of extensive leisure time and a more varied, reliable, and probably nutritious diet than that consumed by numerous farming and herding peoples. Studies of modern foragers show that they typically spend fewer than 20 hours weekly collecting food and devote their considerable free time to extensive socializing and producing works of art—the prolific and beautiful rock art of Africa is largely the creation of foragers—and it is believed that this abundant leisure time was true of foragers in the past also, who actually lived on less marginal land then than they do today. In an additional benefit, hunting and gathering societies appear to have practiced near equality of **women** and men. Foragers had a gendered division of labor in which men mainly hunted wild game and women mostly gathered. Using spears or bows and arrows often tipped with poison to slowly kill large game, snares and nets for small prey and birds, and hooks for fish, men hunted a wide range of animals including ostrich, zebra, buffalo, rhinoceros, giraffe, hippopotamus, wildebeest and quagga.

Women collected wild fruits, vegetables, berries, nuts, seeds, grains, eggs, insects, grubs, and honey and unearthed tubers with digging sticks. On average far more than half, most likely around three-fourths, of the food consumed by foragers came from gathering, making women's contributions highly significant. After farming spread across Africa, a process essentially complete by the early medieval years, foragers often lived in symbiotic and mutually beneficial relationships with their settled neighbors, trading items such as honey and meat for agricultural products and metal wares. This transformation did have the negative effect of slowly pushing foragers off the more fertile land desired by cultivators, and exposing them to the broader range of serious diseases that took root in farming communities as part of the agricultural transition to sedentism. Foragers also had a typically short life span and ran significant risk of accidental injury and early onset of certain illnesses such as arthritis. Given the substantial social and nutritional benefits of foraging, though, it is perhaps not surprising that small populations of Africans continue to practice hunting and gathering to the present in the Congo basin and the Kalahari, resisting all pressures to adopt a settled life. *See also* **Ecological Zones** and **Regions**.

Further Reading

Ingold, Tim, David Riches, and James Woodburn. *Hunters and Gatherers.* Volume I: *History, Evolution and Social Change*. Oxford, UK: Berg Publishers, 1997.

Lee, Richard B., and Richard Daly. *The Cambridge Encyclopedia of Hunters and Gatherers*. Cambridge, UK: Cambridge University Press, 1999.

Ibn Battuta (1304–1368/1377)

Ibn Battuta, the most celebrated of medieval Muslim travelers, traversed virtually all of the Muslim world of his day in epic journeys that totaled over 70,000 miles in length. Born to **Berber** parents in Tangier in today's Morocco, as a young man of 21 who had studied Muslim theology and jurisprudence Ibn Battuta left his home in North Africa to make the *hajj*, or religious pilgrimage, to Mecca in the Arabian Peninsula, a journey which he extended into a 24-year odyssey to Yemen, Oman, East Africa, Central Asia's steppes, the Indian subcontinent, Ceylon, Sumatra, the Maldives, Constantinople, Anatolia, Baghdad, Persia, the Balkans, the Caucasus, Spain, and possibly China too—he claimed to have traveled to the last of these, but all do not find his account of China convincing. In a second, much shorter journey, which lasted from 1352 to 1354 Ibn Battuta traveled from Morocco south across the Sahara to **Mali** in West Africa.

As Dunn's Foreword to Hamdun and King's translation of Ibn Battuta's writings points out, his journeys provide evidence for what the modern world might see as surprisingly frequent intercontinental travel across the medieval Muslim world in an example of "globalization" many centuries old—Ibn Battuta was constantly coming across old friends in even obscure places, served as a diplomat linking far-flung parts of the Muslim world, and at times made a living pedaling his skills as a jurist in diverse Muslim communities widely separated from one another geographically yet unified by the bonds of religion and the common language of Arabic. In addition, Ibn Battuta also left the world extremely important renderings of the fourteenth-century East African coast and West African Sudan; he wrote up his memoirs in his book titled the *Rihla*, or Journey, which was edited by the scholar Ibn Juzayy.

Although Ibn Battuta's descriptions of the places he visited have at times been critiqued for their limited scope—they tend to emphasize trade, political elites, and, because he was a gourmand, food—they also paint vivid portraits of these worlds in the entertaining words of an individual who clearly delighted in his travels and travails, giving us vital and illuminating tidbits of information that can be found nowhere else. *See also* **Islam** and Documents 8 and 9.

Further Reading

Dunn, Ross E. *The Adventures of Ibn Battuta: A Muslim Traveler of the Fourteenth Century.* Berkeley: University of California Press, 1986.

Hamdun, Said, and Noel King. *Ibn Battuta in Black Africa.* Princeton, NJ: Marcus Wiener Publishers, 1994.

Igbo

The Igbo were among the most prominent medieval inhabitants of what is today southeastern Nigeria. Most of the Igbo have lived in the lands to the east of the Niger Delta, which is formed as this mighty river nears the Atlantic, though much smaller numbers of Igbo have also resided to the Delta's west. Although the western Igbo possessed hierarchical governmental structures, the eastern Igbo are a people who with very few exceptions eschewed the formation of centralized political structures in favor of a decentralized system of governance in which responsibility for decision making was spread horizontally across many members of their small, village communities. Many medieval Africans across the continent practiced this decentralized form of government, creating what are often referred to today as a stateless or acephalous societies, of which an additional prominent example can be found in the city of **Jenné-jeno**.

Although past generations of scholars typically saw this decentralized method of political organization as inferior to centralized political authority, increasingly today it is recognized as a highly stable and sophisticated option that often created societies more durable and long-lasting than hierarchically organized states and empires, as well as one that allowed for the emergence of complex social identities and organizations and the accumulation of significant wealth. In regards to their economic base, the Igbo raised domesticated animals and farmed in their lands that lay behind the Delta. They also engaged in trade north in return for the products of the savannah and Sahara, and south with peoples of the Delta and coast who could offer salt and fish in exchange for the kola nuts, meat, and agricultural goods of the Igbo.

Perhaps the best-known medieval Igbo location is the ninth-century burial site of an obviously prominent and wealthy man found at the village of Igbo-Ukwu. Its excavation has provided evidence of connection to intercontinental trading networks, because the grave contained over one-hundred thousand glass beads thought to have been imported from outside of Africa. The excavation has also revealed that, in common with the **Yoruba** and people of **Benin** who lived nearby, the Igbo had a medieval tradition of producing cast metal sculptures of extremely high artistry and technical virtuosity because a variety of cast bronze artworks including basins, pots, and bowls with a rich profusion of delicately worked details were unearthed from this single gravesite.

Further Reading

Falola, Toyin, ed. *Igbo History and Society: The Essays of Adiele Afigbo*. Trenton, NJ: Africa World Press, 2005.

Shaw, Thurstan. *Igbo-Ukwu: An Account of Archaeological Discoveries in Eastern Nigeria*. 2 vols. Evanston, IL: Northwestern University Press, 1970.

Islam

Islam, which means submission (to God) in Arabic, came to the African continent very soon after the religion emerged in the Arabian Peninsula early in the seventh century C.E. when the Prophet Muhammad received from the Angel Gabriel God's revelations, which form the Muslim holy book, the Qur'an. By the early eighth century, Muslim Arabs conquered the North African coast from **Egypt** to Morocco to a depth into the African interior of up to 200 miles, and a substantial though far from universal Islamization followed within several centuries.

From North Africa Islam more slowly moved south, first to the **Berbers** of the Sahara and then into the sahel and northern savannah belts of West Africa. Traders were often the first to convert, recognizing the value of sharing religious ties with their trading partners. In West Africa the next to convert were often political rulers, who typically combined the practice of Islam with indigenous religious observances in recognition of the religious identities and expectations of their mainly non-Muslim subjects—few sub-Saharan commoners embraced Islam medievally. Meanwhile Islam also traveled from its Arabian homeland to the Horn of Africa and the East African seaboard in the first centuries of the faith, again in conjunction with commerce. Although Islam moved very gradually into the Horn's interior medievally, in East Africa it remained solely a coastal phenomenon. In the medieval centuries heterodox forms of Islam often flourished in the Maghrib, which became the new home of immigrants from outside the continent who practiced forms of the religion, such as the Shi'ite and Kharijite sects, unwelcome in the parts of the Muslim world where mainstream Sunni Islam prevailed.

Berbers who embraced Islam but resented overrule by cultural outsiders were also drawn at times to these heterodox sects, as a means of protest and because these forms typically tolerated the common practice which attended the spread of Islam in Africa of retaining elements of pre-Islamic religious traditions. Sufism, an Islamic mysticism, which stresses a more personal spirituality, also found a ready home on the continent, first among North Africans and postmedievally among West Africans. Whatever form was embraced, Islam provided the great benefit of connecting Islamized parts of Africa to the global Islamic world of the medieval centuries, a process facilitated by the fact that the *hajj*, or religious pilgrimage to the sacred city of Mecca on the Arabian Peninsula's Red Sea coast, is one of the Five Pillars of the faith, incumbent upon all Muslims able to fulfill the journey. In another momentous development, Islam also brought to Islamized portions of medieval Africa the Arabic script, and literacy in

Page of Koran. Ayyubid dynasty (1171–1250), School of Yakurt El Musta'simi (12th/13th century). The Art Archive/Museum of Islamic Art Cairo/Gianni Dagli Orti.

Arabic and those African languages whose speakers began writing their vernaculars using this script.

Further Reading

Abun-Nasr, Jamil M. *A History of the Maghrib in the Islamic Period.* 3rd ed. Cambridge, UK: Cambridge University Press, 1993.

Levtzion, Nehemiah, and Randall L. Pouwels, eds. *The History of Islam in Africa.* Athens: Ohio University Press, 2000.

Robinson, David. *Muslim Societies in African History.* Cambridge, UK: Cambridge University Press, 2004.

Jenné-jeno

Jenné-jeno, located in the richly fertile lands of the Inland Niger Delta in today's **Mali**, is a striking example of early West African urbanization. Jenné-jeno emerged premedievally, around 200 B.C.E., was at its peak from the ninth into the eleventh centuries, and then slowly declined before being entirely abandoned by the early fifteenth century. It is the best researched and therefore best understood example of a type of urbanization that appeared in West Africa at this time and was characterized by what the archaeologists Susan and Roderick McIntosh, Jenné-jeno's principal investigators, have labeled the Urban Complex or clustered city.

These Urban Complexes contain one or more primary settlements closely surrounded by a cluster of smaller, physically distinct urban satellites, all of which together form a single city. These urban conglomerations, found at numerous West African locations within and beyond the Inland Niger Delta, were characterized by marked occupational specialization, with the producers of particular craft and subsistence items such as iron wares, copperwares, pottery, and individual foodstuffs living in the separate satellite settlements located in close proximity to the primary settlement(s). The original settlement at Jenné-jeno, for example, had no fewer than 69 of these satellites, all located within 2½ miles of the urban core. In toto they are estimated to have had a population of over ten thousand people at their peak, individuals who exchanged their various products with one another in a system of local exchange. In addition to this trade, Jenné-jeno was also part of a far-reaching system of commerce stretching across West Africa, which involved the exchange of goods specific to the region's various **ecological zones**.

Evidence for this exchange lies, for example, in the iron smelting and working that existed at Jenné-jeno from its inception, though the closest iron ore was located over 30 miles distant, and in the copper working that occurred at Jenné-jeno as early as the fifth century C.E., although the sources of copper ore were some 200 miles away. Because Jenné-jeno lay on the Niger River that gave it relatively easy access to the sahel and Sahara to the north and the forests to the south, and was in a location that also provided ready connections to land routes leading east and west within the Sudan, it was ideally situated to be a major locus of exchange for the goods of all of these areas. In addition to shedding light on the nature of early West African urbanism and long distance trade, Jenné-jeno is significant as an important example of their emergence even in the absence of the hierarchical social structures and centralized governance that Western academics have long assumed are their necessary prerequisites.

The extensive archaeological excavations conducted at Jenné-jeno over the past 30 years have revealed no sign of social or political hierarchies such as monumental architecture, or distinct caches of valuable objects that are the status-conferring possessions of an elite, and the McIntoshes postulated that it possessed a heterarchical structure in which the city's many discrete social groups were not ranked hierarchically but instead shared power horizontally. Thus, Jenné-jeno did not require centralized political authority to achieve any of its developments and, in conjunction with examples of heterarchical social organization and urbanization from other continents, provides a basis for challenging long-held beliefs about the preconditions necessary for cities and long-distance trade to emerge. Jenné-jeno refutes another long-held belief too: that urbanization, long distance trade, and social complexity in West Africa appeared only after the onset of trans-Saharan trade, which brought with it Arab and Islamic external influences long asserted to be necessary stimuli to these West African developments. Instead, Jenné-Jeno demonstrates entirely indigenous West African processes of early urbanization and social complexity, which predated by many centuries trans-Saharan trade and the influence of these outsiders. In fact, the McIntoshes argued persuasively that trans-Saharan trade could eventually flourish as it did in part because of the deeply rooted sub-Saharan trading networks that could now be used to channel the goods of West Africa to more northern markets.

Jenné-jeno declined over the course of the thirteenth and fourteenth centuries, most likely in response to a drying climate, the growing importance of **Islam**, and changes in commercial patterns. As it faded Jenné-jeno was eclipsed by the new city of Jenné, which lay fewer than 2 miles to its northwest and moved into its ascendancy as the medieval period drew to a close.

Further Reading

McIntosh, Roderick J. *Ancient Middle Niger: Urbanism and the Self-Organizing Landscape.* Cambridge, UK: Cambridge University Press, 2005.

McIntosh, Roderick J. *The Peoples of the Middle Niger: The Island of Gold.* Oxford, UK: Blackwell Publishers, 1998.

McIntosh, Susan Keech. *Excavations at Jenné-Jeno, Hambarketolo, and Kaniana (Inland Niger Delta, Mali): The 1981 Season.* Berkeley: University of California Press, 1995.

Judaism

Jews have lived in North Africa since Biblical times, some drawn, like so many individuals and conquerors over the millennia, by the economic opportunities created by the region's involvement in the commerce of the Mediterranean world and its far-reaching trading networks. Other Jews arrived in North Africa after fleeing persecution, for example at the hands of Romans in the first century C.E. and Spaniards during the medieval Reconquista. Although most of these individuals resided in Jewish communities located in innumerable cities and towns across North Africa from **Egypt** to Morocco, some medieval Jews moved further into the continent due to their involvement in trans-Saharan trade, taking up residence in Saharan oases such as **Sijilmasa** and Tuat; they also worked in these communities as goldsmiths.

Often relations between Jews and the dominantly Muslim medieval populations of North Africa and the Sahara were entirely cordial and amicable. At other times, however, they were not; the Almohad Empire was notably intolerant of its Jewish population, and in the 1490s the Muslim scholar Muhammad al-Maghili led a movement to expel the Jews from Tamantit in Tuat (*see* **Almoravid and Almohad Movements**). Jews in medieval Spain played a key role in the creation of the earliest European maps depicting the lands lying beyond North Africa, no doubt receiving information from friends and relatives living in those regions in this era when European knowledge of these lands was infinitesimal. The famous Catalan Atlas of 1375 was the work of the Sephardic Jew Abraham Cresques of Majorca. In addition to these North African and Saharan Jewish communities, the Beta Israel of Ethiopia, formerly called the Falasha though that term is recognized as a pejorative today, formed what has in recent centuries come to be thought of as another medieval African Jewish community. Their origins are the topic of considerable and politicized dispute today; what is indisputable is the evidence that from the beginning of the common era Judaism, most likely introduced from South Arabia, influenced key elements of Ethiopian culture—for example, medieval Ethiopians celebrated their Christian Sabbath on Saturday; followed dietary laws similar to those prescribed by Jewish law; circumcised male infants on the eighth day after birth; incorporated numerous Hebrew loan-words into their language, and much, much more—and that in the fourteenth to sixteenth centuries a segment of the Ethiopian population who came to be known as the Beta Israel embraced an overtly "Israelite" identity as an act of resistance to the imperialist and Christian Solomonid dynasty of Ethiopia that was encroaching upon their territory and marginalizing them economically and socially.

Postmedievally, a sizeable Jewish community has developed in South Africa in the modern era, while in the second half of the 1900s the many vibrant Jewish communities that had for so many centuries and even millennia existed in North Africa, Ethiopia, and Saharan oases largely vanished as a result of out-migration to other parts of the world, casualties of twentieth century politics. *See also* Document 10.

Further Reading

Goitein, S.D. *A Mediterranean Society: The Jewish Communities of the Arab World as Portrayed in the Documents of the Cairo Geniza.* 6 vols. Berkeley: University of California Press, 1967–1993.

Hunwick, John O. *Jews of a Saharan Oasis: The Elimination of the Tamantit Community.* Princeton, NJ: Markus Wiener Publishers, 2006.

Kaplan, Steven. *The Beta Israel (Falasha) in Ethiopia from Earliest Times to the Twentieth Century.* New York: New York University Press, 1992.

Kanem-Bornu

The state of Kanem, located in the central West African Sudan to the north and east of Lake Chad, had emerged by the tenth century C.E. if not considerably earlier, founded by Zaghawa pastoralists and from the eleventh century led by the *mais* or kings of its Saifawa dynasty from their capital at Njimi. Kanem derived much of its wealth from trans-Saharan trade, and the caravan route from its lands through the Fezzan to Tripoli constituted the shortest and most easily traversed of all of the trade routes crisscrossing the Sahara.

Because Kanem lay well to the east of West African sources of gold, unlike the medieval states of **Ghana, Mali**, and **Songhai,** this most precious of metals was not the basis for its trans-Saharan trade. Instead, slaves were Kanem's main export, in return for which they received highly valued horses from North Africa. The horses, used in cavalries, gave Kanem a decisive military edge over the peoples living to their south who Kanem raided and enslaved in a continuous and bloody cycle of violence. Kanem also exported ostrich feathers and ivory, as welling as taxing agriculture and collecting tribute. In the late fourteenth to early fifteenth centuries, as a result of challenges to Saifawa leadership by the Bulala and others, and also perhaps a drying climate, the rulers of Kanem moved to Bornu in the lands, which lay to the south and west of Lake Chad.

Bornu had long been tributary to Kanem; now, from the new Saifawa capital of Gazargamo, it became the seat of power to which Kanem was made subordinate. Among the most prominent of Kanem and Bornu's rulers were Mai Dunama Dibalami who ruled in the first half of the thirteenth century and Mai Idris Aloma who reigned from the 1560s until the end of the sixteenth century. In addition to expanding Kanem, which rose to new heights under his rule, Dunama Dibalami's fame rests on the overt challenge he laid down to local religious practices. Although Kanem emerged as a non-Islamic state, by the later eleventh century its rulers had adopted the new religion. As in most medieval West African polities, Muslim rulers had also to accommodate the beliefs of their non-Muslim subjects, leaving them to walk a constant tightrope between the religious expectations of followers of the two faiths. Dunama Dibalami responded in part by breaking open a sacred religious object from the local religious tradition said to safeguard the dynasty so long as it remained intact, which by infuriating traditionalists furthered the stresses which resulted 250 years later in the Saifawa dynasty's move to Bornu.

Mai Idris Aloma is noted for his military expansion of the empire, facilitated by its fearsome cavalry, whose military leaders emerged as an elite when they were rewarded for their efforts with gifts of large estates. Trans-Saharan trade flourished during Idris Aloma's rule as well. He also gave strong support to **Islam**: New mosques opened, conversion accelerated, and Islamic scholarship in Bornu flourished for centuries to come. Recognizing their power, he also began importing guns from North Africa along with Turks to train his troops in their use. He strengthened diplomatic relationships with important trading partners and coreligionists in Tripoli and far-away Turkey. Bornu, which reached its greatest strength in the sixteenth to seventeenth centuries, continued to be ruled by the Saifawa into the nineteenth century though by then its territory was much shrunken.

Further Reading

Bjorkelo, Anders J. *State and Society in Three Central Sudanic Kingdoms, Kanem-Bornu, Bagirmi and Wadai*. Bergen, Norway: Universitetet i Bergen, 1976.

Hiskett, Mervyn. *The Development of Islam in West Africa*. London: Longman Group Ltd., 1984.

Kilwa

In the fourteenth century Kilwa, an island located just off the coast of present-day Tanzania, was the wealthiest and most renowned of the **Swahili** cities, a prominence it achieved due to its ability to gain a near-monopoly over the export of **gold** from the East African coast. The gold traded by the Swahili was mined far away in the southeastern African interior, on the **Zimbabwe Plateau** located between the Zambezi and Limpopo **rivers**. It was then funneled to the Swahili by the state of Zimbabwe via Sofala, a coastal port town, which lay south of the Swahili coast and due east of Zimbabwe in today's Mozambique. By controlling the coast around Sofala, Kilwa managed to export the lion's share of the gold.

Because of its reputation and wealth Kilwa attracted a steady stream of medieval visitors. In 1331, it was visited by **Ibn Battuta**, a North African from Tangiers, who famously wrote of its coral stone house–lined streets, gardens, and orchards of fruit trees, "Kilwa is one of the most beautiful and well-constructed towns in the world. The whole of it is elegantly built" (Freeman-Grenville, p. 31). Archaeological excavations at Kilwa also reveal the presence of monumental architecture constructed in the coral stone and lime mortar style of the Swahili cities. The Great Mosque, largest of all mosques along the Swahili coast, had magnificent vaulted ceilings. The massive Husuni Kubwa palace complex, which contained over one hundred rooms, stands out for its octagonal bathing pool as well as its terraces, courtyards, and vaulted and domed roofs.

In the 1300s and perhaps earlier Kilwa minted its own coins, at least one of which has been found as far afield as the ruins of Zimbabwe. Kilwa went into a decline in the 1400s following a reduction in the flow of gold exported by Zimbabwe, which was facing crises of its own at this time mostly likely due to environmental degradations resulting from overgrazing and extensive timber harvesting. Kilwa's dénouement came when it was defeated in 1505 by the Portuguese, who attacked Swahili city after city in the early 1500s. Though today it lies in ruins, in its time it was a pearl of East Africa, drawing visitors from afar dazzled by its wealth, beauty, and sophistication.

Further Reading

Chittick, Neville. *Kilwa: An Islamic Trading City on the East African Coast*. Nairobi, Kenya: British Institute in Eastern Africa, 1974.

Freeman-Grenville, G.S.P., ed. and trans. *The East African Coast, Select Documents from the First to the Earlier Nineteenth Century*. Oxford, UK: Clarendon Press, 1962.

Horton, Mark, and John Middleton. *The Swahili: The Social Landscape of a Mercantile Society*. Oxford, UK: Blackwell Publishers, 2000.

Kongo

The Kongo kingdom emerged in the late fourteenth century in the lands immediately south of the Malebo Pool, a widening of the Congo River located some 200 miles inland from the Atlantic coast that represents the end of the easily traversed portion of the Congo that is then marked by rapids and waterfalls as it drops to the sea. Kongo's material base resided in the development of significant trading networks traversing the lands of the forest–savannah fringe, which lay on the southern border of the massive tropical forests of western equatorial Africa.

Important commodities in this system of commerce included salt from the Atlantic shoreline, copper, and raffia cloth of very high quality, which along with other products including ivory and iron were traded between environmental zones in the pattern of ecologically driven exchange found in commercial networks all across medieval Africa. The Kongo kingdom rose rapidly to prominence as a notably large and powerful state exerting very strong centralized control over a range of conquered peoples from its capital of Mbanza Kongo. At its peak the state dominated regional trade utilizing a seashell **currency**, demanded tribute from its vassal states, and contained over a half million people in some 60,000 square miles of territory located in what are today southwestern Zaire and northern Angola, in the lands south of the Congo River that range from the Kwango River in the east to the Atlantic coastline in the west.

At the end of the medieval period the Kongo kingdom developed a complex relationship with the Portuguese, who came to this stretch of Africa's Atlantic coastline in the early 1480s, and Kongo become a prominent supplier of slaves to the Portuguese in return for a range of imports. Members of the Kongo royal family including the king converted to Catholicism, though in a tug-of-war reminiscent of the arrival of **Islam** in West Africa not all citizens supported their leaders' embrace of the new religion. Disagreements with the Portuguese over the increasingly worrisome scope of the burgeoning slave trade proved one distraction, as did the recurring question of succession given the absence of clear-cut rules for choosing new kings, and in the midsixteenth century the state was attacked and defeated by warriors from the east known as the Jaga.

With assistance from the Portuguese, the Kongo kingdom regained its independence and continued to flourish economically. In the seventeenth century, however, new rivals in commerce greatly reduced Kongo's regional dominance of trade, and the once-mighty kingdom faded away by the early 1700s.

Further Reading
Hilton, Anne. *The Kingdom of Kongo.* Oxford, UK: Clarendon Press, 1985.
Vansina, Jan. *Paths in the Rainforests: Towards a History of Political Tradition in Equatorial Africa.* Madison: University of Wisconsin Press, 1990.

Luba

In the late medieval years, a Luba kingdom arose in the savannah lands in and around the Upemba Depression, a swampy valley dotted with lakes that is located along the upper Lualaba River in the region of Lake Kisale in what is today the southern Congo. The Luba kingdom's emergence was preceded by a series of developments in this area that commenced in the early medieval centuries and included extensive and accomplished metalworking utilizing copper and iron, expanded **agriculture** benefiting from the use of iron tools, skillful exploitation of the natural fauna of the area through hunting and fishing, utilization of local salt deposits, and involvement in regional trade.

Evidence of these developments, which positioned the region's inhabitants for the emergence of a large state, comes mainly from archaeological digs conducted at gravesites located in the Upemba Depression, most prominently Sanga. These sites reveal increasing social and economic differentiation over the course of the centuries culminating in the emergence of the first Luba kingdom in the fourteenth century. It possessed a monarchical form of government with kings chosen from among the members of the royal family, who legitimized their rule in part through their royal bloodlines. Women played important roles in the Luba state, for example, as royal spirit mediums, ambassadors, and keepers of royal secrets.

Postmedievally, in the eighteenth century, the Luba expanded their authority into a much larger Luba empire. The Luba are noted for their artistic traditions including pottery; beautifully worked wooden objects including bowstands, headrests, and stools; and metalworking, which produced large quantities of finely worked tools and jewelry, as well as the copper crosses used as a form of **currency** in this region.

Further Reading

Roberts, Mary, and Allen F. Roberts. *Luba: Visions of Africa*. Milan, Italy: 5 Continents Editions, 2007.

Roberts, Mary Nooter, and Allen F. Roberts. *Memory: Luba Art and the Making of History*. New York: The Museum for African Art; Munich: Prestel, 1996.

Vansina, Jan. *Paths in the Rainforests: Towards a History of Political Tradition in Equatorial Africa*. Madison: University of Wisconsin Press, 1990.

Mali

Mali, which emerged around 1235, became an immensely large and powerful West African empire that at its height stretched from the Atlantic Ocean in the west to beyond the Niger Bend in the east, and from the important southern Saharan town of Walata in the north to the forest fringes in the south. Within its expansive borders lay a range of **ecological zones**, including desert, sahel, savannah, and forest, and the empire made full use of the products of each of these environments as one basis for its wealth. A brisk trade between regions existed, exchanging goods such as kola nuts and forest snails from the forest, grains and cereals from the savannah, goats and sheep from the sahel, and salt from the desert. The **agriculture**, which flourished in the savannah, was taxed by the state as one important source of revenue.

Because Mali controlled the Bure goldfields, which lay along the upper Niger, which was also the homeland of the Malinke who founded and ruled this empire, they profited immensely from growing North African and European demand for **gold**. Mali also taxed trans-Saharan trade, which flowed through the kingdom following a shift east in the trade routes that coincided with Mali's rise. Reflecting solid governmental control, the North African traveler **Ibn Battuta**, who visited in 1352 to 1353, wrote of the great security of Mali, through which traders and their valuable goods passed utterly unmolested. Its wealth was reflected in significant urbanization: Important towns and cities included **Timbuku**, Gao, Walata, and Niani, the first of which accelerated down its path toward becoming a very important center of Islamic scholarship in the time of the renowned Malian ruler **Mansa Musa**.

Mali emerged in the Sudan out of the political uncertainty that followed the fading away of **Ghana**, which had ruled over a sahel-based empire until declining gradually over the eleventh and twelfth centuries. For a short time in the early thirteenth century the Soso (alternately, Sosso or Susu), a people who had been conquered and forcibly incorporated into Ghana's empire, filled the power vacuum in the region under the leadership of Sumanguru. At this time the Malinke, who were organized into a number of small, politically independent village-based entities called kafus, fell under onerous Soso overrule. The Malinke threw off Soso domination under the leadership of the brilliant **Sundjata**, whose exploits were chronicled by the bards or griots of Mali who have passed this oral tradition down to the present day through memory and public recitation. Following Sundjata's triumph over Sumanguru in the Battle of Kirina in 1235, the Malinke expanded their authority over more and more people and became the supremely dominant West African power of the day, ruling from their capital at Niani on the Sankarani River. Like Ghana before it, Mali allowed those it conquered substantial internal autonomy in exchange for payments of tribute and recognition of Malian suzerainty.

In addition to its political achievements, Mali stands out for the shift in the locus of power from the sahel to the Sudan that occurred in its time, due to a combination of the drier climate that affected West Africa from the twelfth through fifteenth centuries and drew people to the better watered south, and the exploitation of the Bure and **Akan** goldfields that lay further south than the Bambuk goldfield mined in the days of Ghana. The empire also drew much of West Africa into one vast trading network, and it was during its rule that the group of trader specialists known as the Dyula (or Juula) emerged and traveled far and wide throughout the empire and beyond, drawing even the distant Akan goldfields of the forest zone into this system of commerce. In regards to social stratification, Mali had a system of hereditary castes for select occupations including smiths and bards, whose members were of low status but whose powers were simultaneously feared. Mali is also notable for its kings' adoption of **Islam**, which became of increasing importance with the growth of the trans-Saharan trade, which connected Mali to Muslim merchants in the Sahara, North Africa, and the Middle East. In a pattern found among many other medieval West African polities, Mali's kings simultaneously continued their adherence to the indigenous religious traditions that remained the faith of most of their people, and which they were expected still to practice. Mansa Musa became the most widely known ruler of Mali as a result of his *hajj* or religious pilgrimage to Mecca in 1324 to 1325.

Mali's strength waxed and waned over the centuries of its existence depending upon the skill of its current ruler. The empire began a final, irreversible decline in the late 1300s due to a series of ineffectual rulers and struggles over succession. Seeing weakness at the center, conquered states who had no doubt always resented their lost independence began breaking away and refusing to pay tribute, further weakening Mali. Attacks from the Mossi who lay to the south of the Niger Bend and the Tuareg who swept down from the desert in the north, even seizing the fabled city of Timbuktu in 1433, left the empire vulnerable to the rising power of the **Songhai** who lay to their east, and a weakened Mali faded gradually away over the next 150 or so years, preserved though its memory is to the present in the immortal words of its bards. *See also* Documents 7 and 9.

Further Reading

Bovill, Edward William. *The Golden Trade of the Moors: West African Kingdoms in the Fourteenth Century*. Oxford, UK: Oxford University Press, 1958.

Levtzion, Nehemiah. *Ancient Ghana and Mali*. New York: Africana Publishing Company, 1973.

Mansa Musa (d. 1337)

Mansa Musa, who ruled the West African empire of **Mali** from 1312 until his death in 1337, is best known for the *hajj*, or religious pilgrimage to Mecca,

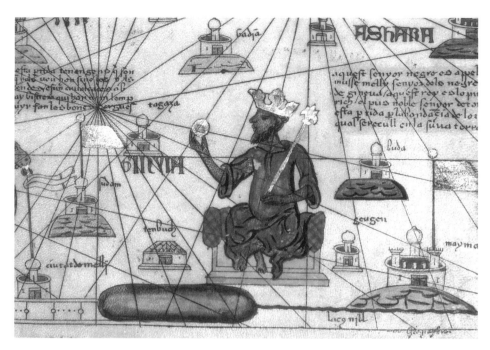

Cresques, Abraham (fl. 1375). King of Mali, 1375. The King, seated on his throne, wearing a crown and holding an orb and sceptre, is portrayed at the centre of a map of his
realm. HIP/Art Resource, NY.

he undertook in 1324 to 1325. Although no doubt he was motivated by piety
and a desire to fulfill the fifth Pillar of **Islam**, which enjoins all Muslims who
can to travel to the holy city of Mecca that lies along the Red Sea in the Arabian Peninsula, the manner in which he journeyed also brought worldwide
attention to his personal power and wealth, and that of his empire. From the
Malian capital of Niani, located on the Sankarani River that flows into the
upper Niger River, Mansa Musa made the long, arduous, and dangerous desert crossing, taking with him an extensive retinue said to include one hundred
camels each carrying 300 pounds of **gold**, over ten-thousand Malian soldiers
and functionaries, his senior wife, and more than five-hundred slaves. Stop-
ping in **Cairo** after successfully navigating the Sahara, Mansa Musa spent
widely and gave munificent gifts of gold so lavishly that it was said that the
price of gold there remained depressed for years following his visit. This drew
the attention of Europe to his empire, and following his *hajj* Mali began ap-
pearing on European maps of the African interior.

On his return home Mansa Musa brought to Mali the Andalusian architect
and poet Abu Ishaq Ibrahim al-Sahili, who designed and built mosques and
other structures in Gao, Niani, and Timbuktu. Mansa Musa also patronized
Islamic literature and scholarship, sending students to North Africa and entic-
ing scholars from afar to teach in Timbuktu, so that under his reign the city
started down its path, fully realized in succeeding centuries, of becoming an
important center of Islamic learning. Mansa Musa is also known for leading
Mali, which had lost control over a number of vassal states since its early days
of glory, to its greatest strength and triumph. Using a military whose cavalry

gave it tremendous advantages over its enemies, he restored the empire's control over outlying districts and enlarged the empire to its greatest-ever territorial extent. He also established diplomatic relations with an important trading partner in North Africa, the Marinids of Morocco, as well as creating less formal ties with **Egypt**. Although his reputation outside of Mali — and European interest in Mali's gold — were sealed as a result of the publicity generated by his *hajj*, within the empire some criticized him for spending so lavishly from the royal treasury, and following his reign Mali gradually declined until it had ceased to exist even in its later, attenuated form by around 1600. *See also* **Islam** and Document 7.

Further Reading

Bovill, Edward William. *The Golden Trade of the Moors: West African Kingdoms in the Fourteenth Century*. Oxford, UK: Oxford University Press, 1958.

Levtzion, Nehemiah. *Ancient Ghana and Mali*. New York: Africana Publishing Company, 1973.

Nubia

Inhabiting a narrow stretch of land straddling the Middle Nile — the portion of the river spanning the first to sixth cataracts or rapids, which stretches from just south of Aswan almost to Khartoum — Nubia was home to three medieval Christian kingdoms. Although the Middle Nile runs mainly through inhospitable desert, because of systems of irrigation and regular deposits of fertile soil during annual **river** flooding the lands right along the river's edge provided an environment in which Nubians farmed, raised animals, and engaged in a system of long-distance trade that moved goods of the African interior north to **Egypt** and points beyond. These activities provided the material base for the early medieval emergence of the Nubian polities Nobatia (or Nobadia), Makuria, and Alwa (or Alodia), which lay from north to south along the Middle Nile. Their capital cities were, respectively, Faras, Old Dongola, and Soba.

These kingdoms adopted **Christianity** very rapidly in the sixth century as a result of the proselytizing activities of missionaries from the competing Byzantine and **Coptic church**es, and Nubian Christianity demonstrated the effects of both sources of influence. Their ecclesiastical art included clearly Byzantine components while also containing stylistic elements very definitively their own. Yet they also embraced Coptic Monophysitism in preference to Byzantine Church Melkitism, and their bishops were appointed by the Egyptian Coptic Church throughout the almost millennium-long history of Nubian Christianity. The Nubians were noteworthy for very successfully repelling Arab Muslim invaders who swooped south immediately after conquering Egypt but proved no match for the formidable Nubian archers who defeated them in 641 and 652, with the result that Nubian Christianity survived even as the Christians of Egypt and the Maghrib were converting to **Islam**. Indeed, so compelling were the Nubian victories that the Arabs entered into a treaty, which recognized their sovereignty in return for the provision of 360 slaves annually. A vital north–south trade beneficial to Nubia and Egypt then flourished for centuries.

The Muslim presence to their north did mean that Nubian Christianity developed in isolation from the rest of the Christian world from this point on.

Religion aside, medieval Nubia was a place of considerable prosperity. The written accounts of medieval visitors and archaeological excavations reveal urbanization; comfortable homes; over one hundred churches and monasteries; imported luxury goods; a literature written in Greek, Coptic, and Nubian; and architectural wonders like Faras Cathedral with its stunning wall murals depicting Nubian bishops and royalty; and Biblical figures and scenes. In addition to its ecclesiastical art, medieval Nubia produced wheel-thrown and beautifully decorated pottery, which is generally considered to be among the finest ever made on the continent. Christian Nubia began crumbling in the later thirteenth century but lasted until the fifteenth, when Christianity disappeared altogether even from the southernmost Alwa, not as a result of conquest but rather due to the steady accrual of Arab and Egyptian Muslim immigrants who, slowly yet inexorably, numerically overwhelmed the local population and assimilated them to their faith, a process that culminated in the emergence of new, Muslim political orders. Sadly, significant portions of medieval Nubia have been submerged under the waters of Lake Nasser, formed in the 1960s when modern Egypt's Aswan Dam was constructed near the Nile's first cataract, making further archaeological explorations of most of Nobatia impossible. *See also* Document 3.

Further Reading

O'Connor, David. *Ancient Nubia: Egypt's Rival in Africa*. Philadelphia: University of Pennsylvania Press, 1993.

Shinnie, Peter L. *Ancient Nubia*. New York: Kegan Paul International, 1996.

Oral Traditions

Oral traditions are the way in which oral cultures have kept their histories and other forms of socially valued knowledge alive through the memorization and performance of oral texts. With the spread of systems of writing, over almost all of Africa in recent centuries, oral traditions have come to coexist with traditions of literacy. For much of Africa across the medieval centuries, however, oral traditions served as the dominant method through which information was passed down through the generations. In societies with oral traditions, various types of knowledge were kept and disseminated to new generations through this technique including political histories; legitimizations of ruling families; knowledge of migrations; epics focused upon a particular cultural hero; stories of origins; genealogies of royal families, social elites, and commoners; and social commentaries and norms.

Some African cultures, more frequently states with centralized political authority, placed the keeping of oral traditions in the hands of a specialist class. A prominent medieval example of this practice is found in the well-known griots of certain West African societies including the empire of **Mali**. In societies that utilized these highly trained specialists, the practitioners of oral traditions often held a complex and contradictory place in society, recognized and feared for the power implicit in the knowledge they held and wielded, yet also stigmatized as a socially marginalized group whose members formed a hereditary occupational caste. In other African societies, however, frequently those that spread political authority broadly throughout their populations rather than concentrating it in the hands of political elites, knowing and reciting an oral tradition could be done by anyone with the requisite talent and expertise. Skills necessary to the successful practice of oral traditions included strong capacities for memorization and the many possible elements of performance: rhetoric and oratory, singing, musical composition, poetic expression, dance, and nonverbal communication were all talents that might be drawn upon while imparting an oral tradition to an audience.

In regards to the reliability of these sources of information about the African past, though core elements of a number of oral traditions have been verified through other sources of information such as archaeology, historical linguistics, art history, and written accounts, and though oral traditions are also very beneficial for the insight they provide into social morés and mentalités, they are simultaneously notorious for chronological inaccuracies and biases toward the rulers of the states whose histories some of them chronicle. Thus historians of Africa analyze oral traditions critically rather than taking them at face value and utilize them in conjunction with other sources of evidence. Oral traditions are only one element of the oral cultures that dominated medieval Africa, other components of which included a deeply held appreciation for the facile use in speech of proverbs, riddles, and puns, and for skilled storytelling, abilities which indicated the speaker's verbal agility and prowess. *See also* **Education**.

Further Reading
Niane, D.T. *Sundiata: An Epic of Old Mali*. 2nd ed. London: Longman, 2006.
Vansina, Jan. *Oral Tradition as History*. Madison: University of Wisconsin Press, 1985.

Regions

The huge continent of Africa, at its greatest extents nearly 5,000 miles in length and width and in area more than three times the size of the United States at almost 11.7 million square miles, is often divided by Africanists into a number of smaller regions: North, West, Central, East, and southern Africa. The regional divisions are not made identically by all scholars, but a typical demarcation places the contemporary nations of Morocco, Algeria, Tunisia, Libya, **Egypt**, and Western Sahara in North Africa; Mauritania, **Mali**, Niger, Senegal, the Gambia, Guinea-Bissau, Guinea, Sierra Leone, Liberia, Cote d'Ivoire, Burkina Faso, Ghana, Togo, **Benin**, and Nigeria in West Africa; Cameroon, Sao Tome e Principe, Equatorial Guinea, Gabon, the Congo Republic, the Central African Republic, Chad, and the Democratic Republic of the Congo in Central Africa; Uganda, Rwanda, Burundi, Kenya, and Tanzania in East Africa; and Angola, Namibia, Malawi, Mozambique, Zambia, Zimbabwe, Botswana, Lesotho, Swaziland, and South Africa in southern Africa.

Reflecting divisions between its north and south of religion, ethnicity, and history, some would put the Sudan in North Africa whereas others would include it in East Africa. And though Ethiopia, Somalia, Eritrea and Djibouti are sometimes considered separately from any of the regions given their location in the Horn of Africa, they too are sometimes placed with East Africa. It is important to note that *West Africa* does not refer to the entire western portion of the continent, but rather that part of it excepting North Africa that extends far west into the Atlantic and runs east until reaching modern-day Cameroon, where the western African coastline makes a right-angle turn and begins running south. Other important subregions include the Horn of Africa, that roughly triangular portion of the continent that juts into the Indian Ocean and is separated from the southern Arabian Peninsula, with which it has a distinctly intertwined history, by the narrow Red Sea; the **Ethiopian Highlands**, a mountainous region within the Horn whose elevation separates it spatially and environmentally as well as in terms of trajectories of human society from the plains below; the Maghrib, which simply means "west" in Arabic and was originally used by Arabs in Egypt to refer to the portion of North Africa stretching along the Mediterranean to their west encompassing the modern states of Tunisia, Algeria, and Morocco (sometimes Libya is included in this designation too); and the Rift Valley, a huge fault line that ruptures the earth's surface and stretches many thousands of miles from the southern African interior north through the Great Lakes region of East Africa and the Ethiopian Highlands before continuing as the bed of the Red Sea and eventually, beyond Africa's borders, the Middle East's Jordan River.

Further Reading

Adams, William M. et al., eds. *The Physical Geography of Africa*. Oxford, UK: Oxford University Press, 1999.

Aryeetey-Attoh, Samuel. *The Geography of Sub-Saharan Africa*. 2nd ed. Englewood Cliffs, NJ: Prentice Hall, 2002.

Cole, Roy, and H.J. De Blij. *Survey of Subsaharan Africa: A Regional Geography*. Oxford, UK: Oxford University Press, 2007.

Rivers

Rivers have played critically important roles in the history of the African continent. Their floodplains and valleys have formed some of the continent's richest farmland, whereas fishing their waters has exponentially increased Africans' sources of often-scarce animal protein. These waterways have also served as key conduits for transportation and the transmission of knowledge and ideas as well as people and trade goods. Some of the characteristics common to many of Africa's rivers stem from the geography of the continent. Plate tectonics and its theory of continental drift proposes that all of the earth's continents formerly existed as one supercontinent known as Pangaea, at the heart of which lay what became the African continent.

When the other continents and landmasses split off from it some 100 million and more years ago, Africa's location at the center of the former supercontinent explains one key feature of the Africa's geography: the steep drop-offs known in places as the Great Escarpment that characterize many of its edges and continue in the abrupt and rapid drops in the ocean depths surrounding the continent, which lack any shallow continental shelf. These sharp drop-offs that occur as the continent's more elevated interior plateaus give way to the surrounding sea level oceans below lead to the existence along many of Africa's rivers of their characteristic waterfalls and cataracts, which allow these waterways to descend from the higher elevations of Africa's interior through the Great Escarpment to the seas. These features also mean that Africa's great rivers cannot be navigated uninterruptedly along their entire lengths due to the impediments imposed by waterfalls and rapids (Table 10).

Table 10. Longest African Rivers

River	Location	Approximate Length in Miles	Details
Nile	Northeastern Africa	4,200	World's longest river; Nile River Valley home to many great civilizations.
Congo	Central Africa	2,720	Second longest river in Africa; flow second in volume only to South America's Amazon.
Niger	West Africa	2,600	Third longest river in Africa; site of very fertile Inland Niger Delta.
Zambezi	Southern Africa	1,700	Fourth longest river in Africa; site of Victoria Falls, among the largest waterfalls in the world.

The most important and majestic African rivers include the Niger, Nile, Congo and Zambezi, found, respectively, in West, northeastern, Central, and southern Africa. West Africa's Niger, which has its headwaters in the Guinea Highlands fewer than 200 miles from the Atlantic coast and at almost 2,600 miles in length is Africa's third longest river, initially runs northeast to what is today the southern Sahara before turning sharply to the southeast and making its way to the Atlantic Ocean at the Gulf of Guinea, forming a vast swamp delta in current-day Nigeria as it nears the sea. The northernmost point on the Niger, known as the Niger Bend, is within 10 miles of the famed city of **Timbuktu**, which in the medieval centuries served a critical role in trans-Saharan trade as the place where commodities moving north and south between the savannah and desert regions were switched from the desert transportation of camel caravans to movement by boat along the broad and mainly gentle stretches of the western half of the Niger as it cut through the savannah belt.

Another critical feature of the Niger is the Inland Niger Delta, formed from the annual overflowing of the river's banks as the runoff caused by the rainy season reaches the portion of the river located in what is today **Mali**. The silt deposited by this annual flooding results in extraordinarily fertile land in this large interior delta, where grains and other crops are produced in abundance. The rapids so characteristic of Africa's rivers are found at Kolikoro on the river's southwestern stretch, whereas to the southeast of the Niger Bend rapids exist near the city of Gao and at Boussa. Important tributaries of the Niger include the Benue, Sankarani, and Bani rivers. The Nile, the best known of Africa's great rivers and the world's longest at almost 4,200 miles in length, has its origins far south in the region of East Africa's Lake Victoria, from where flows the White Nile that is one of the two major tributaries of this mighty waterway.

The second of these tributaries, the Blue Nile, originates near Lake Tana in the **Ethiopian Highlands**, and joins the White Nile at Khartoum in the modern Sudan. From there the Nile continues its way through desert to the Mediterranean, with its mighty triangular delta reaching north from its apex at Cairo to stretch along nearly 200 miles of Egypt's Mediterranean coast. Notable features along the Nile include the sudd, or massive swamps, which lie along the White Nile far south of Khartoum, and the six cataracts or rapids between Khartoum and Aswan, all of which interrupt the river's smooth flow and thus also progress along the Nile by boat. Of profound importance as a source of life-giving water and arable land in portions of its river valley and delta that historically were enriched annually by new deposits of silt, the Nile has been the seat of great civilizations including Ancient Egypt, Kush, and Meroë.

The Congo, known between 1971 and 1997 as the Zaire River, is the second longest river in Africa at over 2,700 miles. The river has its origins in the Lualaba River in what is today the southeastern part of the Democratic Republic of the Congo and the Chambeshi River that originates in today's Zambia, and then crosses the equator twice as it arcs through Central Africa. Flowing through well-watered rainforests and with multiple tributaries, which have different rainy seasons, the Congo is noted for its consistent and high-volume flow that is second only to that of South America's Amazon. Possessing numerous cataracts and waterfalls along its lower reaches, the Congo empties into the Atlantic through its massive and navigable estuary. The Zambezi, which along with the Limpopo and Orange rivers drains southern Africa, is notable for its world-famous Victoria Falls, among the largest waterfalls in the world. As with the Niger and Nile, the Zambezi is marked by floodplains and swamps and creates a sizeable delta as it empties into the Indian Ocean in contemporary Mozambique.

Further Reading
Adams, William M., Andrew S. Goudie, and Antony R. Orme, eds. *The Physical Geography of Africa.* Oxford, UK: Oxford University Press, 1996.
Collins, Robert O. *The Nile.* New Haven, CT: Yale University Press, 2002.

Sijilmasa

Sijilmasa, a walled medieval city located at the expansive Tafilalt oasis in the northwestern Sahara in today's Morocco, was founded in the middle of the eighth century shortly after Arabs moved into North Africa. Among its founders were **Berbers** who had embraced Kharijite **Islam** and sought freedom from mainstream Muslim Arab overrule by moving from North Africa into the desert fringe and creating what became the very important city of Sijilmasa. They also achieved spectacular economic success: A cosmopolitan city of thirty-thousand people at its height that was home to Berbers, Arabs, and Jews from North Africa, the Sahara, and Muslim Spain, Sijilmasa derived its significant wealth from its critical role in trans-Saharan trade. It was the northern entrepôt for the desert crossing from where camel caravans began the long and arduous journey south, a place where goods traded between North and West Africa, including the fabulous quantities of gold exported by the wealthy and powerful medieval sudanic empire of **Ghana**, changed hands as they moved in and out of the desert.

Archaeological excavations have revealed the wealth of Sijilmasa's upper class, indicated by large houses, finely worked jewelry, architectural ornamentation, and luxury goods; these are also attested to in the accounts of medieval visitors to the city. In addition to profits generated by trans-Saharan trade, due to its location and ingenious cistern-based irrigation Sijilmasa produced a rich bounty of oasis crops including dates, grains, fruits, and vegetables; some of its grapes were converted to wine. Sijilmasa was ruled at various points in its long and rich history by Berber and Arab polities, including the eleventh- to thirteenth-century **Almoravid and Almohad** Berber empires. The Almoravids established mints in Sijilmasa and struck large quantities of finely worked dinars, golden coins that gained wide circulation throughout North Africa, Europe, and the Middle East as what many have called that day's coin of the realm. Sijilmasa fell into decline in the late medieval years due to shifts in trans-Saharan trade routes and political unrest, and today this once-vibrant city exists only as ruins in the desert sand. *See also* Document 5.

Further Reading

Messier, Ronald. *Archaeological Survey of Sijilmasa*. Murfreesboro: Middle Tennessee State University, 1989.

Songhai

Songhai (or Songhay) existed from at least the ninth century as a small state, controlled by Songhai-speaking people and centered on the city of Gao that is located along the stretch of the Niger that runs southeast from the Niger Bend. In keeping with many other medieval West African states, Songhai derived its wealth from a combination of locally based fishing and agriculture and involvement in trans-Saharan trade, in its case facilitated by its experienced Sorko fishermen who also moved goods along the Niger with ease. Gao, like Ghana's Kumbi Saleh and **Mali**'s **Timbuktu**, functioned as an important point near the desert–sahel edge where the goods of the Sahara and North Africa were exchanged for the products of West Africa.

In the late tenth century Songhai's rulers embraced **Islam**, the first royals in sub-Saharan West Africa known to have done so. As was true of most medieval West African polities whose leaders adopted the new religion, the bulk of the people continued to practice their previous religious traditions. When Mali was in its prime Gao was forced to accept Mali suzerainty. With Mali's precipitous decline in the fifteenth century, however, Songhai regained its full independence and emerged as the dominant West African empire of the fifteenth and sixteenth centuries and the largest of the entire medieval period. Under the leadership of **Sonni Ali** (r. 1464–1492) of the Sonni dynasty Songhai transformed itself from a state to an empire. In 1468, Sonni Ali took Timbuktu from the Berbers who had wrested it from a fading Mali in 1433. Expanding control further southwest along the Niger, he conquered Jenné in 1473.

Under the ruler **Askiya Muhammad** (r. 1493–1528), who seized power from Sonni Ali's successor and founded the Askiya dynasty, Songhai reached its greatest heights. The empire stretched all the way from the Senegal River in the west to Agades far beyond the Niger in the east, cementing its control of virtually the entire West African end of trans-Saharan trade. Songhai also reached deep into the Sahara, controlling salt-producing Taghaza located far into the desert's northwest, as well as dipping south well into the grasslands beyond **Jenné-jeno**, which gave it control of West Africa's gold routes. Its achievements did not last long, however. In the late sixteenth century, Songhai faced the twin problems of ineffectual rulers and succession disputes so common in West African polities with their flexible rules of succession, which culminated in civil war.

These internal woes coincided with formidable external pressures. First, a change in the manner of exporting West Africa's most valuable commodity, gold, followed the fifteenth-century arrival along the West African coastline of the Portuguese, who created an alternative demand for the precious metal to the south of the goldfields, redirecting some 50 percent of its export away from trans-Saharan channels to Atlantic shipping routes with a predictably negative effect on Songhai's economy. Then came the daring Moroccan invasion of 1591, in which the Sultan Ahmad al-Mansur sent a crack unit of his army south across the Sahara to wrest from Songhai control of the salt mines at Taghaza and the gold trade of West Africa. His soldiers succeeded militarily, defeating the Songhai at the town of Tondibi outside Gao and gaining control, tenuous though it proved, of the lands along the Niger Bend including the important cities of Gao and Timbuktu. The combination of these challenges proved too much for the already weakened Songhai Empire to withstand, and it splintered into a number of smaller states, bringing to a close the era of large West African empires while ushering in the postmedieval rise of smaller sudanic and sahelian states and the heyday of more southerly kingdoms.

Further Reading

Bovill, Edward William. *The Golden Trade of the Moors: West African Kingdoms in the Fourteenth Century*. Oxford, UK: Oxford University Press, 1958.

Hunwick, John O., ed. and trans. *Timbuktu and the Songhay Empire: Al-Sa'dis Ta'rikh al-sudan down to 1613 and other Contemporary Documents*. Leiden, The Netherlands: Brill, 1999.

Sonni Ali (d. 1492)

Sonni Ali (r. 1464–1492), the next-to-last leader of **Songhai**'s Sonni dynasty, is renowned for transforming Songhai from a state into a mighty West African empire expanding outward from its home in the lands lying just southeast of the Niger Bend. Under his leadership, using a formidable cavalry as well as the skills of the Sorko fishermen who readily turned their boating aptitude to military exploits and their fishing boats to war canoes, Songhai captured the critically important city of **Timbuktu** in 1468 and **Jenné-jeno** in 1473, neutralizing the threats posed by the Tuareg of the Sahara and the Mossi who lived south of the Niger Bend and cementing Songhai's ascendancy over a rapidly waning **Mali**.

Although highly successfully militarily, Sonni Ali made bitter enemies of many of the influential Muslim scholars and merchants of Timbuktu and other urban areas, who deeply resented the rough treatment some Muslims received during the conquest of Timbuktu and campaigns against the Tuareg, and viewed him as an upstart of questionably sincere Muslim identity who thereby lacked legitimacy to rule. Many of these scholars moved from Timbuktu to Walata to avoid what they saw as Sonni Ali's persecution, and in their histories he is scathingly denounced. In fact, in keeping with the longstanding practice of the rulers of many medieval West African states, to retain legitimacy Sonni Ali practiced elements of Islam and older, local religious traditions to please not only the economically important Muslim merchants, but also the religious expectations of the overwhelmingly non-Muslim commoners he led, and he had little choice but to do so if he wished to retain the support of the masses. This reality, however, was not persuasive to the scholars of Timbuktu. Sonni Ali is said to have drowned in the Niger in 1492. *See also* **Islam**.

Further Reading

Bovill, Edward William. *The Golden Trade of the Moors: West African Kingdoms in the Fourteenth Century*. Oxford, UK: Oxford University Press, 1958.

Hunwick, John O., ed. and trans. *Timbuktu and the Songhay Empire: Al-Sa'dis Ta'rikh al-sudan down to 1613 and other Contemporary Documents*. Leiden, The Netherlands: Brill, 1999.

Sundjata (c. 1205–c. 1255)

The founder of the great medieval empire of **Mali**, Sundjata (alternately Sundiata) was a son of Nare Maghan, chief of the Keita clan of the Malinke, one of the Mande-speaking peoples of West Africa, and his second wife Sogolon. His life history and exploits, chronicled in the Epic of Sundjata, have been passed down through the centuries by the griots, or oral historians, of Mali, and consequently the events surrounding the emergence of Mali are still well known today. According to these bards, Sundjata, born around 1205, was a backward child, subject to ridicule, who didn't walk for years. But because it had been foretold that he would succeed his father, the ambitious first wife of Nare Maghan harried Sundjata, his mother Sogolon, and his full siblings into exile after the king's death so that her own son, Sundjata's half brother Dankaran Tuma, could inherit the kingship.

In exile, Sundjata grew to maturity, great wisdom, and military prowess. He returned, united the disparate Malinke clans into a single Malinke nation, and, thus fortified, in a series of epic and supernaturally charged encounters with their chief Sumanguru that culminated in the Battle of Kirina in 1235, vanquished the Soso (also Sosso or Susu) who had defeated the Malinke some years earlier and subjected them to very heavy payments of tribute. The depiction in the griots' oral tradition of the battle between Sundjata and Sumanguru is often understood today as an allegorical representation of the clash between **Islam** and indigenous religious beliefs, which was in fact occurring in West Africa around the time of Sundjata's life (*see* **African Traditional Religions**). Both of the protagonists display the magical powers that are central to indigenous religious traditions, yet Sundjata also embodies the "good" Muslim ruler battling the dark powers of Sumanguru, the "evil," non-Muslim, sorcerer king.

Given the need for Mali's rulers to appeal to Islamized urbanites and the overwhelmingly non-Muslim rural dwellers of their empire, it is not surprising that Sundjata, the culture hero of the Malinke, embodies both traditions. It is unlikely that Sundjata himself ever adopted Islam, but kings of Mali succeeding him certainly did, and this is foreshadowed by the Epic of Sundjata. After triumphing over the Soso, Sundjata led a series of successful battles against a wide range of peoples of West Africa, defeating them and demanding annual tribute and recognition of Malinke overrule, resulting in the creation of the vast and mighty empire of Mali. He also founded the Malian capital of Niani on the Sankarani River, a tributary of the upper Niger. Sundjata ruled his empire for some twenty years, dying around 1255 A.D.

Further Reading

Austen, Ralph, ed. *In Search of Sunjata: The Mande Oral Epic as History, Literature and Performance*. Bloomington: Indiana University Press, 1999.

Johnson, John William, Fa-Digi Sisòkò, and Charles S. Bird. *The Epic of Son-Jara: A West African Tradition*. Bloomington: Indiana University Press, 1992.

Niane, D.T. *Sundiata: An Epic of Old Mali*. 2nd ed. London: Longman, 2006.

Swahili

The Swahili, who were in their heyday from approximately 1200 to 1500, arose along the east coast of Africa during the final centuries of the first millennium C.E. and created a string of wealthy towns and cities on the 1,000-mile-long stretch of coastline lying between Mogadishu in the north and northern Mozambique in the south. Their bustling municipalities studded with multistory houses built of coral stone, the larger with populations of up fifteen-thousand people, had harbors filled with visiting dhows from ports around the Indian Ocean as well as the Swahili sewn boats known as *mtepe*. Easily visible from the sea because they were located right along the coastline and on off-shore islands such as Kilwa, Pemba, Pate, Lamu, Zanzibar, and the more distant Comoros, these Swahili cities astounded the Portuguese who, in 1498, encountered the East African seaboard after rounding the Cape of Good Hope.

Since then the Swahili have often been portrayed as deriving their wealth solely from their role as intermediaries in Indian Ocean commerce, trading the goods of the African interior such as **gold**, which they received from Zimbabwe to their southwest to merchants from across the sea. This activity certainly produced an important component of their wealth, as the Swahili exported not only gold but ivory, slaves, rhinoceros horn, leopard skins, tortoiseshell, rock crystal, cloves, mangrove poles, and other commodities to markets in Arabia, Persia, India, Indonesia, China, and the Mediterranean world in return for silks, cottons, and foodstuffs, Chinese porcelain, pottery from the lands around the Persian Gulf, glass beads, and other goods in the vast Indian Ocean trading system that linked East Africa with these far-flung parts of the globe. But in reality the Swahili had a multifaceted economy in which agriculture, fishing, raising **domesticated animals**, maritime trade north and south along the coastline as well as land-based trade west into the interior through which were exchanged goods of the different East African **ecological zones**, and productive activities such as cloth making, iron- and copper-working, bead-making, masonry, woodworking, and boat-building also played prominent roles.

Their cities did indeed contain the architecturally impressive and innovative coral-stone houses for which they are renowned, which provided wealthy Swahili merchants and their families a high degree of material comfort given these buildings' indoor toilets, running water, rooftop terraces, and attention to aesthetically pleasing detail including beautifully carved wooden doors and lintels, decorative plasterwork, and niches in the interior walls of their rooms that allowed for the display of imported Chinese porcelain and copies of the Qur'an. However, archaeological research also indicates that the wood, mud, and thatch homes housing those of lesser wealth and social standing constituted the majority of buildings. In terms of ethnicity, though the Swahili were for centuries erroneously misidentified by outsiders as members of an Arab culture imported from overseas and appended to the very edge of the African continent, today it is recognized that their origins lie predominantly in the African populations of Bantu speakers who peopled the East African coast from early in the Common Era, though immigrants from Arabia did come, settle, and intermarry, most notably contributing to Swahili culture their religion of **Islam** and its traditions of literacy and scholarship, while lesser numbers of immigrants from Indonesia, Persia, and India added additional elements to the emerging culture (*see* **Bantu Expansions**).

The predominantly African origins of the Swahili are reflected not only in this history of settlement but also in their language: The grammar or basic framework of Swahili is Bantu, as is the majority of its vocabulary. The mainly Arab (and secondarily Persian and Hindi) loan-words incorporated into the Swahili language, which so struck early European visitors to the Swahili coastline, are for the most part modern accretions dating from the eighteenth century on, many hundreds of years after the emergence of Swahili culture. Never unified into one Swahili state, the various Swahili cities operated as politically independent units, generally under the rule of a head of state variously referred to as king or sultan (and occasionally queen), though in at least one instance a Swahili city lay under the collective governance of a group of prominent trading families.

Sometimes a more powerful city such as **Kilwa** would exert some control over neighboring towns or shorelines, but this typically proved a temporary state of affairs. The lack of political unity, in concert with the limited military experience of the Swahili who most often competed with one another through trade rather than fighting, contributed to their vulnerability to the heavily armed Portuguese who arrived as the medieval era drew to a close and, backed by the authority of their ship-mounted cannons which they did not hesitate to use in naval bombardments of the Swahili cities, exerted their power over this coastline in the early years of the sixteenth century.

The Swahili cities were already in a decline when the Portuguese arrived, due to a variety of factors including a downturn in the flow of gold from the interior. The Portuguese overrule of sections of the coast was followed by an eighteenth- and nineteenth-century Omani imperialism, with the result that the Swahili never again existed as independent polities though their culture continues to the present. *See also* Documents 8 and 11.

Further Reading

Horton, Mark, and John Middleton. *The Swahili: The Social Landscape of a Mercantile Society*. Oxford, UK: Blackwell Publishers, 2000.

Nurse, Derek, and Thomas Spear. *The Swahili: Reconstructing the History and Language of an African Society, 800–1500*. Philadelphia: University of Pennsylvania Press, 1985.

Pouwells, Randall. *Horn and Crescent: Cultural Change and Traditional Islam on the East African Coast, 800–1900*. Cambridge, UK: Cambridge University Press, 1987.

Takrur

Takrur, one of the earliest West African states to appear in the historical record, was given brief mention in the writings of North African Arabs from the eleventh century. How long it had existed prior to that time is unknown, but certainly it was a part of the tradition of West African state formation that dates back to around the beginning of the Common Era and resulted from the surplus wealth generated by a combination of agriculture, ironworking, herding, fishing, and regional as well as long-distance trade. From its location along the middle and lower Senegal River Takrur was involved in trans-Saharan commerce, exporting gold from the Bambuk goldfields as well as slaves and cotton cloth north along a westerly Saharan trade route that ran from Takrur through **Sijilmasa** to Morocco.

Takrur is most often mentioned for its very early embrace of **Islam**; its king War Jabi, who ruled until 1040 to 1041, adopted the religion during his reign.

In striking contrast to most medieval West African states, in Takrur rural commoners as well as urban elites took up the new religion. A rival of the larger, more powerful, and better documented empire of **Ghana** that lay to its east and that came to control the export of Bambuk gold, in the eleventh century Takrur sided with the Almoravids who were also Muslim rivals of Ghana and flourished as that other empire faded away. Takrur was then incorporated into the vast empire of **Mali**, which rose as Ghana fell (*see* **Almoravid and Almohad Movements**). With Mali's decline, Takrur split into a number of Wolof polities as well as the kingdoms of Futa Toro and Futa Jalon.

Further Reading
Bovill, Edward William. *The Golden Trade of the Moors: West African Kingdoms in the Fourteenth Century*. Oxford, UK: Oxford University Press, 1958.
Levtzion, Nehemiah. *Ancient Ghana and Mali*. London: Methuen and Co. Ltd., 1973.

Timbuktu

Timbuktu, located above the Niger Bend—the northernmost point of the Niger River—in what is today **Mali**, was an extremely important medieval West African city situated where the southern Sahara met the sahel. From the fourteenth century, when it displaced Walata, Timbuktu played a key role in trans-Saharan trade as the most critical transshipment point where goods passed between the control of the desert **Berbers** and the peoples of the savannah. From there gold and a host of other exports were sent north across the Sahara, while salt and many other goods were shipped south down the Niger River as far as **Jenné-jeno** and were then dispersed throughout West Africa.

Founded by Tuareg Berbers early in the second millennium C.E., control of Timbuktu passed into the hands of the great West African empire of Mali in the mid-1300s, though in concert with Mali's decline power reverted to the Berbers in 1433, only to be lost in 1468 to the rising power of **Songhai** as the medieval years drew to a close. The city continued to serve its central role in trans-Saharan trade under all of these authorities. Timbuktu also played a preeminent role in the intellectual life of **Islam** in West Africa, an identity which began to take shape following the 1324–1325 *hajj*, or religious pilgrimage to Mecca, of the Malian ruler **Mansa Musa**, who came back from that journey a devoted patron of Islamic architecture, arts, and scholarship. He underwrote the construction of a new mosque, the Jingere-Ber or Great Mosque, and encouraged Islamic studies, forging intellectual linkages with Muslims in the Maghrib and **Egypt**. Some of these seeds sown by Mansa Musa came to full fruition after his lifetime: the Sankoré Mosque, and its famous Sankoré University whose renown reached far beyond West Africa, date to the late fourteenth century, and Timbuktu reached its greatest heights as a center of Islamic learning in the sixteenth century. *See also* Document 12.

Further Reading
Hunwick, John O., ed. and trans. *Timbuktu and the Songhay Empire: Al-Sa'dis Ta'rikh al-sudan down to 1613 and other Contemporary Documents*. Leiden, The Netherlands: Brill, 1999.
Hunwick, John O. *West Africa, Islam and the Arab World: Studies in Honor of Basil Davidson*. Princeton, NJ: Markus Wiener, 2007.
Saad, Elias N. *Social History of Timbuktu: The Role of Muslim Notables and Scholars 1400–1900*. Cambridge, UK: Cambridge University Press, 1983.

Great Mosque at Timbuktu. It is the oldest mosque south of the Sahara. Constructed of round dried mud-bricks and stone rubble with clay rendering, the foundation of the mosque, in 1325, is attributed to Mansa Musa, king of Mali. Mali-Songhay periods, 14th C.E. Werner Forman/Art Resource.

Warfare

Warfare in medieval Africa was practiced quite differently depending on whether the combatants came from smaller, often lineage-based stateless societies without centralized governments or larger states with hierarchical political structures and identified political leaders. In either case, warfare typically involved hand-to-hand combat using a variety of weapons including knives, spears, and swords. Ehret pointed out that in Central Africa, a dreaded multi-bladed throwing knife was used in the late medieval centuries until the horrors of this weapon led to its banishment by one Central African state in the seventeenth century in an early example of disarmament.

Combatants were usually trained in the techniques of hand-to-hand combat, and in defensive measures, which aimed to minimize the risk of injury when engaged in this type of fighting. In stateless societies the conflicts tended to be fought by people for whom military service was at most an occasional activity and whose wars were typically of very short duration, whereas conflict between states utilized professional soldiers and military leaders whose wars could last for years. Wars of conquest were waged commonly by expansionist medieval states seeking to force neighboring peoples into vassal and tribute-paying statuses. Indeed, some would argue that the lesser frequency and intensity of warfare in stateless societies was one of a number of examples of their benefits relative to states with centralized governance.

Relatively few parts of the continent utilized cavalry, because horses were (and remain) ill suited to the many parts of Africa where the sleeping sickness-transmitting tsetse fly caused rapid equine death. Even in the West African savannah where **Songhai** and the **Hausa** states were using them relatively frequently by the later medieval centuries, the horses tended to be lighter than the ideal cavalry mount making it difficult to outfit them with the body armor that best prolonged their lives in warfare, though some states such as Songhai did utilize such protections. Cavalry allowed some later medieval West African states to more easily enslave neighboring peoples, with Kanem and the Hausa being prime examples of this use of military might (*see* **Kanem-Bornu**).

In stateless societies outstanding success as a warrior conferred heightened status on individual men, whereas some powerful states such as Bornu rewarded particularly proficient military leaders with grants of land. In societies that organized men into age grades, found mainly in East Africa, members of the age grade of young adults served as the designated warriors of their societies—in a pattern still familiar to human societies of the twenty-first century, typically fighting the wars decided upon by the age grade of elders who monopolized political decision making in their societies.

Further Reading
Ehret, Christopher. *The Civilizations of Africa: A History to 1800*. Charlottesville: University Press of Virginia, 2002.

Women

Although it is possible to make generalizations about women in medieval Africa, it is simultaneously an imperative to recognize that the position and status of women, as well as the meanings attached to biological sex, have always varied over space and time: Gendered conditions could and did diverge markedly from place to place, as well as in any one place at different points in time. They also differed depending on a host of social identities other than gender. For example, ethnicity, religion, age, socioeconomic status, family and kinship identities, free or unfree status, and a multitude of other factors likewise influenced any one individual's standing and situation, and intersected with gender in significant ways. Therefore, it is vitally important to recognize the immense value of specificity when talking about gender and women.

Nonetheless, some general points regarding medieval African women can be made. In regards to political authority, it is clear that some African women wielded marked political power in a number of medieval African societies, indeed to a much greater extent than African women have been able to achieve in the most recent hundred years: Medieval African history contains numerous examples of politically powerful women. The institution of queen mother, a woman's political office, existed among the **Yoruba** and was created just postmedievally in **Benin**, whereas in the **Luba** kingdom women fulfilled critically important functions as royal spirit mediums and ambassadors. On the **Swahili** coast and among the Yoruba, women as well as men served as local rulers, whereas in Bornu high-ranking women of the royal family held significant political offices (*see* **Kanem-Bornu**). That numerous female rulers who appeared to be part of the normal order of things rather than anomalies were documented in the late 1400s and 1500s by Europeans visiting Africa is compelling evidence that women were extremely likely to have held such roles medievally also.

Scholars of gender in Africa have also considered the informal mechanisms which, often operating through marriage and lineage ties, allowed women to wield very considerable if indirect influence over affairs of state even in places, which excluded women from formal political positions. For example, the epic of **Sundjata** shows the key roles played in his success by this founder of **Mali**'s mother and sisters, as well as the overt political power wielded by his father's senior wife. Medieval African women played important religious roles too, including spirit medium, healer, and priestess. Even in Muslim and Christian areas where religious authority in these monotheistic traditions was vested in men, the religious syncretism typical of African **Islam** and **Christianity** allowed for the continued practice of numerous aspects of **African traditional religions**, with the result that women still held considerable religiously based authority. This is demonstrated, to give just one example, in medieval women's involvement in spirit possession cults in many Muslim parts of the continent.

In the realm of the economy and work, medieval women played key agricultural roles; they were the main producers of farmed foodstuffs and also saw to their storage and preparation (as they still do today), tasks also requiring them to gather firewood and water for their households, often from considerably distant locations. The gendered division of labor in farming gave men in most African societies responsibility for clearing land, and women responsibility for planting, weeding, and harvesting, activities that were in toto considerably more time-demanding than men's agricultural duties. In foraging societies the dietary contributions women made through their gathering contributed the majority of calories to everyone's daily diet, far eclipsing the share deriving from the meat provided by male hunters. Among herders, women typically bore responsibility for milking cattle and churning butter.

Craft production was gendered too, with female potters and male metalworkers; weaving and dying cloth were the purview of women in some societies and men in others. It has been speculated that some of the great medieval African artwork that has been preserved to the present, the terra-cotta and clay sculptures produced by many different societies, which have generally been presumed by Western art historians of the last century to have been the artistically valued achievements of men, may well have been made by women given their longstanding dominance in working clay. This dominance may have given women a role in the production of some of the most renowned medieval metal sculptures too, because many were produced using the lost-wax method, which requires an original clay mold. Another artistic medium, which women have dominated postmedievally, which may well have been practiced by them in earlier centuries too, is tattooing and other forms of body art.

In regards to children and the creation of the next generation, women were highly valued for their reproductive as well as productive abilities, a fact recognized—to women's detriment—in a general medieval (and modern) African preference for female slaves, who were valued for precisely these capacities.

This emphasis on women's reproductive capabilities could lead to loss of status and personal hardship and sorrow for medieval women who could not or did not bear children, however. Although all of these examples of women's key contributions and agency can be found in the medieval African historical record, it is also clear that medieval African women could be marginalized in certain spheres at certain times in certain places. One example lies in the fact that though women could and did play vitally important political roles, the historical record also indicates that they far less frequently served as heads of state and governmental officials than did men.

It was very likely the case that men typically held significantly greater authority in marriages and families too, though again many individual exceptions doubtless existed. As is often the case in explorations of gender, though women lived with the impediment of a number of socially institutionalized disenfranchisements, individually and collectively medieval African women clearly sought and often achieved ways to assert their authority and realize desired outcomes. *See also* **Agriculture**, **Education**, and **Food**.

Further Reading

Kent, Susan. *Gender in African Prehistory*. Lanham, MD: AltaMira Press, 1998.

Schoenbrun, David. "Gendered Themes in Early African History," in *A Companion to Gender History*. Edited by Teresa A. Meade and Merry E. Wiesner-Hanks. Oxford, UK: Blackwell Publishing, 2004.

Sheldon, Kathleen. "Writing About Women: Approaches to a Gendered Perspective in African History," in *Writing African History*. Edited by John Edward Philips. Rochester, NY: University of Rochester Press, 2005.

Yoruba

Some time in the first millennium C.E., the Yoruba arose in what is today southwestern Nigeria, in the savannah and forest lands that lie to the west of the lower Niger River. Their story of origin relates the appearance from heaven of Oduduwa, who founded the town of Ife (also known as Ile-Ife), which dates to the late first millennium and became the spiritual center of the Yoruba people. In the early centuries of the second millennium the Yoruba radiated out from Ife and established a number of independent city-states, the most important of which were said to be founded by the children and grandchildren of Oduduwa, the founding ancestor.

From early on the Yoruba were an urban people, residing in cities, often walled, which had a palace and a marketplace at the core surrounded by private homes. Each city-state was ruled by an *oni* or king who wielded his power from the centrally located palace, which was nestled in a series of walls, which served to separate the ruler spatially and psychologically from those he ruled. The so-called Pavement Period of Ife, which has been the site of numerous archaeological digs, has revealed their practice, in the first half of the second millennium C.E., of paving areas such as courtyards with mosaics constructed from broken pieces of potsherds and white stones. Agriculture, a key activity of Yoruba men, took place in the farms, which surrounded a given city and were located outside its walls. **Women**, who expected to earn their own incomes, which they kept separate from those of their husbands, dominated local market trading. Craft production of goods such as metal wares, textiles, and woodcarvings formed another important sector of the economy, and the

Yoruba were involved in systems of commerce that stretched north to locations such as Hausaland and **Songhai** in the savannah, and from there connected to Saharan and trans-Saharan trade, as well as south to the coast and east and west within the forest zone (*see* **Hausa**).

Among other achievements, the Yoruba are renowned for a medieval tradition of stunningly graceful artistry in the form of cast metal sculptures worked in brass and copper. The best known of these are a series of human heads that radiate a calm beauty and serene composure and are thought to depict the ideal *oni* or king. An extensive corpus of skillfully and beautifully worked terracotta statuary forms another part of their sophisticated and elegant artistry.

Further Reading

Drewal, Henry John, et al. *Yoruba: Nine Centuries of African Art and Thought.* New York: Center for African Art in association with Henry N. Abrams, Inc., 1989.
Johnson, Rev. Samuel. *The History of the Yorubas from the Earliest Times to the Beginning of the British Protectorate.* London: George Routledge and Sons, 1921.
Willett, Frank. *Ife in the History of West African Sculpture.* London: Thames and Hudson, Ltd., 1967.

Zimbabwe Plateau

The Zimbabwe Plateau, which lies between the Limpopo and Zambezi rivers in southeastern Africa and is located mainly in the modern state of Zimbabwe, was home to a series of medieval polities noted for their construction of striking stone-walled enclosures, the most magnificent of which were built at Great Zimbabwe. Although these stone structures are noteworthy intrinsically given the mastery of dry stone masonry they illustrate and the immense and awe-inspiring design of the largest examples of this tradition, their deeper significance lies in the light they shed on social and political processes occurring on the Plateau in the first half of the second millennium C.E.

Immediately before the medieval age began, from the earliest centuries of the Common Era, the Zimbabwe Plateau was peopled by individuals practicing the agriculture, herding, and craft production typical of Africa's Iron Age. Cattle keeping rose to great prominence here, not only because the Plateau provided extensive grazing lands but because its elevation placed it outside of the range of the trypanosomiasis-transmitting tsetse fly so devastating to livestock and people at lower altitudes. Interregional trade of significant scope and distance also grew to play a role in the local economy, as individuals exchanged the products of one ecological zone for another. For example, the deposits of **gold** and copper ore that lay on the Plateau were both exploited, while its elephant herds supplied ivory.

Added to these activities, and significantly increasing the wealth accruing to emerging elites from farming, herding, and regional trade, was growing involvement as a supplier of ivory and gold to the vast Indian Ocean trading network in which the Swahili of the East African coast, located to the Plateau's northeast, played a prominent role. As a result of all of these sources of wealth, the Zimbabwe Plateau witnessed increased social stratification, urbanization, and centralization of political authority from around 1000. Mapungubwe, located just to the south of the Limpopo River and occupied in the eleventh to midthirteenth centuries, was the first of the Zimbabwe polities to demonstrate these changes. This state constructed stone-walled structures that appear to have enclosed the living quarters of social and probably political elites, attested to by the presence at their burial sites of luxury goods including a gold-plated wooden carving of a rhinoceros, glass beads, and finely worked gold and copper objects.

Succeeding Mapungubwe was the greatest of these polities, Zimbabwe, headquartered at the archaeological site known as Great Zimbabwe, where the traditions of dry stone masonry using blocks of local granite reached their greatest heights with the construction of the Great Enclosure, Valley Complex, and Hill Complex. The scale and technological artistry of this monumental architecture—the massive walls of the Great Enclosure reach heights of 30 feet and the sophistication of the stonework increased markedly over time—bespeaks the ability of Zimbabwe's rulers to mobilize labor and resources to construct monuments that, lacking defensive fortifications as they did, appear to have existed mainly as an expression of the power and strength of these political elites. Although archaeological research has until recently focused on these more spectacular architectural elements of Zimbabwe Plateau societies, there is growing recognition of the need to consider also the more humble homes of commoners, constructed of a very hard clay known as daga.

When one takes these into account, for example, estimates of the population of Great Zimbabwe alone climb markedly, to a population of perhaps eighteen thousand inhabitants at its peak. After its monumental structures were built in the thirteenth and fourteenth centuries, Zimbabwe went into a decline in the first half of the fifteenth century and was largely abandoned by the midfifteenth century, probably due to environmental degradation resulting from an overexploitation of local sources of timber as well as grazing and agricultural lands, and changes in long-distance trade routes that did not work to its advantage. The economic linkages between Zimbabwe and Indian Ocean trade are attested to not only by finds at Great Zimbabwe of Chinese porcelain, Persian faience, more than fifty-thousand glass beads, and a coin minted at the prominent **Swahili** city of **Kilwa**, all imported from the coast; they are also illustrated by the fact that Kilwa, which received the lion's share of the ivory and gold exported by Zimbabwe (the latter of which was mined in the lands lying to Zimbabwe's north and west) before exporting it across the Indian Ocean, rose in tandem with Zimbabwe in the early fourteenth century and declined in tandem with it in the early decades of the 1400s.

The sociopolitical developments occurring in the Zimbabwe Plateau that Mapungubwe and Zimbabwe embodied survived these states and found expression in Zimbabwe's immediate successors of Torwa and Mutapa (also known as Munhumutapa). Torwa though not Mutapa also continued and even further developed the Zimbabwean architectural traditions of stone-built settlements. Indeed, these traditions extended far beyond the Zimbabwe Plateau: To date over one-hundred-fifty sites demonstrating dry stone wall architecture have been located not only on the Plateau but in the neighboring Transvaal region of today's South Africa, as well as in Mozambique and eastern Botswana.

Further Reading

Beach, D.N. *The Shona and Zimbabwe, 900–1850: An Outline of Shona History*. New York: Holmes and Meier Publishers, 1980.

Pikirayi, Innocent. *The Zimbabwe Culture: Origins and Decline of Southern Zambezian States*. Lanham, MD: AltaMira Press, 2001.

Primary Documents

1. Indian Ocean Trade (first century C.E.)

This account of Indian Ocean trade, which dates from very early in the Common Era, shows the deep historical roots of this intercontinental network, which, in the medieval centuries, linked Africa, the Middle East, India, and points as far east as the ports of southern China. This commercial network utilized not only the Indian Ocean, but also the Red Sea and the Persian Gulf, both of which fed into it. This selection was written by a Greek-speaking mariner from Egypt, most likely Alexandria. The portion excerpted here describes the East African coast from around Mogadishu to Mozambique, here called Azania, and the towns involved in Indian Ocean trade that dotted its shoreline.

Beyond Tabæ, after four hundred stadia, there is the village of Pano. And then, after sailing four hundred stadia along a promontory, toward which place the current also draws you, there is another market-town called Opone, into which the same things are imported as those already mentioned, and in it the greatest quantity of cinnamon is produced, (the *arebo* and *moto*), and slaves of the better sort, which are brought to Egypt in increasing numbers; and a great quantity of tortoiseshell, better than that found elsewhere. The voyage to all these far-side [beyond the Red Sea, into the Indian Ocean proper] market-towns is made from Egypt about the month of July, that is Epiphi. And ships are also customarily fitted out from the places across this sea, from Ariaca and Barygaza [Red Sea ports], bringing to these far-side market-towns the products of their own places; wheat, rice, clarified butter, sesame oil, cotton cloth . . . and girdles, and honey from the reed called *sacchari*. Some make the voyage especially to these market-towns, and others exchange their cargoes while sailing along the coast. This country is not subject to a King, but each market-town is ruled by its separate chief. Beyond Opone, the shore trending more toward the south, first there are the small and great bluffs of Azania; this coast is destitute of harbors, but there are places where ships can lie at anchor, the shore being abrupt; and this course is of six days, the direction being southwest. Then come the small and great beach for another six days' course and after that in order, the Courses of Azania, the first being called Sarapion and the next Nicon; and after that several rivers and other anchorages, one after the other, separately a rest and a run for each day, seven in all, until the Pyralaæ islands and what is called the channel; beyond which, a little to the south of south-west, after two courses of a day and night along the Ausanitic coast, is the island Menuthias, about three hundred stadia from the mainland, low and wooded, in which there are rivers and many kinds of birds and the mountain-tortoise. There are no wild beasts except the crocodiles; but there they do not attack men. In this place there are sewed boats, and canoes hollowed from single logs, which they use for fishing and catching tortoise. In this island they also catch them in a peculiar way, in wicker baskets, which they fasten across the channel-opening between the breakers. Two days' sail beyond, there lies the very last market-town of the continent of Azania, which is called Rhapta; which has its name from the sewed boats (*rhaptôn ploiariôn*) already mentioned; in which there is ivory in great quantity, and tortoise-shell. Along this coast live men of piratical habits, very great in stature, and under separate chiefs for each place. The Mapharitic chief governs it under some ancient right that subjects it to the sovereignty of the state that is become first in Arabia. And the people of Muza now hold it under his authority, and send thither many large ships; using Arab captains and agents, who are familiar with the natives and intermarry with them, and who know the whole coast and understand the language. There are imported into these markets the lances made at Muza especially for this trade, and hatchets and daggers and awls, and various kinds of glass; and at some places a little wine, and wheat, not for trade, but to serve for getting the good-will of the savages. There are exported from these places a great quantity of ivory, but inferior to that of Adulis [a great port city on the Red Sea's African coast], and rhinoceros-horn and tortoise-shell (which is in best demand after that from India), and a little palm-oil. And these markets of Azania are the very last of the continent.

Source: Schoff, Wilfred H., trans. *The Periplus of the Erythræan Sea: Travel and Trade in the Indian Ocean by a Merchant of the First Century.* New York: Longmans, Green, and Co., 1912, 27–29.

2. An Account of Trade with the Etiopian Kingdom of Aksum, 525

Cosmos Indicopleustes, believed to have been a Greek born in Alexandria who first worked as a merchant and later in life became a monk, journeyed to Aksum in what is today Ethiopia in 525. He has left us a record of the trade—including the export of frankincense, in demand in the Mediterranean world for its use in burials—which flowed in and out of this powerful state through Adulis, its port on the Red Sea.

From Byzantium, again, to Alexandria there are fifty stages, and from Alexandria to the Cataracts [of the Nile] thirty stages; from the Cataracts to Axômis [Aksum], thirty stages; from Axômis to the projecting part of Ethiopia, which is the frankincense country called Barbaria, lying along the ocean, and not near but at a great distance from the land of Sasu which is the remotest part of Ethiopia, fifty stages more or less. . . . The region which produces frankincense is situated at the projecting parts of Ethiopia, and lies inland, but is washed by the ocean on the other side. Hence the inhabitants of Barbaria, being near at hand, go up into the interior and, engaging in traffic with the natives, bring back from them many kinds of spices, frankincense, cassia, calamus, and many other articles of merchandise, which they afterwards send by sea to Adulê [Adulis], to the country of the Homerites [in Arabia], to Further India, and to Persia. This very fact you will find mentioned in the Book of Kings, where it is recorded that the Queen of Sheba [Saba, in the southwestern Arabian Peninsula], that is, of the Homerite country, whom afterwards our Lord in the Gospels calls the Queen of the South, brought to Solomon spices from this very Barbaria, which lay near Sheba on the other side of the sea [Red Sea], together with bars of ebony, and apes and gold from Ethiopia which, though separated from Sheba by the Arabian Gulf [Red Sea], lay in its vicinity. . . . For the Homerites are not far distant from Barbaria, as the sea which lies between them can be crossed in a couple of days . . . The country known as that of Sasu is itself near the ocean, just as the ocean is near the frankincense country, in which there are many gold mines. The King of the Axômites accordingly, every other year, through the governor of Agau [another Ethiopian people], sends thither special agents to bargain for the gold, and these are accompanied by many other traders—upwards, say, of five hundred—bound on the same errand as themselves. They take along with them to the mining district oxen, lumps of salt, and iron, and when they reach its neighbourhood they make a halt at a certain spot and form an encampment, which they fence round with a great hedge of thorns. Within this they live, and having slaughtered the oxen, cut them in pieces, and lay the pieces of the top of the thorns, along with the lumps of salt and the iron. Then come the natives bringing gold in nuggets like peas, called *tancharas*, and lay one or two or more of these upon what pleases them—the pieces of flesh or the salt or the iron, and then they retire to some distance off. Then the owner of the meat approaches, and if he is satisfied he takes the gold away, and upon seeing this its owner comes and takes the flesh or the salt or the iron. If, however, he is not satisfied, he leaves the gold, when the native seeing that he has not taken it, comes and either puts down more gold, or takes up what he had laid down, and goes away. Such is the mode in which business is transacted with the people of that country, because their language is different and interpreters are hardly to be found. The time they stay in that country is five days more or less, according as the natives more or less readily coming forward buy up all their wares. On the journey homeward they all agree to travel well-armed, since some of the tribes through whose country they must pass might threaten to attack them from a desire to rob them of their gold. The space of six months is taken up with this trading expedition, including both the going and the returning. In going they march very slowly, chiefly because of the cattle, but in returning they quicken their pace lest on the way they should be overtaken by winter and its rains. For the sources of the river Nile lie somewhere in these parts, and in winter, on account of the heavy rains, the numerous rivers which they generate obstruct the path of the traveller.

Source: McCrindle, J.W., trans. and ed. *The Christian Topography of Cosmas, an Egyptian Monk.* London: Hakluyt Society, 1897, 50–53.

3. A Letter Illustrating Relations Between Muslim Egypt and Christian Nubia, 759

After Arab Muslims conquered Egypt between 639 and 642, they attempted to spread their power southward into the Christian states of Nubia, which lay further into the African interior along the Middle Nile. However, the Muslims met their match in the famed archers of Nubia, who repelled them in battle in 641 and 652. In consequence, Nubia retained its independence and its Christianity for many centuries to come, although not without occasional disagreements with its northern neighbor, as this 759 "Letter from the Governor of Egypt to the King of the United Kingdom of Makouria and Nobatia" illustrates. The letter refers to the *baqt*, or pact, which was made between Nubia and Egypt following Nubia's seventh-century victories, an agreement that recognized Nubian sovereignty and set the terms for peaceful relations between the two states.

God, blessed and exalted is he, says in His book "Fulfill the compact of God when you make a compact, and do not break the oath after it has been affirmed and you have made God your guarantor . . . " We have fulfilled for you that which we took upon ourselves for you in turning away from your blood and your property and you know your security in our land and your dwelling wherever you wish in it and the repairing of your merchants to us; no oppression or harm comes to them from us; no one of you who is among us is attacked by us nor is he denied his right; no obstacle is placed between your merchants and what they want—they are safe and contented wherever they go in our land, this being in fulfillment of our compact, in truth to our word. . . . You, however, in that which lies between us, behave otherwise. You do not bring to us that to which you are liable according to the *baqt* on the basis of which agreement was made with you; nor do you return those of our slaves who run away to you; nor are our merchants safe among you; nor do you hasten to permit our messengers to return to us. You know that the people of all religions and the persuasions which neither know a lord, nor believe in a resurrection, nor hope for recompense, nor fear punishment, even these do not attack a merchant or detain a messenger. You make manifest to the people of your persuasion belief in Him who created the heavens and the earth and what is between them, you believe in Jesus the son of Mary and his book, and you make manifest to them justice and the doing of what is right, while what you do in that which is between you and us is contrary to that which you make manifest. One of the merchants of the people of our country, Sa'd by name, came to you with much wealth, having made off with it from its owners, and you detained him among you, stood between him and the one who rightly pursued him . . . Secondly, a man of the people of Aswan, named Muhammad b. Zayd, sent to you a merchant of his, on his business and seeking rights for him. You detained him and the wealth that he had with him. . . . So look into that about which I have written to you and hasten the dispatching to us of your remaining liability according to the *baqt* for the years for which you owe . . . send to us the merchant of Muhammad b. Zayd and the wealth which was with him . . . and send to us Sa'd the merchant who is among you and be not tardy in that in any respect if you wish us to fulfill for you our compact and to continue as we did in dealing correctly with you.

Source: Burstein, Stanley, ed. *Ancient African Civilizations: Kush and Axum.* Princeton, NJ: Markus Wiener Publishers, 1998, 128–131.

4. A Muslim Account of Ghana, 1067–1068

The following excerpts are from Al-Bakri's mid-eleventh-century account of the West African empire of Ghana. He gives obvious precedence to the question of Islamicization, which was dear to the heart of this Spanish-born Muslim, but also provides insight into the physical geography of Ghana's capital city. The city of Ghana had a quarter for Muslim visitors to this sub-Saharan polity whose people had not yet widely adopted Islam but which conducted vitally important commerce with Muslim merchants from North Africa. Al-Bakri also speaks to Ghana's indigenous religious practices and trade.

The city of Ghana consists of two towns in a plain. One of these towns is inhabited by Muslims. It is large with a dozen mosques in one of which they assemble for the Friday prayer. . . . Around the town are wells of sweet water from which they drink and near which they cultivate vegetables. The royal town, called al-Ghaba ["the grove"], is six miles away [from the Muslim town], and the area between the two towns is covered with houses. Their houses are made of stone and accacia wood. The king has a palace and conical huts, surrounded by a wall-like enclosure. In the king's town, not far from the royal court of justice, is a mosque where pray the Muslims who come there on missions. . . . Around the king's town are domed huts and groves where live the sorcerers, the men in charge of their religious cult. In these are also the idols and the tombs of their kings. These groves are guarded, no one can enter them nor discover their contents. The prisons of the king are there, and if anyone is imprisoned in them, no more is ever heard of him. . . . Their religion is paganism and the worship of idols. When the king dies, they build a huge dome of wood over the burial place. Then they bring him on a bed lightly covered, and put him inside the dome. At his side they place his ornaments, his arms and the vessels from which he used to eat and drink, filled with food and beverages. They bring in those men who used to serve his food and drink. Then they close the door of the dome and cover it with mats and other materials. People gather and pile earth over it until it becomes like a large mound. Then they dig a ditch around it so that it can be reached only from one place. They sacrifice to their dead and make offerings of intoxicating drinks. . . . The best gold in the country [of the king of Ghana] comes from the town of Ghiyaru, eighteen days traveling from the king's town . . . Gharantal [on this route] is a large territory and an important kingdom. Muslims do not live there, but the people treat them with respect, and come out to meet them, when they enter the country. . . . The town of Ghiyaru is twelve miles distant from the Nile [Niger], and there are many Muslims. . . . West of Ghiyaru on the Nile [Niger] the town of Yaresna is inhabited by Muslims, but is surrounded by pagans. . . . From Yaresna Sudanese, known as Banu Naghmartah, trade in gold to [all] countries.

Source: Levtzion, Nehemiah. *Ancient Ghana and Mali.* New York: Africana Publishing Company, 1980, 22–26, 187.

On every donkey-load of salt when it is brought into the country their king levies one golden dinar, and two dinars when it is sent out. From a load of copper the king's due is five mithqals, and from a load of other goods ten mithqals. . . . The nuggets found in all the mines of his country are reserved for the king, only this gold dust being left for the people. But for this the people would accumulate gold until it lost its value.

Source: Levtzion, N., and J.F.P. Hopkins, eds. *Corpus of Early Arabic Sources for West African History.* Cambridge, UK: Cambridge University Press, 1981, 81.

The king of Ghana can put two hundred thousand warriors in the field, more than forty thousand being armed with bow and arrow. . . . When he gives audience to his people . . . he sits in a pavilion. . . . on his right hand are the sons of the princes of his empire, splendidly clad and with gold plaited into their hair. . . . The gate of the chamber is guarded by dogs of an excellent breed, who never leave the king's seat: they wear collars of gold and silver.

Source: Davidson, Basil. "Al Bekri: Ghana in 1067," in *The African Past: Chronicles from Antiquity to Modern Times.* Boston: Little, Brown and Company, 1964, 72.

5. Accounts of the Saharan City of Sijilmasa (tenth-twelfth centuries)

Sijilmasa, located at an oasis in the northwestern Sahara, played a key role in trans-Saharan trade as the northern entrepôt to which camel caravans came and went as they made the desert crossing. The three selections below speak to various elements of this important medieval city, including commerce, wealth, agriculture, and international diplomacy. These accounts, written in the order in which they appear below, are by Ibn Hawqal (based on his travels to the Maghrib in 947–951), al-Bakri (who penned his history in the eleventh century), and al-Maqqari (quoting al-Sarakhsi, who met individuals from Sijilmasa when he was in Marrakech between 1197 and 1203).

Ibn Hawqal

. . . there is at Sijilmasa an uninterrupted trade with the land of the Sudan and other countries, abundant profits, and the constant coming and going of caravans. . . . I saw at Awdaghust a warrant which was the statement of a debt owed to one of them [the people of Sijilmasa] by one of the merchants of Awdaghust, who was [himself] one of the people of Sijilmasa, in the sum of 42,000 dinars. I have never seen or heard anything comparable to this story in the East. . . . Mu'tazz, during the period of his emirate there, continuously received revenue from taxes on caravans setting out . . . as well as tithes, land tax, and old-established dues from what was bought and sold there . . . to a total of about 400,000 dinars and this from Sijilmasa and its district alone.

Al-Bakri

The town of Sijilmasa is situated on a plain the soil of which is salty. Around the town are numerous suburbs with lofty mansions and other splendid buildings. There are also many gardens. The cathedral mosque of the town is strongly built. . . . The water in the town is brackish as it is in all the wells of Sijilmasa. The cultivated land is irrigated with water from the river collected in basins like those used for watering gardens. There are many date-palms, grapes, and all sorts of fruit. The grapes grown on trellises which the sun does not reach do not turn into raisins except in the shade, and for this reason they are known as *zilli* "shady", but those which the sun does reach become raisins in the sun.

Al-Maqqari

These are some of his [the Governor of Sijilmasa's] words in a letter of reply to the king of the Sudan in Ghana, complaining to him of the detention of some traders: "We are neighbors in benevolence even if we differ in religion;

we agree on right conduct and are one in leniency towards our subjects. It goes without saying that justice is an essential quality of kings . . . tyranny is the preoccupation of ignorant and evil minds. We have heard about the imprisonment of poor traders and their being prevented from going freely about their business. The coming to and fro of merchants to a country is of benefit to its inhabitants and a help to keeping it populous. If we wished we would imprison the people of that region who happen to be in our territory but we do not think it right to do that. We ought not to 'forbid immorality while practicing it ourselves'. Peace be upon you."

Source: Levtzion, N., and J.F.P. Hopkins, eds. *Corpus of Early Arabic Sources for West African History.* Cambridge, UK: Cambridge University Press, 1981, 47–48, 64–65, 372.

6. The *Kebra Negast:* An Account of the Origins of the Christian Kings of Ethiopia (c. thirteenth-fourteenth centuries)

Ethiopia's Christian Solomonid dynasty legitimized its rule in part through its assertion that its rulers were descended from King Solomon and the Queen of Sheba. This story is told in the *Kebra Negast* or "Book of the Glory of Kings," which also relates how Ethiopians became God's chosen people who gained possession of the Ark of the Covenant, and Ethiopia was anointed the new Zion.

And the Queen [of Sheba] said . . . "I desire wisdom and my heart seeketh to find understanding" . . . by the Will of God, her heart desired to go to JERUSALEM so that she might hear the wisdom of SOLOMON . . . And seven hundred and ninety-seven camels were loaded, and mules and asses innumerable were loaded, and she set out on her journey . . . And she arrived in JERUSALEM . . . And King SOLOMON answered and said unto her, "Wisdom and understanding spring from thee thyself. As for me, [I only possess them] in the measure in which the God of ISRAEL hath given [them] to me because I asked and entreated them from Him. And thou, although thou dost not know the God of ISRAEL, hast this wisdom which thou hast made to grow in thine heart, and [it hath made thee come] to see me, the vassal and slave of my God" . . . And the Queen [said] . . . "From being a fool, I have become wise by following thy wisdom, and from being a thing rejected by the God of ISRAEL, I have become a chosen woman because of this faith which is in my heart; and henceforth I will worship no other god except Him." . . . the King rose up and he went to the Queen, and he said unto her . . . "Take thou thine ease here for love's sake until daybreak." . . . he worked his will with her and they slept together. And after he slept there appeared unto King SOLOMON [in a dream] a brilliant sun, and it came down from heaven and shed exceedingly great splendour over ISRAEL. And when it had tarried there for a time it suddenly withdrew itself, and it flew away to the country of ETHIOPIA, and it shone there with exceedingly great brightness for ever, for it willed to dwell there. And [the King said], "I waited [to see] if it would come back to ISRAEL, but it did not return." . . . And the Queen departed and . . . nine months and five days after she had separated from King SOLOMON. . . . the pains of childbirth laid hold upon her, and she brought forth a man child . . . And when he was two and twenty years old . . . he said unto the Queen, "I will go and look upon the face of my father, and I will come back here by the Will of God" . . . And then SOLOMON the King . . . said . . . "Come, let us make him king of the country of ETHIOPIA" . . . And they made ready the ointment of the oil of kingship . . . And they brought the young man into the Holy of Holies, and he laid hold upon the horns of the altar, and sovereignty was given unto him . . . And behold, the Angel of the Lord appeared . . . and said . . . "Stand up, be strong . . . and take the pieces of wood and I will open for thee the doors of the sanctuary. And take thou the Tabernacle of the Law of God" . . . and it was taken away by them forthwith, in the twinkling of an eye, the Angel of the Lord being present and directing. And had it not been that God willed it ZION could not have been taken away.

Source: Budge, E.A. Wallis, trans. *The Queen of Sheba and Her Only Son Menyelek* (I), 2nd ed. London: Oxford University Press, 1932, 21, 23, 25–26, 32, 33, 35, 37–39, 51, 53, 71–72.

7. Mansa Musa's Pilgrimage to Mecca, 1324

Mansa Musa, king of the great medieval empire of Mali, which controlled the flow of West African gold to North Africa and points beyond, made the long and arduous journey from his capital in the West African Sudan to Mecca, located near Arabia's Red Sea shore, in 1324. For Mansa Musa, the trip fulfilled one of the Five Pillars of Islam, the *hajj* or religious pilgrimage. On the way, Mansa Musa stopped in Cairo, where his fabulous wealth and lavish spending made a lasting impression on that great city's citizens (and its gold exchange). The following selection was written by Al-Umari, who was in Cairo a dozen years later and recorded impressions of Mansa Musa's visit.

The Emir . . . spoke of the sultan's noble appearance, dignity and trustworthiness. "When I went out to greet him in the name of the glorious Sultan [of Egypt]," he told me, "he gave me the warmest of welcomes and treated me with the most careful politeness. But he would talk to me only through an interpreter . . . although he could speak perfect Arabic. He carried his imperial treasure in many pieces of gold, worked or otherwise. I suggested that he should go up to the palace and meet the Sultan. But he refused, saying: 'I came for the pilgrimage, and for nothing else . . . ' He argued about this. However, I well understood that the meeting was repugnant to him because he was loath to kiss the ground [before the Sultan] or to kiss his hand. I went on insisting, and he went on making excuses. But imperial protocol obliged me to present him, and I did not leave him until he had agreed. When he came into the Sultan's presence we asked him to kiss the ground. But he refused and continued to refuse, saying, 'However can this be?' Then a wise man of his suite whispered several words to him that I could not understand. 'Very well,' he thereupon declared, 'I will prostrate myself before Allah who created me and brought me into the world.' Having done so, he moved towards the Sultan. The latter rose for a moment to welcome him and asked him to sit beside him: then they had a long conversation. After Sultan Musa had left the palace the Sultan of Cairo sent him gifts . . . This man [Mansa Musa] . . . spread upon Cairo the flood of his generosity: there was no person, officer of the [Cairo] court or holder of any office of the [Cairo] sultanate who did not receive a sum in gold from him. The people of Cairo earned incalculable sums from him whether by buying and selling or by gifts. So much gold was current in Cairo that it ruined the value of money." Let me add [continues Omari] that gold in Egypt had enjoyed a high rate of exchange up to the moment of their arrival. The gold *mitqal* that year had not fallen below twenty-five drachmas. But from that day [of their arrival] onward, its value dwindled; the exchange was ruined, and even now it has not recovered. The *mitqal* scarcely touches twenty-two drachmas. That is how it has been for twelve years from that time, because of the great amounts of gold they brought to Egypt and spent there.

Source: Davidson, Basil. "Al Omari: Mali in the Fourteenth Century," in *The African Past: Chronicles from Antiquity to Modern Times*. Boston: Little, Brown and Company, 1964, 75–77.

8. Ibn Battuta's Description of East Africa's Swahili Coast, 1331

Ibn Battuta, a world traveler, journeyed to Mogadishu, Mombasa, and Kilwa along the East African shoreline in 1331. Among other things, the sub-Saharan African tradition of hospitality to strangers—including those with whom one may conduct business—is evidenced in these passages. Given his familiarity with many of the great cities of his day, Ibn Battuta's praiseworthy description of Kilwa deserves particular notice.

From there we sailed fifteen nights and arrived at Mogadishu, which is a very large town . . . The merchants are wealthy . . . Among the customs of the people of this town is the following: when a ship comes into port, it is boarded from *sanbuqs*, that is to say, little boats. Each *sanbuq* carries a crowd of young men, each carrying a covered dish, containing food. Each one of them presents his dish to a merchant on board, and calls out: "This man is my guest." And his fellows do the same. Not one of the merchants disembarks except to go to the house of his host among the young men, save frequent visitors to the country. In such a case they go where they like. When a merchant has settled in his host's house, the latter sells for him what he has brought and makes his purchases for him. Buying anything from a merchant below its market price or selling him anything except in his host's presence is disapproved of by the people of Mogadishu. They find if of advantage to keep to this rule. . . . The food of these people is rice cooked with butter, served on a large wooden dish. With it they serve side-dishes, stews of chicken, meat, fish, and vegetables. They cook unripe bananas in fresh milk, and serve them as a sauce. They put curdled milk in another vessel with peppercorns, vinegar, and saffron, green ginger and mangoes, which look like apples but have a nut inside. Ripe mangoes are very sweet and are eaten like fruit; but unripe mangoes are as acid as lemons, and are cooked in vinegar. When the Mogadishu people have taken a mouthful of rice, they take some of these pickles. . . . Then I set off by sea . . . for the land of the Swahili. . . . We arrived at Mombasa, a large island two days' journey from the land of the Swahili. The island is quite separate from the mainland. It grows bananas, lemons, and oranges. . . . The people . . . follow the Shafi'i rite, and are devout, chaste, and virtuous. Their mosques are very strongly constructed of wood. Beside the door of each mosque are one or two wells . . . Anyone who wishes to enter the mosque first washes his feet; beside the door is a piece of heavy material for drying them. Anyone who wishes to perform the ritual ablutions, takes the vessel between his thighs, pours water on his hands, and so makes his ablutions. Everyone here goes barefoot. We spent a night on the island and then set sail for Kilwa, the principal town on the coast, the greater part of whose inhabitants are Zanj of very black complexion . . . A merchant told me that Sofala is half a month's march from Kilwa, and that between Sofala and Yufi in the country of the Limiim is a month's march. Powdered gold is brought from Yufi to Sofala. Kilwa is one of the most beautiful and well-constructed towns in the world. The whole of it is elegantly built. The roofs are built with mangrove poles.

Source: Freeman-Grenville, G.S.P. *The East African Coast: Select Documents from the first to the earlier nineteenth century.* Oxford, UK: Clarendon Press, 1962, 27–31.

9. Ibn Battuta's Descriptions of Mali, 1352–1353

These descriptions of Mali come from the widely traveled Ibn Battuta, who journeyed across the Sahara to the West African Sudan in the mid-fourteenth century. Clearly his descriptions are colored by the assumptions and values he brought with him as a North African Muslim visiting a Mali whose rulers were Islamized yet practiced a mix of Muslim and indigenous religious and social traditions, and whose citizens had, for the most part, not embraced the new faith.

The sultan has a raised cupola which is entered from inside his house. He sits in it a great part of the time. It has on the audience side a chamber with three wooden arches, the woodwork is covered with sheets of beaten silver and beneath these, three more covered with beaten gold . . . When the sultan has sat down three of his slaves go out quickly to call his deputy . . . The *farari-yya* [commanders] arrive, and they are the *amirs* [officers], and among them are the preacher and the men of *fiqh* [jurisprudence], who sit in front of the armed men on the right and left of the place of audience. The interpreter Dugha stands at the door of the audience chamber wearing splendid robes . . . On his head is a turban which has fringes, they have a superb way of tying a turban. He is girt with a sword whose sheath is of gold . . . In his hands there are two small spears, one of gold and one of silver with points of iron. The soldiers, the district governors, the pages and the Massufa and others are seated outside the place of audience in a broad street which has trees in it. Each *farari* [commander] has his followers before him with their spears, bows, drums and bugles made of elephant tusks. Their instruments of music are made of reeds and calabashes, and they beat them with sticks and produce a wonderful sound . . . Inside the audience chamber under the arches a man is standing; he who wants to speak to the sultan speaks to Dugha, Dugha speaks to the man who is standing, and he speaks to the sultan.

The blacks are the most humble of men before their king and the most extreme in their self-abasement before him. . . . When he calls one of them while he is in session in his cupola . . . the man invited takes off his clothes and wears patched clothes, takes off his turban, puts on a dirty cap, and goes in raising his clothes and trousers up his legs half-way to his knees. He advances with humility looking like a beggar. He hits the ground with his elbows, he hits it hard. He stands bowed . . . When one of them speaks to the sultan and he gives him an answer, he removes his clothes from his back and throws dust on his head and back, as a person does when bathing with water. . . . If the sultan says to him that he has spoken the truth or thanks him, he takes off his clothes and dusts. This is good manners among them.

Source: Hamdun, Said, and Noel King. *Ibn Battuta in Black Africa*. Princeton, NJ: Markus Wiener Publishers, 1994, 46–50.

Sometimes the sultan holds meetings in the place where he has his audiences. There is a dais in that place, situated under a tree, with three big steps called *penpi*. The dais is covered with silk and embellished with cushions, and above it is placed a parasol that looks like a silken dome. On the top of the parasol is a golden bird as big as a sparrow hawk. . . . On his head he wears a gold hat that is held in place by a band, also of gold . . . Most often he is dressed in a red velvet tunic . . . The singers come out in front of the sultan . . . Behind him are about 300 armed slaves. The sovereign walks patiently, advancing very slowly. . . . As soon as the sultan is seated, drums are beaten, a horn is sounded, and trumpets blare.

What I Found to Be Praiseworthy About the Conduct of the Negroes in Contrast to What I Found to Be Bad.

Among the good qualities of this people, we must cite the following:

1. The small number of acts of injustice that take place there [in Mali], for of all people, the Negroes abhor it the most. . . .
2. The general and complete security that is enjoyed in the country. The traveler, just as the sedentary man, has nothing to fear of brigands, thieves, or plunderers.
3. The blacks do not confiscate the goods of white men who die in their country, even when these men possess immense treasures. On the contrary, the blacks deposit the goods with a man respected among the whites, until the individuals to whom the goods rightfully belong present themselves and take possession of them.

Some of the actions of these people are:

1. The female servants and slaves, as well as little girls, appear before men completely naked. . . .
2. All the women who come into the sovereign's house are nude and wear no veils over their faces; the sultan's daughters also go naked. . . .

The Copper Mine

The copper mine is situated outside Takedda. Slaves of both sexes dig into the soil and take the ore to the city to smelt it in the houses. As soon as the red copper has been obtained it is made into bars one and one-half handspans long—some thin, some thick. Four hundred of the thick bars equal a ducat of gold; six or seven hundred of the thin bars are also worth a ducat of gold. These bars serve as a means of exchange, in place of coin. With the thin bars, meat and firewood are bought; with the thick bars, male and female slaves, millet, butter, and wheat can be bought. The copper of Takedda is exported to the city Couber [Gobir], situated in the land of the pagan Negroes. Copper is also exported to Zaghai [Dyakha—western Masina] and to the land of Bernon [Bornu], which is forty days distant from Takedda and is inhabited by Muslims . . . Beautiful slaves, eunuchs, and cloth dyed with saffron are brought from Bernon to many different countries.

Source: Collins, Robert O. *Western African History.* New York: Markus Wiener Publishing, 1990, 22–23.

10. Jews in the Sahara and Sudan (fifteenth–sixteenth centuries)

By the later medieval centuries, Jews had moved south from communities in North Africa, first into Saharan oases and eventually into some sub-Saharan cities, including Timbuktu. As the excerpt from Antoine Malfante's letter written in 1447 indicates, relations between Muslims and Jews were amicable in the Saharan community of Tuat in the midfifteenth century. John Hunwick's book, however, tells how, around 1490, at the behest of Muhammad al-Maghili, a Muslim from North Africa, the Jews of Tuat became the targets of a successful campaign to eliminate their community—though it is vital to note that al-Mahili had to search far and wide to find Islamic scholars who sanctioned this act. Al-Maghili also journeyed further south, beyond the desert, where he persuaded the king of Songhai to purge Jews from his lands, resulting in the attitudes and decrees the traveler Leo Africanus found extant in the early sixteenth century.

There are many Jews, who lead a good life here [Tuat], for they are under the protection of the several rulers, each of whom defends his own clients. Thus they enjoy very secure social standing. Trade is in their hands, and many of them are to be trusted with the greatest confidence. . . . In the lands of the blacks [however], as well as here, dwell the Philistines [Tuareg Berbers] . . . They are sworn enemies of the Jews, who do not dare to pass hither.

Source: Crone, G.R., trans. and ed. "The Letter of Antoine Malfante," in *The Voyages of Cadamosto and Other Documents on Western Africa in the Second Half of the Fifteenth Century.* London: Hakluyt Society, 1932, 86, 87.

This is an epistle from the servant of God Most High, Muhammad . . . al-Maghili . . . to every Muslim man and woman . . . One of the goodly folk asked me about the obligation for Muslims to steer clear of unbelievers, and about the necessity for 'protected persons' to pay *jizya* [a tax levied on Jews and Christians] and to receive humiliation and abasement . . . I say—and God it is whose help is sought, and upon whom dependence is placed: . . . The essence is that one brings no unbeliever close to himself or his relatives, nor employs him for jobs of his, and puts any money of his in his hands, unless one has no religion, no intelligence, and no manly virtue. . . . God—Exalted is He— said: "O you who believe, do not take Jews and Christians as friends. They are friends one to another. Whoever among you befriends them is indeed one of them. God does not guide wrongdoing people [Qur'an, 5:51]. . . . He who is

Exalted also said: "You see many of them befriending those who disbelieve. Surely ill for them is what they send on before themselves, that God's wrath will be upon them, and in doom shall they abide." . . . On this topic I [al-Maghili] uttered these [poetry] verses:

In love for the Prophet, hatred of the Jews is necessary;
Have regret for what has passed. Don't repeat it.
Whoso befriends the enemies of the Prophet,
How will it be for you in the grave,
And resurrection into the flaming Fire?
Who will plead on behalf of him if [the Fire] comes close
To the face of him who gave satisfaction to the Jews?

. . . it is obligatory for every believer to procure hatred for all unbelievers of our Prophet—our lord, our beloved one and intercessor—and to call to mind the greatness of their demands on us, and their challenge against us over our religion. Surely every unbeliever is a friend of the cursed Demon, the obvious enemy. . . . God—Exalted is He—said: "Fight those who do not believe in God . . . until they pay tribute readily, being brought low" [Qur'an, 9:29]. . . . As for humiliation, the occurrence is that they adhere to depravity and humility in their talk and actions and all their conditions, so that by that they will be taken over by every Muslim—male or female, free or slave.

Source: Hunwick, John. *Jews of a Saharan Oasis: Elimination of the Tamantit Community.* Princeton, NJ: Markus Wiener Publishers, 2006, 14–15, 19, 22–23, 24, 26.

He [the king of Songhai] so deadly hateth all Iewes [Jews], that he will not admit any into his citie: and whatsoeuer Barbarie merchants he understandeth haue any dealings with the Iewes, he presently causeth their goods to be confiscate.

Source: Leo Africanus. *The History and Description of Africa and of the Notable Things Therein Contained.* Edited by Robert Brown. Translated by John Pory. Vol. III. London: Hakluyt Society, 1896, 825.

11. A European Description of the East African Coast, 1500–1518

Duarte Barbosa traveled to East Africa more than once in the first two decades of the sixteenth century. He gives detailed eyewitness accounts of a number of Swahili cities as they appeared in the earliest years of contact with the Portuguese. Note his use of the term *Moors* to denote Muslims.

Sofala

Having passed the Little Vciques . . . there is a river . . . whereon is a town of the Moors called Sofala . . . These Moors established themselves there a long time ago on account of the great trade in gold which they carry on with the Gentiles of the mainland: these speak somewhat of bad Arabic (garabia), and have got a king over them . . . And the mode of their trade is that they come by sea in small barks which they call zanbucs (sambuk), from the kingdoms of Quiloa, and Mombaza, and Melindi; and they bring much cotton cloth of many colours, and white and blue, and some of silk; and grey, and red, and yellow beads, which come to the said kingdoms in other larger ships from the great kingdom of Cambay [in India], which merchandise these Moors buy and collect from other Moors who bring them there, and they pay for them in gold by weight, and for a price which satisfied them; and the said Moors keep them and sell these cloths to the Gentiles of the kingdom of Benematapa [Mutapa, also known as Munhumutapa, located in the East African interior] who come there laden with gold, which gold they give in exchange for the before mentioned cloths without weighing, and so much in quantity that these Moors usually gain one hundred for one. They also collect a large quantity of ivory, which is found all round Sofala, which they likewise sell in the great kingdom of Cambay at five or six ducats the hundred weight, and so also some amber, which these Moors of Sofala bring them from the Vciques. They are black men, and men of colour — some speak Arabic, and the rest make use of the language of the Gentiles of the country. They wrap themselves from the waist downwards with cloths of cotton and silk, and they wear other silk cloths above named, such as cloaks and wraps for the head, and some of them wear hoods of scarlet, and of other coloured woollen stuffs and camelets, and of other silks. And their victuals are millet, and rice, and meat, and fish. In this river near to the sea there are many sea horses, which go in the sea, and come out on land at times to feed. These have teeth like small elephants, and it is better ivory than that of the elephant, and whiter and harder, and of greater durability of colour. In the country all round Sofala there are many elephants, which are very large and wild, and the people of the country do not know how to tame them: there are also many lions, ounces, mountain panthers, wild asses, and many other animals. It is a country of plains and mountains, and well watered.

Island of Quiloa [Kilwa]

After passing this place and going towards India, there is another island close to the mainland, called Quiloa, in which there is a town of the Moors, built of handsome houses of stone and lime, and very lofty, with their windows like those of the Christians; in the same way it has streets, and these houses have got their terraces, and the wood worked in with the masonry, with plenty of gardens, in which there are many fruit trees and much water. This island has got a king over it, and from hence there is trade with Sofala with ships, which carry much gold, which is dispersed thence through all Arabia Felix, for henceforward all this country is thus named on accounts of the shore of the sea being peopled with many towns and cities of the Moors; and when the King of Portugal discovered this land, the Moors of Sofala, and Zuama, and Anguox, and Mozambique, were all under obedience to the King of Quiloa, who was a great king amongst them. And there is much gold in this town, because all the ships which go to Sofala touch at this island, both in going and coming back. These people are Moors, of a dusky colour, and some of them are black and some white; they are very well dressed with rich cloths of gold, and silk, and cotton, and the women also go very well dressed out with much gold and silver in chains and bracelets on their arms, and legs, and ears.

Island of Mombaza [Mombasa]

Passing Quiloa, and going along the coast of the said Arabia Felix towards India, close to the mainland there is another island, in which there is a city of the Moors, called Bombaza [Mombasa], very large and beautiful, and built of high and handsome houses of stone and whitewash, and with very good streets, in the manner of those of Quiloa. And it also has a king over it. The people are of dusky white, and brown complexions, and likewise the women, who are much adorned with silk and gold stuffs. It is a town of great trade in goods, and has a good port, where there are always many ships, both of those that sail for Sofala and those that come from Cambay and Melinde, and others which sail to the islands of Zanzibar, Manfia, and Penda . . . This Monbaza is a country well supplied with plenty of provisions, very fine sheep, which have round tails, and many cows, chickens, and very large goats, much rice and millet, and plenty of oranges, sweet and bitter, and lemons, cedrats, pome-granates, Indian figs, and all sorts of vegetables, and very good water.

Melinde

After passing the city of Mombaza, at no great distance further on along the coast, there is a very handsome town on the mainland on the beach, called Melinde, and it is a town of the Moors, which has a king. And this town has fine houses of stone and whitewash, of several stories, with their windows and terraces, and good streets. The inhabitants are dusky and black, and go naked from the waist upwards, and from that downwards they cover them-selves with cloths of cotton and silk, and others wear wraps like cloaks, and handsome caps on their heads. The trade is great which they carry on in cloth, gold, ivory, copper, quicksilver, and much other merchandise, with both Moors and Gentiles of the kingdom of Cambay, who come to their port with ships laden with cloth, which they buy in exchange for gold, ivory, and wax. Both parties find great profit in this.

Source: Stanley, Henry E.J., trans. *A Description of the Coasts of East Africa and Malabar in the Beginning of the Sixteenth Century by Duarte Barbosa, A Portuguese.* London: Hakluyt Society, 1866, 4–6, 10–13.

12. A Description of Timbuktu in the Early 1500s

Leo Africanus's description of Timbuktu in the era of Songhai reveals the wealth and sophistication of this city, which for centuries played such an important role in trans-Saharan trade and was a center of Islamic schol-arship. It also notes the linkages between this sub-Saharan city, North Africa, and Europe. (Note the reversal of the letters "u" and "v" in this translation produced in 1600.)

Howbeit there is a most stately temple to be seene, the wals whereof are made of stone and lime; and a princely palace also built by a most excellent workeman of Granada [Spain]. Here are many shops of artificers, and mer-chants, and especially of such as weaue linen and cotton cloth. And hither do the Barbarie-merchants bring cloth of Europe. All the women of this region except maid-servants go with their faces couered, and sell all necessarie vict-uals. The inhabitants, & especially strangers there residing, are exceeding rich, insomuch, that the king that now is, married both his daughters unto two rich merchants. Here are many wells, containing most sweete water; and so often as the riuer Niger ouerfloweth, they conueigh [convey] the water thereof by certaine sluces into the towne. Corne, cattle, milke, and butter this region yeel-deth in great abundance: but salt is verie scarce here; for it is brought hither by land from Tegaza, which is fiue hundred miles distant. When I my selfe was here, I saw one camels loade of salt sold for 80 ducates. The rich king of Tom-buto [Timbucktu] hath many plates and scepters of gold, some whereof weigh 1300 poundes: and he keepes a magnificent and well furnished court. When he trauelleth any whither he rideth vpon a camel, which is lead by some of his noblemen; and so he doth likewise when hee goeth to warfar, and all his souldiers ride vpon horses. Whosoeuer will speake vnto this king must first fall downe before his feets, & then taking vp earth must sprinkle it vpon his owne head & shoulders: which custom is ordinarily obserued by them that neuer saluted the king before, or comes as ambassadors from other princes. He hath always three thousand horsemen, and a great number of footmen that shoot poisoned arrows, attending vpon him. They haue often skirmishes with those that refuse to pay tribute, and so many as they take, they sell vnto the merchants of Tombuto. Here are verie few horses bred, and the merchants and courtiers keepe certaine little nags which they vse to trauell vpon: but their best horses are brought out of Barbarie. And the king so soone as he heareth that any merchants are come to towne with horses, he commandeth a certaine number to be brought before him, and chusing the best horse for himselfe, he payeth a most liberall price for him. . . . Here are great store of doctors, iudges [judges], preists, and other learned men, that are bountifully maintained at the kings cost and charges. And hither are brought diuers [diverse] manuscripts or written bookes out of Barbarie, which are sold for more money than any other merchandize. The coine of Tombuto is of gold without any stampe or superscription: but in matters of small value they vse certaine shells brought hither out of the kindome of Persia, fower hundred of which shells are worth a ducate: and six peeces of their golden coine with the third parts weigh an ounce. The inhabitants are people of a gentle and cheerful disposition, and spend a great part of the night in singing and dancing through all the streets of the citie: they keep great store of men and women-slaues [slaves], and their towne is much in danger of fire: at my second being there halfe the town al-most was burnt in fiue howers space. Without the suburbs there are no gar-dens nor orchards at all.

Source: Leo Africanus. *The History and Description of Africa and of the Notable Things Therein Contained.* Vol. III. Edited by Robert Brown. Translated by John Pory. London: Hakluyt Society, 1896, 824–826.

Appendix: Dynasties of Medieval Africa

Rulers of Mali

Sundjata (Mari Djata) (c. 1235–1255)
Uli
Wati
Khalifa
Abu Bakr
Sakura (c. 1300)
Qu
Muhammad (?–1312)
Mansa Musa (1312–1337)
Magha (1337–1341)
Sulayman (1341–1360)
Qasa (1360)
Mari Djata II (1360–1373/4)
Musa II (1373/4–1387/8)
Magha II (1387/8)
Sandaki (1388/9–1390)
Mahmud (1390–?)

Sources: Adu Boahen, with Jacob F. Ade Ajayi and Michael Tidy. *Topics in West African History.* Harlow, UK: Longman Group, 1986, pp. 27–32; Nehemiah Levtzion. *Ancient Ghana and Mali.* New York: Africana Publishing Company, 1973, p. 71; Mark R. Lipschultz and R. Kent Rasmussen. *Dictionary of African Historical Biography.* 2nd ed. Berkeley: University of California Press, 1986, p. 134.

Rulers of Songhai

Sonni Ali (1464–1492)
Sonni Baru (1492–1493)
Askiya Muhammad (1493–1528)
Musa (1528–1531)
Muhammad Bankan (1531–1537)
Ismail (1537–1539)
Ishaq I (1539–1549)
Daud (1549–1582)
Muhammad II (1582–1586)
Muhammad Bani (1586–1588)

Ishaq II (1588–1591)
Muhammad Gao (1591–1592)

Sources: Adu Boahen with Jacob F. Ade Ajayi and Michael Tidy. *Topics in West African History.* Harlow, UK: Longman Group, 1986, pp. 36–42; Mark R. Lipschultz and R. Kent Rasmussen. *Dictionary of African Historical Biography.* 2nd ed. Berkeley: University of California Press, 1986, pp. 222–223.

Rulers of the Solomonid Dynasty of Ethiopia

Yekuno Amlak (1270–1285)
Salomon I (1285–1294)
Bahr Asgad, Senfa Asgad, Hezba (1294–1299)
Ared, Kedma Asgad, Zhin Asgad (ca. 1296–ca. 1299)
Wedem Ared (1299–1314)
Amda Seyon I (1314–1344)
Newaya Krestos (1344–1372)
Newaya Maryam (1372–1382)
Dauti (David) I (1382–1413)
Tewodros (Theodore) I (1413–1414)
Yeskaq (1414–1429)
Endreyas, Takla Maryam, Sarwa (1429–1434)
Iyasus, Amda Iyasus (1433–1434)
Zara Yaqob (1434–1468)
Baeda Maryam (1468–1478)
Eskender (1478–1494)
Amda Seyon II (1494)
Naod (1494–1508)
Lebna Dengel (Dauti II) (1508–1540)
Galawdewos (Claudius) (1540–1559)
Minas (1559–1563)
Sarsa Dengel (1563–1597)
Yaqob (I) (1597–1603)
Za Dengel (1603–1604)
Yaqob (2) (1604–1607)

Susneyos (1607–1632)
Fasiladas (1632–1667)
Yohannes I (1667–1682)
Iyasu I (1682–1706)
Takla Haymanot (1706–1708)
Tewoflos (1708–1711)
Yostos (1711–1716)
Dauti III (1716–1721)
Bakaffa (Asma Giorgis) (1721–1730)
Iyasu II (with Menetewab as regent)
(1730–1755)
Iyoas I (1755–1769)

"Era of the Princes" (1769–1855)
Tewodros (Theodore) II (1855–1868)
Takla Giorgis II (1868–1872)
Yohannes (John) IV (1872–1889)
Menelik II (1889–1913)
Iyasu V (Lij Iyasu) (1914–1916)
Zauditu (1916–1930)
Haile Selassie (1930–1974)

Source: Mark R. Lipschultz and R. Kent Rasmussen. *Dictionary of African Historical Biography.* 2nd ed. Berkeley: University of California Press, 1986, p. 65.

NORTH AFRICA AND THE MIDDLE EAST

James E. Lindsay

Chronology

c. 570   Muhammad is born in the Arabian city of Mecca

c. 610–622   Muhammad is called to prophethood and begins preaching in Mecca

622   Muhammad makes his *Hijra* (*Hegira*, meaning "Migration") from Mecca to Medina; the Hijra marks the official beginning of the religion of Islam and this year counts as year 1 of the Muslim calendar

628–632   Islam is consolidated and expands within Arabia

632   Death of the prophet Muhammad; Abu Bakr is proclaimed the first Muslim caliph

638   Muslims conquer Jerusalem

650s   Compilation of the Qur'an (Koran), the holy scripture of Islam

661   Assassination of 'Ali ibn Abi Talib, the cousin and son-in-law of Muhammad and fourth and last Rashidun caliph (r. 656–661); Mu'awiya ibn Abi Sufyan (r. 661–680) established the Umayyad dynasty: this dispute eventually splits the Islamic community into Sunni and Shia branches, with Shia Muslims considering Ali and his descendents as rightful heirs of Muhammad

661–750   Umayyad caliphate is based in Damascus

680   Martyrdom of Husayn at Karbala; Husayn becomes the model of protest and suffering for Shia Muslims down to the present day

690s   Muslims conquer Byzantine North Africa

691   Completion of the Dome of the Rock in Jerusalem; the venerated mosque is built on the site of the original Jewish temple

705–715   Construction of the Umayyad Mosque in Damascus

711   Muslims conquer most of the Iberian Peninsula, thus establishing a strong presence in Europe

732   Muslim expansion into western Europe is halted by the Frankish leader Charles Martel at the Battle of Tours

744–750   Third civil war in the Islamic world results in the defeat of the Umayyads by the Abbasids

750–1258   Long rule of the Abbasid caliphate marks the golden age of Islamic civilization

762   Baghdad is founded and becomes the capital of the Abbasid caliphate

786–809   Reign of Harun al-Rashid marks the height of the Abbasid caliphate

833–945   Emergence of regional states within Abbasid territories

836	Abbasid capital is moved from Baghdad to Samarra, a new city lying about 80 miles to the north
909–969	Fatimid caliphate rules in North Africa
945	Buyid dynasty occupies Baghdad; end of direct rule by Abbasid caliphs
969–1171	Fatimid caliphate of North Africa also rules Egypt and Syria
1038–1194	Seljuk dynasty rules in Iraq and Iran
1071	Muslim Turks crush a Byzantine army at the Battle of Manzikert, forcing the Byzantine emperor to seek help from the West
1099	European knights conducting the First Crusade capture Jerusalem and establish the Latin Kingdom of Jerusalem
1171	Muslim ruler Saladin conquers Egypt, thus threatening the Latin Kingdom of Jerusalem and leading to calls in Europe for a new Crusade
1187	Saladin defeats the Franks at the Battle of Hattin and reconquers Jerusalem for Islam
1189–1192	Third Crusade, know as the Kings' Crusade because it was led by Richard I of England and Philip II of France, tries unsuccessfully to wrest Jerusalem from Saladin
1219–1221	Mongols conquer Persia
1250–1517	Mamluk dynasty rules in Egypt and Syria
1258	Mongols sack Baghdad
1260	Mamluks defeat Mongols at Ayn Jalut in Palestine
1281–1924	Ottoman Empire, a Turkish Muslim state, is established in Asia Minor
1291	Mamluks capture Acre, the last Frankish stronghold in Syria, thereby ending the Crusader presence in the Holy Land
1402	Ottoman ruler Bayezit I is defeated by the Turko-Mongol invader Timur at the Battle of Ankara
1421	Mehmet I begins expansion of the Ottoman Empire
1453	Byzantium falls to the Ottomans
1481	Beyezit II ascends the Ottoman throne
1512	Selim I comes to the Ottoman throne and expands the empire to the east and south
1520–1566	Rule of the Ottoman Sultan Suleyman the Magnificent; who expands the Ottoman dominions into southeastern Europe

Mohammad's Missions and Campaigns to 632

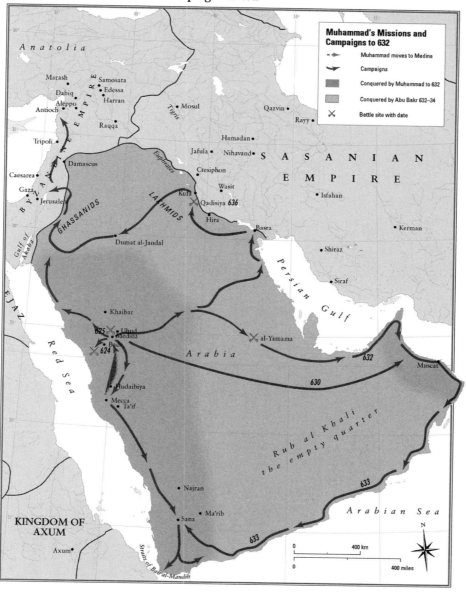

519

The Middle East on the Eve of the Muslim Era

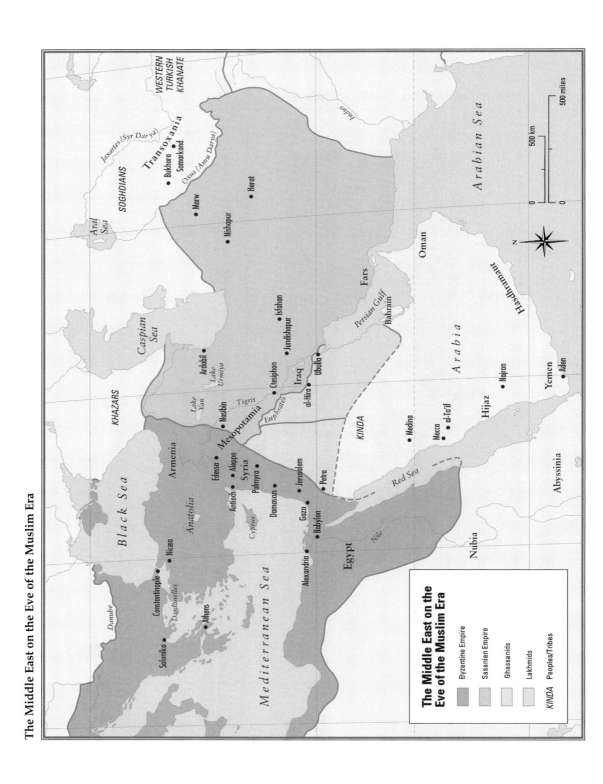

Expansion of Islam, 624–c. 750

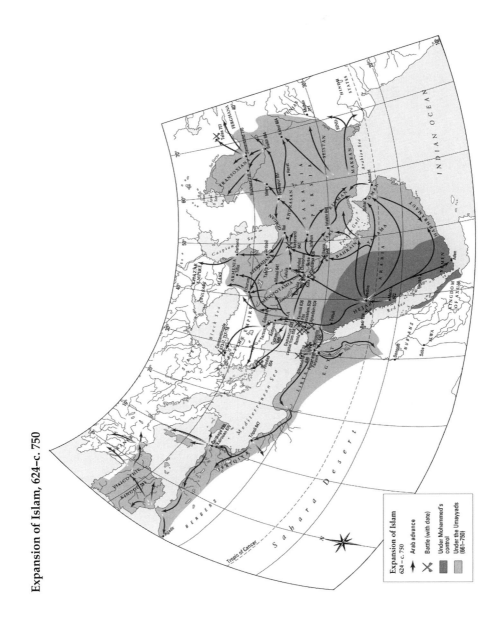

The Middle East in the late Eleventh Century

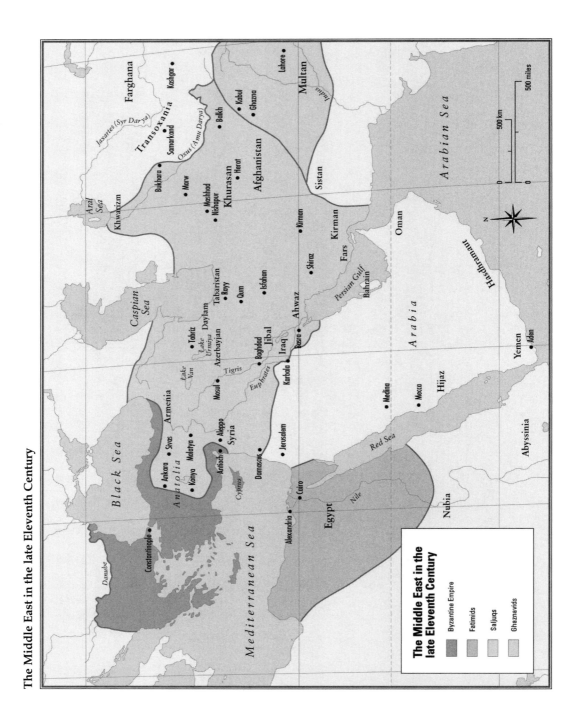

Byzantine Empire, c. 1270

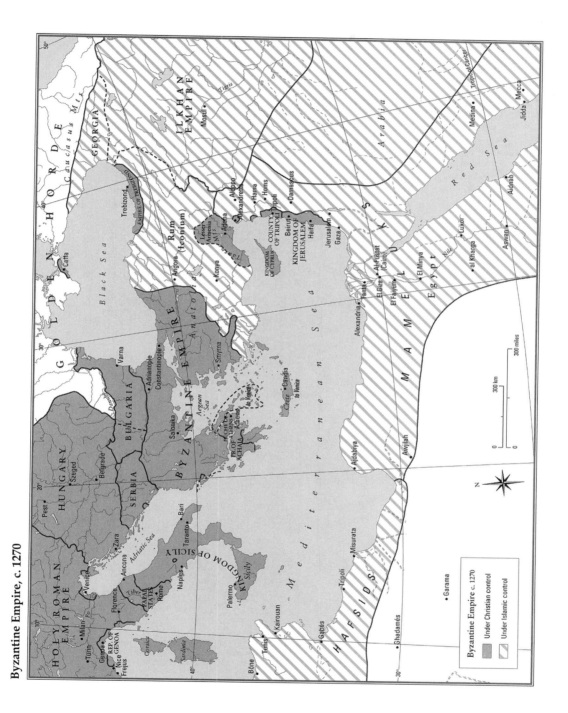

Byzantine Empire c. 1270
Under Christian control
Under Islamic control

The Islamic World in 1500

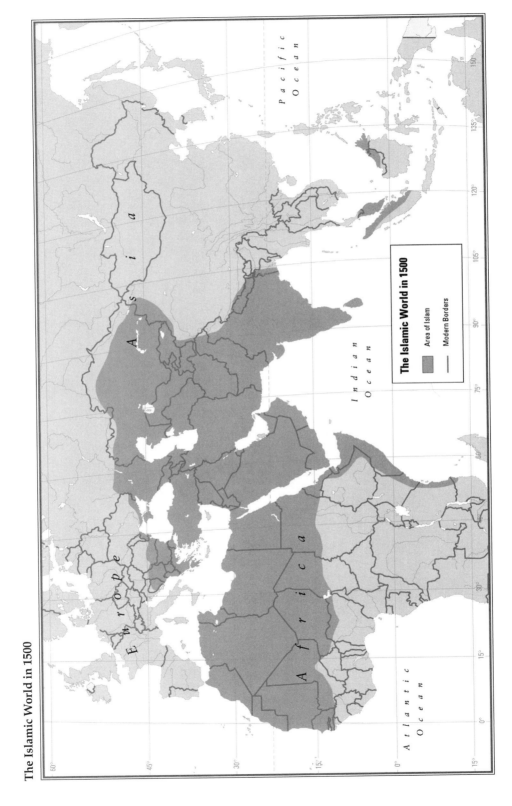

Overview and Topical Essays

1. HISTORICAL OVERVIEW

Although most of the great world religions have their origins in the Ancient and Classical worlds, Islam was born some two centuries after the Middle Ages commenced (at least according to the dates used in this series). According to Islamic tradition, Islam began around the year 610 with a revelation from God to Muhammad ibn Abd Allah in the brackish settlement of Mecca in Western Arabia. By 750, Islam had become the religion of the military and political elite of a vast empire that spanned from Spain in the west to the Indus Valley in the east and parts of Central Asia to the north. Although Anatolia—Constantinople in particular—was a target of Islamic expansion since the late 600s, it did not begin to be incorporated into the Islamic world until the eve of the Crusader period in the eleventh century. It was not brought under complete Muslim political domination until the conquest of Constantinople by the Ottoman sultan, Mehmed II, in 1453.

Initially, Islam was the religion of a small elite, but by the mid-900s, Islam had become the majority religion in most of the places where Islamic political authority held sway. By the mid-900s as well, the Arabic language had become the preferred language of science and learning for nearly every ethnic and religious group under Muslim rule. Arabic served to unite the educated elites in the Islamic world in much the same way that Latin did in medieval Western Europe or English does in the modern world. That is, in the tenth century, an educated Jew in Baghdad wrote in Arabic (often with Hebrew characters), while he employed Hebrew for religious purposes, and possibly a dialect of Aramaic in everyday speech. An educated Muslim or Zoroastrian in Iran could speak and write Arabic but used a dialect of Persian for everyday speech. Educated Christians in Cairo were fluent in Arabic but used Coptic for religious purposes and possibly everyday speech. The same held true for educated Christians in Damascus. They knew Arabic but used a dialect of Aramaic for religious purposes and possibly everyday speech as well. Similar situations existed among the educated Muslim and non-Muslim populations of Spain, North Africa, Central Asia, and Sind (the Indus River plain).

How is it then that a small—even minor—religious movement in Western Arabia in the early seventh century could be transformed into a far-flung Islamic empire by the early eighth century and a sophisticated Islamic civilization by the tenth century and beyond? In a sense this is the very question that early Muslim historians grappled with. Not surprisingly, Muslim historians—like their Jewish and Christian predecessors—credit God with their success and for the miraculous victories of the early Islamic conquests. What the Muslim historians did is reminiscent of what one finds in the historical books of the Tanakh (Hebrew Bible/Old Testament), in which God is portrayed as having entered into a covenant relationship between Himself and the Children of Israel, often intervening on their behalf against their enemies. One also finds examples of this in the Acts of the Apostles in the New Testament, in which persecutions of early Christians are portrayed as ordained by God for the purpose of dispersing the community and spreading the Gospel around the Mediterranean basin. Most modern historians do not claim (at least in public) to see the hand of God in history. Ancient Jewish and Christian writers as well as early Muslim writers could not help but see it nor did they hesitate to write about it. Needless to say, caution is required of modern historians, who must rely on accounts that were written by people with worldviews so different from our own.

The Life of Muhammad (c. 570–632)

According to the Islamic sources, Muhammad's prophetic career spanned some two decades, beginning around the year 610 when he was about 40 years old and lasting right up to the year of his death in 632. These sources also agree that Muhammad was a reluctant prophet when the angel Gabriel brought him the first revelation. However, he soon realized that he was a prophet in the mold of the ancient Hebrew prophets; and like Moses, Isaiah, and Jeremiah of old, he knew that he could not refuse to preach. After all, in a world where people still believed very concretely in the supernatural and were aware of at least the gist of the Biblical stories of God's powerful and miraculous dealings with the Children of Israel and their enemies, one simply could not ignore a summons from the very creator and sustainer of the universe.

Muhammad's biographers tell us far more about Muhammad's career after he received his revelations than about his childhood and early adulthood. Nevertheless, what they do have to say about his early years tells us a great deal about the values of the Arabian kinship-based society into which Muhammad was born, as well as the desire on the part of his biographers to demonstrate that Muhammad was indeed the Messenger of God. Like Abraham, Isaac, Jacob, Moses, and Jesus—to name but a few of the Biblical prophets—Muhammad is portrayed as having a prophetic pedigree. He, too, could trace his lineage to Abraham, though unlike the Biblical prophets, his genealogy went through Abraham's son Ishmael rather than Isaac. In addition to genealogy, Muhammad's biographers include numerous stories in which Christian and Jewish holy men gave their stamp of approval to Muhammad's prophethood. What better ways to prove to one's audience that God's chosen messenger was indeed who he claimed to be? Not only did he belong to a long line of prophets, but the very holy men who had access to the special knowledge that only holy men possess agreed that he was in fact who he claimed to be.

Muhammad was born in Mecca around the year 570 to a woman named Amina. Most accounts indicate that his father, Abd Allah, died before Muhammad was born. Muhammad's mother died while he was a young boy, after which he came under the protection of his father's brother, Abu Talib, the leader of Muhammad's clan, the Banu Hashim—an honorable, though certainly not the most important, branch of the Banu Quraysh. The dominant group in Mecca at the time, the Banu Quraysh derived much of its prestige and wealth from two things. First, it was the custodian of the principal pagan shrine of the town: the Kaaba. Second, it was involved in regional trade. It is doubtful that Mecca was a major player in long-distance trade at the time, but its trading activities and shrine custodianship did serve as the basis for the group's relations with outlying tribal confederations in the Hijaz and other regions of Arabia.

Muhammad's biographers portray him as a trustworthy young man who participated in the religious and commercial activities of Mecca. In fact, his trustworthiness in business affairs ultimately led to his first marriage (c. 600) to a wealthy widowed businesswoman named Khadija. Khadija provided significant moral support to Muhammad during the early years of his prophetic career—after he received his first revelations around the year 610 and especially after he received the revelation to begin his public preaching 3 years later. She remained his sole wife until her death in 619, the year that his uncle and protector, Abu Talib, also died.

Muhammad's prophetic career can be divided into two roughly equal periods. The first took place in his hometown of Mecca from about 610 to 622. By 622, he had fallen out of favor with the leaders of Mecca and negotiated a move for himself and his followers to the oasis settlement of Medina approximately 250 miles to the north. Those early Meccan converts who moved to Medina with Muhammad are referred to as *muhajirun* (emigrants). The people of Medina who embraced Muhammad and his message and who welcomed him to Medina are referred to as *ansar* (helpers). These two groups and their descendants played major roles in the course of Islamic history during Muhammad's career in Medina as well as after his death in 632.

It was only after Muhammad had made his **hijra** to Medina in 632 that he was in a position to implement his vision of a society governed by God's law, for according to the Qur'an, Islam is the perfect divinely established religion and was to be the sole authority in Muhammad's new state in Arabia. Muhammad's role would no longer be limited to proclaiming God's revelations. He now added to his duties the role of political and military leader of the new order in Medina. In fact, Muhammad's *hijra* and the establishment of his new political order in Medina is of such importance that Muslims established Muhammad's *hijra* as year one of the Islamic **calendar**.

Muhammad's agenda during his career in Medina was much like that of King David in the establishment of Ancient Israel as well as the later Hebrew prophets who proclaimed the word of the Lord (YHWH) and summoned the Children of Israel to obedience. Unlike modern U.S. society—the basis of which is supposed to be our Constitution written by men—Muhammad's principal goal was to create a society that lived in accordance with God's commandments in part by persuasion, but also by coercion and even warfare as necessary. Like King David, Muhammad was a very successful and at times bloody-minded warlord in his mission to establish himself as God's designated ruler of the Hijaz. Although violence in the name of religion tends to make modern Westerners uncomfortable, the idea that brutality and bloodshed could be an expression of piety was neither new nor unique to the seventh-century Near East.

Muhammad spent his first 2 years in Medina organizing its residents into a new community based on the revelations he had already received and a document that modern historians call "The Constitution of Medina." The year 624 marks the beginning of a series of bloody conflicts between Muhammad and his supporters in Medina and the Banu Quraysh of Mecca. It also marks the beginning of a number of conflicts between Muhammad and three of the major Jewish clans of Medina, which by 627 had resulted in the expulsion of two Jewish clans and the extermination of the adult males and the enslavement of the women and children of a third. The conflict with Mecca ended in 630 when the leaders of Mecca agreed to accept Muhammad as the Messenger of God along with his religion and to restore Mecca to its rightful place as a pilgrimage center as established by Adam and Abraham. (Obviously, the Islamic tradition's depiction of Adam and Abraham differs considerably from that of Genesis.)

By the time Muhammad died in 632, he had become the ruler of the Hijaz and had established tributary alliances with a number of the outlying tribes in Arabia. At his death, Muhammad's senior associates reached a consensus about a successor and proclaimed Muhammad's close friend, early convert, and father-in-law — **Abu Bakr** — as the head of the community. As such, Abu Bakr enjoyed all of Muhammad's authority except prophethood. The earliest sources refer to the holders of this office by three titles: (1) *Khalifat Rasul Allah* (**caliph**: deputy or successor of the Messenger of God), (2) *Amir al-Mu'minin* (commander of the believers), and (3) *imam* (religious leader).

For all intents and purposes, these titles emphasize different aspects of the caliph's political, military, and religious authority. Whatever the title, there was a general consensus about the basic responsibilities of the office: (1) the caliph should be the sole leader of the community, (2) all political power was to be invested in this one man, and (3) this office was to be a lifetime office. Most of the major Muslim factions agreed with the above positions. The basic problem was related to the criteria for determining who was qualified to hold this office. Although there was and remains a great deal of diversity of opinion within the Muslim community on this issue, during the first century or so of Islamic history three broad factions emerged that came to be known the **Sunnis**, the Shi'is (*see* **Shiism**), and the **Kharijis**.

The Early Islamic Conquests (632–750)

Whereas the Tanakh's (Hebrew Bible/Old Testament) ancient vision of a just society living in accordance with God's instruction (*torah*) was limited by ethnicity and geography to the People of Israel, the Land of Israel, and the Temple at Jerusalem where the God of Israel caused his name to dwell, the vision articulated in the Qur'an and the early Islamic historiographical tradition is much more ambitious in that it is neither limited by ethnicity nor geography. Rather, it is to strive in the path of God (*jihad fi sabil Allah*) until the whole world and its people are subjugated under Islamic authority and rule. That is, Muhammad and his community were commanded to "fight them until there is no sedition [*fitna*] and the religion is Allah's entirely" (Qur'an 8:39). After Muhammad's death, it fell to Abu Bakr and his **Rashidun**, **Umayyad**, and **Abbasid** successors to undertake the conquest and subjugation of Arabia and far beyond. And as they did, they sought and easily found inspiration for their religious, political, and military policies in the life and deeds of the most perfect of examples: Muhammad the son of Abd Allah, known to his followers as Muhammad the Messenger of Allah.

Abu Bakr's principal objective during his short reign (r. 632–634) was to subdue a rebellion in Arabia among the tribes who believed that their agreements with Muhammad died with him or who did not think that Abu Bakr was worthy of their allegiance. Abu Bakr and Muhammad's companions obviously disagreed. For them, the tribes' submission to Muhammad during his lifetime was equal to their submission to God; therefore, they did not have the option of seceding from the new political and religious community. Hence, the wars to subjugate the peoples of the peninsula are known as the *Ridda* Wars—or the Wars of Apostasy, although not all of those who were compelled to accept Islam and submit to Muslim political authority were actual apostates. That is, some had never been Muslims nor had they submitted to Muhammad's authority during his lifetime.

By the early 650s, the Arabian Muslim armies had conquered the Iranian Plateau, Syria, Egypt, and part of North Africa, primarily under the leadership **Umar ibn al-Khattab** (r. 634–644). After Umar's assassination, the conquests continued under his successor, **Uthman ibn Affan** (r. 644–656); however, they were interrupted by internal disputes over Uthman's policies in Iraq and Egypt that ultimately led to Uthman's assassination in 656. **'Ali ibn Abi Talib**'s (r. 656–661) caliphate was torn apart by the first civil war. Ali's death—also by an assassin's hand—marked the end of the Rashidun (or rightly guided) caliphate according to what came to be known as the Sunni tradition. The Shi'i tradition, however, argued that Muhammad had designated Ali (and his progeny) to be his successor at a place called Ghadir Khumm in 632. Consequently, according to the Shi'i conception of the caliphate/imamate, the first three caliphs were usurpers of Ali's rightful position.

After Ali's assassination, leadership of the Islamic empire shifted to **Mu'awiya ibn Abi Sufyan** (r. 661–680), the first of the Umayyad caliphs (661–750) to rule from Damascus. Mu'awiya reinvigorated the conquest and extended the frontiers of the empire further into North Africa in the west and Eastern Iran and Afghanistan in the east. In the 710s, the Muslim forces began the conquest of Spain in the west and Sind in the east. It is worth noting, that the point of the conquests—apart from the *Ridda* Wars in Arabia—was not conversion of the local populations to Islam per se. Rather, it was to spread Islamic political authority and rule throughout the world. Not surprisingly, the phenomenal success in this project only served to convince the conquerors that theirs was a divinely sanctioned mission: a mission that would be renewed throughout Islamic history with calls for jihad to expand the borders of Islamic rule. Although it is impossible to determine the precise number of Arabian Muslim troops involved in the conquests during the first century of Islamic history, it is abundantly clear that the Arabian Muslim conquerors were a very small minority in a vast non-Muslim sea.

Fragmentation of the Caliphate

The political fragmentation of the Islamic empire and of the institution of the caliphate had its beginnings under the Abbasid caliphs (750–1258). The Abbasids came to power by manipulating a Shi'i revolt against their predecessors, the Umayyads (661–750), in the late 740s. But once the Abbasids assumed power they began to follow the Sunni paradigm for the caliphate. The second Abbasid caliph, **al-Mansur** (r. 754–775), founded Baghdad in 762 as his new capital. Initially established as a palace complex, Baghdad soon grew into one of the most cosmopolitan cities of the medieval Islamic world. The Abbasid caliphate never fully recovered from the civil war between **Harun al-Rashid**'s (r. 786–809) two sons, al-Amin (r. 809–813) and **al-Ma'mun ibn Harun al-Rashid** (r. 813–833). By the 860s and 870s, many petty states had established themselves under Muslim rulers in North Africa and Spain to the west and in Iran and lands further east. In fact, by the tenth century, there were three caliphates at the same time: the Abbasid caliphate with its capital at Baghdad and the **Fatimid** caliphate (909–1171) with its capital at Cairo; whereas in Cordoba, the Umayyad Abd al-Rahman III (r. 912–961) claimed the title of caliph for himself.

In 945, Baghdad was sacked by the **Buyids**—a group of Shi'i soldiers of fortune from the region of Daylam on the southern shores of the Caspian Sea. From 945 onward, the Abbasid caliphs remained subordinate to a series of Muslim warlord regimes until 1258, when the invading Mongol armies sacked Baghdad and, for all intents and purposes, brought an end to the Abbasid caliphate. A version of the Abbasid caliphate continued under the tutelage of the **Mamluk Sultanate** (1250–1517) in Cairo, but it amounted to little more than a means to provide a veneer of legitimacy for the Mamluk sultans. In spite of the failure of the political ideal of a single community of believers under the universal government of Muhammad's successors, it was during the tenth through the fifteenth centuries that we see Islam's capacity to expand, geographically as well as in the intellectual, cultural, and economic spheres.

There was an important ethnic shift also, because by the tenth century Islam had begun to lose its close and almost exclusive association with those who traced their lineage to the first Arabian Muslim warriors. In the political realm, people who could trace their lineage to the Arabian Muslim conquests had lost their leading role by 900 as well. Throughout the following centuries (and in fact into the twentieth century), dynasties of Turkic origin dominated the political life of the Islamic world from modern Algeria to India. In fact, it was the Turkish Ghaznavids who initiated the definitive Islamic conquest of northern India from Afghanistan. The Delhi Sultanates (1206–1526) had their origins in inner Asia as well. This Turkish political domination reflected a substantial migration of Turkic peoples from Inner Asia into the Middle East, though only in a few areas did these immigrants come to constitute a majority of the population: Transoxiana (Central Asia north of the Oxus River), Northwestern Iran, and eventually Anatolia. The newcomers did not drive out or assimilate the old Muslim populations in the lands they ruled, and in many respects the Turkic conquerors became the firmest advocates of the established cultural and religious traditions of Sunni Islam.

One faction of these immigrants, named after a man called Seljuk, belonged to the great Oghuzz confederation of Turkic tribesmen. In 1040, under the leadership of two of Seljuk's grandsons—Toghril Beg and Chagri Beg—the Seljukids defeated the Ghaznavids at the Battle of Dandanqan in Afghanistan and established themselves in Afghanistan and eastern Iran. Leaving his younger brother, Chagri, to administer the family lands in the east, Toghril turned his attention westward. In 1055, Toghril and his Sunni Seljukid Turkoman tribesmen overthrew the Shi'i Buyids in Baghdad. The Abbasid caliph conferred on Toghril the title of sultan.

Toghril and his successors determined early on that if they were to administer a thriving urban and agrarian society in Iraq and Iran they would need a disciplined standing army. Toghril's successor, Sultan Alp Arslan (r. 1063–1073), pursued an aggressive policy of removing the fiercely independent Turkomans and replacing them with his own Mamluk slave troops. Some of the Turkomans migrated north and east; others migrated to the northwest and pursued their nomadic raiding practices along the Byzantine frontier. For the Byzantines, these Turkomans were nothing but bandits and genuinely threatened their territory and subjects. The Turkomans, on the other hand, legitimated their raiding and pillaging in eastern and central Anatolia as the righteous work of holy warriors (*ghazis*) engaged in jihad against the Byzantines. After all, from the Turkomans' point of view, they were merely striving in the path of God (*jihad fi sabil Allah*) against the preferred infidel enemy of Islam since the seventh century. Things came to a head in 1071 as the Byzantine emperor Romanus Diogenes (r. 1068–1071) led several Byzantine columns eastward to deal with this Turkish menace once and for all. Already on campaign in Syria, Alp Arslan turned his forces north to come to the aid of his fellow Turkomans and fellow Muslims. A pitched battle between the two sides took place at Manzikert, near Lake Van, in the summer of 1071. Alp Arslan's forces were victorious, and Romanus Diogenes was taken captive. He was ultimately ransomed and deposed. The Battle of Manzikert marks the beginnings of the process by which Anatolia became Turkey.

In 1095, Pope Urban II preached a sermon in Clermont, France, in which he called on the interminably feuding nobility of Western Europe to turn their energies to the cause of Christ and his Church. Urban II was by no means the first to call on them to use their military skills in aide of their Byzantine Christian brothers who, since the Battle of Manzikert, were increasingly threatened by Muslim Turkish marauders in eastern and central Anatolia. In fact, Pope Gregory VII had proposed that he himself lead a force of some fifty-thousand men to liberate their Eastern brethren in 1074. More important, however, Urban called on the Frankish nobility to take up the cross of Christ and make an armed pilgrimage to Jerusalem to redeem their Lord's patrimony, which had been stolen by the infidel Saracens some four centuries earlier. By the summer of 1099, Jerusalem was in the hands of the Crusaders. Unfortunately for Pope Urban II, he died shortly after Jerusalem was taken, but before word reached Western Europe.

In 1092, the Seljukid wazir, **Nizam al-Mulk**, was murdered by Nizari Ismailis (better known in the west as the Assassins). A month later, the Seljukid Sultan Malikshah died under suspicious circumstances. Two years later, "the year of the death of caliphs and commanders," brought with it the death of al-Mustansir, the Fatimid caliph in Egypt, and his wazir Badr al-Jamali. In Baghdad, the Abbasid Caliph al-Muqtadi died in 1094 as well. Consequently, Egypt, Syria, and Iraq were largely devoid of effective political leadership during the last decade of the eleventh century. Although there is no evidence that the Franks had been briefed on the disarray in Syria when they responded to Urban's call, they could not have arrived at a more auspicious time.

There is evidence that some Syrian preachers and scholars decried the loss of Jerusalem and even undertook missions to Baghdad for assistance from the Abbasid caliphs and Seljukid sultans. But neither was in a position to respond favorably to such requests. It was not until 1144 when a Turkish commander named Zengi (d. 1146) captured the Frankish city of Edessa (ostensibly

on behalf of his Abbasid overlords) that the first successful Muslim counter offensive against the Franks took place. His son Nur al-Din (d. 1174), after occupying Damascus in 1154, was able to unite the Muslim-controlled areas of
Syria and undertook his own jihad against the Franks as well as against the
domestic enemies of Sunni Islam: the Shi'i Fatimids in Egypt and their coreligionists in Syria. But his successor and Kurdish protégé, **Saladin** (d. 1193),
was finally able to bring an end to the Fatimid caliphate in Cairo in 1171. He
also dealt the Franks a decisive defeat at the Battle of Hattin in 1187 and re-
took Jerusalem shortly thereafter.

Under Saladin's leadership, Egypt and Syria were ruled as a family confederation, with members of his extended family administering various provinces
throughout the realm. Named after Saladin's father, Ayyub (Job), the Ayyubid
family confederation did have some success against the Franks. The nearly six
decades after Saladin's death were characterized by a series of shifting alliances and accommodations among various Ayyubid and Frankish princes.
Not until the Egyptian branch of the Ayyubid house was overthrown in 1250
and the Mamluk forces defeated the Mongols at Ayn Jalut on September 3,
1260 did the policy of accommodation with the Franks begin to change. The
transition from the Ayyubid family confederation to the Mamluk sultanate
took a good decade to complete. One of the more fascinating aspects of this
transition is the brief tenure of Shajar al-Durr, the widow of Sultan al-Salih
Ayyub, as sultana in her own right.

Overcome by illness, Sultan al-Salih Ayyub died in the midst of Louis IX's
invasion of Egypt on November 21, 1249. His only living son and successor,
Turanshah, was a governor in northern Mesopotamia at the time. Shajar al-
Durr kept her husband's death a secret from all save his commander-in-chief,
Fakhr al-Din ibn al-Shaykh, and a few others. They held things together until
Turanshah reached Egypt to assume the sultanate. By the time he arrived on
February 23, 1250, Fakhr al-Din had been killed in battle with the Franks and
things looked bleak. Turanshah had, however, arrived in time to lead a victory
over Louis IX and even captured the French king on April 6. In a "last will and
testament" letter to Turanshah, the sick Sultan al-Salih Ayyub advised his son
to stay away from alcohol and to be generous to his father's Mamluks. As sons
often do, Turanshah chose to ignore his father's wise counsel and sought to
replace his father's Mamluks with those of his own. In the end, his disloyalty
cost him his life as his father's Mamluks killed him on May 2, 1250. But what
to do now that al-Salih Ayyub and his only surviving son were gone?

Enter Shajar al-Durr who became sultana in May 1250, one of the few Muslim women who held real political authority in premodern Islamic history.
The minting of coins (*sikka*) and the invocation of the ruler's name in the Friday sermon (*khutba*) were two of the most important symbols of political legitimacy in the medieval Islamic world. Hence, Sultana Shajar al-Durr's name
was invoked in Friday sermons, and coins were minted in her name. The coins
referred to her as the Queen of the Muslims; they also declared her fealty to
the Abbasid caliph in Baghdad. However, her sultanate was neither popular
in Cairo nor was it acceptable to the caliph who offered to send a man from
Baghdad to rule the country if none could be found in Egypt. So in July 1250,
she abdicated in favor of her new husband, al-Salih Ayyub's former food-
taster, Izz al-Din Aybak al-Turkomani, chosen primarily because of his apparent malleability. Five days later, he was replaced by an Ayyubid child prince,

al-Ashraf Musa, whom he served as *atabeg*, that is, as guardian of the prince and as commander of the army. It would take another decade and the defeat of the Mongols at Ayn Jalut before the Mamluk sultanate was firmly established in Egypt and Syria under Sultan Baybars and his successors.

Sultan Baybars (r. 1260–1277) aggressively pursued a remarkably effective, multifaceted foreign policy to achieve his goals of fending off renewed Mongol incursions and removing the Franks from Syria. He cultivated good relations with the Golden Horde branch of the Mongol empire in Russia that controlled the reservoir for the regime's new Mamluk recruits and also served as a counter to the Mongol Il-Khans in Iraq and Iran with whom the Golden Horde and the Mamluk Sultanate were frequently at war. He concluded a commercial treaty with Genoa, whose merchants held a near monopoly on trade in the Black Sea. The treaty supplied the Mamluk Sultanate with new recruits who could no longer be transported by land through Il-Khan territory, but it had the added benefit of strengthening the Genoese in their competition with the Venetians. In addition, he established a commercial treaty with the Byzantine Empire that controlled access from the Black Sea to Alexandria via Constantinople. It too had an added benefit for the Mamluk Sultanate in that it served as a counter to the Papacy's efforts to support the Franks in Palestine. In the end, the Mamluks were able to drive the Franks from Acre in 1291, thus ending nearly two centuries of Frankish presence in the Near East. By the end of the twelfth century the Il-Khans had converted to Islam and by the 1320s were no longer a major threat to the Mamluk regime in Syria and Egypt. *See also* Documents 4 and 5.

Further Reading

Esposito, John L., ed. *The Oxford History of Islam*. New York: Oxford University Press, 1999.

Hodgson, Marshall G.S. *The Venture of Islam*. 3 vols. Chicago: University of Chicago Press, 1974.

Hourani, Albert. *A History of the Arab Peoples*. Cambridge, MA: Harvard University Press, 1991.

Lapidus, Ira. *A History of Islamic Societies*. Rev. ed. Berkeley: University of California Press, 2002.

Lewis, Bernard. *The Middle East: A Brief History of the Last 2,000 Years*. New York: Simon & Schuster, 1995.

Lindsay, James E. *Daily Life in the Medieval Islamic World*. Westport, CT: Greenwood, 2005.

Robinson, Francis, ed. *Cambridge Illustrated History of the Islamic World*. New York: Cambridge University Press, 1996.

2. RELIGION

Muslim scholars have long described the five basic ritual practices of Islam in architectural terms. They refer to them as Five Pillars: the supports that define one's submission (*islam*) to God. The Five Pillars upon which the entire edifice of Islam rests are the statement of belief (*shahada*), ritual prayer (*salat*), almsgiving (*zakat*), fasting (*sawm*) during the daylight hours of Ramadan (the ninth month of the Islamic **calendar**), and the pilgrimage (*hajj*) to Mecca during the twelfth month of the Islamic calendar. Islam as a religion comprises Five Pillars (for many, *jihad* is equally important and functioned essentially as a sixth pillar) as an idea that was developed and implemented by scholars and jurists decades and more after Muhammad's death. Nevertheless, these Five Pillars are the instruments that for centuries have produced the rhythms and the melodies of daily life in all Islamic societies.

As with most issues concerning the first Islamic centuries, when precisely each of the Five Pillars began to be practiced in a way recognizable to us and to medieval Islamic scholars is a matter of some debate and conjecture. It is clear that each developed in its own way and had its own history. It is also clear that the sources allow us to speak with greater confidence about Islamic ritual practices by the time we get to the third Islamic century, when we observe a tremendous deepening of Islamic culture and identity within the old Islamic lands of North Africa and the Middle East. For the great majority of the population in this region, Islam came to provide not only a system of beliefs, but also a framework for social action and cultural expression.

Whether in the city or the countryside, the subject populations had wide areas of autonomy in daily life. Still, relations among individuals and relations between individuals and a regime were, in principle, governed by *shari'a*, one of the many Arabic words that convey the idea of pathway. Although shari'a is sometimes translated as Islamic law, it is not a formal body of legislation in the modern sense; rather, it is an all-encompassing code of behavior worked out over the centuries by religious scholars (*ulama*), who sought to determine how Muslims could best fulfill the Qur'anic admonition to "obey God and His messenger" (Qur'an 3:132)

Shahada—Statement of Faith

The first of the Five Pillars, the *shahada* or statement of belief is a simple two-part statement that is at the center of Islamic belief, ritual, and worship. This statement declares: There is no god but God (*la ilaha illa'llah*); Muhammad is the messenger of God (*Muhammadun rasul Allah*). Both of these statements are in the Qur'an, but not side by side as in the *shahada* formula. Nevertheless, versions of both phrases begin to appear on coins in the late seventh century. Because we do not find the *shahada* formula per se on earlier coins, it appears that the *shahada* had not been officially established as a ritual statement of faith until the end of the first Islamic century.

The inscriptions on the Dome of the Rock in Jerusalem (est. 692) provide additional early examples of the sentiments of the *shahada*. One overtly anti-Trinitarian, hence, anti-Byzantine Christian inscription reads, "There is no god but God alone; He has no partner with Him; Muhammad is the messenger of God." Another reads, "Muhammad is the servant of God and His messenger whom He sent with the guidance and the religion of truth." This latter phrase is the same one embossed on **Umayyad** coins after the reign of **Abd al-Malik** (r. 685–705), the Umayyad caliph who built the Dome of the Rock.

Although the *shahada* is the simplest of the Five Pillars to perform because of its brevity, it is arguably the most important of all. For to recite the *shahada* publicly with proper intent in front of Muslim witnesses is to accept one's obligation to perform the remaining four as well. The *shahada* is the very wellspring from which the remaining four flow. That is, without belief in the one God and that Muhammad is His messenger, the remaining four pillars are without meaning. Moreover, though any monotheist can proclaim the first part of the *shahada* (there is no god but God), it is from the second part of the *shahada* (Muhammad is the messenger of God) that the entirety of Islamic ritual and practice is ostensibly derived. And as noted above, the whole process of the sharia can be viewed as an effort to determine how best to fulfill the Qur'anic admonition to "obey God and His messenger" (Qur'an 3:132).

Salat—Ritual Prayer

Although the *shahada* is the most important of the Five Pillars, in practice, it is the *salat* — the ritual prayer performed five times per day — that is the ubiquitous symbol of Islamic ritual and piety. Qur'an 11:14 provides general guidance as to when and how often one should perform the *salat*: "Attend to your prayers, morning and evening, and in the night-time too." What we do not find in the Qur'an are instructions that one should perform the *salat* five times per day (rather than three), the precise hours of the day in which the *salat* should be performed, the specific procedures for **ablutions** necessary to make one ritually clean (*tahara*) so that one's prayers can be valid, the exact words that should be said in the *salat*, or the physical acts that should be performed during the *salat*. Rather, we learn these things — and in great detail — from the *hadith* literature about Muhammad's life and teachings.

For example, one of the most famous episodes in these biographies is Muhammad's night journey, during which Muhammad was taken from Mecca to Jerusalem on Buraq — a winged horse with a human face. From Jerusalem he was taken up to the seventh heaven where God informed him that his community would be required to perform fifty prayers per day. According to Ibn Ishaq (d. 767), Muhammad described his return journey as follows:

> On my return, I passed by Moses and what a fine friend of yours he was! He asked me how many prayers had been laid upon me and when I told him fifty he said, "Prayer is a weighty matter and your people are weak, so go back to your Lord and ask Him to reduce the number for you and your community." I did so and He took off ten. Again I passed Moses and he said the same again; and so it went on until only five prayers for the whole day and night were left. Moses again gave me the same advice. I replied that I had been back to my Lord and asked Him to reduce the number until I was ashamed, and I would not do it again. He of you who performs them in faith and trust will have the reward of fifty prayers. (Ibn Ishaq, 186–187)

Ibn Ishaq's account of Muhammad's negotiations with God to reduce the number of prayers from fifty to five is reminiscent of Abraham's negotiations with God to reduce the number of righteous men necessary to save Sodom from fifty to ten (Genesis 18:22–30). More important, Ibn Ishaq's account provides a powerful narrative explanation for why the faithful should perform the ritual prayer five times per day.

Prior to his *hijra* to Medina, Muhammad had instructed his followers to pray toward Syria, which was understood to mean toward Jerusalem. He continued this practice after his arrival in Medina as well. After encountering stiff opposition from a number of the Jewish clans of Medina, Muhammad received a revelation instructing him to henceforth pray facing Mecca. The importance of determining the direction of Mecca is evidenced by the fact that each mosque has a *mihrab*, which usually takes the form of a niche in a wall to indicate the direction (*qibla*) of Mecca. Near the *mihrab* is a *minbar*, or elevated pulpit, from which the sermon (*khutba*) is preached.

The five designated prayer times are the morning, noon, afternoon, evening, and night prayers. Each of the five prayers (if possible) is to be performed during specific periods determined according to the position of the sun, not a time on the clock. Thus, the period for the morning prayer begins with the crack of dawn and ends at sunrise; the noon prayer when the sun is at its midpoint, not at noon. The afternoon prayer is usually performed when an object's shadow is slightly longer than itself. The evening prayer can be performed at any time after sunset and before the disappearance of the last light over the horizon; the night prayer at any time between the end of the time period for the evening prayer and beginning of the time period for the morning prayer.

Although each prayer is valid during its appointed time frame, it is preferable to perform the *salat* shortly after the muezzin calls the faithful to prayer if possible. Once one has performed the appropriate ablution he or she is ready to perform the *salat*. The five daily prayers may be recited in the privacy of one's home (the customary practice among women), though it is more meritorious to say them with others in a mosque, especially on Friday, which is the designated day for congregational prayer.

The act of ritual prayer is the same whether one performs it by oneself or with others. It consists of a series of precise bowings and prostrations, which together are called a *raka* (lit., bowing) or prayer cycle. In a congregational setting, those performing the *salat* line up behind an imam (prayer leader) in straight rows facing the direction (*qibla*) of Mecca. Hence, those performing the *salat* in Syria face south, in Yemen they face north, in India they face west, and in Morocco they face east. Men line up behind the imam; if women are present, they line up at the back of the mosque behind the men or in an antechamber of some sort. Following the imam's lead, the worshipers stand erect and recite the first chapter of the Qur'an, the *Fatiha* (lit., opening), which is always recited in Arabic, even if the person reciting it is not an Arabic speaker.

> In the name of God the Compassionate the Merciful. Praise be to God, Lord of the Universe, the Compassionate, the Merciful, Sovereign of the Day of Judgment! You alone we worship, and to You alone we turn for help. Guide us to the straight path, the path of those whom you have favored, not of those who have incurred Your wrath [Jews], nor of those who have gone astray [Christians]. (Qur'an 1:1–7)

After a minute or so they briefly bow at the waist with their back straight (roughly 90 degrees) and their hands on their knees; they then stand erect again, and almost immediately place their knees, hands, and forehead on the ground. They hold this position for a few moments and then assume a sitting position. They then prostrate themselves a second time, all the while reciting short prayers. This completes the first *raka*, after which they stand erect and begin the cycle all over again for as many times as required for each daily prayer. The evening prayer consists of three *raka*s, the night four, the morning two, the noon four, and the afternoon four. After the final *raka* is performed the worshipers remain seated and turn to their right and to their left and say *al-salam alaykum* (peace be upon you).

Those who are unable to perform the *salat* because of a physical malady should perform those aspects of the *salat* that they can and recite the appropriate passages at the appropriate times. The five daily *salat*s represent the *required* ritual prayers in Islamic ritual and worship. They do not represent the full extent of prayer in Islamic practice. Additional passages from the Qur'an may be recited during the *salat*, and additional greetings and blessings may be said. Supererogatory *salat*—that is, additional *rakas*—are highly recommended as expressions of piety and devotion as well. In addition to the ritual prayer of the *salat*, more open-ended supplications are part of Muslim worship. However, such petitions are referred to as *duat* and do not fall under the rubric of *salat*, nor do they require the performance of a *raka*. Additional types of prayer are also found as part of the Shi'i and Islamic mystical (Sufi) traditions.

Zakat—The Giving of Alms

Despite its frequent admonitions to give alms, the Qur'an does not specify what percentage of one's wealth should be given as *zakat* beyond that one should give "what you can spare" (Qur'an 2:219). The Qur'an does, however, set forth who the legitimate recipients of alms are.

> Alms (*zakat*) shall be only for the poor and the destitute, for those that are engaged in the management of alms and those whose hearts are sympathetic to the Faith, for the freeing of slaves and debtors, for the advancement of God's cause, and for the traveler in need. That is a duty enjoined by God. God is all-knowing and wise. (Qur'an 9:60)

Because the very concept of the Five Pillars of Islam was worked out by scholars and jurists decades or more after Muhammad's death, it reflects the vision of right religion as understood by educated and relatively well-to-do individuals. As the scholars and jurists extrapolated from the Qur'an and the *hadiths* what the specific obligations of the *zakat* were for the faithful, they determined that they only applied to those Muslims who possessed wealth and that the *zakat* should be paid from one's profit, not necessarily the totality of one's wealth. Consequently, the poor and destitute are under no obligation to give it. A consensus also emerged that the portion of one's profit that should be given as *zakat* can range anywhere from 2.5 percent of one's gold, silver, or merchandise to 10 percent of one's crops to be paid at harvest time. How the *zakat* was actually collected and/or distributed is difficult to ascertain. While the Qur'an speaks of giving *zakat* to those "engaged in the management of alms," individuals could legitimately give their *zakat* directly to the deserving recipients.

Sawm—Fasting

Fasting as an integral part of religious observance certainly was not new with Islam in seventh-century Arabia. It had long been part of the religious observances of Ancient Rome, Greece, Babylon, Egypt, and India. Moreover, it is abundantly clear from even a cursory examination of the Bible that it was essential to the religious life of Ancient Israel and the early Christian Church as an act of repentance, contrition, atonement, mourning, prayer, supplication, and devotion. According to the Bible, Moses (Deuteronomy 9:9–10), Elijah (1 Kings 19:7–9), and Jesus (Matthew 2:1–11) each fasted 40 days as preparation for major supernatural encounters at the beginning of their public careers.

It was during the Medinan phase of his career (when Muhammad encountered a large Jewish community that practiced fasting) that Muhammad received the revelation that established the month of Ramadan as the time for the Muslim fast (Qur'an 2:183–187). Ramadan came to take on a special sanctity in Islamic religious practice as well. According to Qur'an 2:185, it was during the month of Ramadan that Muhammad received his first revelation. This correlation between revelation and fasting parallels the connection between the giving of the tablets to Moses on Mt. Sinai and the fast on the Jewish Day of Atonement.

Based on Qur'an 2:183–87 and the *hadith* tradition, Muslim scholars developed lengthy and elaborate treatises that addressed a host of questions regarding the Ramadan fast, including how and when it was to be performed, who should perform it, what exempted one from it, which behaviors and consumable products were to be avoided, and what invalidated one's fast. Scholars argued that the fast was obligatory for all adult Muslims (generally defined as those who had fully entered into puberty) who were in good physical and mental health. For one's fast to be valid, one is required to begin each day by declaring one's intention to abstain from those things that are forbidden from that point when "you can tell a white thread from a black one in the light of the coming dawn" until nightfall. Many Muslims break their fast each evening by eating dates, which according to Islamic tradition was how Muhammad used to break his fasts.

During the fast, one should abstain from all food and drink, even swallowing spittle that could be expectorated. As specified in Qur'an 2:187, sexual relations with one's legitimate sexual partners (wives and female slaves for men; husbands and masters for **women**) are forbidden during this period. Deliberate seminal emission, menstruation, and bleeding in the wake of childbirth all invalidate one's fast. Those who could not perform it because of illness, travel, warfare, or other exigent circumstances should make up the fast at a later time; the same applies to women who are menstruating, pregnant, or nursing. Those who simply break the fast without good reason are required to fast for 2 months to make up for each day. The moral importance of the fast as an act of worship and piety is amplified by a *hadith* according to which Muhammad said, "Five things break the fast of the faster—lying, backbiting, slander, ungodly oaths, and looking with passion" (Murata and Chittick, 17). Here it is engaging in morally reprehensible activities that are always forbidden, rather than failing to temporarily abstain from activities normally permitted, that invalidates one's fast.

Ramadan begins on the first day of the ninth month of the Islamic lunar calendar; that is, when the new crescent moon is sighted. The Ramadan fast, of course, begins the following morning. It ends with the Festival of Fast Breaking (*Id al-Fitr*) when the next crescent moon is cited at the beginning of the tenth month, Shawwal. Because lunar months generally last 29 or 30 days, if the skies are too cloudy to see whether there is in fact a crescent moon, the first of Ramadan is deemed to be 30 days after the first of the preceding month.

Those accustomed to the 365-day Gregorian Christian solar calendar tend to find the 354-day Islamic lunar calendar rather frustrating since the Islamic calendar does not employ any mechanism to ensure that it coincides with the four seasons of the year. According to the Gregorian calendar, the ninth month (September) always straddles the end of summer and the beginning of autumn. According to the Islamic calendar, the ninth month (Ramadan) can correspond to September. But because Ramadan comes 11 days (give or take a day) earlier each year, it would take another 33 years or so before it would correspond with September again.

Hajj—Pilgrimage

What ultimately became the rituals of the Islamic *hajj* represent a combination of several preexisting Arabian practices associated with two uninhabited sacred pilgrimage areas outside of Mecca: Arafat and Mina. Visitations to the Kaaba in Mecca were later added to these rituals. Other pre-Islamic pilgrimage practices that were incorporated into the Islamic *hajj* include the inviolability of the pilgrim, particular dress called the *ihram*, performances of certain rituals and sacrifices, and commerce. In time, these rituals came to be associated with Abraham who, according to Qur'an 2:127, built the Kaaba with his son Ishmael as a place of veneration of the One God.

The annual pilgrimage takes place in and around the precincts of Mecca, and it begins on the eighth and ends on the thirteenth day of the last lunar month of the Islamic calendar, Dhu l-Hijja (The *Hajj* Month). The annual *hajj* is required of those adult Muslims who are able to undertake it and can withstand the many physical and financial hardships required of the pilgrims who come from the entire Islamic world. In addition to the required annual *hajj*, many Muslims perform another pilgrimage (*umra*), which can be performed at any time of the year. Although the *umra* is considered praiseworthy, it is neither obligatory nor is it considered a substitute for the *hajj*.

Prior to entering and after months, even years in transit, pilgrims remove their regular clothes, performed the necessary ablutions, and donned a special garment consisting of two rectangular pieces of unstitched white cloth, called an *ihram*. Men wrap one piece of cloth around their waists. This piece should be large enough that it reaches to the ankles. The second piece of cloth is wrapped around the torso and draped over the left shoulder. The *ihram* is worn throughout the entire *hajj*. Pilgrims either go barefoot or wear sandals without heels. Women's *ihram*, consists of clean, modest, and plain clothes. Although women cover their heads, they are not required to wear a face veil as is the custom in some of their home countries.

Upon entering Mecca, the pilgrim enters the Haram mosque and walks counterclockwise around the Kaaba seven times—three times quickly and four times slowly. The pilgrim then proceeds to the Station of Abraham, which is opposite the Kaaba. Standing behind the Station, the pilgrim performs two *rakas*, after which he or she goes to the well of Zamzam, drinks some of the water, and performs additional ablutions. According to Islamic tradition, at Zamzam the Angel Gabriel miraculously brought forth water for Hagar and Ishmael after Abraham had left them at Mecca and headed into the desert. The Bible records a similar story; however, according to Genesis 21:8–21, Hagar and Ishmael's exile, their thirst, and the angel of God's miraculous provision of water occurred in the wilderness near Beersheba in the northern Negev desert of modern Israel.

Next, the pilgrim leaves the Haram complex through the southeastern gate and proceeds to a small hill called Safa and then he or she runs or jogs about a quarter mile to another rise called Marwa. The pilgrim repeats this seven times, all the while reciting prayers in commemoration of Hagar's frantic search for water. After completing this ritual, the pilgrims enter the bazaar and have their hair cut, concluding the rituals of the *umra*. Those performing the *hajj* have only just completed the preliminary rituals. Instead of having their hair cut, they leave the Haram complex and find their lodgings, for there are many more journeys and rituals to be fulfilled.

First, pilgrims travel east through the desert some four miles to Mina where they spend the night on the eighth day of Dhu l-Hijja. They set out the next day for the plain of Arafat, about 7 miles further east. Although the wealthy could afford to hire camel transport, most walked the whole way. Some even walked barefoot as an act of piety. At noon on the ninth day of Dhu l-Hijja, pilgrims begin the part of the *hajj* that is called "The Standing" at Arafat. That is, they keep vigil around the Mount of Mercy until sundown, all the while reciting, "What is Your command? I am here!" and listening to sermons preached from the summit where, according to Islamic tradition, the first man, Adam, had prayed and Muhammad had preached his farewell sermon. At sunset, the pilgrims pack up and begin their return to Mecca. By tradition, the pilgrims wait until they have reached Muzdalifa, some 3 miles behind them toward Mina, to perform their evening prayers. Although most of the pilgrims sleep at Muzdalifa overnight, women, children, and the infirm can continue the trip to Mina.

At Mina, on the tenth of the month, the pilgrims perform a series of rituals in remembrance of God's instruction to Abraham to sacrifice a ram instead of his son (Qur'an 37:103–109). Three stone pillars are located east to west along the valley. The first ritual act at Mina is for pilgrims to throw pebbles at the westernmost pillar. This "stoning of the devil" symbolically identifies the pilgrim with Abraham, who threw stones at the devil as he sought to convince Abraham not to sacrifice his son as God commanded. Because the Qur'an does not name which son Abraham was commanded to sacrifice, there was disagreement among the earliest commentators as to whether the son in question was Isaac or Ishmael. Eventually, majority opinion came to be that (unlike the Biblical account in Genesis 22) it was Ishmael.

After the stoning, the pilgrim purchases a goat or a sheep (or a camel if he or she can afford it) to sacrifice. The pilgrim then turns the face of the animal toward Mecca and slits its throat as Abraham did. Slitting the animal's throat is the final act of the *ihram* phase, after which the pilgrim finds one of the many barbers present at Mina and has his head shaved, or at least has some of his hair cut. After this, he is free to put on his regular clothes. He then returns to Mecca where he circumambulates the Kaaba once again. In the remaining days of the *hajj*, pilgrims return to Mina to throw pebbles at all three pillars, sacrifice additional animals, and enjoy the festivities with fellow pilgrims.

Although it is not required, many (if not most) pilgrims also make the trek northward to Medina to visit Muhammad's mosque there before returning home.

Although one must be in Mecca and its surroundings to perform the annual *hajj* rituals, markets in villages, towns, and cities throughout the medieval Islamic world teemed with animals in the days leading up to the day on which pilgrims sacrificed at Mina as Muslims prepared to sacrifice and feast in solidarity with their brothers and sisters in the Arabian desert. (For nonpilgrims, this is known as the Feast of Sacrifice or *Id al-Adha*.) In addition, as the Islamic conquests vastly expanded the territories under Islamic political authority, the *hajj* caravans from the furthest reaches of the Islamic world proved to be indispensable to Islamic learning and international commerce.

In addition to themes discussed in this volume there are two other important strains of Islamic religious thought and practice that developed in the middle ages—**Shiism** and **Sufism**. Important to each of these expressions of Islamic religion is pilgrimage and the visitation (*ziyara*) of the shrines and tomb complexes of the Shi'i imams and Sufi saints. These traditions will be discussed in detail below in Global Ties. *See also* **Sunnis** and Document 1.

Further Reading

Berkey, Jonathan. *The Formation of Islam: Religion and Society in the Near East, 600–1800.* New York: Cambridge University Press, 2003.

Denny, Frederick M. *Islam and the Muslim Community.* Prospect Heights, IL: Waveland Press, 1998.

Elias, Jamal. *Islam.* Upper Saddle River, NJ: Prentice Hall, 1998.

Gibb, H.A.R. *Muhammadanism.* 2nd ed. New York: Oxford University Press, 1972.

Guillaume, Alfred, trans. *The Life of Muhammad: A Translation of Ibn Ishaq's Sirat Rasul Allah.* Oxford, UK: Oxford University Press, 1955.

Peters, F.E. *Islam: A Guide for Jews and Christians.* Princeton, NJ: Princeton University Press, 2003.

Rahman, Fazlur. *Islam.* 2nd ed. Chicago: University of Chicago Press, 1979.

Rippin, Andrew. *Muslims: Their Religious Beliefs and Practices.* Rev. ed. New York: Routledge, 2001.

3. ECONOMY

Daily life in the medieval Islamic world revolved around its markets and its mosques—two institutions essential to the hustle and bustle of daily life in every city and town—for it was in the local markets that goods were manufactured and food was bought and sold. In the major cities such as Damascus, Baghdad, Cairo, and others everything imaginable from all over the Abode of Islam and beyond could be found as well. Consequently, the bulk of this section will be devoted to markets of three major cosmopolitan centers—Damascus, Baghdad, and Cairo—and the provinces of Syria, Iraq, and Egypt. Whereas Damascus is one of the oldest continuously inhabited cities in the world, Baghdad (est. 762) and Cairo (est. 969) were founded as palace cities for new imperial dynasties: the **Abbasids** (750–1258) and **Fatimids** (909–1171), respectively. The main congregational mosque—the center of official religious and political life—was always located within or next to a market. In those instances where congregational mosques were constructed in new garrison towns such as Basra and Kufa or in new palace cities such as Baghdad and Cairo, new markets soon sprung up adjacent to the principal gathering place for the faithful.

Syria and Damascus

As the administrative center of Syria after the initial conquests in the 630s and as the seat of the **Umayyad caliphate** (661–750), Damascus oversaw the consolidation and continued expansion of the Islamic empire and the development of many of the administrative policies and institutions that would be employed by the Umayyads' successors. With the conclusion of the first civil war (656–661) and **Mu'awiya ibn Abi Sufyan**'s consolidation of his position in Syria, Islamic expansion was renewed—in Iran to the east as well as in North Africa and Spain in the west. During this early period, the Umayyads also initiated a number of policies to consolidate their administrative control over the new empire. Most notable are the reforms undertaken by **Abd al-Malik** (r. 685–705) to issue a distinctive currency and to establish Arabic as the principal administrative language of the regime. It was under Abd al-Malik's direction that the Dome of the Rock in Jerusalem was constructed as a symbol that the new Islamic regime had permanently replaced that of the Byzantines. Abd al-Malik's son, al-Walid (r. 705–715), continued with this theme as he transformed the ancient church of St. John the Baptist in Damascus into the great Umayyad mosque in the center of the city. He also refurbished and re-built Muhammad's mosque in Medina.

Although the Syria of the medieval Muslim geographers and travelers included the modern state of Syria, it also included the modern states of Lebanon, Jordan, Israel, and the Palestinian territories of the West Bank and Gaza Strip—that is, everything north of the western Arabian Peninsula. In addition, they rarely used the word *Syria* to describe the region; rather, they generally referred to it as *al-Sham*. The tenth-century geographer, **al-Muqaddasi**, explains the meaning of *al-Sham* as follows:

> It has been said that Syria is called "Shâm" because it lies on the left of the Ka'bah, and also because those who journey thither (from the Hijaz) bear to the *left* or *north*; or else it may be because there are in Syria so many Beauty-spots, such as we call *Shâmât*—red, white, and black—(which are the fields and gardens held to resemble the moles on a beauty's face). (Le Strange, 14; Collins, 129)

The rather mundane directional etymology of *al-Sham* is certainly correct. Nevertheless, the fact that al-Muqaddasi takes the trouble to include his fanciful "beauty-spot" etymology is indicative of the lengths that scholars were willing to go to praise the merits of their home provinces or cities.

Al-Muqaddasi describes in detail the physical geography of Syria and then turns his attention to Syria's climate, which is generally temperate, but because of its mountains and valleys it is also subject to the extremes of bitter cold and debilitating heat. Baalabakk in the mountains of Lebanon qualifies as the coldest place in Syria, while the Jordan Valley ranks as the hottest. In the tenth century, al-Muqaddasi could not have known that the Dead Sea, just south of Jericho in the Jordan valley, is the lowest place on the planet (1,300 feet below sea level). However, he was well aware that the Jordan Valley rift stretched south past the Hijaz and that it was a "Wâdy of heat and of palm-trees" (Le Strange, 15; Collins, 150).

As a good geographer al-Muqaddasi is rather fond of lists. A list of particular importance for our purposes is his list of the agricultural bounty and other goods produced in Syria. For it is from his list (arranged according to region and town) that we can know what people ate in tenth-century Syria and what they manufactured and sold in their local markets. Many of these foodstuffs and manufactured goods were purchased by merchants and other middlemen for sale in Damascus, but also in the markets of Cairo and Baghdad. Some may have even been purchased by long-distance traders for sale in the markets of Cordoba in Andalusia, Isfahan in Iran, and even Constantinople, the capital of the Byzantine Empire.

Al-Muqaddasi's list of Jerusalem's produce is the longest and most detailed. As one might expect, some of his hometown's produce is celebrated, excellent, and without equal.

> From Jerusalem come cheeses, cotton, the celebrated raisins of the species known as 'Ainûnî and Dûrî, excellent apples, bananas—which same is the fruit in the form of a cucumber, but when the skin is peeled off, the interior is not unlike the water-melon, only finer flavored and more luscious—also pine-nuts of the kind called "Kuraish-bite," and their equal is not found elsewhere; further mirrors, lamp-jars, and needles. (Le Strange, 18; Collins, 151)

Elsewhere, al-Muqaddasi reports that Palestine was known for olives, dried figs, raisins, the carob-fruit, textiles of mixed silk and cotton, soap, and kerchiefs; Jericho for excellent indigo; Amman for grain, lamb, and honey; Tiberias for carpet stuffs, paper, and cloth; Beit Shean for indigo, dates, and rice; Tyre for sugar, glass beads, as well as cut and blown glass vessels; Aleppo for cotton, clothes, dried figs, dried herbs, and a red chalk called *al-maghrah* (that is, the mineral *Rubrica Sinopica*). Al-Muqaddasi's list for Damascus is fuller, though not as long as his list for his hometown. "From Damascus come all these: olive-oil fresh-pressed, the *Bal'îsiyyah* cloth, brocade, oil of violets of an inferior quality, brass vessels, paper, nuts, dried figs, and raisins" (Le Strange, 19; Collins, 151).

In addition to the wide variety of foodstuffs produced in Syria, al-Muqaddasi's list illustrates very nicely the types of local manufactured goods found in Syria: various types of textiles made from locally grown silk and cotton, soap, carpets, cotton paper, glass wear, brass vessels, and *al-maghrah*. Similar types of manufactured products dominated the lists of goods produced in Iraq and Egypt as well. Of particular importance for our purposes is the extensive presence of a range of textiles, cotton paper, and *al-maghrah*. Textiles were important staples of trade in the medieval Islamic world. Paper production exploded in the medieval Islamic world after the introduction of paper-making technology in the eighth century. Finally, the red chalk called *al-maghrah* was thought to have curative powers for a range of liver disorders and is an example of the type of medicine employed in large part on the recommendation of Galen (d. 203 A.D.) and other ancient medical practitioners whose works had been translated into Arabic between the eighth and tenth centuries under the patronage of the Abbasids. In the medieval Islamic world, textiles, paper, and medicines were particularly attractive to long-distance traders because of their great value and the relative ease with which they were transported by ship as well overland by camel caravan.

Iraq and Baghdad

Despite their many successes, including extensive conquests in North Africa, Spain, Sind, and Central Asia, the Umayyad caliphate (661–750) was riddled with internal divisions by the 740s. In the end, the Umayyad house was toppled by a clandestine revolutionary movement, which operated in the name of "the approved one from the house" of Muhammad. During a Friday sermon in late October or early November 749, Abu l-Abbas Abd Allah ibn Muhammad al-Saffah (r. 749–754) publicly declared himself "the approved one from the house" in the main congregational mosque in Kufa in Iraq. Al-Saffah and his Abbasid successors based their claims principally on their kinship with Muhammad because they were descendants of his paternal uncle, Abbas.

Whereas Syria was the home province of the Umayyad caliphate and Damascus its capital, the Abbasids found their center of gravity in Iraq. Although the political discontent of Kufa had proved advantageous during the revolutionary phase of the movement, al-Saffah's brother and successor, al-**Mansur** (r. 754–775), determined that the movement's consolidation phase required the establishment of a new palace city in more stable surroundings. Al-Mansur searched along the Tigris River for the ideal location, and in 762, he settled on the site of the ancient Persian village of Baghdad. According to one report preserved by al-Tabari (839–923), when al-Mansur settled on Baghdad he said the following:

> This is a good place for an army camp. Here's the Tigris, with nothing between us and China, and on it arrives all that the sea can bring, as well as provisions from the Jazira, Armenia and surrounding areas. Further, there is the Euphrates on which can arrive everything from Syria, al-Raqqah, and surrounding areas. The caliph therefore dismounted and pitched his camp on the Sarat Canal. He sketched a plan of the city and put an army commander in charge of each quarter. (McAuliffe, 238)

Unlike medieval Syria, which encompassed much more than the modern state of Syria, medieval Iraq was far smaller than modern Iraq. Medieval geographers divided the land between the Tigris and Euphrates rivers (Mesopotamia) into two broad regions that roughly corresponded to the ancient designations of Lower and Upper Mesopotamia. Generally, when medieval geographers spoke of Iraq, they meant Lower Mesopotamia—the land between the Tigris and Euphrates rivers south of the town of Tikrit. The territory between the two rivers north of Tikrit (Upper Mesopotamia) was generally referred to as the Jazira (The Island).

Not surprisingly, al-Muqaddasi's description of Iraq and the Jazira focuses on the Tigris and Euphrates rivers and how they affected agriculture and daily life from the Persian Gulf to their headwaters in Eastern Anatolia. According to al-Muqaddasi, the waters of the Tigris are "feminine, pleasant and excellent, favorable to jurists. . . . Indeed, two-thirds of the charm of Baghdad derives from this river" (Collins, 103). The Euphrates, on the other hand, "is a masculine river: it has a hardness about it" (Collins, 104). An ancient network of canals from the Euphrates had long watered the fertile black (*sawad*) agricultural lands between the rivers that gave Lower Mesopotamia its other name: the Sawad. In the region of Baghdad a network of four canals connected the Euphrates to the Tigris. South of Kufa, the Euphrates winds its way toward Wasit where it begins to disperse into a vast marshland. The waters of the Tigris were used to irrigate the lands to its east, primarily by means of the ancient Nahrawan canal that ran from Tikrit in the north and reconnected to the Tigris about 50 miles north of Wasit in the south. By the time the rivers converged at Basra, they had so intermixed with the sea tides and waste that drinking water had to be brought from up-river by boat. According to al-Muqaddasi, there was a saying that the water in Basra "is one-third seawater, one third tidewater, and one third sewage. This is because at ebb tide the canal banks are laid bare and people relieve their bowels there: then the tide coming in carries the excrement with it" (Collins, 108).

Textiles, fish, luxuries, dates, and figs are what caught al-Muqaddasi's eye in Iraq. Basra was renowned for its silks and linens, twenty-four varieties of fish, for pearls, gems, antimony, cinnabar, verdigris, and litharge of silver and for forty-nine types of dates which were exported along with henna, silk, essence of violet, and rosewater. Kufa was renowned for silk turbans, essence of violet, and *azadh* dates; Hulwan for figs; Wasit for fish and draperies; Numani-yya for "superb garments and cloths of wool the colour of honey;" Baghdad for strong cloth, silks, fine apparel, mats, as well as "shawls and turbans of special *yakanaki* fabrics" (Collins, 107–108). The Jazira, whose climate is similar to northern Syria's, was a land of far greater agricultural diversity and was especially renowned for horses, soap, chains, leather straps, cotton, balance scales, and a preserve called *qubbayt* made from locust fruit and nuts. More specifically, Mosul was renowned for grains, honey, dried meats, coal, fats, cheese, honeydew, sumac, pomegranate seeds, pitch, iron, metal buckets, knives, arrows, salted fish, and chains; Nasibin for chestnuts, dried fruits, scales, inkstands, and rods for fulling carpets; Raqqa for soap, olive oil, and reed pens; Harran for *qubbayt*, honey, earthen wine jars, cotton, and balance scales; Malathaya for dairy products, coal, grapes, fresh fruit, cannabis seeds, hemp, and dried meat (Collins, 123).

Once again al-Muqaddasi's lists illustrate the importance of textiles (cotton, silks, linens, garments, fine apparel, and draperies) to the economy of the medieval Islamic world. Although al-Muqaddasi does not mention paper, the first paper mill in the Islamic world was established in Baghdad in 794 to 795 during the reign of **Harun al-Rashid**. Paper's production and its many uses spread from Baghdad throughout the region and ultimately, via Muslim Spain, to Europe (Bloom, 48). Antimony, cinnabar, verdigris, and litharge of silver were minerals thought to have special medicinal powers. And finally, dates, salted fish, dried meats, dried fruits, and nuts were easily preserved and exported well beyond the regions where they were produced.

Egypt and Cairo

In the wake of a clandestine revolutionary movement among the Berbers of North Africa, Ubayd Allah al-Mahdi proclaimed himself the first Fatimid imam in 910. Despite the similarities between the methodology and rhetoric of the Fatimids and that of the Abbasids, the Fatimid imams belonged to the Ismaili branch of Shi'i Islam, which was openly hostile to the **Sunni** Abbasid caliphate in Baghdad (*see* **Shiism**). In fact, the Fatimids' intent had long been to use North Africa as a staging ground for their ultimate goal of conquering Baghdad and unseating the Abbasids. To that end, and after several failed attempts, Fatimid forces finally conquered Egypt in 969. Almost immediately, the Fatimid general, Jawhar, began laying the foundations for the new palace city, al-Qahira (Cairo). The Fatimids never were able to overthrow the Abbasid caliphs, but under their tutelage Egypt and its new capital became one of the wealthiest and most important cosmopolitan way stations for international trade and culture in the Mediterranean world, southwest Asia, and the Indian Ocean. Saladin brought an end to the Fatimid caliphate in 1171, but Cairo and Egypt continued to flourish under his leadership and that of his Ayyubid successors (1171–1250) and of the **Mamluk** sultans (1250–1517).

Egypt, too, played an important role in Islam's sacred past. It was the land of the evil Pharaoh and the beautiful Joseph. It was the land in which Moses performed many of his miracles; it was the land of prophets, the wilderness, and Mount Sinai; and the land where Mary took refuge with her son Jesus (a claim made by Damascus as well). Despite al-Muqaddasi's great affection for his home province, as far as he was concerned, "Syria, with all its greatness, is just a rural district of [Egypt]; and [the] Hijaz, with its inhabitants, depends on it" (Collins, 163). There are a number of legends about the founding of al-Qahira and the etymology of its name.

According to one legend, Jawhar had staked out the perimeter of the city with wooden stakes and ropes with bells on them but wanted to wait to break ground until the astrologers determined the most propitious time. When a crow lit on one of the ropes, the workmen took the sound of the ringing bells as the signal to begin their work. Although the astrologers determined that Mars (al-Qahir, the Ruler) was in the ascendant—a bad sign—work commenced nevertheless. Another legend relates that the Fatimid imam, al-Muizz, had instructed Jawhar before he left North Africa to build a new walled city and call it al-Qahira for it would rule the world. According to yet another legend, the city was first called al-Mansuriyya (the Victorious; the name of the Fatimid capital in North Africa), but al-Muizz changed it to al-Qahira after his arrival 4 years later. Whatever the truth of these stories, Jawhar built the new Fatimid capital on a sandy plain north of Fustat where it was protected on the east by the Muqattam Hills and on the west by a canal running along the east bank of the Nile.

Because al-Muqaddasi visited Cairo only a few decades after its founding, Cairo had yet to become the bustling cosmopolitan city that travelers would later find under the Fatimids and their successors, the Ayyubids and the Mamluk Sultans. According to al-Muqaddasi,

> Al-Qahira (Cairo) is a town which Jawhar the Fatimid built after he had conquered Egypt, and subjugated [*qahara*] its inhabitants. It is large and well-built, with a splendid mosque. The imperial palace stands in its center. The town is well fortified, having iron-plated gates. It is on the main road to Syria, and no one may enter al-Fustat except through here, as both places are situated between the mountains and the river. The *Musalla* (place of prayer), where public prayers in connection with the two festivals [Ghadir Khumm and Ashura] are said, is beyond the town, while the burial grounds are between the metropolis and the mountain. (Collins, 169)

In al-Muqaddasi's day, Fustat was still the principal city of Egypt and the center of commerce and culture. According to al-Muqaddasi, "It has superceded Baghdad, and is the glory of Islam, and is the marketplace for all mankind. It is more sublime than the City of Peace [Baghdad]. It is the storehouse of the Occident, the entrepôt of the Orient, and is crowded with people at the time of the Pilgrimage festival" (Collins, 166–167). Fustat's markets were without equal, its baths were the peak of perfection, its mosques were crowded with the faithful, and its teeming population lived in four- and five-story tenements, which housed as many as two hundred people. In addition, "Victuals here are most appetizing, their savories superb. Confectionaries are cheap, bananas plentiful, as are fresh dates; vegetables and firewood are abundant. The water is palatable, the air salubrious. It is a treasury of learned men; and the winter here is agreeable" (Collins, 167). Clearly, in al-Muqaddasi's mind, there was no finer city in the entire Islamic world.

He was particularly struck by the abundance of ships plying their trade along the Nile and those anchored at Fustat's port. When a man asked al-Muqaddasi where he was from, he told him that he was from Jerusalem. The man proceeded to tell him that if the vessels along the shore of Fustat were to go to Jerusalem, they could carry away all its people, all their possessions as well as all the stones and timbers that made up the city; such was the capacity of the ships at Fustat that when they were full, nothing of Jerusalem would remain. One gets the impression that this man told a version of this story to many a stranger, but al-Muqaddasi relates it to convey his sense of wonder about Egypt's teeming economic prosperity in the tenth century.

Many of these ships were small ferries for local use. Some sailed north to the Mediterranean ports of Alexandria and Damietta. Others traveled south to Aswan where they took on goods that had been transported across the desert from the Red Sea port of Aydhab. Still others were ships that plied the waters of the Mediterranean Sea, and had sailed down the Nile to offload their goods and passengers—pilgrims, traders, artisans, Muslims, Christians, and Jews—from throughout the Mediterranean world. Some of these Mediterranean ships flew Muslim flags; others flew Byzantine or various "Frankish" flags. Clearly, political sensibilities were not to interfere with business in Fatimid Egypt. The abundance brought to Fustat by these many ships can be seen in the eleventh-century traveler, **Naser-e Khosraw**'s, glowing description of one of the markets near the mosque of Amr ibn al-As, named after the general who conquered Egypt and became its first Muslim governor in 642.

> On the north side of the mosque is a bazaar called Suq al-Qanadil [Lamp Market], and no one ever saw such a bazaar anywhere else. Every sort of rare goods from all over the world can be had there: I saw tortoise-shell implements such as small boxes, combs, knife handles, and so on. I also saw extremely fine crystal, which the master craftsmen etch beautifully. [This crystal] had been imported from the Maghreb, although they say that near the Red Sea, crystal even finer and more translucent than the Maghrebi variety had been found. I saw elephant tusks from Zanzibar, many of which weighed more than two hundred maunds. There was a type of skin from Abyssinia that resembled a leopard, from which they make sandals. Also from Abyssinia was a domesticated bird, large with white spots and a crown like a peacock's. (Thackston, 53)

The frontiers of medieval Syria and Iraq were different than their modern counterparts; medieval Egypt, however, basically corresponds to modern Egypt. Al-Muqaddasi divides Egypt into seven districts. He begins with the settled areas along the Mediterranean coast of the Sinai Peninsula, then lists three districts in the Nile Delta region ranging westward from modern day Suez to Alexandria; the fifth region is immediately south of the delta, the capital of which is Fustat. The sixth district is Upper Egypt, which lies to the south of Fustat, and its capital is Aswan, just north of the first cataract on the Nile. The seventh district is the desert and its oases.

Al-Muqaddasi devotes a great deal of attention to the Nile, its annual rise and fall, the public ceremonies held each year to break the dykes when it reached the appropriate level, as well as canals and water wheels used to irrigate farmers' fields and bring water to villages. He was particularly impressed with the crocodile, which looked like a lizard, was terrifyingly dangerous, was invulnerable to all weapons, and could snatch a whole person in its mouth. Even more impressive, though far less dangerous, were the lighthouse at Alexandria and the Pyramids at Giza, Sakkara, and elsewhere along the Nile.

But most important of all for al-Muqaddasi was the produce, because Egypt was a country of commerce as well as agriculture. Its goods included incomparable reed pens and their vitriol, vinegar, wool, canvas, cloth, flax, linen, leather, shoes, leggings, geese, plantains, bananas, sugar cane, dies, apparel, spun yarn, water skins, and fish. In particular, Fustat was renowned for its fine leather, leggings, and cloth made from a three-ply yarn of camelhair and goat's wool; Upper Egypt was known for rice, wool, dates, vinegar, and raisins; Tinnis for multicolored cloth; Damietta for sugar cane; Fayyum for rice and inferior linen; Busir for shrimp and superior cotton; Farama and its villages for fish, baskets, fine ropes, fine white cloth, wraps, canvas, mats, grains, jasmine, and other oils (Collins, 171–172).

Once again, we see the importance of textiles (dies, canvas, spun yarn, cloth, linen, wool, and fine white and multicolored cloth) to international trade in the medieval Islamic world. Paper was also produced in Egypt by al-Muqaddasi's day, having by then largely replaced parchment and papyrus. Although al-Muqaddasi focuses his attention on Egypt as a center for the production of textiles, leather, grain, and other foodstuffs, Egypt had long been a major center for the production of metal works (gold, silver, copper, tin, and lead), fine glass products, as well as pottery (Goitein, 1:108–111).

Money and Markets

Essential to the economic prosperity of the far-flung medieval Islamic world was a degree of political stability, traders' confidence that their persons and property would be generally secure along caravan and sea routes, and a stable currency with which they could buy and sell their goods. In the wake of the Islamic conquests, Muslim rulers and their subjects continued to employ the currency already in use in the conquered Byzantine and Sassanian territories. New coins were struck as well. Medieval Islamic rulers minted three types of coins. For the most part a gold coin was called a *dinar*, a silver coin was called a *dirham*, and a base metal coin (usually copper) was generally called a *fals*. There were other regional (even slang) names for the coins, but *dinar*, *dirham*, and *fals* were the customary terms used throughout the medieval Islamic world.

Because at any given time one could find merchants from Damascus, Baghdad, Cairo, Cordoba, Isfahan, Tashkent, Bukhara, Delhi, Constantinople, and a host of other Afro-Eurasian cities in the markets of the medieval Islamic world, one of the most important men in any market was the *sayrafi*, usually translated as money-changer. But his job entailed far more than simply making change: It was also to determine the precise value of a coin, especially foreign coins that traveling merchants needed to exchange for Islamic issues. In addition to the *sayrafi*, the *muhtasib* (market inspector or public censor) was essential to the smooth functioning of markets, long-distance trade, and the overall economy in any given region. His job was to ensure that the weights and measures in the market (including those used by the *sayrafi*) were correct and that business was transacted honestly, but also that public morality in the very public space of the market was upheld. *See also* Document 10.

Further Reading

Bloom, Jonathan M. *Paper Before Print: The History and Impact of Paper in the Islamic World*. New Haven, CT: Yale University Press, 2001.

Collins, Basil, trans. *The Best Divisions for Knowledge of the Regions: Ahsan al-taqasim fi ma'rifat al-aqalim*. Reading, UK: Garnet Publishing, 2001.

Dunn, Ross E. *The Adventures of Ibn Battuta: A Muslim Traveler of the 14th Century*. Berkeley: University of California Press, 1989.

Goitein, S.D. *A Mediterranean Society: The Jewish Communities of the World as Portrayed in the Cairo Geniza*. 6 vols. Berkeley: University of California Press, 1967–1993.

Le Strange, Guy, trans. *Palestine under the Moslems: A Description of Syria and the Holy Land from* A.D. *650 to 1500*. Beirut, Lebanon: Khayats Oriental Reprints, 1965 [1890].

McAuliffe, Jane Dammen, trans. *The History of al-Tabari*. Vol. 28: *Abbasid Authority Affirmed*. Albany: State University Press of New York, 1995.

Schultz, Warren C. "The Monetary History of Egypt, 642–1517," in *The Cambridge History of Egypt*, vol. 1. ed. Carl F. Petry. New York: Cambridge University Press, 1998, pp. 318–338.

Thackston, Wheeler M., trans. *Naser-e Khosraw's Book of Travels (Safarnama)*. Albany: State University of New York Press, 1986.

4. THE ARTS

Before we turn our attention to examples of art in the medieval Islamic world, it is important to dispel a common myth about "Islamic art" that one frequently finds in nonspecialist discussions of the subject. That is, the assertion that Islam forbids depictions of Muhammad or the representation of the human form—especially in religious settings. There were and are strains—particularly the more puritanical **Sunni** strains—of Islamic thought that held and still hold to such views. However, early Islamic coins, ceramics, palace inscriptions, manuscript illuminations, and so forth make it abundantly clear that though such depictions were never ubiquitous as in Byzantine and Latin Christian art, the notion that such depictions are absolutely forbidden is one of those myths that apparently cannot be dispelled no matter how much evidence there is to the contrary.

As in most premodern societies, the arts in the medieval Islamic world tended to be expressions of the artists' and craftsmen's religious and political patrons' interests. That is not to say that art was purely utilitarian in nature. Rather, it stood in stark contrast to the rather modern notion of art for art's sake or as an expression of an artist's narcissistic notions of reality. In this section, we examine a range of art forms that flourished in the medieval Islamic world, including monumental architecture, calligraphy, metalwork, woodwork, ceramics, textiles, literature, and manuscript illuminations.

The Mosque

Probably the most recognizable examples of art in the medieval Islamic world fall under the umbrella of monumental architecture: mosques, palaces, citadels, caravanserais, and so forth. Because the mosque is central to the practice of the Islamic religion and the primary example of monumental architecture in all Islamic societies, it is fitting that we begin our discussion of Islamic art with the mosque. The Arabic word for mosque (*masjid*) literally means "place of prostration." Its function was essentially the same as a synagogue or church in the ancient world; that is, it was a place for the formal worship and assembly of the community of faith.

The first mosque was actually the courtyard of Muhammad's house in Medina. Once the Islamic forces began their conquests of Arabia, Syria, Iraq, Iran, Egypt, and North Africa, we find that the armies built congregational mosques in their newly established military bases such as Kufa and Basra in Iraq as well as Fustat in Egypt and Qayrawan in North Africa. It was around these congregational mosques that these military bases served as administrative centers and gradually developed into full-fledged cosmopolitan cities.

Unlike medieval cathedrals, which tended to be long and narrow to accommodate the procession of the liturgy of the mass from the back of the church to the altar at the front, mosques tended to be broad to accommodate the rows of worshipers who lined up in prayer behind the imam. Because the faithful are required to face Mecca wherever they perform their five daily prayers (*salat*), the prayer hall of a mosque was constructed to face the direction (*qibla*) of Mecca. The front wall contained a *mihrab* that indicated the *qibla*. To the right of the *mihrab* was the *minbar* or pulpit from which the sermon would be preached. Frequently the *mihrab* took the form of a niche in the wall that was decorated with verses of the Qur'an in elaborate calligraphy as well as naturalistic and geometric designs. (For Islamic prayer rituals, *see* "Religion" section.)

In early Islamic history, the entire male Muslim population was required to worship together during the Friday noon prayer in each city's local congregational mosque. Such attendance was a defining marker of membership in and allegiance to the Muslim political and military ruling class. With the passage of time and eventual conversion of much of the local population to the religion of the conquerors, it became necessary to construct several congregational mosques in each large city. Most mosques were built as mosques from the start. However, there were instances where existing religious structures or holy sites were selected as the location for a mosque. Probably the most famous example of this is the transformation of the Cathedral of St. John the Baptist in Damascus into the main congregational mosque in the city. This transformation also presents a fascinating example of how monumental religious architecture illustrates dramatic changes in political and religious authority in the early Islamic period.

The eleventh-century Andalusian traveler **Ibn Jubayr** describes the Umayyad Mosque in Damascus as "one of the most celebrated mosques of the world," located in the center of the city (Broadhurst, 272). Initially constructed in 375 as the cathedral of St. John the Baptist by Emperor Theodosius I, the church had long been a place of veneration and pilgrimage for Christians, because the main building housed the tomb of John the Baptist. In the early 700s, al-Walid ibn Abd al-Malik (r. 705–715) appropriated the cathedral and transformed it into a congregational mosque symbolizing **Umayyad** and Islamic supremacy. However, in the years between the Islamic conquest of Damascus (635) and al-Walid's reign, the cathedral of St. John the Baptist had served as a place of worship for the majority local Christian population and the relatively few Islamic forces.

Legend has it that the early Islamic armies conquered Damascus from the west and the east. Abu Ubaydah ibn al-Jarrah (the general in charge of the conquest of Syria) had made peace with the city's Christians prior to entering the city and the church from the west. However, Khalid ibn al-Walid (hero of the *Ridda* Wars and early Islamic conquests) had made no such peace and conquered the city and the church from the east. Henceforth, the eastern part of the cathedral belonged to the Muslims, the western part to the Christians. The cathedral's gradual transition to cathedral/mosque and then to mosque illustrates the degree to which Syria's early Muslim rulers were required to accommodate the majority local Christian population until their own position was solidified by Abd al-Malik and his son, al-Walid.

As one might expect, Ibn Jubayr's account of al-Walid's construction of the new cathedral mosque paints Islam and al-Walid in the best possible light. According to Ibn Jubayr, al-Walid initially asked the Christians for the church in exchange for compensation. When they refused his generous offer, he seized the building by force and razed it. When he began to rebuild it anew as a mosque, al-Walid wrote to the "king of Rum at Constantinople ordering him to send twelve thousand craftsmen from his country, offering threats in case he should delay" (Broadhurst, 272). Of course, the Byzantine Emperor submissively obeyed the caliph and complied. The details of this story have long been disputed, especially the nature of the cathedral's joint use and whether the Christians were fairly compensated for it or whether it was seized by force. Whatever the actual truth of the details, al-Walid's mosque in Damascus is an impressive example of early Islamic monumental architecture. It soon became an object of veneration and pilgrimage for Muslims of the Middle Ages and remains so to this day. Subsequent to al-Walid's transformation, it took on even greater importance as an Islamic pilgrimage site because the head of al-Husayn ibn Ali (Muhammad's martyred grandson) was buried in the eastern side of the courtyard after he was killed at Karbala, Iraq in 680.

Palaces

The earliest remains of palace architecture—the most elaborate of the **housing** for Muslims—date to the Umayyad period. Most of these appear to have served primarily as desert retreats from the city, from plague outbreaks, as well as from the prying eyes of the Umayyads' more pious subjects. In the wake of the Abbasid seizure of power, we begin to see a change in the use of palatial architecture; that is, the **Abbasids** established their new palace cities of Baghdad (est. 762) and later Samarra (est. 836) not as retreats but as monumental edifices designed to legitimate their claims to the caliphate and leadership of the entire Islamic world. Palaces provided center for **entertainment** in the Muslim world.

A keen devotee of astrology, **al-Mansur** consulted his astrologers to ensure that the heavens agreed with his choice of Baghdad as the location for his new palace city. According to al-Khatib al-Baghdadi, after the city was completed al-Mansur had Ibrahim ibn Muhammad consult the stars. The astrologer obeyed and was pleased to inform his caliph that the horoscope was indeed auspicious; the city would be long lived, it would be the home of a great civilization, and the world and its people would gravitate to it. Moreover, he said, "May God honour you, O Commander of the Faithful. I bring you good tidings of yet another gift indicated by the stars. No Caliph shall ever die in the city" (Lassner, 46–47). Needless to say, Ibrahim's pronouncement greatly pleased al-Mansur, though assassins and civil wars would clarify for subsequent caliphs that the astrologer's forecast was not entirely accurate.

The **Fatimids** pursued a similar policy with their establishment of palace cities at Mahdiyya and al-Mansuriyya in North Africa and of course Cairo after their conquest of Egypt in 969. The Umayyads in Spain challenged the Fatimids and Abbasids to caliphal leadership in the tenth century, in part, by constructing Madinat al-Zahra (est. 936) — a new palace city within the traditional capital of Cordoba. Unfortunately for our purposes, it was customary for new rulers to destroy the palaces of their predecessors and use the material to build their own edifices. Such was the fate of Abbasid palaces in Baghdad and Samarra, Fatimid palaces in North Africa and Cairo, as well as Madinat al-Zahra in Cordoba. Hence, no palaces prior to the fourteenth century have been preserved intact.

The only palace constructed in the medieval Islamic world that remains largely intact today is the famous Alhambra (Red Fortress) built by the fourteenth-century Nasrid rulers in Granada, Spain. Ironically, it was the Christian forces that had long warred against Granada and finally subdued it in 1492 that preserved the palace. The magnificent Ottoman Topkapi Palace in Istanbul was constructed in the wake of Mehmed II's conquest of Constantinople in 1453 (after the time frame of this book) and was henceforth the home of the Ottoman sultans down to the reign of Sultan Abdulmecid (r. 1839–1860). Fortunately, detailed descriptions of palaces from throughout the medieval Islamic world have been preserved in a wide range of literary sources. Most palaces were built from stone, brick, and stucco. Some are even said to have been built out of sweets, glass, and ceramics. It should also be noted that it was common for huge and elaborate tents to be constructed specifically to serve as a ruler's palace as well. A massive palace tent used by the Fatimids was famously known as "The Slayer" because at least two men are said to have died each time it was set up.

The Written Word—Calligraphy

For the vast majority of Muslims, the Qur'an is the eternal uncreated speech of God, flawlessly recited to mankind in Arabic by His messenger, Muhammad. It should come as no surprise then that the Qur'an and the study of the Arabic language were the fundamental building blocks of education in the medieval Islamic world. Nor should it come as a surprise that the medieval Islamic world was a world in which the written word was ubiquitous, after all we learn in the Qur'an that "your Lord . . . taught by the pen, taught man what he did not know" (Qur'an 96:3–5).

The oldest form of the Arabic script is what is known as Kufic, which is rather blockish and stubby in shape. Kufic was the most commonly used script in early Islamic history and was the only script used for transcribing the Qur'an for centuries. In time, Kufic was replaced by Naskhi as the most common script used for the production of books, including the Qur'an. One of the highest examples of artistic expression in the medieval Islamic world was calligraphy—the use of the written word in highly decorative forms. By the tenth century the six classical scripts of Islamic calligraphy had been established: Kufic, Naskhi, Muhaqqaq, Raihani, Tawqi, and Riqa. Other scripts were employed as well, especially in much later Persian and Turkish calligraphic productions, both of which are written with the Arabic alphabet.

The exteriors and interiors of mosques and other public buildings were decorated with Qur'anic inscriptions. Elaborate and sophisticated inscriptions often were used to decorate the *mihrab*, or niche in the wall of a mosque that indicates the direction (*qibla*) of prayer toward Mecca. Some of the earliest artifacts of the Qur'anic text are the inscriptions on the Dome of the Rock in Jerusalem that date to the late seventh century. Presumably, **Abd al-Malik** could have selected whatever verses he wished from the Qur'an to decorate his new shrine; however, he saw fit to employ passages that assert the finality of Muhammad's prophethood and the superiority of Islam over Christianity, themes that emphasize the change in the religious and political landscape more than half a century after the initial Islamic conquest of formerly Byzantine Christian Syria.

In addition to pious and laudatory inscriptions on public buildings, coins, swords, textiles, carpets, ceramics, lamps, and so forth, one could find inscriptions, poetry, and belles-lettres with far less noble themes as well. Fine calligraphy was such a highly regarded and sought-after art form that trade in the works of famous calligraphers was a highly lucrative business, so lucrative in fact that there are numerous reports of highly skilled calligraphers passing off their own forgeries as authentic works of earlier masters.

Metalwork

Unlike medieval Europe, where metalwork tended to be viewed as a rather minor art form, metalwork—especially work in precious metals—was one of the leading art forms in the medieval Islamic world. Artists who worked in metal were of such repute that it was quite common for metalworkers to actually sign their works. Major centers of metalwork were located in northern and eastern Iran, where artists employed techniques that were inherited for the most part from their Sassanian predecessors. In the wake of the Mongol conquests in the thirteenth century, many skilled artisans understandably fled to the **Mamluk** lands of Syria and Egypt. Nevertheless, Iran continued to produce high-quality metalwork and other types of art, especially after the Ilkhanids embraced Islam and Persianate culture in the fourteenth century and presented themselves as patrons of Islamic learning and art. Iran continued to be a center of Islamic arts under the Timurids as well. Very few examples of gold and silver work have survived from the early period. Given the value of the metals themselves, it should not be surprising that many of these artifacts were melted down so that the metals could be reused. Much of what has survived is made of brass decorated with elaborate geometric designs and calligraphy of gold and silver inlay. Many of these pieces have been stripped of the gold and silver, with only the grooves where the precious metals had once been inserted. Examples of this kind of work that have survived include large water basins, candlesticks, lamps used in mosques, incense burners, hand warmers, and so forth.

Woodwork

Medieval artisans developed sophisticated ways to carve, turn, and embellish wood. We see this especially in the detailed woodwork in some of the elaborate *minbar*s (stepped pulpits in mosques), Qur'an stands, chests, and other domestic furnishings that have survived. One common means of achieving ventilation and privacy in domestic and public buildings is what is known as *mashrabiyya*: a wooden grill or grate that was used to cover windows or balconies. The grills or lattice work were usually made of turned wood that was joined together with carved blocks or spheres of wood to create intricate patterns. (In the homes of the very wealthy or for use in public buildings, the screen was occasionally made of metalwork.) There are also numerous example of intricate inlay work. Depending on available materials as well as the stylistic tastes of patrons or craftsmen, elaborate geometrical patters constructed with different types of woods, mother of pearl, ivory, and so forth.

Ceramics

The medieval Islamic world produced a tremendous range of pottery and ceramics styles, types, and designs. Rather simple earthenware vessels were, of course, abundant for utilitarian purposes such as storing water, wine, olive oil, grain, and so forth. Basic methods of decorating pottery included coating it with a white clay slip or coating it with a glaze before firing it. In time more sophisticated glazing techniques were developed that allowed for more detailed decorative motifs. Display ware employed similar decorative designs to those used by metalworkers, manuscript illuminators, calligraphers, and woodworkers. That is, there was a fondness for elaborate geometric patterns and calligraphy. We also find artifacts that were decorated with depictions of the natural world as well as scenes from literature. Such decorative techniques were employed most notably in the ceramic tile work that decorates mosques, palaces, homes, bathhouses, fountains, and so forth throughout the medieval Islamic world. In addition to working with clay, craftsmen also produced similar decorative vessels with glass as well as carved them from crystal, jade, and ivory.

Textiles and Rugs

The textile and dying industries were two of the most important industries in the medieval Islamic world. Obviously, most of what was produced would not be classified as art. But some of what was produced were luxury items made of silk as well as gold and silver threads. Such items were intended as art as well as symbols of status and were treated as such. Fine textiles were major commodities in long-distance trade and because of its value could even serve as a kind of currency. Unfortunately, because textiles are made from biodegradable materials, very little from the early period has survived; the earliest examples are quite difficult to date. Probably the most famous example of Islamic art in the Western world is the "Persian carpet" or "Oriental rug." Such pile carpets have long been favored as luxury items in the West since they were first introduced by Italian merchants in the later middle ages. In the Islamic world carpets were used as floor coverings, but also as decorative wall hangings, for cushions, pillows, bags, and sacks of all types. The *sajjada* or prayer rug was ubiquitous as well, because it provided a clean place to perform one's ritual prayers (*salat*).

The most famous textile in the medieval Islamic world was the *kiswa* or tapestry that covers the Ka'ba in Mecca. At the end of each *hajj*, the old *kiswa* was removed and replaced with a new one, a pilgrimage practice that has pre-Islamic origins as well. In Islam's early years, it became customary for the caliph to supply the new *kiswa* each year. Ibn Jubayr made the pilgrimage in 1184 and records the installation of the new *kiswa* in his *Book of Travels*.

> On Saturday, which was the Day of Sacrifice, the *Kiswah* ["Robe" or covering] of the holy Ka'bah was conveyed on four camels from the encampment of the Iraqi Emir to Mecca. Before it walked the new Qadi, wearing the black vestment given to him by the Caliph, preceded by banners and followed by rolling drums. . . . The *Kiswah* was placed on the venerated roof of the Ka'bah, and on Tuesday the 13th of the blessed month the Shaybites were busily employed in draping it. It was of a ripe green colour, and held the eyes in spell for its beauty. In its upper part it had a broad red band (that ran around the Ka'bah), and on the side that faces the venerated Maqam [Station of Abraham], the side that has the venerated door and that is blessed, there was written on this band, after the Bismillah [the invocation "In the name of God"] the words "Surely the first Sanctuary appointed for mankind (was that at Bekkah [Mecca])" [Koran III, 95]. On the other side was written the name of the Caliph with invocations in his favour. Running round the band were two reddish zones with small white roundels containing inscriptions in fine characters that included verses from the Koran as well as mentions of the Caliph. (Broadhurst, 185)

The *bismilla* is the opening sentence of all but one of the 114 chapters of the Qur'an, "In the name of God, the Merciful, the Compassionate." It was customary for an author to write only a few phrases of a Qur'anic passage with the assurance that his reader had the Qur'anic text memorized and would fill in the blanks himself. Qur'an 3:96–97 in its entirety reads as follows, "The first temple [house] ever to be built for mankind was that at Bakkah, a blessed site, a beacon for the nations. In it there are veritable signs and the spot where Abraham stood. Whoever enters it is safe. Pilgrimage to the House is a duty to God for all who can make the journey. As for the unbelievers, God can surely do without them." *Bakkah* is another name for Mecca.

Poetry

One of the most popular events at trade fairs in seventh-century Arabia was the poetry competition among the leading poets of the clans present. For to the best poet went not only a financial reward, but his entire clan benefited from the prestige of his poetic prowess. Arabic poetry performances continued to be extremely popular throughout the medieval Islamic world and remain so today, often selling out large auditoriums. Persian reemerged as a language of literature and administration in the tenth century. Public recitations of Ferdowsi's (ca. 940–1020) *Shahnameh* (Book of Kings)—one of the earliest and greatest examples of new Persian epic poetry—were quite popular throughout the Persian-speaking world. Turkish poetry began to become popular as well by 1400 after the rise of the Ottoman house in Anatolia and southeastern

Europe. It should come as no surprise that poetry often dealt with themes of honor, glory, and heroism among men, but also the beauty of one's beloved, the passions of unrequited love, and the romantic benefits of wine. Among the ruling elites as well as among the wealthy classes, poetry performances were often accompanied by music and performed by singing girls, many of whom were slaves purchased expressly for their beauty, voices, and dancing abilities.

Illuminations

The introduction of paper to the Islamic world in the eighth century made the production and reproduction of knowledge much easier and over time significantly cheaper. By the tenth century paper-making technology had been diffused throughout the Islamic world to such an extent that we see a major increase in the production of books, and with it the practice of illuminating texts with images. Examples of illustrated manuscripts that have survived include technical manuals on warfare, medicine, plants, human anatomy, astronomy, and so forth. *Kalila wa-Dimna* (a popular Arabic translation of Indian animal fables) and Ferdowsi's *Shahnameh* (one of the longest epic poems in world literature with some fifty-thousand couplets) provided a great deal of material for the illustrator's imagination and talents. The earliest complete illustrated manuscripts of the *Shahnameh* were commissioned under the Mongol Ilkhans in the fourteenth-century Iran. The tradition of patronizing the illumination of the *Shahnameh* continued under the Timurids and Safavids as well. Finally, there is the illustrated "tales of the prophets" tradition that rather explicitly flies in the face of the assertion that Islam forbids the depiction of Muhammad or other prophets. Some of these manuscripts portray Muhammad with his face visible; some with his face veiled or effaced in some fashion; and others with flames about his head similar to the nimbus (or halo) above or around sacred figures in Christian iconography.

Further Reading

Allen, Roger. *The Arabic Literary Heritage*. New York: Cambridge University Press, 1998.

Bloom, Jonathan M., and Sheila Blair. *Islamic Arts*. London: Phaidon, 1997.

Bloom, Jonathan M. *Paper before Print: The History and Impact of Paper in the Islamic World*. New Haven, CT: Yale University Press, 2001.

Broadhurst, R.J.C., trans. *The Travels of Ibn Jubayr*. London: J. Cape, 1952.

Ettinghausen, Richard, and Oleg Grabar. *The Art and Architecture of Islam, 650–1250*. New Haven, CT: Yale University Press, 1987.

Hillenbrand, Robert. *Islamic Art and Architecture*. London: Thames and Hudson, 1999.

Irwin, Robert. *Islamic Art in Context*. New York: Harry N. Abrams, Inc., 1997.

Lassner, Jacob, trans. *The Topography of Baghdad in the Early Middle Ages: Texts and Studies*. Detroit: Wayne State University Press, 1970.

5. SOCIETY

Full membership and participation in the medieval Islamic world was based on religion—an absolutely universal idea in the premodern world, whether in

Byzantium, Sasanian Iran, or fifteenth-century France. That is, if one had any hopes of being a full participant in Byzantine society, he had to be an Orthodox Christian; if one had any hopes of being a full participant in Sassanian Iranian society, he had to be a Zoroastrian; if one had any hopes of being a full participant in fifteenth-century France, he had to belong to the Latin rite of Christianity. Issues of superiority and inferiority are not limited to religion. Few themes in Islamic history cut against the grain of modern American social and cultural values than the role and status of women and men in Islamic societies. Hence, in this section we will use the themes of proper relations between Muslims, Christians, and Jews as well as proper relations between men and women to gain a broad understanding of the social order (real and ideal) in the medieval Islamic world. One of the physical marks of participation in Muslim society was **circumcision**, of both men and women. But before we turn our attention to these issues, a few words on the role of the *muhtasib* (market inspector or public censor) are in order.

The *muhtasib's* responsibility was to ensure that the weights and measures in the market were correct and that business was transacted honestly, but equally (if not more) importantly that public morality in the very public space of the market was upheld. **Nizam al-Mulk** (d. 1092) emphasizes all three roles in his advice to the Seljukid Sultan Malikshah (r. 1073–1092):

> In every city a censor must be appointed whose duty is to check scales and prices and to see that business is carried on in an orderly and upright manner. He must take particular care in regard to goods which are brought from outlying districts and sold in the bazaars to see that there is no fraud or dishonesty, that weights are kept true, and that moral and religious principles are observed. (Darke, 45)

According to Nizam al-Mulk, maintaining the integrity of the marketplace is "one of the foundations of the state and is itself the product of justice" (Darke, 45). For if the sultan does not give his full support to his *muhtasib*s and ensure the integrity of the markets in his realm, the poor will suffer, merchants will buy and sell as they see fit without regard to honesty, "sellers of short weight will be predominant; iniquity will be rife and divine law set at naught" (Darke, 45). Nizam al-Mulk's moral vision of the marketplace with its emphasis on the importance of honest weights and measures is strikingly reminiscent of the Biblical admonition that "the LORD abhors dishonest scales, but accurate weights are his delight" (Proverbs 11:1).

Another of the *muhtasib's* many responsibilities was to remove or repair anything that might hinder the free passage of goods, beasts, merchants, and customers throughout the market. The absence of wheeled vehicles contributed to the warrens of relatively narrow streets and alleys of the medieval Islamic world's bazaars and neighborhoods. Although some streets were wide, most only needed to be wide enough for two fully loaded camels, horses, or donkeys to pass one another. Needless to say, traffic jams, filthy streets, and open sewage were the bane of merchants in the medieval Islamic world as much, if not more so, as they are today. Rainstorms, floods, bad weather, and natural disasters created obvious traffic flow problems that were beyond the control of any *muhtasib*. Manmade congestion was another story. In fact, *muhtasib*s had to maintain constant vigilance against shop owners who were fond of arranging their wares well outside their storefronts, making the streets impassable for beasts of burden and sometimes even fellow merchants and customers.

Nizam al-Mulk wrote his *Book of Government* in a time when no ruler could even imagine the kind of inspection and enforcement tools that modern Americans take for granted. Hence, the only way that a sultan could ensure that his markets were honest and that public morality was upheld was to appoint *muhtasib*s who were beyond reproach and who could not be bought off. The best candidates for such jobs in Nizam al-Mulk's mind, of course, were the kinds of men that Mahmud of Ghazna (r. 998–1030) had selected. A nobleman was a good candidate, but even better would be a "eunuch or an old Turk, who having no respect for anybody, would be feared by nobles and commoners alike" (Darke, 45).

Nizam al-Mulk illustrates the near absolute authority of the *muhtasib* and the importance of public morality in the medieval Islamic world with a story. Mahmud and several of his boon companions had been up all night drinking together. When morning came, Ali Nustigin, who was still feeling giddy with drink, decided that it was time for him to go home. He asked Mahmud if he could take leave of the sultan, but Mahmud advised him that he should stay indoors until he had sobered up because it was inappropriate to go out in public intoxicated. "If the censor sees you like this in the bazaar, he will arrest you and give you the lash. You will be put to shame, and I shall be very embarrassed and unable to help you" (Darke, 45).

Ali was a general in the sultan's army and a military hero and assumed that no *muhtasib* would dare approach him in public no matter how drunk he might be. As luck would have it, when he was in the middle of the bazaar, the *muhtasib* appeared with a hundred men. The *muhtasib*, who was an old and venerable Turkish eunuch, ordered his men to drag Ali off his horse. The inspector then dismounted his own horse and proceeded to beat Ali forty times with a stick until he fell to the ground while everyone silently watched. When the *muhtasib* left, Ali's men carried him home. The next day Mahmud asked him if the *muhtasib* had seen him. When Ali showed him the stripes on his back, he laughed and said, "Now repent and resolve never to go outdoors drunk again" (Darke, 46).

Jews and Christians: People of the Book

Relations between Muslims and non-Muslims were ostensibly governed by Qur'anic pronouncements, *hadith*s about Muhammad's words, deeds, and attitudes towards non-Muslims, as well as the practice of the early Muslim community. Together, they provide the basis for the Islamic concept of *dhimma*, a term that means "protected people," those who agree to pay a special tax and accept the rule of Muslim leaders. Through this concept, Muslims offer hospitality to those of other religions living in their lands. Muslim scholars considered Jews, Christians, Zoroastrians (Magians), Samaritans, and Sabeans to be adherents of "other revealed religions"; that is, *ahl al-kitab* (People of the Book). As such, only they were afforded *dhimmi* status. As Muslim armies conquered new territories and for reasons of political expediency, other groups such as Buddhists in Central Asia and Hindus in India were afforded de facto *dhimmi* status. However, Buddhism and Hinduism were not considered de jure revealed religions.

The Qur'an venerates Noah, Abraham, Moses, Jesus, and other Biblical figures as prophets who had preached the same monotheistic message that Muhammad proclaimed to his kinsmen and followers in Mecca and Medina. Although the Qur'an concedes that there are some individual Jews and Christians who are righteous, it condemns Jews and Christians in general as willfully errant communities of faith. "Had the People of the Book accepted the Faith, it would surely have been better for them. Some are true believers, but most of them are evil-doers" (Qur'an 1:111).

Jews are condemned in the Qur'an for having corrupted the *Tawrah* (Torah) given to Moses, for having killed God's prophets, and for falsely claiming to have crucified Jesus (Qur'an 4:154–157). Christians are condemned for having corrupted the *Injil* (Gospel) given to Jesus, for claiming that Jesus is God's son, and especially for the doctrine of the Trinity, which the Qur'an describes as polytheism, the worst of all sins (Qur'an 4:171). In spite of the Qur'an's veneration of Abraham, Moses, and Jesus, its attitude toward the People of the Book is explicitly aggressive and hostile, as follows:

> Fight against such of those to whom the Scriptures were given [*ahl al-kitab*] as believe neither in God nor the Last Day, who do not forbid what God and His apostle have forbidden, and do not embrace the true Faith, until they pay tribute [*jizya*] out of hand and are utterly subdued. (Qur'an 9:29)

Accordingly, once the People of the Book were properly subdued and had paid the *jizya* (tribute or poll-tax, essentially protection money), there was no need to continue to fight them.

As one might expect, how these and other texts were interpreted by jurists and how they were applied by rulers varied according to time period and region. Nevertheless, in exchange for their submission and tribute all members of these communities were supposed to be afforded protection of life and property as well as limited religious freedoms, at least in those areas such as marriage, divorce, and inheritance where their activities did not impinge on the ruling Muslim classes. Certain disabilities were imposed on them as well, including distinctive dress, restrictions on the construction of new places of worship, even prohibitions against riding horses.

According to *The Book of the Islamic Market Inspector*, compiled in the twelfth century by the Syrian jurist al-Shayzari (d. c. 1193),

> The *dhimmi*s must be made to observe the conditions laid down for them in the treatise on *jizya* written for them by Umar b. al-Khattab, and must be made to wear the *ghiyar* [a distinctive piece of cloth]. If he is a Jew, he should put a red or a yellow cord on his shoulder; if a Christian, he should tie a *zunnar* [distinctive girdle] around his waist and hang a cross around his neck; if a woman she should wear two slippers, one of which is white and the other black. When a protected person goes to the baths, he must wear a steel, copper or lead neckband to distinguish him from other people. (Buckley, 121–122)

As a manual for *muhtasib*s, al-Shayzari's admonitions are more prescriptive of what should be enforced rather than descriptive of what actually occurred. There is plenty of evidence that specific restrictions on *dhimmi*s differed according to time, place, regime, and class. Sometimes they were not enforced at all; at other times, they were enforced with draconian cruelty.

Some of the most famous examples include the arbitrary policies of the Fatimid Caliph al-Hakim (r. 996–1021), who was thought to be mad, and the Almohad regime in North Africa and Spain (1130–1269) which was particularly brutal to Jews and Christians, but also to Muslims who did not conform to its particularly strict version of Islam. However *dhimma* regulations were enforced, their purpose was twofold: (1) to ensure that, as commanded in the Qur'an, the People of the Book properly submitted to Islamic authority and paid the *jizya* and (2) to demonstrate publicly the superiority of Islam and Muslims to the inferior *dhimmi* religions and communities.

In light of Muhammad's conflicts with the leading Jewish clans of Medina *hadith*s such as the following were favorites of jurists who supported strict enforcement of *dhimma* regulations: "You will fight the Jews to such a point that if one of them hides behind a rock, the rock will say: Servant of God, here is a Jew behind me! Kill him" (al-Bukhari, volume 4, book 52, number 176). So too were Qur'anic passages that declare that those who violated the Sabbath and opposed God would be turned into apes and pigs (Qur'an 2:65; 5:60; 5:78; 7:166). In addition, the prolific ninth-century author, al-Jahiz (777–869), marshaled many of the standard Muslim arguments against Jews and Christians in his anti-Christian polemic, *The Refutation of Christianity* (Colville, 71–94). He begins his treatise with an account of why, despite their perversions and Trinitarian polytheism, Christians are "more trustworthy, more sociable, less pernicious, lesser infidels and generally, less of a torment, than Jews" (Colville, 73). His basic arguments against Jews are based on Muhammad's negative encounters with the Jews of Medina. According to al-Jahiz, because the Christian Arab tribes and the lands of Christendom were far removed from Mecca and Medina, Christians "never resorted to intrigue, vilification and open hostility against Muslims. This is the principal reason why Muslim opinion became set against Jews but remains tolerant of Christians" (Colville, 73). Nevertheless, "the Christian is at heart, a foul and dirty creature. Why? Because he is uncircumcised, does not wash after intercourse and eats pig meat. His wife does not wash after intercourse, either, or even after menstruation and childbirth, which leaves her absolutely filthy. Furthermore she, too, is uncircumcised" (Colville, 79).

Jewish and Christian attitudes toward Muslims and toward each other were equally contemptuous. After all, all three religions claimed to possess the sole revealed truth. Polemics aside, demographic realities necessitated intercommunal contact between the superior Muslim community and the inferior Jewish and Christian communities. It should come as no surprise that the history of Muslim/non-Muslim relations varied considerably from the first Islamic centuries when the Muslim military and ruling elite represented such a small minority of the population to the later centuries after the majority of the local population had converted to the religion of the conquerors.

Muslim rulers had little choice but to retain non-Muslim peoples (Christians but also Jews in the formerly Byzantine lands; Zoroastrians and some Christians and Jews in the formerly Sassanian lands) in bureaucratic positions such as revenue collectors and administrators of various types. In fact, one of al-Jahiz's reasons for writing his *Refutation of Christianity* was the presence of influential Christians and Jews in Baghdad in his day. Christians and Jews continued to be employed in government service during the **Fatimid** (969–1171) and Ayyubid (1171–1250) periods in Egypt as well.

Despite their inferior status, Jews and Christians were not consigned to ghettos as they were in parts of medieval Christian Europe. Jews, Christians, and Muslims often lived in the same neighborhoods and in adjoining properties. Muslims and non-Muslims rented apartments, warehouses, and market stalls from one another. Jewish and Christian congregations even occasionally rented space from Muslim landlords to use as synagogues or churches to circumvent the laws against the construction of non-Muslim places of worship. Occasionally, other legal ruses were used to permit the construction of new churches and synagogues. Muslims and non-Muslims entered into business transactions with one another, whether in the local market or long distance trade.

The frequency and type of such intercommunal contacts does not mean that the medieval Islamic world was a model of religious diversity and toleration in the modern American sense. Again, according to al-Shayzari,

> The *muhtasib* [market inspector] must take the *jizya* from them according to their social status. Thus, at the beginning of the year a poor man with a family pays one dinar, while someone of middling wealth pays two dinars and a rich man pays four dinars. When the *muhtasib* or his agent comes to collect the *jizya*, he should stand the *dhimmi* in front of him, slap him on the side of the neck and say: "Pay the *jizya*, unbeliever." The *dhimmi* will take his hand out of his pocket holding the *jizya* and present it to him with humility and submission. (Buckley, 122–123)

As the Cairo **Geniza** records make abundantly clear, the poll tax (*jizya*) was the *dhimmi*'s inescapable burden and clear marker of inferiority in any and all relations with Muslims. Hence, religious diversity in the medieval Islamic world was characterized by Jewish and Christian communities that essentially functioned as separate nations within the Abode of Islam, and which were tolerated only because they had little choice but to accept the terms of their inferior status.

The documents of the Geniza also make it abundantly clear that Jews were involved in extensive and profitable long-distance trade throughout the Mediterranean Basin, East Africa, India, and even as far as Indonesia in Southeast Asia. In fact, the Geniza records indicate that Jews owned many of the ships that operated in the Mediterranean Sea, the Nile, and the Indian Ocean, though there is little evidence that Jews actually piloted very many of them. S.D. Goitein discusses one case in which an Egyptian Jewish merchant had died in India after a 9-year sojourn there. After the merchant's death, his brother paid his poll tax for the whole 9 years. He and others had little choice. Failure to pay the poll tax could result in beatings and/or imprisonment, where one faced starvation and even death. Needless to say, people of modest means found the poll tax particularly onerous. Wealthy Jews and Christians, of course, could more easily afford to pay it. In fact, petitions to wealthy Jews and/or to the head of the local Jewish community for assistance in paying the poll tax represent one of the most common themes in the many letters preserved in the Cairo Geniza.

Finally, **al-Muqaddasi**'s brief comment that "most of the assayers, the dyers, cambists, and tanners in [al-Sham] are Jews; while the physicians and the scribes are generally Christians" brings us to the important issue of the role of the *dhimmi* physician in the medieval Islamic world (Collins, 153). In keeping with the general distrust of Jews and Christians, Muslim jurists argued that Muslims should abstain from using the services of Jewish and Christian doctors or pharmacists on the grounds that an unbeliever might prescribe medicines that would do them physical or spiritual harm. However, there is probably no *dhimma* regulation that was more frequently ignored than this. Jewish and Christian prohibitions against consulting physicians who did not belong to their own faith communities were widely ignored as well.

It appears that because many Muslims, Christians, and Jews (like many modern Americans) were far less concerned with their physician's religion than with his medical knowledge and the quality of his practice, it was the medical profession in particular that transcended religious boundaries in the medieval Islamic world. According to S. D. Goitein, physicians were "the torchbearers of secular erudition, the professional expounders of philosophy and the sciences. . . . [They] were the disciples of the Greeks, and as heirs to a universal tradition formed a spiritual brotherhood that transcended the barriers of religion, language, and countries" (Goitein, 2:240–241).

Women and Men in the Family and Society

Few themes in Islamic history cut against the grain of modern American social and cultural values than the role and status of women and men in the Qur'an. In traditional Islamic thought, concepts that modern Americans take for granted—individual liberty, individual choice, personal fulfillment—necessarily lead to moral chaos because they are not informed by the admonitions and guidance of God's revelation to mankind in the Qur'an. Although the Qur'an has very little material that may be consider legal in nature, the bulk of the legal material in the Qur'an deals with the proper role and status of women and men in the family and in society as a whole. For a more detailed discussion of women and men in medieval Islamic thought see **Women** and **Clothing and Modesty** in the "Short Entries" section.

The discussion below intends to clarify what the role and status of women and men were supposed to be (especially in the context of the family), at least according to the Qur'an and its later interpreters as they worked out the requirements of *shari'a*, or Islamic law. Using the building blocks of shari'a—the Qur'an, the sunna of Muhammad, and Arabian custom—scholars in Medina and the urban culture of Iraq, Syria, and elsewhere during the first Islamic centuries sought to discern precisely what one's submission (*islam*) to God entailed. In principle, at least, the role and status of women and men in Islamic thought are governed by three concepts that if not explicitly stated in the Qur'an, are certainly implied therein.

The first principle is embodied in the *shahada*—the simple two-part creedal declaration that is at the very center of Islamic belief, ritual, and worship. "There is no god but God; Muhammad is the messenger of God (*la ilaha illa'llah; Muhammadun rasul Allah*)." Each man and each woman is personally responsible for making this declaration (*shahada*) and submitting (*islam*) to the one God and acknowledging Muhammad as His messenger. Consequently,

> Those who surrender themselves to God and accept the true Faith; who are devout, sincere, patient, humble, charitable and chaste; who fast and are ever mindful of God—on these, *both men and women*, God will bestow forgiveness and a rich reward. It is not for true believers—*men or women*—to take their choice in their affairs if God and His apostle decree otherwise. He that disobeys God and His apostle strays far indeed. (Qur'an 33:35–36) (Emphasis added)

The second principle is that though the Qur'an condemns many of the practices of seventh-century Mecca and Medina including idolatry, polytheism, gambling, drinking wine, the abuse of the poor by the rich, and female infanticide, it accepts the *patrilineal* kinship system of Arabia and many of its values as the natural order of things. "Men have authority over women because God has made the one superior to the other" (Qur'an 4:34a). The third principle — that a man must provide for every member of his household (wives, children, servants, and slaves) from his own resources — is closely connected to the second, "because they [men] spend their wealth to maintain them [women]" (Qur'an 4:34b).

Although every man and woman is morally responsible before God for his or her beliefs and actions (and despite modern interpretations, polemics, and protestations to the contrary), medieval commentators interpreted the Qur'an as uncompromisingly patriarchal in its description of proper relations between men and women. One of the most important elements of the system of patrilineal kinship is paternal certainty, for without it the entire system would fall apart. According to this structure, chastity (especially *female* chastity) before marriage and fidelity in marriage are essential in guaranteeing *paternal* certainty. Sexual activity outside of marriage was not a matter of individual choice, but a violation of family honor and the Qur'anic sexual ethic that embraced it (Qur'an 24:2–5). In theory, the Qur'anic requirements of chastity and fidelity applied equally to men and women; however, the physical consequences of a man's illicit sexual activity were less readily apparent and less strictly enforced. Related to chastity are the issues of modesty and separation of the sexes, which were rigorously observed in the public sphere; that is, essentially everywhere outside of the home and apart from one's kin. In the most prominent of public spaces, the mosque and the market, this separation of the sexes consisted of the physical separation of women from men (e.g., congregational prayers in the mosque) as well as by means of modest dress.

Fundamental to family life in any society are the conditions under which new families are established in marriage. Unlike in the American ideal of marital bliss, where many believe one's spouse should be one's best friend and soul mate, the purpose of marriage in the Qur'an and the medieval Islamic world was the procreation of children and the strengthening of ties between two extended families. In principle, the man or the woman was able to decline a proposed match, but rarely was there an opportunity for such an arrangement to be initiated on the basis of mutual affection or common interests and certainly not after a period of courtship as in the American ideal of the institution.

Another way in which marriage differs from the modern American model is that according to the Qur'an, a man may take up to four wives at the same time, with the proviso that he treat each wife fairly to avoid injustice (Qur'an 4:3). Whether a man took one wife or as many as four, it is clear from the Qur'an that in return for his protection and provision, he was owed obedience. If a wife was not obedient, her husband was allowed to chastise her and even to beat her into submission.

> Good women are obedient. They guard their unseen parts because God has guarded them. As for those from whom you fear disobedience, admonish them and send them to beds apart and beat them. Then if they obey you, take no further action against them. (Qur'an 4:35)

Not surprisingly, this passage often produces embarrassment among some modern Muslims, especially in the West, where women and men (at least according to the laws in most Western countries) are supposed to be equals in a marriage relationship. According to the Qur'anic worldview, however, "men have authority over women because God has made the one superior to the other, and because they spend their wealth to maintain them" (Qur'an 4:34).

Whereas a man was limited to having four wives at any given time, he could possess as many female slaves as he could afford. According to shari'a, in exchange for his maintenance and support, the head of the household had the right to obedience as well as sexual relations with his female slaves. Unlike the American slave system, the child of a free Muslim man and a female slave received the status of the father not the mother. That is, the child was a legally free Muslim and bore no stigma of illegitimacy. In addition, once a female slave had borne a child, she could not be put out of the house, she could legally expect maintenance and support, and she had to be granted her freedom upon the death of her owner. A wife on the other hand could bear her husband as many children as physically possible, and he could divorce her without cause.

Slavery

Slavery of some sort is a nearly universal constant in human societies. It should come as no surprise then that it was a key element in medieval Islamic societies as well. Certainly the most famous example of slavery in the medieval Islamic world is military slavery, known as the **Mamluk** institution. *Mamluk* is an Arabic word that means "one who is owned"; however, it is almost always used as a technical term for a particular type of military slavery designed to produce an elite force of mounted warriors. *Abd* and *khadim* are the Arabic words generally used to describe field hands, domestic servants, day laborers, concubines, singing girls, tutors—some of which evoke images of slavery and servitude that more closely resemble the history of slavery in the United States. In fact, there is plenty of evidence that the kinds of abuses that are equated with slavery in the United States were inflicted on field hands, domestic servants, day laborers, concubines, and so forth in Islamic history as well.

In the medieval Islamic world, however, having been enslaved as a young boy and raised to the profession of arms was anything but degrading. In fact, Mamluks served in a number of important offices on behalf of the ruler—personal attendants, cup bearers, officers charged with attending to and training the ruler's horses and hunting falcons, even as provincial governors. Moreover, being a Mamluk was a position of privilege that opened the door to many avenues of wealth and status in society, even to the highest offices in the regime. It appears that in the ninth through eleventh centuries, it was not required for Mamluks who rose to such high positions to be manumitted. Thereafter, it was much more common that they were.

Although the preferred route for developing Mamluk regiments was to purchase boys and to train them in barracks apart from the rest of society in the sciences of horsemanship, warfare, and religion, some adults were incorporated into Mamluk regiments, especially during the early years of the institution. According to Islamic law, a free person could only be enslaved if he was a non-Muslim and resided outside the Abode of Islam; that is, in the Abode of War. Hence, slaves were acquired by various means (purchase, conquest, as gifts, etc.) from peoples who lived on the fringes of the Abode of Islam: sub-Saharan Africans, Eastern Europeans, Greeks, Armenians, Circassians, Indians, and so forth. However, the preferred practice for creating Mamluk units was to purchase boys from the slave markets along the Central Asian frontier north of the Oxus River. These boys were generally referred to as "Turks"—a kind of shorthand for anyone who was a pastoral nomad from the Central Asian steppe, and it was this steppe that served as a vast military reservoir for many of the regimes in the medieval Islamic world.

In addition to their military prowess and horsemanship, Turkish slaves were renowned for their beauty, which served some in good stead in their service as pages, personal attendants, and occasional bedfellows. Turkish slave girls were prized as singing girls and concubines. We learn from the geographer, Ibn Hawqal (fl. 943–977), just how much people were willing to pay for the very best Turkish slaves—male and female—in the tenth century.

> The most valuable slaves are those which come from the land of the Turks. Among all the slaves in the world, the Turks are incomparable and none approach them in value and beauty. I have not infrequently seen a slave boy sold in Khurasan for 3000 dinars; and Turkish slave girls fetch up to 3000 dinars. In all the regions of the earth I have never seen slave boys or girls which are as costly as this, neither Greek nor one born in slave status. (Bosworth, 209)

The Ottomans (c. 1300–1923) took non-Muslim slaves from neighboring Russia and the Caucasus region as well. However, they also undertook a policy that was a dramatic departure from the traditional practice of slave procurement; in the late fourteenth century they began to levy a rather peculiar tax on their (primarily) Balkan Christian subjects, which involved drafting Christian children into service to the sultan. This tax, called the *devshirme*, produced the elite janissary corps as well as so many high government officials in the Ottoman regime that there are instances where Muslim families in the Balkans presented their own children as Christians so that they too might benefit from such prestigious and lucrative opportunities.

Further Reading

Bosworth, C.E. *The Ghaznavids: Their Empire in Afghanistan and Eastern Iran, 944–1040.* Beirut, Lebanon: Librairie du Liban, 1973.

Buckley, R.P., trans. *The Book of the Islamic Market Inspector: Niyayat al-rutba fi talab al-hisba (The Utmost Authority in the Pursuit of Hisba) by 'Abd al-Rahman b. Nasr al-Shayzari.* New York: Oxford University Press, 1999.

al-Bukhari. *Sahih al-Bukhari: The Translation of the Meanings of Sahih al-Bukhari.* 9 vols. Translated by M. Muhsin Khan. Riyadh, Saudia Arabia: Darussalam Publishers, 1997, volume 4, book 52, number 176.

Cahen, Claude. "Dhimma," in *Encyclopaedia of Islam, New Edition.* P.J. Bearman et al., eds. Boston: Brill Academic Publishers, 2005.

Collins, Basil, trans. *The Best Divisions for Knowledge of the Regions: Ahsan al-taqasim fi ma'rifat al-aqalim.* Reading, UK: Garnet Publishing, 2001.

Colville, Jim, trans. *Sobriety and Mirth: A Selection of the Shorter Writings of al-Jahiz.* London: Kegan Paul, 2002.

Darke, Hubert, trans. *The Book of Government or Rules for Kings: The Siyar al-Mulk or Siyasat-nama of Nizam al-Mulk.* Richmond, UK: Curzon Press, 2002.

Goitein, S.D. *A Mediterranean Society: The Jewish Communities of the World as Portrayed in the Cairo Geniza.* 6 vols. Berkeley: University of California Press, 1967–93.

Lewis, Bernard. *The Jews of Islam.* Princeton, NJ: Princeton University Press, 1984.

6. SCIENCE AND TECHNOLOGY

Islamic Science

Frequently introductory discussions of science, technology, medicine, and so forth in the medieval Islamic world highlight the contributions of thinkers whose work was eventually translated into Latin (e.g., al-Khwarizmi, al-Razi, al-Biruni, Ibn Sina) and which found a following in the Latin west during the later Middle Ages. Although such an approach is certainly valid, it frequently overlooks the processes by which the Arabic language—the language of obscure Arabian tribesmen in late antiquity—became the vehicle by which some of the finest examples of classical science and learning were made accessible in the Islamic empire between the eighth and tenth centuries. Many of the earliest translators of this learning were in fact Christian scholars who knew the relevant languages, the most famous being the Assyrian scholar, physician, and scientist, Hunayn ibn Ishaq (809–873). It was only after Arabic had become the lingua franca of the educated classes and after many of the classics of Greek (and other) learning were made available in Arabic that Arabic-speaking Jews, Christians, and Muslims could undertake to transform this learning into a body of literature that is generally classified under the rubric of "Islamic science."

As our sources make clear, what we now call Islamic science can only be classified as such because it was developed largely under the patronage of medieval Islamic rulers as well as their officials and associates. For medieval Muslims, the "Islamic sciences" were those subjects devoted to understanding the broad principles as well as the minutia of right religion—the Qur'an and its interpretation, hadith studies, the roots of jurisprudence (*usul al-fiqh*, legal theory), the branches of jurisprudence (*furu'al-fiqh*, practical application), the intricacies of Islamic mysticism, and so forth (*see* **Shari'a** and **Sufism**).

Subjects such as astronomy, medicine, mathematics—what we call the physical and natural sciences—belonged to the sciences shared by all peoples. The fourteenth-century North African historian and philosopher Ibn Khaldun (d. 1406) addresses this distinction in his monumental *Muqaddima*, or "Introduction" to the science of history and civilization.

> The intellectual sciences are natural to man, inasmuch as he is a thinking being. They are not restricted to any particular religious group. They are studied by the people of all religious groups who are all equally qualified to learn them and to do research in them. They have existed (and been known) to the human species since civilization had its beginnings in the world. (Ibn Khaldun, 3:113)

Elsewhere in his *Muqaddima*, Ibn Khaldun draws a connection between Greek and Persian learning—a connection that highlights Persian self-conceptions of their intellectual and imperial heritage:

> Among the Persians [in antiquity], the intellectual sciences played a large and important role, since the Persian dynasties were powerful and ruled without

interruption. The intellectual sciences are said to have come to the Greeks from the Persians, (at the time) when Alexander killed Darius and gained control of the Achaemenid empire. At that time, he appropriated the books and sciences of the Persians. (Ibn Khaldun, 3:113–114).

But what concerns us here are the conditions that made it possible—even necessary—for Greek and other classical learning to be transformed into scientific knowledge composed in the Arabic language. Or to paraphrase Dimitri Gutas, how is it that Greek knowledge became part of Arabic culture?

Two major reforms that the **Umayyad** caliph, **Abd al-Malik** (r. 685–705), undertook in the late seventh century were the minting of a new currency with distinctively Islamic themes and Arabic inscriptions (*see* **Money and Coinage**) and the establishment of Arabic as the principal language of administration throughout his domains. No longer would markets employ Byzantine and Sasanian coins. Nor would Umayyad bureaucrats (most of whom belonged to families that had served similar functions prior to the Islamic conquests) use Greek in the former Byzantine territories or Persian in the former Sasanian lands. Such changes in economic and administrative policy reflect a high degree of religious and political self-confidence on the part of Abd al-Malik a mere half century after the death of Muhammad.

In the wake of the **Abbasid** revolution in the 740s, the political and administrative center of the Islamic world shifted from Syria and Damascus to Mesopotamia, where the second Abbasid caliph, **al-Mansur** (r. 754–775), established Baghdad in 762 as his new palace city and capital. The move from Damascus to Baghdad represented much more than a simple change in geography, for it was in Baghdad and Mesopotamia that al-Mansur initiated the translation of Greek and other classical astronomical, philosophical, medical, mathematical, and scientific texts into Arabic, a monumental intellectual undertaking that would continue well into the tenth century.

Of course, some translations of classical texts had been produced in the Umayyad period, but al-Mansur's policy went far beyond that of new rulers' needs for pragmatic administrative or military knowledge. Although the specific circumstances and concerns of al-Mansur's caliphate and those of his successors are complex, the essential need for any regime to legitimate itself can help clarify why such extensive translations of classical scientific works were undertaken.

The Abbasids' claim that they were the legitimate successors to Muhammad by virtue of their descent from Muhammad's clan of Hashim met the demands of their Muslim subjects (at least in theory); however, the majority of the population was not Muslim. With their center of gravity in Mesopotamia, the Abbasids also presented themselves as the successors of "the ancient imperial dynasties in Iraq and Iran, from the Babylonians to the Sasanians, their immediate predecessors. In this way they were able to incorporate Sasanian culture, which was still the dominant culture of large masses of the population east of Iraq, into mainstream Abbasid culture" (Gutas, 29).

Al-Mansur and his son al-Mahdi (r. 775–785) were the principal early architects of the translation program, whose intent, in part, was to appeal to the Sasanian cultural self-conception that all knowledge is derived from the Zoroastrian canon, but also to provide the intellectual and argumentative tools to buttress Abbasid political claims as well as to aid the proselytization efforts designed to defend the superiority of Islam against other religions—namely

Judaism, Christianity, and Zoroastrianism. According to the tenth-century historian al-Masudi (d. 956):

> [Al-Mansur] was the first caliph to favor astrologers and to act on the basis of astrological prognostications. He had in his retinue the astrologer Nabakht the Zoroastrian, who converted to Islam upon his investigation and who is the progenitor of this family of the Nawbakhts. Also in his retinue were the astrologer Ibrahim al-Fazari, the author of an ode to the stars and other astrological and astronomical works, and the astrologer Ali ibn-Isa the Astrolabist.
>
> [Al-Mansur] was the first to have books translated from foreign languages into Arabic, among them *Kalila wa-Dimna* and *Sindhind*. There were also translated for him books by Aristotle on logic and other subjects, the *Amlagest* by Ptolemy, the *Arithmetic* [by Nicmachus of Gerasa], the book by Euclid [on geometry], and other ancient books from classical Greek, Byzantine Greek, Pahlavi [Middle Persian], Neopersian, and Syriac. These [translated books] were published among the people, who examined them and devoted themselves to knowing them. (Gutas, 30–31)

By the end of the tenth century, hundreds of ancient Greek, Persian, and Sanskrit works on philosophy, medicine, mathematics, astronomy, astrology, geography, and other sciences had been translated into Arabic under the patronage of the Abbasids. Muslim (as well as Jewish and Christian) scholars studied these classics and built upon them, making such Greek learning distinctively their own in the Arabic language. Hence the need for new translations into Arabic abated by the end of the tenth century. Many of these ancient as well as new Arabic language classics were eventually translated into Latin and made their way into the medieval European curriculum. The pantheon of philosophers, polymaths, physicians, and others contains far too many personalities to be addressed here. I briefly address the four scholars mentioned above merely to illustrate that, building on the work of the ancients, scholars in the medieval Islamic world (Jews, Christians, and Muslims) made important advancements in all areas of science and learning.

The ninth-century mathematician al-Khwarazmi (c. 800–c. 847) played a major role in the introduction of "Hindu numerals" into the Islamic world. This numbering system was later adopted and modified in the West resulting in what are now known as "Arabic" numerals. Al-Khwarazmi also wrote an important mathematical text *Kitab al-mukhtasar fi hisab al-jabr wa l-muqabila* (*Compendium on Calculation by Transposition and Reduction*) in which he developed methods for solving quadratic equations in which words and letters were used to represent numerical values. In 1145, Robert of Ketton began his Latin translation of al-Khwarazmi's *Compendium* (*Liber Algebras et Almucabola*) with the phrase *dixit Algorithmi*; that is, "Algorithmi says." It is from Ketton's transliteration of al-Khwarazmi's title (*Algebras* for *al-jabr*; transposition) that we get our word *algebra*; from Ketton's transliteration of his name (Algorithmi for al-Khwarazmi) that we get our term for the step-by-step process of working out mathematical problems, algorithm.

Al-Razi (865–925), who was known in the West as Rhazes, is most famous for his medical works but was also an accomplished alchemist, chemist, and philosopher. He was known as a pioneer in the fields of pediatrics, obstetrics, and ophthalmology. Theoretical diagnoses of illness and their treatments held little interest for him. Rather, he was a meticulous observational diagnostician and clinician who served as head of hospitals in his hometown of Rayy in Iran as well as in the Abbasid capital, Baghdad. Al-Razi is said to have authored nearly two hundred books and treatises on scientific, medical, and philosophical topics. His *Kitab fi l-jadari wa l-hasba* (*The Book of Smallpox and Measles*) is the first detailed diagnostic and treatment regimen for both diseases, which carefully catalogues the differences in their symptoms. He also wrote a general medical handbook, *Kitab al-tibb al-Mansuri* (*The Mansuri Book of Medicine*). His most important medical work, *al-Hawi fi l-Tibb* (*The Comprehensive Book on Medicine*), is an encyclopedia of clinical medicine and certainly lived up to its title since it comprised more than twenty volumes. However, his general medical handbook was much more broadly influential because of its brevity and organization made it readily accessible to students and medical practitioners.

Al-Biruni (973–1048) was one of the most important scientists, mathematicians, astronomers, geographers, ethnographers, physicians of the medieval Islamic world. A true polymath, al-Biruni composed more than one hundred fifty books and treatises and is one of the most studied scholars in the Arabic scientific tradition. He has been a frequent recipient of praise for his breadth of expertise and pursuit of scientific knowledge down to the present. His *al-Qanun al-Masudi* (*The Canon of Masudi*) is a model synthesis of Greek, Indian, and Persian astronomy. Frequently compared to Ptolemy's synthesis of Greek astronomy in his *Almagest*, al-Biruni's *Canon* also serves as a history of Arabic astronomy down to his own day. The importance of al-Biruni's enduring contributions to the science of astronomy is illustrated by the fact that an impact crater on the far side of the moon is called the al-Biruni Crater. Al-Biruni's pursuit of knowledge moved well beyond the physical and natural sciences. His treatise based on his travels in India is a sympathetic depiction of Indian society and religion is largely free of the blistering polemics so characteristic of the age. His sensitivity and determination to describing his observations as objectively as possible has led modern scholars to call him the first anthropologist.

Al-Biruni's contemporary Ibn Sina (980–1037), who was known in the West as Avicenna, had a tremendous influence on philosophy, theology, and medicine in the medieval Islamic world as well as in Europe. Ibn Sina's proof for the existence of God, based on the distinction between possible and necessary existence, was equally influential among Jewish and Christian thinkers. The Jewish philosopher and physician, Moses Maimonides (d. 1204), a native of Muslim Spain (who relocated to Egypt in the wake of Almohad persecutions) read Ibn Sina's work in Arabic and adapted it to his own theological writings. The Christian theologian, St. Thomas Aquinas (d. 1274) studied it in Latin translation and incorporated it into his own systematic theology. Ibn Sina's proof remains the starting point for many rational proofs for the existence of God to this day. I even remember learning a greatly simplified version of this proof as a child in Sunday school.

In addition to his major contributions to philosophy and theology, Ibn Sina is most famous for his comprehensive and systematic medical text, *al-Qanun fi l-tibb* (*The Canon of Medicine*) based in large part on the works of Galen (d. 203 C.E.) and his disciples in the medieval Islamic world. After all, when human beings are ill or injured, they tend to be more interested in their immediate physical health than the eternal fate of their souls. About a century after Ibn Sina's death, Gerard of Cremona translated Ibn Sina's *Canon* into Latin. In Europe, his *Canon* was a favorite of doctors and medical schools until the rise of experimental medicine in the sixteenth and seventeenth centuries. It was translated into Hebrew, was retranslated into Latin again in the early sixteenth century, and was the subject of countless commentaries in European and Islamic languages.

Although al-Khwarizmi, al-Razi, al-Biruni, and Ibn Sina were all Muslims and wrote their works in the Arabic language, each of them hailed from the Persianate world—what is now Iran, Afghanistan, and parts of Central Asia. Al-Khwarizmi hailed from Khwarizm, which roughly corresponds with modern day Uzbekestan; al-Razi was born in Rayy, near modern Tehran; al-Biruni was born in Kath, a city in Khwarizm that no longer exists; and Ibn Sina was born in Bukhara, the modern capital of Uzbekistan. That such important scholars, writing in the Arabic language, were not Arabs illustrates the extent to which non-Arab peoples had been assimilated into the learned classes of the medieval Islamic world. In fact, as stated in volume one, by the tenth century, the Arabic language had become the preferred language of science and learning for nearly every ethnic and religious group under Muslim rule. Arabic served to unite the educated elites in the Islamic world in much the same way that Latin did in medieval Western Europe or English does in the modern world.

Astronomy

Given al-Mansur's fascination with astrology, it should come as no surprise that we see advances in technology and methods designed to more effectively map and study the heavens. Early Arabic astronomers were influenced by Indian and Persian thought. In time they realized that Greek astronomy was far superior. One of the most important Greek texts on the development of astronomy in the medieval Islamic world was Ptolemy's (83–161 C.E.) *Almagest*, which, as noted by al-Masudi above, was first translated under the auspices of al-Mansur himself. Ptolemy's elaborate geocentric mathematical theories remained tremendously influential on Arabic astronomy down to the eventual replacement of the geocentric view with the heliocentric system. Under the auspices of **Harun al-Rashid**'s son, **al-Ma'mun** (813–833), programs of observation were organized in Baghdad and Damascus, which naturally resulted in enhanced prestige for the science throughout the realm, but also new translations of astronomical texts as well as the composition of original treatises in Arabic that sought to reconcile Ptolemy's work with the collective observational and theoretical research conducted in Baghdad, Damascus, and elsewhere.

The science of astronomy was not merely an intellectual exercise. There were a number of very practical implications derived from its study. Some of the practical astronomy issues dealt with specific aspects of Islamic religious observance and practice; others addressed a wide range of more practical or secular day-to-day concerns. Because the Islamic **calendar** is a lunar calendar, each month begins immediately after sundown with the sighting of the new crescent moon. To sight the crescent moon one needs to know where to look in the sky, which varies based on celestial coordinates, issues of latitude and longitude, the brightness of the sky, season of the year, and so forth. One very important sighting of the new moon initiates the observance of Id al-Fitr; that is, the feast held to commemorate the end of the annual Ramadan Fast. Another practical concern was determining the direction (*qibla*) of Mecca for proper observance of the five daily ritual prayers (*see* the "Religion" section). Detailed calculation methods and tables were developed to aide in determining the shortest arc along the great circle of the globe from Mecca to the locality in question. Obviously, such calculations required the precise geographical coordinates of Mecca as well as the locale. Related to the direction of prayer is determining the times of prayer, which required the development of timekeeping methods, the earliest known text on which was composed by al-Khwarizmi. While observing the heavens to sight the new crescent moon, determining the direction of Mecca, and keeping time had specific ritual implications, the science and technology necessary to make such determinations had significant applications in other areas of life. Such problems spurred renewed research and experimentation in the science and the art of constructing instruments such as astrolabes, quadrants, compasses, sextants, grid locators, surveying equipment, map making, and so forth.

Medicine

Medicine in the medieval Islamic world was based on Hellenistic medicine. As Ptolemy's *Almagest* influenced astronomy, so did Galen's (d. 203 C.E.) and other Greek medical treatises, which were translated into either Arabic or Syriac by Hunayn ibn Ishaq (808–873) and his students. By the end of this process, the Galenic model of the four bodily humors (blood, phlegm, yellow bile, black bile) in relation to the four elements (air, water, fire, earth) and the four qualities (hot, moist, cold, dry) had become the foundation of Arabic medicine. Health was defined as balance or equilibrium among these humors and qualities. Disease and sickness were caused by an imbalance. The goal of the physician was to aid his patients in maintaining balance and treatment of disease required the restoration of equilibrium. Hence, a great deal of theoretical discussion in the end tended to be superimposed on direct observation. A major exception to this approach was al-Razi mentioned above, who put forth a number of criticisms of the inherited medical wisdom based on his own keen and detailed observations of his patients. What we see then developing throughout the Middle Ages is the construction of new methods and practices built on the foundation of Galenic medicine.

The list of important and innovative physicians in the medieval Islamic world is far too long to address here. However, *Kitab al-manazir* (*The Book of Optics*) by Ibn al-Haytham (965–1039), who was known in the West as Alhazen, bears mention as the most important and influential Arabic treatise on optics. In it he rejected the traditional Hellenistic emission theory of optics and set forth what is known as the intromission theory of vision; that is, visual perception occurs when rays of light are reflected from objects into the eyes. He also developed numerous optical experiments on lenses and mirrors, as well as the refraction, reflection, and dispersion of light. Finally, as noted above, Ibn Sina's *Canon* was a favorite medical manual of physicians and students down to the rise of experimental medicine in the sixteenth and seventeenth centuries. He is also known for many of his contributions to the history of medicine, not the least of which were his diagnostic and experimental methods, his understanding of pharmacology, infectious diseases, as well as the benefits of quarantine in preventing their spread.

Military Implications

Maintaining military superiority over one's enemies is necessary to retaining power as well as extending the borders of one's domains. Medieval Muslim rulers were keen to adapt tactics and technologies that might assist them in achieving their goals. An early example of such adaptation is the incorporation of iron stirrups in the first Islamic century from Iran. After Muslim forces encountered Greek fire for the first time in their siege of Constantinople in the late seventh century, there was an understandable desire to learn its secrets and incorporate it into their arsenal as well. Siege warfare was little practiced in Arabia, but it too was a tactic that Muslim armies in time learned to employ. Military manuals include detailed plans for constructing siege engines, catapults, battering rams, and so forth. During the twelfth century we begin to see the use of the counterweight trebuchet in addition to the traction trebuchet, which had already been used quite effectively for centuries in the Islamic world.

Although the mechanics of siege warfare were vital to any army's success, it was the cavalrymen, archers, and foot soldiers that were essential to bring victory as well as holding territory conquered. Such warriors required quality equipment and skilled smiths to fashion them, and it is in the foundries and smiths' forges that we see important developments for improving the quality of steel from which to fashion such weapons. The fourteenth-century Egyptian alchemist, al-Jidalki (d. 1342), describes the technique for turning low-grade cast iron into steel via carbonization. According to al-Jidalki, after the cast iron is heated in the foundry to the point that it is like water:

> They nourish it with glass, oil and alkali until light appears from it in the fire and it is purified of much of its blackness by intensive founding, night and day. They keep watching while it whirls for indications until they are sure of its suitability, whereupon they pour it out through channels so that it comes out like running water. Then they allow it to solidify in the shape of bars or in holes made of clay fashioned like crucibles. They take out of them refined steel in the shape of ostrich eggs, and they make swords from it, and helmets, lanceheads and all tools. (Hill, 217–218)

In the late fourteenth and early fifteenth centuries, siege engines began to be made obsolete by the introduction of cannon, which could fire more rapidly. The early days of cannon were not entirely successful, especially when the cannon was defective, resulting in considerable loss of life (on the wrong side) as well as expense. In due course founding techniques were considerably improved, so too were the size, range, and accuracy of the weapon as can be seen in their Mehmed I's successful use of them in his conquest of Constantinople in 1453, nearly eight centuries after the first Muslim siege of the city.

Further Reading

al-Biruni. *Alberuni's India: An Account of the Religion, Philosophy, Literature, Geography, Chronology, Astronomy, Customs, Laws and Astrology of India, about* A.D. *1030.* 2 vols. Translated by Edward C. Sachau. New Delhi, India: Munshiram, 2002.

Conrad, Lawrence I. "The Arab-Islamic Medical Tradition," in *The Western Medical Tradition, 800* BC *to 1800* AD. New York: Cambridge University Press, 2000, pp. 93–138.

Gutas, Dimitri. *Greek Thought, Arabic Culture: The Graeco-Arabic Translation Movement in Baghdad and Early Abbasid Society (2nd–4th/8th–10th Centuries).* London: Routledge, 1998.

Hill, Donald R. *Islamic Science and Engineering.* Edinburgh, Scotland: Edinburgh University Press, 1993.

Ibn Khaldun. *The Muqaddimah.* 3 vols. Translated by Franz Rosenthal. Princeton, NJ: Princeton University Press, 1967.

Roshdi, Rashed, ed. *Encyclopedia of the History of Arabic Science.* 3 vols. New York: Routledge, 1996.

Turner, Howard R. *Science in Medieval Islam: An Illustrated Introduction.* Austin: University of Texas Press, 1995.

7. GLOBAL TIES

Global ties within the medieval Islamic world and between the Islamic world and its neighbors were extensive. By the tenth century, the Islamic world had become the primary transit zone for such ties—at least throughout Afro-Eurasia. We see these connections especially in the extensive travel networks throughout the Islamic world. The major impetuses for travel fell into four broad categories: (1) travel for the purposes of making the obligatory *hajj* and other pilgrimages; (2) travel in the pursuit of religious knowledge, particularly to study with leading scholars of the Qur'an, *hadith*, theology and so forth; (3) travel in the pursuit of mystical (Sufi) knowledge and experience; and (4) travel as part of the vast international trade networks of Muslim Africa and Asia (*see* **Sufism**). As Ross E. Dunn has so ably demonstrated, the famous fourteenth-century Moroccan traveler, **Ibn Battuta** (1304–1368), spent three decades crisscrossing the Islamic world under the umbrella of all four categories at various times. In part, Ibn Battuta was able to do this because of what Dunn called the *Pax Mongolica* that was established throughout much of the Islamic world and East Asia in the fourteenth century.

As we see below, earlier travelers such the tenth-century Syrian geographer, **al-Muqaddasi** (c. 945–c. 1000), the eleventh-century Persian traveler, **Naser-e Khosraw** (d. c. 1075), and the twelfth-century Andalusian traveler, **Ibn Jubayr** (1145–1217), also covered a great deal of territory. Like Ibn Battuta, each was an educated man who traveled extensively throughout the Abode of Islam for religious as well as scholarly purposes. It is difficult to ascertain whether their urge to travel was a result of fulfilling the ritual obligation to undertake the pilgrimage to Mecca or whether their desire to make the pilgrimage was rooted in their own wanderlust. Whatever their true motivations, al-Muqaddasi, Naser-e Khosraw, Ibn Jubayr, and Ibn Battuta began their travels with the expressed intent of making the pilgrimage, and each left for posterity a detailed record of his travels. As one might expect, their professions and interests color what they thought important to record from their travels throughout the region. That these men hailed from Syria, Iran, Spain, and Morocco, respectively, illustrates the extent to which they and many others benefited from and contributed to the establishment and strengthening of the far-flung religious, scholarly, and economic networks of the medieval Islamic world. Before we turn our attention to the reasons for travel it is important first to describe the methods of how people actually traveled when they chose to do so.

Travel and Transportation

Most modern forms of transportation require wheeled vehicles of some sort. The notable exceptions, of course, are traveling by foot, boat, or beasts of burden.

However, those who use beasts as their primary means of transportation usually employ them to pull wheeled buggies, carts, carriages, or wagons. Flat tires and broken axles essentially render these as well as cars, trucks, trains, bicycles, and motorcycles useless as modes of transportation. Air travel, too, would be impossible without the wheels necessary for planes to take off and land. (Pontoon planes, ski planes, and some helicopters are the exceptions here.) Compared to the medieval Islamic world, or any premodern era or region, modern modes of transportation are the epitome of ease, speed, and comfort.

Because wheeled transport had disappeared throughout much of the Middle East and North Africa prior to the Islamic conquests, the peoples of the medieval Islamic world traveled from one city to another on the back of a donkey or mule, as part of a camel caravan in desert regions, or by ship. Many could not afford to travel by any other means than by foot. Unlike the Romans who built extensive networks of paved roads and elaborate grid-like cities with wide throughways, medieval Islamic rulers had little use for such massive expenditures. Donkeys, mules, horses, and camels simply did not need paved roads to traverse the trade routes that crisscrossed the Islamic world and beyond. Medieval Muslim rulers did, however, devote a great deal of attention to the construction of bridges so that people, camels, horses, donkeys, and other animals could cross rivers and wadis that were either too deep or too swift to ford, especially during flood seasons. Baghdad, in particular, was famous for its pontoon bridges that spanned the Tigris River.

Although the camel caravans that traversed the Sahara between North Africa and the trading towns along the Niger River as well as across the Sahara from Morocco to Egypt played vitally important roles in the international trade networks of the Islamic world, merchants, traders, pilgrims, and others who hailed from Spain (e.g., Ibn Jubayr) or the port cities along the southern shores of the Mediterranean preferred to travel by ship whenever they could. The winds and waters of the Mediterranean were relatively calm, especially compared to the Indian Ocean where travel was much more dangerous. Of course, the Nile, Tigris, and Euphrates rivers were the primary highways and preferred means of travel in Egypt and Mesopotamia.

Whatever the means of transportation, travelers were always susceptible to raiders, brigands, and pirates. Consequently, only a fool would travel alone. In fact, it was considered bad form, even disgraceful, to allow a friend or relative to travel even short distances without a *rafiq*, or traveling companion. A famous Arabic proverb, "the companion is more important than the route taken" clarifies that the dangers, discomforts, and duration of travel in the medieval Islamic world necessitated the careful selection of a *rafiq* who was resourceful, trustworthy, and hopefully a pleasant conversationalist.

Because medieval merchants and travelers—like their counterparts in antiquity—required places to provision themselves and their beasts, hostelries or inns were constructed along trade networks, pilgrimage routes, in small towns, and major cities. Major trading cities often had dozens, even hundreds of them within their walls. *Funduq*, the Arabic term for inn, is derived from the Greek word, *pandocheion*, that had been employed throughout the pre-Islamic Mediterranean world. Medieval European travelers and merchants used *fondaco*, a cognate derived from *funduq*. Terms such as *caravansarai* and *khan* were also used to describe inns and hostelries throughout the medieval Islamic world, often interchangeably.

In the eleventh century, the Persian traveler Naser-e Khosraw recorded that in Cairo, "there are no end of caravanserais [Persian, *karawansaray*], bath houses, and other public buildings—all property of the sultan" (Thackston, 45). Around 1150, the geographer al-Idrisi reported that there were 970 (!) *funduqs* in the Spanish port of Almería. Three decades later, Ibn Jubayr described the customs house in Damascus at the other end of the Mediterranean as "a *khan* prepared to accommodate the caravan" (Broadhurst, 317). In the tenth century, al-Muqaddasi observed that "taxes in Syria are light, except for those levied on the caravanserais, in which case they are absolutely oppressive" (Collins, 159). Whether in Damascus, Baghdad, Cairo, Almería, or elsewhere, *funduqs*, *khans*, and caravansaries were extremely important tax revenue producers for rulers throughout the medieval Islamic world.

Because of the importance of travel and trade to the international economies of the medieval Islamic world, Muslim rulers took it upon themselves to ensure that the trade routes that passed through their territories were well protected and dotted with secure inns for what they hoped would be many travelers and merchants. In the eleventh century, **Nizam al-Mulk** emphasizes the importance of such initiatives in his description of a just ruler as one who devotes his attention to that which advances civilization, such as the following:

> constructing underground channels, digging main canals, building bridges across great waters, rehabilitating villages and farms, raising fortifications, building new towns, and erecting lofty buildings and magnificent dwellings; he will have inns [*ribats*] built on the highways and schools for those who seek knowledge; for which things he will be renowned forever; he will gather the fruit of his good works in the next world and blessings will be showered upon him. (Darke, 10)

Nizam al-Mulk advises the construction of inns (*ribats*) on the highways to facilitate trade in the realm, but also to protect merchants and travelers from brigands and highway robbers. It should be noted that though *ribat* can be used in lieu of *funduq*, *khan*, or *caravansarai*, by the later Middle Ages *ribat* tended to be used exclusively to describe a dwelling for mystics or a fortified retreat along the frontier for ghazi warriors (many of whom were mystics as well).

The nuances of terminology for inns and hostelries based on geography and chronology are beyond the scope of our discussion here. What is important for our purposes is that medieval travelers could expect to find a great deal of similarity among *funduqs*, *khans*, and caravanserais throughout the medieval Islamic world. Architecturally, they tended to be rectangular—even square—buildings with a solitary entrance. Inside the building was a central courtyard surrounded by porticos or stalls where travelers could refuel their beasts and store them and their goods overnight. They could also find food and lodging for themselves. *Funduqs* also provided charitable services such as indigent housing, soup kitchens, even medical care. Most *funduqs* in towns and cities were near a mosque. Those located on the overland travel routes between cities had a mosque built into the structure or nearby. Some *funduqs* in Cairo or in the ports of the Mediterranean served Jewish or Christian merchants and contained or were built near to synagogues and churches. In addition, there were opportunities for travelers, merchants, and pilgrims to worship at other altars, since *funduqs* often served as taverns and brothels as well.

Pilgrimages

The details of the obligatory annual *hajj* are discussed in the "Religion" section. Here we address other types of pilgrimages that drew Sunni and Shi'i Muslims from throughout the medieval Islamic world. Veneration of the imams and visitation (*ziyara*) to their tombs were essential to Shi'i piety. When these and other practices became part of the Shi'i tradition is not entirely clear, but we do know that after the Shi'i **Buyids** conquered Baghdad in 945, they encouraged the open and public performance of three public rituals that were fundamentally important to daily life in Shi'i Islam—the commemoration of Ghadir Khumm, the commemoration of the martyrdom of **Husayn ibn 'Ali ibn Abi Talib**, and visitation to the Shi'i imams' tombs (*see* **Shiism**). The Ismaili **Fatimids** in Egypt (969–1171) encouraged the public performance of these rituals also.

Without a basic understanding of the role of the Shi'i doctrine of the imamate, it is difficult to understand the importance and the meaning of the very public rituals of Shi'i Islam that were part of daily life in the medieval Islamic world, especially in Iraq under the Buyids and in Egypt under the Fatimids. There are three basic doctrines that developed among the Shi'is. First, the rightful **caliph** or imam had to be a lineal descendant of Muhammad, in particular through the line of **'Ali ibn Abi Talib** and Muhammad's daughter, Fatima. The second is that the caliph or imam was not only the political head of the community, but also an infallible religious teacher—guaranteed to be without error in matters of faith and morals. Because of this emphasis on the religious and theological role of the head of the community, Shi'i texts tend to use the title *imam* for this office more frequently than caliph (*Khalifa*) or commander of the believers (*Amir al-Mu'minin*).

Third, according to Shi'i doctrine, all of the imams except the twelfth died as martyrs. Some were slain in battle, while others were poisoned or died in prison. The most dramatic martyrdom, of course, is that of Husayn in 680. Because all the imams are seen as the "sinless ones," their suffering and martyrdom is understood to exemplify their willingness to voluntarily take on a portion of the suffering and punishment of mankind, which brings us to the third, and controversial, doctrine. That is, because of their suffering, mankind can be spared the severity of God's justice. Moreover, the imams' martyrdom qualifies them to serve as intercessors between the faithful and God himself. Such an understanding of redemptive suffering parallels the sacrifice of Jesus Christ for the sins of the world in Christian theology. However, unlike Christian theology, Islamic theology rejects the notion of original sin. Therefore, the suffering of the imams benefits the faithful only for the specific sins they have committed. Because **Sunnis** reject the Shi'i doctrine of the imamate, they reject the idea that the Shi'i imams play any redemptive role at all.

The faithful can benefit from the imams' suffering and martyrdom by their willingness to become martyrs themselves, but also by visiting the tombs of the imams and weeping over them. There are reports of the faithful weeping over Husayn's grave almost immediately after his tomb was constructed. In 850, the **Abbasid** Caliph al-Mutawakkil had the shrine destroyed to put an end to Shi'i pilgrimages to it. His efforts proved unsuccessful as pilgrims continued to go to Karbala even though there was no shrine. The Buyid ruler Adud al-Dawla restored Husayn's tomb at Karbala and Ali's tomb at Najaf in 990.

Over time, elaborate rituals developed as part of the faithful's visitation and public mourning at the imams' tombs, whether at Husayn's tomb in Karbala, Ali's tomb in Najaf, or at the tombs of the imams buried in Baghdad, Samarra, Medina, or Mashhad in Iran. According to the thirteenth-century theologian Ta'usi (d. 1266), the faithful expressed their longing for the imams and their suffering as they cried over their graves, as follows:

Could I but be your ransom! Since the Lord of the future life takes pleasure in sorrow and since it serves to purify God's servants—behold! we therefore don mourning attire and find delight in letting tears flow. We say to the eyes: stream in uninterrupted weeping forever! (Halm, 140)

The most elaborate of the lamentations is for Husayn, and the rituals of the Ashura festival date at least to the Buyid period. Sources indicate that the oldest Ashura ritual is for pilgrims to Husayn's tomb to request a sip of water in commemoration of one of Husayn's final acts prior to his martyrdom. Near the end of the battle, as Husayn pleaded for water for his infant son (whom he held in his arms), an arrow pierced the baby's throat and killed him. Undeterred by his child's death, Husayn continued to fight until he was finally slain. The elaborate passion plays and public processions where mourners beat and cut themselves in identification with Husayn's suffering so common in modern Iran, Iraq, and Lebanon appear to date from the Safavid (1501–1722) and Qajar (1779–1925) periods in Iran, well after the period covered in this book.

Although visitation (*ziyara*) to the tombs of the imams did not constitute formal legal substitutes for making the obligatory annual pilgrimage (*hajj*), Shi'is considered their spiritual benefits and rewards to be greater than those of the *hajj*. This is clearly illustrated in a brief exchange in which a certain Shihab ibn Abd Rabbihi was asked how many obligatory annual pilgrimages he had made. When he replied that he had made the pilgrimage nineteen times, his interlocutor responded, "Should you complete twenty-one Pilgrimages, they will be counted for you as a *ziyara* to Husayn" (Meri, *Cult of Saints*, 141).

When **Saladin** deposed the Fatimids in 1171, state support for Ismaili Shiism and its rituals ended, the name of an Abbasid caliph was invoked in the Friday sermon for the first time in two centuries, and Fatimid institutions of learning were transformed into Sunni ones. Because Ismaili Shiism had never taken deep root in Egypt outside the ruling elite and a few others, it soon withered away. Although the Seljukid conquest of Baghdad in 1055 ended state sponsorship of Twelver Shiism in Iraq, this form of Shiism did not wither away at all in that region. After all, Iraq was the Shi'i Holy Land of sorts. Karbala and Najaf housed the tombs of Imam Husayn and Imam 'Ali ibn Abi Talib, whereas Baghdad and Samarra housed the tombs of other imams as well. Pilgrimage to these shrines continued, though not as freely as had been the case under the Buyids.

Other Pilgrimages

In addition to the obligatory *hajj*, the praiseworthy *'umra*, and the distinctive Shi'i pilgrimages (*ziyara*; lit. visitation) to the tombs of the Shi'i imams, there were countless local pilgrimages that became part of the fabric of daily life throughout the medieval Islamic world. The tombs of Muhammad's companions, Sufis, saints, scholars, martyrs, virtuous rulers, even sacred objects such as copies of the Qur'an, or more mundane items that ostensibly belonged to Muhammad himself were venerated and visited by the faithful hoping to benefit from the *baraka* (divine blessing) they possessed.

Jerusalem and other sacred sites associated with pre-Islamic prophets and patriarchs in Syria, Egypt, and Iraq were especially popular destinations for pilgrims of all types. Understandably, Jerusalem and the Biblical Holy Land (the site of the ancient Jewish Temple and the Church of the Holy Sepulchre) held pride of place for Jews and Christians. However, Muslims considered Syria to be a holy land (*ard muqaddasa*) as well. Not only was Syria the home of Abraham, Moses, Joseph, David, Solomon, and Jesus, its most holy city, Jerusalem, was the destination of Muhammad's night journey as well as the home of the al-Aqsa Mosque and the venerable Dome of the Rock.

An important subgenre of the merits (*fada'il*) of places literature is the pilgrimage guide or manual, which described important pilgrimage sites in a particular town or province of the medieval Islamic world. One such manual for Syria is Ibn al-Hawrani's (d. 1592) *Guide to Pilgrimage Places*, which draws extensively on earlier sources such as al-Raba'i's (d. 1052) *Merits of Syria and Damascus* and Ibn Asakir's (d. 1176) *History of Damascus*. Like his predecessors, Ibn al-Hawrani praises the merits of Syria and its sacred history, including stories about more than 100 sacred sites in Damascus and Syria such as the location of Moses' (Musa) tomb, the site where Jesus (Isa) will descend to earth at the end of time, the place where John the Baptist's (Yahya ibn Zakariya) head was discovered, the location of the shrine of Husayn ibn Ali's head, the tomb of Nur al-Din (d. 1174), even the presence of one of Muhammad's sandals, which is buried in the southern wall above the *mihrab* of the *Dar al-Hadith*, near the Citadel of Damascus.

Ibn al-Hawrani emphasizes the importance of visiting the tombs of saints and other holy persons based on hadiths in which Muhammad is reported to have visited the graves of his companions. He concludes his *Guide to Pilgrimage Places* as follows, with a section on proper pilgrimage etiquette:

> It is customary practice to position oneself facing the face of the tomb's inhabitant, to approach, and greet him. The pilgrim stands near the tomb, comporting himself, humbling himself, surrendering himself, bowing his head to the ground with dignity, God-inspired peace of mind, and awe, casting aside power and chieftainship. He should imagine himself as if he were looking at the tomb's inhabitant and he at him. Then he should look with introspection to what God has granted to the one visited of loftiness, dignity and divine secrets and how God has made him a locus of sainthood, for secrets, closeness, obedience, and divine gnostic truths. (Meri, "Pilgrimage Guide," 76)

Al-Hawrani further advises the pilgrim to read from the Qur'an and to devote himself to prayer and the remembrance of God. The purpose of these meditations and supplications is to focus the pilgrim's attention on his sins (which prevent him from drawing close to God) and the virtues and spiritual blessing of the saint (which will be rewarded at the end of days).

It should be noted that some Sunni scholars denounced as heretical innovations any pilgrimage other than the obligatory and praiseworthy pilgrimages to Mecca (*hajj* and *'umra*). The famous Syrian scholar Ibn Taymiyya (1263–1328) is representative of such opinion. Based on the practice of Muhammad, Ibn Taymiyya argued that it was permissible for the faithful to invoke God's blessings on the deceased. However, he adamantly opposed the visitation of tombs for the purpose of petitioning a deceased person (or an object connected to him or her) to intercede with God on one's behalf. As far as Ibn Taymiyya was concerned, such supplication was a form of polytheism. Moreover, based on a hadith attributed to Muhammad, Ibn Taymiyya also argued that the veneration of tombs was forbidden because Jews and Christians had originally instituted the practice. "It is for this reason that the Prophet . . . said in a [sound] tradition: 'May God curse the Jews and Christians. They have taken the tombs of their prophets as places of prayer (lit. prostration). Such behaviour is to be warned against'" (Meri, *Cult of Saints*, 131).

Condemnation of religious practices and doctrines because of their real or alleged connections to Jews and/or Christians was standard practice in medieval Islamic polemics. Nevertheless, the Middle East and North Africa had been home to saints, ascetics, mendicants, and miracle workers (Jewish, Christian, and others) since antiquity. Holy men, with their divine blessing, special knowledge, and miracles were part and parcel of daily life in the pre-Islamic Mediterranean world centuries before Muhammad's birth. Moreover, as evidenced by Ibn al-Hawrani's *Guide to Pilgrimages* (and despite the objections of Ibn Taymiyya and his ilk), pilgrimage (*ziyara*) to the tombs and shrines of prophets, scholars, Sufis, saints, and even some virtuous rulers and others was "the very center and pivot of popular religious life" in the medieval Islamic world (Goitein, 188).

Further Reading

Broadhurst, R.J.C., trans. *The Travels of Ibn Jubayr.* London: J. Cape, 1952.

Collins, Basil, trans. *The Best Divisions for Knowledge of the Regions: Ahsan al-taqasim fi ma'rifat al-aqalim.* Reading, UK: Garnet Publishing, 2001.

Constable, Olivia Remie. *Housing the Stranger in the Mediterranean World: Lodging, Trade, and Travel in Late Antiquity and the Middle Ages.* New York: Cambridge University Press, 2003.

Darke, Hubert, trans. *The Book of Government or Rules for Kings: The Siyar al-Mulk or Siyasat-nama of Nizam al-Mulk.* Richmond, UK: Curzon Press, 2002.

Dunn, Ross E. *The Adventures of Ibn Battuta: A Muslim Traveler of the 14th Century.* Berkeley and Los Angeles: University of California Press, 1989.

Goitein, S.D. *Jews and Arabs: Their Contacts through the Ages.* Rev. ed. New York: Shocken Books, 1974.

Halm, Heinz. *Shiism.* Edinburgh, Scotland: Edinburgh University Press, 1991.

Meri, Josef W. "A Late Medieval Syrian Pilgrimage Guide: Ibn al-Hawrani's *al-Isharat il Amakin al-Ziyarat (Guide to Pilgrimage Places)*." *Medieval Encounters: Jewish, Christian and Muslim Culture in Confluence and Dialogue* 7.1 (2001): 3–79.

Meri, Josef W. *The Cult of Saints among Muslims and Jews in Medieval Syria.* New York: Oxford University Press, 2002.

Momen, Moojan. *An Introduction to Shi'i Islam.* New Haven, CT: Yale University Press, 1985.

Thackston, Wheeler M., trans. *Naser-e Khosraw's Book of Travels (Safarnama).* Albany: State University of New York Press, 1986.

Short Entries: People, Ideas, Events, and Terms

Abbasid Caliphate (750–1258)

The second caliphal dynasty in Islamic history, the Abbasids overthrew the **Umayyads** in 750 and ruled primarily from Baghdad (est. 762) until the Mongol conquest of the city in 1258. The Abbasids claim to the caliphate is rooted in their decent from Muhammad's paternal uncle, Abbas. The Abbasids had come to power by manipulating a Shi'i revolt against their predecessors, the Umayyad caliphs (661–750), in the late 740s, but once the Abbasids took power they began to follow the Sunni paradigm for the caliphate. In 945, Baghdad was sacked by the **Buyids**—a group of Shi'i soldiers of fortune from the region of Daylam on the southern shores of the Caspian Sea. From 945 onward, the Abbasid caliphs remained subordinate to a series of Muslim warlord regimes until 1258, when the invading Mongol armies sacked Baghdad and, for all intents and purposes, brought an end to the Abbasid caliphate. *See also* **Shiism** and **Sunnis**.

Further Reading
Gordon, Matthew. *The Rise of Islam*. Westport, CT: Greenwood, 2005.
Kennedy, Hugh N. *When Baghdad Ruled the World: The Rise and Fall of Islam's Greatest Dynasty*. Cambridge, MA: Da Capo Press, 2005.

Abd al-Malik (c. 646–705)

Ruling from 695 to 705, Abd al-Malik was the fifth of the **Umayyad** caliphs to rule from Damascus. While **Mu'awiya ibn Abi Sufyan** (r. 661–680) is credited with preserving the early Islamic Empire after the assassination of '**Ali ibn Abi Talib** during the first Civil War, Abd al-Malik is credited with establishing Arabic as the language of administration throughout the Empire, issuing a new coinage that explicitly asserts the dominance of Islam, and constructing the Dome of the Rock in Jerusalem, which is a vivid example that Islam and Muslim rule had replaced Christianity and Byzantine rule in Syria. *See also* Document 3.

Further Reading
Gordon, Matthew. *The Rise of Islam*. Westport, CT: Greenwood, 2005.
Robinson, Chase. *Abd al-Malik*. Oxford, UK: Oneworld, 2005.

Great Palace, Aanjar, Umayyad City. Built by Calpih Walid I Abd al-Malik, c. 705–715 A.D., Lebanon. Courtesy of photos.com.

Ablutions

Before one can actually perform the *salat*, he or she needs to perform a series of major or minor ablutions to enter into a state of ritual purity (*tahara*). Therefore, it was essential that medieval mosque complexes at the very minimum had access to clean water; some had simple water faucets, others has elaborate and ornate fountains, while still others even housed complete bathing facilities. The major ablution (*ghusul*) is required when one is in a state of major ritual impurity in which one cannot perform the *salat* nor should he or she enter a mosque or even touch a Qur'an. Activities that required a man or woman to perform a major ablution to be restored to a state of ritual purity include sexual intercourse and touching a human corpse. In addition, men must perform a major ablution after any emission of semen; women must do so after menstruation and after childbirth.

The major ablution requires that one bathe from head to foot, making sure that every part of one's body is made wet. The minor ablution (*wudu'*) is less complete but is required after one has entered a state of minor ritual impurity from a range of unavoidable daily activities such as sleeping, relieving oneself, and passing gas. The minor ablution involves washing certain body parts with water in the following order: hands, mouth, nose, right forearm, left forearm, face, head, ears, right foot, left foot. Both the major and the minor ablution can be performed with sand or with a stone in those instances where one has no access to clean water or if one should not touch water for medical or other reasons.

Further Reading
Rippin, Andrew. *Muslims: Their Religious Beliefs and Practices*. New York: Routledge, 2001.

Abu Bakr (d. 634)

Abu Bakr was a native of Mecca and a member of the Banu Quraysh. He was the first adult male convert to Islam, a close companion of Muhammad, made the *hijra* with Muhammad in 622, and hid in a cave with him as Muhammad's Meccan opponents pursued them and their Bedouin guide. When his daughter, **'Aisha bint Abi Bakr**, was nine years old, Abu Bakr gave her to Muhammad to be his third wife. After Muhammad established himself in Medina, Abu Bakr continued to be one of Muhammad's closest advisers until he died in 'Aisha's house in the summer of 632. While Muhammad's body was being prepared for burial, a heated debate took place over who should succeed him as the leader of the new *umma*. In the end, Abu Bakr was acclaimed the leader and is known as the first of the **Rashidun** or rightly guided caliphs in the Sunni tradition (*see* **Sunnis**). The Shi'i tradition rejects Abu Bakr and argues that Muhammad had in fact designated **'Ali ibn Abi Talib** to be his successor (*see* **Shiism**).

Abu Bakr's principal objective during his short reign (r. 632–634) was to subdue a rebellion in Arabia among the tribes who believed that their agreements with Muhammad died with him or who did not think that Abu Bakr was worthy of their allegiance. Abu Bakr and Muhammad's companions obviously disagreed. For them, the tribes' submission to Muhammad during his lifetime was equal to their submission to God; therefore, they did not have the option of seceding from the new political and religious community. Hence, the wars to subjugate the Arabic-speaking tribes of the peninsula are known as the *Ridda* Wars—or the Wars of Apostasy, although not all of those who were compelled to accept Islam and submit to Muslim political authority were actual apostates. That is, some had never been Muslims nor had they submitted to Muhammad's authority during his lifetime.

Further Reading

Crone, Patricia, and Martin Hinds. *God's Caliph: Religious Authority in the First Centuries of Islam.* New York: Cambridge University Press, 1986.

Gordon, Matthew. *The Rise of Islam.* Westport, CT: Greenwood, 2005.

Kennedy, Hugh. *The Great Arab Conquests: How the Spread of Islam Changed the World We Live in.* Philadelphia, Da Capo, 2007.

Madelung, Wilferd. *The Succession to Muhammad: A Study of the Early Caliphate.* New York: Cambridge University Press, 1998.

Afterlife. *See* Death and Afterlife

Agriculture

The diet of even the lowliest peasant in the medieval Islamic world was generally varied and quite healthy, certainly far healthier than what most classes had access to in medieval Europe. The staple grains in most areas were wheat and in areas with more saline soil, barley. Sorghum was grown widely as well, but it appears that only the lower classes used it as a **food** crop for themselves and their animals. Rice could only be cultivated in those areas where there was an abundance of water, such as the southern shores of the Caspian Sea, in parts of Spain, in the Nile Delta and along the Nile in Egypt, the lower Euphrates in southern Iraq, even along the Jordan River near Beit Shean. In such areas it competed with wheat and sorghum as a staple. However, in many other areas it was an imported luxury that only the wealthier could afford.

Along the Mediterranean coastlands, olive orchards were as thick on the ground as they had been in antiquity. Vineyards were cultivated as well; however, after the Islamic conquests, they gradually became less important to the local diet than they had been in late antiquity as more and more of the population converted to Islam and adopted the Islamic prohibition against the consumption of wine. Nevertheless, grapes continued to be used in Bilad al-Sham to produce raisins (*zabib*) and molasses (*dibs*), which were staples of the local diet, especially in the winter months. Ba'labekk was famous for its molasses and Darayya (southeast of Damascus) for its grapes and raisins.

Some of the oasis settlements of Arabia as well as some of the settlements along the rivers in Iraq and Egypt cultivated vast date palm groves. A wide array of fruits and vegetables native to the region were cultivated along with others such as bananas, citrus, sugar cane, eggplants, watermelons, and mango trees that entered the Middle East from India and Africa in late antiquity or during the early Islamic period. Precisely how these foods spread westward across the Mediterranean to Spain is difficult to ascertain. There are numerous stories about rulers who encouraged the cultivation of exotic foods in their palace gardens and orchards. I mention but three examples here. 'Abd al-Rahman I (r. 756–788), one of the few **Umayyads** to survive the **Abbasid** revolution, surrounded his palace in Spain with trees from around the world, including date palms and pomegranate trees ostensibly brought to Spain by men he had sent to Syria for the purpose of bringing back all sorts of seeds and plants to be grown in his garden.

The Abbasid caliph **al-Ma'mun ibn Harun al-Rashid** (r. 813–833) is said to have brought sour orange trees from northeastern Iran to Rayy near modern Tehran. A century later, the Abbasid caliph al-Qahir (r. 932–934) reportedly had sour orange trees brought to Baghdad from India via Yemen. Whether or not rulers were the principal agents for the transfer of such foods from region to region, it is clear that the extensive overland and seaborne trade networks of the vast medieval Islamic world facilitated their transfer. Many foods likely began to be cultivated in new regions simply because a traveling merchant or scholar developed a taste for them in his travels and brought some plants or seeds home with him.

Essential to the flourishing cities and states of the medieval Islamic world were the sophisticated and varied irrigation technologies that made it possible to grow crops, such as sugar cane, bananas, mangos, rice, and cotton. These and other crops that originated in tropical or semitropical climes required intensive irrigation, especially during the summer months for the simple reason that in much of the region (as in southern California and the American southwest) it rained only during the winter months. Consequently, one of the major expenditures of any regime was for the construction and maintenance of irrigation technologies.

Dams were built to contain rainwater in low lands or to divert rivers and streams. Trenches and canals were dug to channel rainwater to above ground reservoirs as well as underground cisterns. Some canals were made of brick and stone, others were elaborate aqueducts, still others included pipes made of tile or lead. Underground aquifers were tapped by digging wells, creating new springs, and in some places (especially in parts of Iran and Afghanistan) by carving tunnels that ran for miles through the bedrock. Each of these methods employed gravity to move water from higher ground to lower.

Whereas gravity-driven water transport requires little human labor beyond initial construction, raising water to higher ground is generally far more labor intensive than the routine maintenance of a trench, canal, aqueduct, or cistern. Lifting water from a well with a bucket on the end of a rope is hard work, and variations on this bucket and rope theme had been employed since antiquity. Pulling the rope through a pulley made the job much easier. So too did attaching a bucket to a pole with a weight on the other end (*shadhuf*) to counterbalance it.

The Archimedes Screw or Archimedes Snail, ostensibly invented by Archimedes (287–212 B.C.E.) himself, had been used since antiquity as well. An Archimedes Screw comprises a screw placed inside a cylinder. The lower end is placed in water and as the screw is turned water is raised to the top. Another important means of raising water was the water wheel, which had the labor-saving advantage of being powered by the current of the river on which it was built. None of this technology was really new, but it certainly was improved upon by the hydrologists of the medieval Islamic world.

Further Reading

Watson, Andrew M. *Agricultural Innovation in the Early Islamic World: The Diffusion of Crops and Farming Techniques, 700–1100.* New York: Cambridge University Press, 1983.

'Aisha bint Abi Bakr (d. c. 678)

'Aisha bint Abi Bakr was the daughter of Muhammad's close companion, **Abu Bakr**, the first caliph. She was betrothed to Muhammad at age 9 and is the only one of his wives who was not a widow when she married him, a virginal virtue of which she reminded her fellow wives often. She was also accused of adultery when she was 14 but exonerated by divine intervention with the revelation of Qur'an 24:11 — at least according to the Sunni tradition (*see* **Sunnis**). It should be noted that Shi'i commentators do not accept the Sunni interpretation of Qur'an 24:11 (*see* **Shiism**). Finally, because of 'Aisha's closeness to Muhammad, she is one of the most revered transmitters of hadiths or reports about Muhammad's teachings and behavior. Despite being admired as a transmitter of hadiths about her husband, attitudes about 'Aisha were ambivalent in the Middle Ages and remain so today in large part because she was one of the principal figures on the losing side in the first civil war that broke out in the wake of the assassination of the third caliph, Uthman, and the contested succession of **'Ali ibn Abi Talib**.

Of all the women in battle in the early Islamic period, few are more memorable than 'Aisha bint Abi Bakr. The best example of 'Aisha's opposition to Ali is her participation in the Battle of the Camel in 656. Her presence there can be viewed as an example of a woman inciting her clan's men to victory. Rather than beating a tambourine, 'Aisha was there in a closed litter atop her camel, around which the fiercest fighting occurred (hence the name of the battle). In the end, Ali's forces were victorious that day. Two of 'Aisha's allies—Talha and al-Zubayr—were killed. 'Aisha's life was spared, but she spent the rest of her days at her home in Medina, quietly transmitting hadiths about her husband.

Because 'Aisha was not the only woman present at the Battle of the Camel and because the sources indicate that there were other women at subsequent battles as well, what offended later commentators was not so much the fact that women per se were present that day. Rather, they were offended that 'Aisha—a wife of Muhammad—had inserted herself in the politics of succession and had violated the Qur'anic injunction that Muhammad's wives should remain in their homes (33:28–34). As Denise A. Spellberg demonstrated, many later commentators used 'Aisha's involvement in the Battle of the Camel to argue that women should never participate in the community's political life. Some accounts actually portray 'Aisha on her deathbed acknowledging the error of her ways and expressing regret that she ever participated in the Battle of the Camel.

Further Reading

Spellberg, Denise A. *Politics, Gender and the Islamic Past: The Legacy of 'A'isha bint Abi Bakr.* New York: Columbia University Press, 1996.

'Ali ibn Abi Talib (d. 661)

'Ali ibn Abi Talib's father, Abu Talib, raised Muhammad after he was orphaned as a young boy. Hence Ali was Muhammad's paternal cousin. Although Ali was a minor child when Muhammad received his first revelations, our sources record that he was one of the first to accept Muhammad's preaching. He was one of Muhammad's closest companions and confidants throughout his prophetic career. The partisans (*shi'a*) of Ali believe that Muhammad had designated Ali to succeed him as leader (*imam*) of the new Muslim community upon his death. The Shi'i doctrine of the imamate is based on the events of 18 Dhu l-Hijja A.H. 10 (March 16, 632 C.E.) (*see* **Shiism**).

According to the Islamic sources, Muhammad stopped at a place called Ghadir Khumm (Pool of Khumm) on his way back to Medina after he had made his final pilgrimage to Mecca. His followers gathered in a grove of trees to escape the suffocating heat and to perform the noon prayers. At the conclusion of the prayers, Muhammad raised Ali's hand in front of the assembly and asked them if they recognized that he, Muhammad, had a claim on each of the believers that supersedes any claim they might have on themselves. They, of course, responded in the affirmative. He then took Ali's hand again and said, "Of Whomsoever I am Lord [*Mawla*], then Ali is also his Lord. O God! Be Thou the supporter of whoever supports Ali and the enemy of whoever opposes him." **Umar ibn al-Khattab** then said to Ali, "Congratulations, O son of Abu Talib! Now morning and evening [i.e., forever] you are the master of every believing man and woman" (Momen, 15).

'Ali ibn Abi Talib, holding up the body of the killed Imam. Scenes from the schism within Islam (7th c.). Safavid fresco, 17th century. SEF/Art ReBridgeman Art Library.

Because the version cited above comes from Ibn Hanbal's (d. 855) *Musnad*, a Sunni hadith collection, it is clear that the Sunni tradition does not deny that the events of Ghadir Khumm actually occurred (*see* **Sunnis**). Where they differ, and differ significantly, is on the interpretation of the event itself. According to Shi'i doctrine, the above story proves beyond a shadow of a doubt that not only had Muhammad designated 'Ali ibn Abi Talib and his descendants to succeed him upon his death (which occurred only three months later on 13 Rabi' al-Awal A.H. June 8/11, 632 C.E.), but that he had bestowed his own political and religious authority on them as well. Although Sunnis afford Ali a tremendous amount of respect and prestige as an early convert, as Muhammad's cousin and son-in-law, and as the fourth of the **Rashidun** or rightly guided caliphs, they simply reject the Shi'i interpretation of the events of Ghadir Khumm altogether.

As things turned out, Muhammad's close companion and father-in-law, **Abu Bakr** (r. 632–634), became the first caliph. He was followed by two more companions, Umar ibn al-Khattab (r. 634–644) and **Uthman ibn Affan** (r. 644–656). After Uthman's assassination, 'Ali ibn Abi Talib (r. 656–661) became caliph/imam. However, the entirety of his caliphate/imamate was disrupted by the first civil war in Islamic history (656–661), ultimately ending in his assassination at the hands of a **Khariji** dissident.

Further Reading

Crone, Patricia, and Martin Hinds. *God's Caliph: Religious Authority in the First Centuries of Islam*. New York: Cambridge University Press, 1986.
Gordon, Matthew. *The Rise of Islam*. Westport, CT: Greenwood, 2005.
Kennedy, Hugh. *The Great Arab Conquests: How the Spread of Islam Changed the World We Live In*. Philadelphia: Da Capo, 2007.
Madelung, Wilferd. *The Succession to Muhammad: A Study of the Early Caliphate*. New York: Cambridge University Press, 1998.
Momen, Moojan. *An Introduction to Shi'i Islam*. New Haven, CT: Yale University Press, 1985.

Buyids (945–1055)

In 945, the Buyids, a group of Twelver Shi'i soldiers of fortune from Daylam on the southern shores of the Caspian Sea, occupied Baghdad and placed the **Abbasid** caliphs under house arrest and ruled as the Abbasids' deputies. Buyid control of Baghdad and much of modern Iraq and Iran continued until the Seljukids conquered Baghdad in 1055. The Buyid period in Iraq marks a period of revived public observances of Shiite ritual and practice (*see* **Shiism**). When precisely the veneration of the imams, visitation to their tombs, and other practices became part of the Shi'i tradition is not entirely clear but we do know that after the Buyids conquered Baghdad in 945, they encouraged the open and public performance of three public rituals that were fundamentally important to daily life in Shi'i Islam: the commemoration of Ghadir Khumm, the commemoration of the martyrdom of **Husayn ibn 'Ali ibn Abi Talib**, and visitation to the Shi'i imams' tombs.

Further Reading

Kabir, Mafizullah. *The Buwayhid Dynasty of Baghdad*. Calcutta, India: Iran Society, 1964.
Mottahedeh, Roy. *Loyalty and Leadership in an Early Islamic Society*. rev. ed. London: I.B. Tauris, 2001.

Calendar (Islamic)

The system for reckoning years from the birth of Jesus as A.D., *Anno Domini* (or more correctly *Anni Domini Nostri Jesu Christi*, meaning "In the Year of Our Lord Jesus Christ") was instituted by the Roman Abbot Dionysius Exiguus in about 527 A.D. The calendar was further revised in a papal bull (edict) by Pope Gregory XIII in 1582. Consequently, the A.D. dating system is known as the Gregorian Christian calendar. Although C.E., Common Era, has recently come into fashion for some, and is used in this volume, the only thing truly common about the Common Era is that most modern countries now use the Gregorian Christian calendar.

The Islamic calendar is known as the *hijri* calendar, because it begins with the year in which Muhammad (c. 570–632) made his **hijra** or migration from Mecca to Medina (622). According to Islamic tradition, the *hijri* calendar was instituted in 638, by the second **Rashidun** caliph, **Umar ibn al-Khattab** (r. 634–644). Under this system, 01/01/01 A.H. was calculated as July 16, 622 A.D/C.E. Most Western scholars employ the abbreviation A.H., *Anno Hejirae*, to distinguish the *hijri* calendar from Gregorian calendar (A.D.; *Anno Domini*).

The Islamic calendar, like many other calendars, is based on a lunar year of 12 months totaling approximately 354 days, or about 11 days fewer than a solar year's 365 days. To keep the lunar months in alignment with the four seasons, most users of lunar calendars periodically add an extra or 13th month. In fact, it was customary in seventh-century Arabia to insert a leap month every few years to ensure that the sacred months (in which pilgrimages to shrines took place, fighting was forbidden, and trade flourished) occurred roughly at the same time each year.

The Jewish tradition also follows a lunar calendar composed of 12 lunar months. However, because many Jewish holy days and festivals have their origins in the agricultural practices of Ancient Israel, they are tied to the seasons of the year as well as a particular Jewish month. Hence, a leap month—called the Second Adar—is added after the sixth Jewish month (Adar) in the following 19-year cycle: 3rd, 6th, 8th, 11th, 14th, 17th and 19th years. Thus, a particular holiday such as the Jewish New Year may vary by as many as 28 days from year to year, but it will always occur in the fall, and usually in September.

According to the biographical literature, during his last pilgrimage to Mecca Muhammad received a revelation forbidding the practice of inserting an extra month.

> God ordained the months twelve in number when He created the heavens and the earth. Of these, four are sacred, according to the true Faith. Therefore, do not sin against yourselves by violating them. But you may fight against the idolaters in all these months, since they themselves fight against you in all of them. Know that God is with the righteous. The postponement of sacred months is a grossly impious practice, in which the unbelievers are misguided. They allow it one year and forbid it in the next, so that they may make up for the months which God has sanctified, thus making lawful what God has forbidden. Their foul acts seem fair to them: God does not guide the unbelievers. (Qur'an 9:36–37)

Some scholars have argued that this passage is speaking against the Quraysh leaders' practice of manipulating the sacred months of the year for their own economic and political advantage; how this was done remains a mystery. Others have argued that another reason for this may have been related to the fact that the annual pilgrimage in and around Mecca had been held during the spring season. That is, forbidding the practice of intercalation may have been done specifically to ensure that the new Islamic pilgrimage would no longer coincide with the Jewish Passover and Christian Easter holidays, which also occurred in the spring season. In any case, one of the results of this prohibition is that none of the Islamic religious holidays—including the Ramadan fast and the annual pilgrimage—corresponds in any way to the seasons.

Reasons for this prohibition aside, there is no easy way to make the Islamic lunar calendar match up with the Gregorian Christian solar calendar. Subtracting 622 from the Gregorian year can provide a rough approximation of the Islamic year in which an event occurred, especially for the first decades of Islamic history. For example, the Caliph Umar conquered Jerusalem in the year 637 A.D./C.E. or 15 A.H (637 – 622 = 15). However, by the time we reach the Crusader period, things are more complicated. The Franks conquered Jerusalem in the summer of 1099 A.D./C.E. or 492 A.H. (1099 – 622 = 477 not 492); Saladin re-conquered it in the summer of 1187 A.D./C.E. or 583 A.H. (1187 – 622 = 565 not 583).

One can calculate the rough equivalents between the Gregorian (C) and Islamic (H) years with the following formulas:

$$H \cdot 32/33 + 622 \; C$$
$$(C - 622) \cdot 33/32 \; H$$

A few words of caution are necessary before using any formula or table to calculate the exact Gregorian date for an Islamic date (or vice versa). Formulas and tables can only provide imprecise estimates because the beginning of an Islamic month varies from region to region depending on when the religious scholars ('ulama) first sighted the crescent moon. For example, the first day of Ramadan 400 A.H. in Cairo may or may not be the same day of the week in Baghdad, or Cordoba, or Delhi, or any other city.

The Islamic Months

1. Muharram
2. Safar
3. Rabi' al-Awwal
4. Rabi' al-Thani
5. Jumada l-Ula
6. Jumada l-Akhira
7. Rajab
8. Sha'ban
9. Ramadan
10. Shawwal
11. Dhu l-Qa'da
12. Dhu l-Hijja

Select Muslim Holidays

- Muharram 1 (*Ras al-sana*: The New Year) is the first day of the first month. It is celebrated throughout the Islamic world, though it is not a particularly religious holiday, nor was it much observed in the medieval Islamic world.

- Muharram 10 (*'Ashura*: The Tenth) is the day on which many pious Muslims fast from dawn to sunset. For Shi'i Muslims this day is of particular importance, as it commemorates the assassination of **'Ali ibn Abi Talib**'s son, **Husayn ibn 'Ali ibn Abi Talib** (*see* **Shiism**).
- Rabi' al-Awwal 12 (*Mawlid al-nabi*: The Prophet's Birthday) is a holiday associated with festivities and exchanging of gifts. Often passages eulogizing Muammad are read.
- Rajab 27 (*Laylat al-isra' wa l-mi'raj*: The Night of Journey and Ascent) commemorates Muhammad's night journey from Mecca to the Haram al-Sharlf area in Jerusalem and his ascent to Heaven and return to Jerusalem, and then Mecca—all in one night. This night is traditionally celebrated by prayers.
- Sha'ban 14 (*Laylat al-bara'a*: Night of Remembrance) is, according to Muslim tradition, the night God approaches Earth to grant forgiveness for an individual's sins.
- Ramadan (9th month of the Muslim year) is devoted to spiritual purification through the abstinence from food, drink, and physical pleasures from dawn until dusk.
- Ramadan 27 (*Laylat al-qadar*: Night of Power and Greatness) is considered a particularly holy time, as it is the night, by tradition, on which Muhammad received the first revelation.
- Shawwal 1 (*'Id al-fitr*: The Feast of Fastbreaking; or The Lesser Feast) is the most joyous festival in the Islamic calendar and marks the end of abstinence during Ramadan.
- Dhu-l-Hijja 1–10: The period in which Muslims are to undertake a pilgrimage (*hajj*) to Mecca and its environs in imitation of Muhammad's last pilgrimage.
- Dhu-l-Hijja 10 (*'Id al-adha*: The Feast of Sacrifice; or The Greater Feast) is the high point of the pilgrimage and is celebrated by Muslims throughout the world even if not actually participating in the pilgrimage. It commemorates Abraham's willingness to sacrifice his son (Qur'an 37:103–109). The Feast of Sacrifice is most often marked by the slaughtering of lambs and the distribution of meat to the needy.
- Dhu-l-Hijja 18 (Ghadir Khumm) is a Shi'i festival commemorating the date when, according to the Shi'is, Muhammad bestowed his own political and religious authority on 'Ali ibn Abi Talib at a place called Ghadir Khumm on his way back to Medina after he had made his final pilgrimage to Mecca in 632 A.D./C.E. or 10 A.H.

Further Reading

Freeman-Grenville, G.S.P. *The Muslim and Christian Calendars*. London: Oxford University Press, 1963.

Lindsay, James E. "Christian and Islamic Calendars with Conversion Table," in *Daily Life in the Medieval Islamic World*. Westport, CT: Greenwood, 2005, pp. 253–279.

Caliph

After Muhammad's death, the early community (*umma*) agreed on the need for a leader and selected **Abu Bakr** as Muhammad's first successor. The earliest sources refer to the holders of this office by three titles: (1) *Khalifat Rasul Allah* (caliph—deputy or successor of the Messenger of God; *Khalifat Allah*

[God's Deputy] was used as well); (2) *Amir al-Mu'minin* (commander of the believers); and (3) *imam* (religious leader). For all intents and purposes, these titles simply emphasize different aspects of the caliph's political, military, and religious authority. Whatever the title, there was a general consensus about the basic responsibilities of the office: (1) the caliph should be the sole leader of the community, (2) all political power was to be invested in this one man, and (3) this office was to be a lifetime office.

Most of the major Muslim factions agreed with the above positions. The basic problem was related to the criteria for determining who was qualified to hold this office. Needless to say, there was and remains a great deal of diversity of opinion within the Muslim community on this issue. What began as a dispute over leadership of the community eventually developed into distinct religious and theological factions within the larger Islamic community, the most notable of which are known as **Sunnis**, Shi'is (*see* **Shiism**), and **Kharijis**.

Further Reading

Crone, Patricia, and Martin Hinds. *God's Caliph: Religious Authority in the First Centuries of Islam*. New York: Cambridge University Press, 1986.
Gordon, Matthew. *The Rise of Islam*. Westport, CT: Greenwood, 2005.
Madelung, Wilferd. *The Succession to Muhammad: A Study of the Early Caliphate*. New York: Cambridge University Press, 1998.

Children

Childhood in the medieval Islamic world was generally defined as lasting from birth to the onset of puberty. In the absence of any physical signs of maturity, 14 to 15 were the generally accepted ages by which the age of majority (adulthood) was defined. Such a determination was important because, neither sexual segregation nor the requirements for **women** to wear the veil applied to prepubescent girls for the simple reason that girls and boys were not yet considered sexual beings in that they were physically unable to reproduce.

The four stages of childhood were generally defined as (1) from birth to teething; (2) from teething to about age 7, or the age of discernment; (3) from 7 to 14; and (4) the transitional phase from fourteen to the onset of puberty. Medieval treatises on marriage admonished parents to receive the births of boys with restrained joy, and to avoid demonstrating disappointment at the birth of girls. They also emphasized the importance of breastfeeding, which was the basic right of an infant for the first 2 years of its life.

Child mortality rates were high in the medieval Islamic world, as they were in all premodern societies. It was common for parents to lose one or more children in infancy or later to childhood diseases as was the case during outbreaks of plague (or Black Death), which hit the medieval Islamic world especially hard during the fourteenth century. Shortly after birth, it was customary to whisper in the child's ear the call to prayer (*adhan*) and the Islamic statement of faith (*shahada*)—"There is no god but God; Muhammad is the Messenger of God." Seven days later, when the child's prospects for survival were more certain, a public feast was held during which the child was named, had some hair cut, and a sheep or goat was slaughtered to express gratitude for the child's birth. The public nature of these ceremonies confirmed the father's parentage and his responsibility to provide for the child.

Although children were able to discern between right and wrong, they were generally seen to have certain legal disabilities that parallel those who are mentally deficient. For example, children could not make binding contracts. Nor were they subject to the same punishments for criminal offenses as adults. In addition, most jurists argued that children were not required to fulfill the rituals of Islamic worship—prayer (*salat*), fasting (*sawm*) during Ramadan, paying alms (*zakat*), or making the pilgrimage (*hajj*). Rather, they should be taught these as part of their religious education in preparation for adulthood.

The marriage age for females tended to coincide with the onset of puberty, but it was common for prepubescent girls to be given in marriage as well. Although there is evidence of marriages being arranged between children, most males married after they had entered into adulthood and tended to be older than their brides. It was common for much older men to marry very young girls. In fact, when Muhammad was in his fifties, he contracted a marriage to his favorite wife, **'Aisha bint Abu Bakr**, when she was 9 years old (some accounts say that she was 6 or 7 years old).

Based on Muhammad's example, the reverse occurred as well. His employer and first wife, Khadija (d. 619), was some 15 years his senior. It was she who initiated the marriage proposal, and Muhammad took no other wives as long as she was alive. Despite Khadija's trust in Muhammad as a businessman and her steadfast moral support for him once he began to receive his revelations, it is possible that Muhammad's monogamy may have been motivated by more than his deep affection for his wife. Although the specific details of their marriage contract remain a mystery, we do know that it was common for a woman of means to contract a marriage on the condition that her husband take no other wives.

One of the more famous examples of such a restriction in a marriage contract is the oath that wealthy widow, Umm Salamah, extracted from the youthful, Abu l-'Abbas (who later became the first **Abbasid** caliph al-Saffah). Umm Salamah made him swear an oath that he would neither take another wife nor a concubine. Abu l-'Abbas agreed to Umm Salamah's terms and, by all appearances, he kept his vow even after he ascended to the caliphate, despite his aides' advice and encouragement that he should partake of the abundantly rich variety of women at his beck and call.

Further Reading

Giladi, Avner. *Children of Islam: Concepts of Childhood in Medieval Muslim Society*. New York: St. Martin's Press, 1992.

Circumcision

The most famous example of circumcision in the Ancient Near East is the institution of male circumcision as the sign of God's covenant with Abraham as described in Genesis:

> Then God said to Abraham, "As for you, you must keep my covenant, you and your descendants after you for the generations to come. This is my covenant with you and your descendants after you, the covenant you are to keep: Every male among you shall be circumcised. You are to undergo circumcision, and it will be a sign of the covenant between me and you. For the generations to come every

male among you who is eight days old must be circumcised. . . . My covenant in your flesh is to be an everlasting covenant. Any uncircumcised male, who has not been circumcised in the flesh, will be cut off from his people; he has broken my covenant." (Genesis 17:9–14)

The early Christian community debated at length whether this physical sign of God's covenant with Abraham should be required under the New Covenant or New Testament. In the end, the Church embraced St. Paul's argument (made in many of his epistles) that "circumcision is circumcision of the heart, by the Spirit, not by the written code" (Romans 2:29).

Despite the fact that circumcision is not mentioned in the Qur'an, classical poetry as well as the biographical literature (sira) on the life of Muhammad indicate that male and female circumcision were practiced in pre-Islamic Arabia. Male circumcision, understandably, was linked to Abraham. According to one account, female circumcision, too, had its origins in the Abraham story — that is, in Sarah's animosity toward Hagar, the mother of Ishmael. After Sarah had sent Hagar away and called her back several times,

She swore to cut something off of her, and said to herself, "I shall cut off her nose, I shall cut off her ear — but no, that would deform her. I will circumcise her instead." So she did that, and Hagar took a piece of cloth to wipe the blood away. For that reason women have been circumcised and have taken pieces of cloth [sanitary napkins?] down to today. (Brinner, 72)

In his famous anti-Christian polemic, "Contra Christianorum," al-Jahiz (777–869) minced no words as to his opinion of the ritual and hygienic merits of male and female circumcision:

[T]he Christian is at heart, a foul and dirty creature. Why? Because he is *uncircumcised*, does not wash after intercourse and eats pig meat. His wife does not wash after intercourse, either, or even after menstruation and childbirth, which leaves her absolutely filthy. Furthermore she, too, is *uncircumcised*. (Colville, 79) (Emphasis added)

Four centuries later, the Damascene Shafi'i scholar al-Nawawi (d. 1233–1277), summarized the views on circumcision advocated by the various *madhhabs* (schools of Islamic jurisprudence) in a treatise on ritual purity (*tahara*), proclaiming that circumcision was obligatory for both men and women. Men had to cut off the full foreskin, and women simply had to cut a small part of the skin off. The ambiguity in the proscription for women left a good deal of latitude for how it was implemented.

Although there was general agreement on the procedure itself, there was little consensus as to timing. Some scholars advocated circumcision on the 7th or 8th day; others at around 7 years of age (when the boy began his formal **education**); others forbade it before 10 years of age. Still others argued in favor of circumcision even later as a right of passage to mark the onset of puberty and in preparation for adulthood and marriage. At whatever age it was performed, circumcision was understood as an essential act of Islamic ritual purification (*tahara*). In fact, a common colloquial term for the practice is *tahara*.

The circumcision of Muslim boys was very much a public affair. Those parents who could afford it, paraded their sons through neighborhood streets on horseback, accompanied by family, friends, and other well-wishers. Less well-to-do parents often scheduled their son's circumcision to coincide with a wedding procession to defray costs. When the child and his entourage had finished their procession, the local barber performed the operation.

Public celebrations and festivities did not accompany the circumcision of a girl. Rather, female circumcision was a private affair attended by the women of the family and the woman who performed the operation. In addition to ritual purity, some of the rationales for female circumcision included the preservation of chastity and the inhibition of sexual desire, but it was also thought to promote fertility and to ensure the birth of sons. Despite the admonitions of scholars, female circumcision was apparently not observed in much (possibly most) of the medieval Islamic world. However, in Egypt, where it had long been observed prior to the Islamic conquest, female circumcision was widely practiced among Muslims and Christians. Finally, despite the scholarly arguments in favor of it, female circumcision (unlike its male counterpart) had a decidedly shameful and secretive connotation attached to it. We see this clearly evidenced by the contemptuous and vulgar epithet, "son of a cutter of clitorises" (*ibn muqatti'at al-buzur*).

Further Reading

Berkey, Johnathan P. "Circumcision Circumscribed: Female Excision and Cultural Accommodation in the Medieval Near East," *International Journal of Middle East Studies* 28.1 (1996): 19–38.

Brinner, William M., trans. *The History of al-Tabari.* Vol. 2: *Prophets and Patriarchs.* Albany: State University Press of New York, 1987.

Colville, Jim, trans. *Sobriety and Mirth: A Selection of the Shorter Writings of al-Jahiz.* London: Kegan Paul, 2002.

Wensinck, J. "*Khitan*" [Circumcision], in *Encyclopaedia of Islam, New Edition.* P.J. Bearman et al., eds. Boston: Brill Academic Publishers, 2005.

Clothing and Modesty

How modest dress was specifically defined in early Islamic history is yet another contested issue among historians because of the paucity of contemporary evidence as well as the allusive (and elusive) character of many Qur'anic passages. This issue is also vigorously debated among modern Muslims because of the implications that the practice of the early community has for Muslim **women** and men today. Fundamental to this discussion is the proper interpretation of the concept of modesty as well as the precise meaning of the Arabic words for veil or covering that are used in the Qur'an (*khimar*, pl. *khumur*; *hijab*, pl. *hujub*).

> Enjoin believing men to turn their eyes away from temptation and to restrain their carnal desires. This will make their lives purer. God has knowledge of all their actions. Enjoin believing women to turn their eyes away from temptation and to preserve their chastity; to cover their adornments (except such as are normally displayed); to draw their veils [*khumur*] over their bosoms and not to reveal their finery except to their husbands, their fathers, their husbands' fathers, their sons, their step-sons, their brothers, their brothers' sons, their sisters' sons, their women-servants, and their slave-girls; male attendants lacking in natural vigour, and children who have no carnal knowledge of women. (Qur'an 24:30–31)

In modern Muslim countries and among Muslim communities in the West, the meaning of veiling is understood in a variety of ways. Some Muslims, especially in the West or among more Westernized communities in the Islamic world, argue that simply covering one's bosom and dressing modestly (usually according to Western standards of modesty) meets the requirement. Others argue that, despite the admonition to "draw their veils [*khumur*] over their bosoms," the subsequent admonition not to "reveal their finery except to their husbands, their fathers" requires not only modest dress, but also the use of a headscarf or shawl to cover one's hair either partially or completely in the presence of all except kin, servants, slaves, and impotents. Others argue that the proper interpretation of this passage requires the complete covering of a woman's body, hands, feet, hair, and face—even to the point of wearing gloves and a veil with sheer material where a woman's eyes are covered so that she can see, but that nobody can see any part of her body, including her eyes.

Although many modern Americans understand the veil as a uniquely Islamic form of women's dress, there is evidence that face veiling was practiced in some pre-Islamic Arabian towns as a sign of high social status. According to the biographical literature, Muhammad required his wives to cover their faces. This was in addition to the Qur'anic injunction that they should remain in their homes. In fact, one of the meanings of the phrase *darabat al-hijab* (She took the veil) is, "She became one of Muhammad's wives."

It remains unclear when precisely face veiling for women became part of broader Islamic practice. Nevertheless, we do know that seclusion and veiling were practiced as symbols of economic wealth and high social status before the advent of Islam in some parts of Arabia, among the urban upper classes in Byzantium, and in Sasanian Iran. It seems entirely plausible that as these areas and their populations were incorporated into the Islamic empire in the first Islamic centuries, the new Islamic order easily adapted this elite urban custom to the new Islamic standards of sexual morality and segregation of the sexes. Finally, whatever the proper interpretation of Qur'anic passages on dress may be for the modern world, it is clear that the dress—especially the public dress—of women and men in early Islamic history as well as throughout much (though not all) of the medieval Islamic world was modest by any modern American standards and included shirts, undergarments, robes, wraps, cloaks, shawls, mantles as well various types of head covering.

Further Reading

Stillman, Yedida Kalfon. *Arab Dress: From the Dawn of Islam to Modern Times*. Leiden, The Netherlands: Brill, 2000.

Coinage. *See* **Money and Coinage**

Death and Afterlife

Muslim burial rituals are fairly simple and, if possible, should occur on the day the person died. First, the corpse is washed and its orifices plugged. It is then wrapped in a shroud in preparation for burial (coffins are not used). The ritual prayer (*salat*) is performed, followed by the recitation of funeral prayers (*janaza*). The shrouded corpse is then carried on a bier or kind of stretcher to the cemetery, where it is placed on its right side with its face toward Mecca in a relatively

The Angel of death asking permission to take Muhammad's life while daughter Fatimah stands by. Turkish painting. The Art Archive/Topkapi Museum Istanbul/ HarperCollins Publishers.

shallow grave so that the deceased can hear the muezzin's call to prayer. According to most Muslim scholars, cremation was not an acceptable practice because of the importance of the physical bodily resurrection of the dead at the end of time. Traditionally, it had also been unacceptable according to Jewish and Christian scholars for similar reasons.

Although the rather modest procedures for properly burying a corpse are important, it is the theology of death itself and the rewards and punishments in the afterlife that are of eternal consequence. One of the most common themes in the Qur'an is the necessity of belief in the One God and the Last Day (The Day of Judgment; or Day of Resurrection). The importance of this theme is made abundantly clear in the seventh chapter of the Qur'an, which describes an event that ostensibly occurred at the beginning of human time when God brought forth Adam's descendants from the loins of his children and made them testify that He was their Lord so that on the Last Day they could not claim ignorance of His Oneness nor could they claim that they were blameless in their polytheism or idolatry because they had learned such false beliefs from their parents (Qur'an 7:171).

Of course, only God knows the moment when each individual will inevitability encounter the angel of death, known as 'Izra'il. A common belief was that God determined the location of each person's death by commanding an angel to put a speck of the soil from the territory where a person was destined to die into the semen in his or her mother's womb. There are many stories told about people who for some unexplained reason felt compelled to visit a particular place, only to die once they arrived there. According to many scholars, once a person is in the grave, two angels (often referred to as Munkar and Nakir) arrive to conduct an interrogation about the content of his or her faith, after which they meet out rewards to the righteous and punishments to the wicked. As noted above, the grave needs to be shallow enough for the deceased to be able to hear the muezzin's call to prayer; however, it also needs to be deep enough for the deceased to be able to sit up and answer the angels' questions.

As the appointed time and location of one's death is known only to God, so too is the exact moment when another angel, Israfil, will sound the trumpet announcing the resurrection of the dead and the ingathering of souls for the final Day of Judgment. However, there are certain events or signs that are expected to occur prior to the Last Day such as natural disasters, the sun rising in the west, a triple eclipse of the moon, and the arrival of Yajuj and Majuj (the Biblical Gog and Magog) to wreak havoc on the earth. Jesus will also return at the end of days to do battle with the Anti-Christ (al-Dajjal). After Jesus defeats the Anti-Christ, he will die for the first time (according to Qur'an 4:157, Jesus only appeared to die on the cross) and be buried in a tomb near Muhammad in Medina.

In addition, a messianic figure called the Mahdi will come and defeat God's enemies, the world will be destroyed, and a new millennial age ushered in. Most Sunni scholars argue that the Mahdi is a member of Muhammad's family; a minority position is that Jesus and the Mahdi are one and the same (*see* **Sunnis**). Twelver Shi'is, of course, believe that Muhammad al-Mahdi—the Hidden Imam—is the Mahdi. Prior to the Day of Judgment, the physical resurrection of the dead will occur (*see* **Shiism**). The righteous and the wicked will then be summoned before God, their vices and virtues recited by angels who recorded them in special books, and God's final judgment given. Essentially, God's final judgment is a formal, ominous, and public vindication of the reward or punishment that He decreed for each person at the moment he or she died.

According to some Muslim scholars, the Final Judgment will occur in the Valley of Jehosephat to the east of Jerusalem (as it will in Judaism and Christianity) and the Ka'ba will be transported from Mecca to witness it. The reward for the righteous and the punishment for the wicked also parallel those found in Judaism and Christianity. The righteous are rewarded with a garden (*janna*), while the wicked are condemned to the fire (*nar*). According to some commentators, the wicked will access the fire via Gehenna (Heb., *gehinom*; Ar., *jahannam*), Jerusalem's garbage dump that used to smolder south of the city. Although the Qur'an speaks of two gardens "for those who fear to stand before God" (Qur'an 55:46) and "two more gardens" beyond them (Qur'an 55:62), some commentators expanded the number from four to seven gardens or "heavens" culminating in the "Garden of Eden."

Whatever the specific number of gardens for the righteous or precise routes to the fire taken by the wicked, the Qur'an makes perfectly clear what is in store for those who obey God and His messenger and those who do not.

> This is the Garden which the righteous have been promised. Therein shall flow rivers of water undefiled, and rivers of milk forever fresh; rivers of wine delectable to those that drink it, and rivers of clarified honey. They shall eat therein of every fruit and receive forgiveness from their Lord. Is this like the lot of those who shall abide in the Fire forever, and drink scalding water which will tear their bowels? (Qur'an 47:15)

Further Reading

Smith, Jane Idleman, and Yvonne Yazbeck Haddad. *The Islamic Understanding of Death and Resurrection*. Albany: State University of New York Press, 1981.

Education

For the vast majority of Muslims, the Qur'an is the eternal uncreated speech of God, flawlessly recited to mankind by His messenger, Muhammad. It should come as no surprise then that the Qur'an was the fundamental building block of education in the medieval Islamic world. Nor should it come as a surprise that the medieval Islamic world was a world in which the written word was ubiquitous. In addition to pious and laudatory inscriptions on public buildings, coins, swords, textiles, carpets, ceramics, and lamps, one could find inscriptions, poetry, and belles-lettres with far less noble themes as well.

Despite the importance of the written word, it was the word that was committed to memory that was held in highest regard. One could not claim to have studied the Qur'an, or any text for that matter, unless he had committed the text to memory. Therefore, beginning around the age of 6 or 7, children were taught to memorize the Qur'an (beginning with the shortest chapters, which are only a few lines) and to study the basics of Islamic beliefs and practices with their teachers. In addition, students learned the basics of Arabic grammar, for without a solid understanding of the Arabic language one could not truly understand the speech of God. Although paper was introduced to the Middle East during the early Islamic period and eventually made its way to Europe, it was only the wealthiest who could afford to waste it. Therefore, students did their lessons with a reed pen and ink on a washable tablet (usually made of wood). Very young boys and the mentally ill were generally discouraged from learning to write in a mosque because they "scribble on the walls and soil the floor, not bothering about urine and other kinds of dirt" (Buckley, 119).

In the early centuries of Islamic history, elementary education was a very informal affair where young children studied with their fathers, uncles, or brothers (and occasionally mothers, aunts, or sisters) at home and, as they matured, with local scholars in the mosque. More advanced students then moved on to study hadiths (statements attributed to or about Muhammad), which along with the Qur'an formed the basis of Islamic jurisprudence and theology. The primary place to study hadith in the early centuries of Islam was the mosque. Scholars also taught in their homes, which allowed them to offer hospitality to their students. It also made it easier for some scholars to charge for their services, despite the fact that it was considered bad form.

The education of boys received a great deal of attention in medieval treatises on education. Al-Shayzari (d. c. 1193) summarizes the sentiments of many in his *Book of the Market Inspector*. Based on a hadith attributed to Muhammad, all boys who have reached the age of 7 should be ordered to pray with the congregation in the mosque. "Teach your children to pray when they reach seven, and when they are ten, beat them if they neglect it" (Buckley, 119). According to al-Shayzari, teachers should employ corporal punishment with what he viewed as moderation:

> The educator should beat them when they are ill-manered, use bad language, and do other things against Islamic law, such as playing with dice, [decorated] eggs, backgammon and all other kinds of gambling. He should not beat a boy with a stick so thick that it will break a bone, nor with one so thin that it will cause too much pain. Rather, the stick should be of middling size. The educator should use a wide strap and aim at the buttocks, the thighs and the lower part of the legs, because there is no fear of injury or harm happening to these places. (Buckley, 119–120)

Teachers should teach their charges to honor and obey their parents. They should avoid using their students for their own needs, for performing demeaning chores such as moving manure or stones; they should also avoid any appearance of impropriety with their students.

Of course, medieval Muslim scholars and educators were well aware of the sentiment that "all work and no play make little Muhammad a dull boy." According to the extremely influential scholar, al-Ghazali (d. 1111 A.D.), "Prevention of the child from playing games and constant insistence on learning deadens his heart, blunts his sharpness of wit and burdens his life; he looks for a ruse to escape them (his studies) altogether" (Giladi, 58). The kinds of games al-Ghazali mentions include, puppet theater, games with balls, toy animals, and toy birds on strings.

In a mosque, teachers generally sat on a mat and against a pillar facing the direction (*qibla*) of Mecca. Their students sat in a circle (*halaqa*) in front of them. Some early scholars thought the use of mats an inappropriate innovation and sat on the bare ground. More renowned scholars often sat on cushions or pillows, which elevated them to a place of honor above their students. As one might expect, the better or more popular teachers attracted larger circles of students than some of their lesser colleagues. In such situations, a teacher might sit on a bench so that his audience could hear him better.

Students intent on mastering the material were expected to faithfully copy out a teacher's lectures, which generally consisted of the teacher dictating a text to which he added his own commentary as well as the commentaries of his teachers. This method of learning from a teacher, who learned from his teachers, who learned from his teachers, illustrates the fundamental importance that medieval Muslims placed on direct personal interaction between teacher and pupil. Once a scholar determined that his student had mastered a given text, he granted him (or her) an *ijaza* (diploma) certifying that he (or she) was now qualified to teach that particular text to others. In part because of this emphasis on the interpersonal, we find scholars and students traveling hundreds, even thousands of miles to study with the leading lights throughout the medieval Islamic world.

There were opportunities for girls to study, to earn *ijazas*, and to become learned enough that eminent scholars sought them out as teachers. This was especially the case among learned families who often made special efforts to ensure high-quality education in the Qur'an and hadith for their sons and daughters. Hadith transmission was the primary field in which women could make their mark as teachers of men. After all, one could hardly argue that women were inadequate to the task of transmitting hadith because **'Aisha bint Abi Bakr**, Muhammad's favorite wife, was one of the most important hadith transmitters in early Islamic history. In addition, Muhammad is reported to have praised the women of Medina because of their desire for religious knowledge. "How splendid were the women of the *ansar*; shame did not prevent them from becoming learned in the faith" (Berkey, 161).

Understandably, religious education for girls tended to be strongest within scholarly families. However, despite 'Aisha's example and despite Muhammad's praise for the women of Medina, educating girls and women was not universally supported. Opponents could even make their case by citing an apparently contradictory statement attributed to Muhammad. "It is said that a woman who learns [how to] write is like a snake given poison to drink" (Berkey, 161). Al-Shayzari warns against teaching women to write as well. "The educator must not teach a woman or a female slave how to write, because this makes a woman worse, and it is said that a woman learning to write is like a snake made more venomous by being given poison to drink" (Buckley, 120).

Nevertheless, it is clear that girls and women could be and were educated in the Qur'an and hadith, some very considerably. Although women did not enroll as students in formal classes, we do know that they did attend ad hoc lectures and study sessions in mosques, *madrasas*, and other public places. It should come as no surprise that some men did not approve of women's public participation. The dyspeptic fourteenth-century scholar, Muhammad

Ibn al-Hajj (d. 1336), was appalled by the behavior of some women who informally audited lectures in his day:

> [Consider] what some women do when people gather with a shaykh to hear [the recitation of] books. At that point women come, too, to hear the readings; the men sit in one place, the women facing them. It even happens at such times that some of the women are carried away by the situation; one will stand up, and sit down, and shout in a loud voice. [Moreover,] private parts of her body will appear; in her house, their exposure would be forbidden—how can it be allowed in a mosque, in the presence of men? (Berkey, 171–172)

The Arabic term translated here as "private parts of her body" (*'awra*) refers to "that which is indecent to reveal," generally understood to mean anything other than a woman's face and hands. Some extended the definition to include even these as well.

The relationship between travel and education is illustrated eloquently by a hadith in which Muhammad is reported to have told his followers that they should seek religious knowledge (*talab al-'ilm*) even unto China; that is, to the ends of the earth. This desire to travel to study with the masters was often coupled with the obligation to undertake the pilgrimage to Mecca at least once if one is able. In addition to being the means for many to fulfill one of the Five Pillars of Islam, pilgrimage caravans from such distant places as Spain, West Africa, Central Asia, India and elsewhere functioned as informal traveling universities that continually added new scholars as they made their way to Mecca and back each year. As such, these pilgrimage caravans played a very important role in spreading new ideas and reinforcing old ones throughout the Islamic world.

Although the *madrasa* existed as early as the late-ninth century, by the late-eleventh century it had become much more prevalent throughout the Islamic world. Funded by pious endowments (made by private individuals and members of royal families), the *madrasa* was more than a mere change in venue from the mosque (or private residence) and its informal instruction. The better-endowed *madrasas* provided salaries for teachers and stipends for students. Many were built with apartments for students and teachers as well. One of Islam's greatest medieval scholars, al-Ghazali (d. 1111), taught at Baghdad's Nizamiyya *madrasa*, founded by the Seljukid wazir, **Nizam al-Mulk** (d. 1092).

Education in the medieval Islamic world, of course, was not limited to religious subjects—Qur'an, hadith, jurisprudence, theology, and so forth. Ancient Greek, Persian, and Sanskrit works on philosophy, medicine, mathematics, astronomy, geography, and other sciences were translated into Arabic between the eighth and tenth centuries under the patronage of the **Abbasid caliphs**. Muslim (as well as Jewish and Christian) scholars studied these classics and built upon them. Many of these ancient classics were eventually translated into Latin and made their way into the medieval European curriculum.

Further Reading

Berkey, Jonathan. *The Transmission of Knowledge in Medieval Cairo: A Social History of Islamic Education*. Princeton, NJ: Princeton University Press, 1992.

Buckley, R.P., trans. *The Book of the Islamic Market Inspector: Niyayat al-rutba fi talab al-hisba (The Utmost Authority in the Pursuit of Hisba) by 'Abd al-Rahman b. Nasr al-Shayzari*. New York: Oxford University Press, 1999.

Giladi, Avner. *Children of Islam: Concepts of Childhood in Medieval Muslim Society*. New York: St. Martin's Press, 1992.

Makdisi, George. *The Rise of Colleges: Institutions of Learning in Islam and the West*. Edinburgh, Scotland: Edinburgh University Press, 1981.

Melchert, Christopher. "The Etiquette of Learning in the Early Islamic Study Circle," in Joseph Lowry, Devin Stewart and Shawkat M. Toorawa, eds. *Law and Education in Medieval Islam: Studies in Honor of Professor George Makdisi*. Cambridge, UK: E.J.W. Gibb Memorial Trust, 2004, pp. 33–44.

Entertainments

Common children's entertainments in the medieval Islamic world included puppet theaters and see-saws as well as games played with balls, dolls, toy animals, and birds. Board games such as chess and backgammon were popular games among all sectors of society. So too were card games. Entertainments that involved tests of physical prowess were quite popular, including wrestling, races, polo, mock military competitions, and other displays of horsemanship—a sort of medieval rodeo.

Not all popular entertainments involved toys, puppets, or physical competitions. One of the most popular events at trade fairs in seventh-century Arabia was the poetry competition among the leading poets of the clans present. For to the best poet went not only a financial reward, but his entire clan benefited from the prestige of his poetic prowess. Arabic poetry performances continued to be extremely popular throughout the medieval Islamic world and remain so today, often selling out large auditoriums. Persian reemerged as a language of literature and administration in the tenth century. Public recitations of Ferdowsi's (c. 940–1020) *Shahnameh* (Book of Kings)—one of the earliest and greatest examples of new Persian epic poetry—were quite popular throughout the Persian-speaking world. Turkish poetry began to become popular as well by 1400 after the rise of the Ottoman house in Anatolia and southeastern Europe.

It should come as no surprise that poetry often dealt with themes of honor, glory, and heroism among men, but also the beauty of one's beloved, the passions of unrequited love, and the romantic benefits of wine. Among the ruling elites as well as among the wealthy classes, poetry performances were often accompanied by music and performed by singing girls, many of whom were slaves purchased expressly for their beauty, voices and dancing abilities.

Hunting in the medieval Islamic world was done for sport as well as for food. It was a favorite entertainment for the wealthy and a necessity for the diet of some of the less well-to-do. Given the specific regulations for butchering domesticated animals for them to be *halal*; that is, permitted according to shari'a or Islamic law, Muslim scholars devoted their attention to determining which game was permissible for consumption and when. Essentially, any wild animal killed by a hunter was considered *halal*, with the notable exception of pigs, which are forbidden under any circumstances. However, it is forbidden for pilgrims to eat game during the annual pilgrimage (*hajj*). Finally, whereas according to the Jewish tradition only fish with scales are considered kosher, all fish and seafood are permissible to Muslims at any time.

Hunting was a common theme in medieval Islamic literature, whether in poetry or in descriptions of a ruler's fondness for spending time on his horse as he and his companions pursued hares, partridges, quail, geese, and other small game with their hunting falcons and hounds. In his memoir, Usama ibn Muhqidh (1095–1188) includes a section about his father's exploits as a hunter near the family estate at Shayzar in the mountains between Hama and the Syrian coast. Because his was a well-to-do family, they had broad access to land on which to hunt. In fact, Usama reports that in Shayzar "we had two hunting fields, one for partridges and hares, in the mountain to the south of town; and another for waterfowl, francolins, hares and gazelles, on the bank of the river in the cane fields to the west of town" (Hitti, 228).

Falcons and hawks are birds of prey that were essential to a successful hunt, so too were hunting hounds. In fact, Usama's father used to dispatch some of his men to distant lands to purchase choice falcons as well as pigeons to feed them. He even sent some of his aides as far as Constantinople, the Byzantine capital, to purchase his falcons and hounds. Falcons and hawks were also purchased from locals who had set up trapping stations nearby to meet the demand for the birds. Although falcons and hawks were excellent hunters of small game and other birds, cheetahs were often used when hunting larger game such as gazelles, antelopes, deer, wild donkeys, and wild boar.

Falcons, hawks, hounds, cheetahs, and horses were a keeper's livelihood as well as essential to his employer's successful hunts. Hence, a great deal of care and attention was paid to a man's hunting animals. In fact, it was common for a hunter to keep his birds of prey in his home. Usamah reports that his father even kept his prize cheetah in their house.

> He had a special maid who served it. In one side of the courtyard she had a velvet quilt folded, with dry grass beneath. In the wall was an iron staple. After the hunt, the cheetah trainer would bring it to the door of the house in which its couching place lay, and leave it there. It would then enter the house and go to that place where its bed was spread and sleep. The maid would come and tie it to the staple fastened to the wall. (Hitti, 237)

Usamah also reports that gazelles, rams, goats, and fawns were born in the same courtyard, but that the cheetah so well behaved that it never touched them.

Further Reading
Hitti, Philip K., trans. *An Arab-Syrian Gentleman and Warrior in the Period of the Crusades: Memoirs of Usamah Ibn-Muhqidh.* Princeton, NJ: Princeton University Press, 1987 [1929].

Fatimids (910–1171)

In the wake of a clandestine revolutionary movement among the Berbers of North Africa, Ubayd Allah al-Mahdi proclaimed himself the first Fatimid imam in 910. Despite the similarities between the methodology and rhetoric of the Fatimids and that of the Abbasids, the Fatimid imams belonged to the Isma'ili branch of Shi'i Islam, which was openly hostile to the Sunni **Abbasid caliphate** in Baghdad (*see* **Shiism** and **Sunnis**). In fact, the Fatimids' intent had long been to use North Africa as a staging ground for their ultimate goal of conquering Baghdad and unseating the Abbasids. To that end, and after several failed attempts, Fatimid forces finally conquered Egypt in 969. Almost immediately, the

Fatimid general, Jawhar, began laying the foundations for the new palace city, al-Qahira (Cairo).

The Fatimids never were able to overthrow the Abbasid caliphs, but under their tutelage Egypt and its new capital became one of the wealthiest and most important cosmopolitan way stations for international trade and culture in the Mediterranean world, southwest Asia, and the Indian Ocean. Saladin brought an end to the Fatimid caliphate in 1171, but Cairo and Egypt continued to flourish under his leadership and that of his Ayyubid successors (1171–1250) and of the **Mamluk** Sultans (1250–1517).

Combat with staffs. Watercolor on parchment, Fatimid period (10th–12th century), Fostât, Egypt. The Art Archive/Museum of Islamic Art Cairo/Gianni Dagli Orti.

Further Reading

Daftary, Farhad. *The Isma'ilis: Their History and Doctrines.* New York: Cambridge University Press, 1990.

Walker, Paul E. *Exploring an Islamic Empire: Fatimid History and Its Sources.* London: I.B. Tauris, 2002.

Food

The diversity of fruits, vegetables, grains, and meats that were available in the medieval Islamic world is truly impressive. Markets throughout the medieval Islamic world were full of local fruits, vegetables, meats, and fish as well as preserved foods that had been brought from afar. Some of these were preserved by cooling as well as drying. The most common method of preservation, however, was to pickle them in vinegar and salt along with a range of condiments, including honey, sugar, lemon juice, olive oil, mustard, nuts, and all sorts of spices and herbs. Although any meat can be made into sausage, sausages made from mutton and semolina were preferred. Muhammad is said to have been particularly fond of milk, but given the difficulties of preserving fresh milk, it was converted into a wide variety of soft and hard cheeses.

In the countryside women generally ground the flour. In the cities, there were mills that ground flour for sale. Some urban marriage contracts have survived that specify that the bride (usually from a wealthy family) was to be exempt from grinding flour. Because only the wealthiest individuals could afford to have an oven built into their residences, foods prepared at home had to be taken to a local bake house to be cooked. In addition, there were shops, which sold breads, pastries, and sweetmeats, as well as restaurants where one could purchase all sorts of prepared dishes.

Islamic dietary laws are limited to but a few items, including blood, meat from animals that are not slaughtered properly, carrion, pork, and animals that have been consecrated to pagan gods. Although there are many similarities between Islamic and Jewish dietary laws, Islamic dietary laws are generally less restrictive than Jewish ones. (Most Christian traditions abandoned Jewish dietary laws in their entirety.) A general rule of thumb is that nearly everything that is permissible (kosher) for Jews to eat is permissible (*halal*) for Muslims to eat. The major exception to this rule is that while wine is kosher and is absolutely essential to Jewish ritual and practice, it is explicitly forbidden in the Qur'an.

However, many things that are *halal* are not kosher. For example, all seafood is permissible (*halal*) for Muslims to eat; however, only fishes with scales are permissible (kosher) for Jews—shell fish, lobster, shrimp, and so forth are forbidden. In addition, certain meat dishes made with milk or yogurt are said to have been some of Muhammad's favorites and hence are permissible for Muslims to eat. However, Jewish kosher regulations state that meat may not be cooked in or eaten with any milk product. An obvious example of a meat dish that is not kosher is the ubiquitous American cheeseburger washed down with a tall glass of milk.

Dietary regulations are more restrictive for pilgrims to Mecca as well. To remain in a state of ritual purity (*tahara*) during the pilgrimage, pilgrims must abstain from killing or eating game (though seafood is permissible) and of course from those foods and drinks that are always forbidden. It should be noted that though the Qur'an specifically forbids the above foods and drinks, the pragmatic side of most schools of Islamic law recognizes exigent circumstances when one might involuntarily or even forcibly be compelled to eat or drink forbidden things.

Although scholars generally extended the Qur'anic prohibition on wine to all alcoholic beverages, it is clear that there were a range of near beers and other "soft" or lightly fermented fruit drinks that could be commonly found throughout the medieval Islamic world. As such, a great deal of ink was spilled defining which types of drinks were in fact "soft" (lightly fermented) and permitted and which were "hard" (real intoxicants) and forbidden. As one might expect, water was an essential drink, though the quality of water was often determined by how much one was willing and or able to pay a water seller who carried water around in a jug on his back for sale in the market. The wealthiest even purchased snow from snow vendors who brought in snow from afar and kept it in storehouses. Fruit juices mixed with water were very common, including drinks made from lemons, oranges, apples, tamarinds, dates, grapes, and pomegranates.

Various coffees can be found throughout the modern Islamic world, and Arabica beans are a favorite in American coffee houses. However, coffee was only introduced to the Islamic world from Yemen and east Africa in the fifteenth century. There are several legends about who was the first to bring coffee beans to Yemen, and most of them revolve around one or more Sufis (Islamic mystics) who praised the drink as an inhibitor of sleep and an aide to mystical devotional rituals (*see* **Sufism**). Tea is ubiquitous in the modern Islamic world as well but was introduced from India even later, and often by European merchants. For example, it was a French merchant who had business dealings in East Asia who first introduced tea to Morocco around 1700. *See also* Document 11.

Further Reading

Hattox, Ralph S. *Coffee and Coffeehouses: The Origins of a Social Beverage in the Medieval Near East*. Seattle: University of Washington Press, 1985.

Zubaida, Sami, and Richard Tapper, eds. *Culinary Cultures of the Middle East*. New York: I.B. Tauris, 1994.

Geniza (Cairo)

According to Jewish custom, documents on which the personal name of God is written should not be destroyed. Hence, the Egyptian Jewish community placed such documents in a storeroom (*geniza*) in the Ibn Ezra synagogue in Fustat until they were supposed to be buried. Most of these documents were written in what is known as Judeo-Arabic, that is, Arabic written in the Hebrew script. The documents from this particular geniza were never buried and were eventually discovered quite by accident in the nineteenth century. These documents (most of which date from 1002 to 1266) are particularly useful for understanding daily life among greater Cairo's Jewish community; however, as S.D. Goitein has so ably demonstrated, these documents can also be used to construct a very detailed picture of daily life in Egypt, the Mediterranean world, and beyond.

Further Reading

Goitein, S.D. *A Mediterranean Society: The Jewish Communities of the World as Portrayed in the Cairo Geniza*. 6 vols. Berkeley: University of California Press, 1967–93.

Lassner, Jacob. *A Mediterranean Society: An Abridgement in One Volume*. Berkeley: University of California Press, 1999.

Harun al-Rashid (d. 809)

Harun al-Rashid (r. 786–809) was the son of the al-Mahdi (the third **Abbasid** caliph) and a former slave girl named al-Kharzuran. Harun al-Rahid's reign and the life at his court at Baghdad are frequently hailed as one of the high points of medieval Islamic history. They are subject of many stories and legends. Many of the stories in the famous *Thousand and One Nights* are likely inspired by the world of his court. In addition to supporting the arts, education, culture, religion, and so forth, Harun was noted for his fulfillment of the religious obligation of jihad, especially against the Byzantines on the Syrian frontier. In the early 800s, Harun arranged for two of his sons, al-Amin and **al-Ma'mun ibn Harun al-Rashid**, to succeed him as caliph in succession. Not surprisingly, the succession was not orderly. In fact, the Abbasid caliphate never fully recovered from the civil war between al-Amin (r. 809–813) and al-Ma'mun (r. 813–833). By the 860s and 870s, many petty states had established themselves under Muslim rulers in North Africa and Spain to the west and in Iran and lands further east.

Kamal al-Din Bihzad. Harun al-Rashid at the barbers. Illustration from Khamsa or Quintet by Nizami, 1141–1209, Azarbaijani poet, produced in 1494, Safavid court at Herat, Afghanistan. The Art Archive/British Library.

Further Reading
Gordon, Matthew. *The Rise of Islam*. Westport, CT: Greenwood, 2005.
Kennedy, Hugh N. *When Baghdad Ruled the Muslim World: The Rise and Fall of Islam's Greatest Dynasty*. Cambridge, MA: Da Capo Press, 2005.

Hasan ibn 'Ali ibn Abi Talib (d. 669)

Hasan was the eldest son of **'Ali ibn Abi Talib** and Fatima (Muhammad's daughter) and second Shiite imam. According to Shi'i tradition, after Ali's assassination in 661, the imamate then passed to Hasan (*see* **Shiism**). However, Hasan abdicated his claim to the caliphate in 661 and did not oppose **Mu'awiya ibn Abi Sufyan** (r. 661–680), who established the **Umayyad caliphate** (661–750) with Damascus as its capital. Despite Hasan's abdication, there remained a faction (*shi'a*) of Muslims who continued to argue that only someone from Muhammad's house (in particular a descendant of Ali and Fatima) could legitimately lead the Muslim community. Hasan died in 669 under mysterious circumstances, possibly on the orders of Mu'awiya. According to Shi'i belief, Ali, Hasan, his brother **Husayn ibn 'Ali ibn Abi Talib**, and all the Shiite imams died as martyrs.

Further Reading
Gordon, Matthew. *The Rise of Islam*. Westport, CT: Greenwood, 2005.
Momen, Moojan. *An Introduction to Shi'i Islam*. New Haven, CT: Yale University Press, 1985.

Hijra

Muhammad's prophetic career can be divided into two roughly equal periods. The first took place in his hometown of Mecca from about 610 to 622. By 622, he had fallen out of favor with the leaders of Mecca and negotiated a move for himself and his followers to the oasis settlement of Medina approximately 250 miles to the north. This move from Mecca to Medina in 622 is referred to as his *hijra* (migration) and is of such importance to his prophetic career that the year 622 of the Gregorian calendar marks the year one of the Muslim calendar.

Further Reading
Freeman-Grenville, G.S.P. *The Muslim and Christian Calendars*. London: Oxford University Press, 1963.

Housing

Housing in the medieval Islamic world included tents, mud huts, reed huts, single-story residences, multistoried tenements, and elaborate palaces. In the deserts of Arabia, Syria, Iraq, Iran, and North Africa tents predominated among the pastoral nomadic populations. These were generally made from the hair, wool, and leather of the nomads' herds and flocks, whether sheep, goats, or camels. In the settled oases of the region, most homes were built from mud or reeds simply because wood and stone were rarely available in sufficient quantities to be practicable. Homes tended to be huts built of mud-bricks in Muhammad's hometown of seventh-century Mecca, whereas in other oases reed huts were more common. In the highlands of Yemen many of the residents lived in villages and towns made up of multistory tenement buildings.

In the major cities such as Damascus, Baghdad, and Cairo wood, stone, and brick were the preferred building materials in part because they were more readily available but also because they are far more durable than tents and mud or reed huts. Although some residents lived in single-story homes, many lived in multistoried apartment buildings. The tenth-century geographer, **al-Muqaddasi**, records that Fustat's (Old Cairo's) teeming population lived in four- and five-story tenements, which housed as many as 200 people. Medieval Muslim rulers also built elaborate stone palaces, mosques, madrasas, caravansaries, bathhouses, and hospitals. Depending on the locale, some of the stones and columns used in constructing such examples of monumental architecture were recycled from Pharaonic, Roman, and Sasanian ruins or from Christian churches and monasteries. Some of the buildings constructed during the Middle Ages still bear the graffiti and other inscriptions from earlier eras.

Typical of most **housing** at the time was a central courtyard or common area of some sort around which salons, bedrooms, and kitchens were constructed. Only the wealthy could afford indoor plumbing or ovens as part of their residences. Outhouses or outdoor latrine facilities of some sort were the order of the day. Men often simply urinated in a street or alley in a manner reminiscent of the Biblical euphemism for men as those "who pisseth against the wall" (I Samuel 25:22, 34). Public baths were essential to every city. If there was only one bathhouse in a town, certain days or parts of days were designated for women and others for men. Larger cities had women's bathhouses, which were usually physically separate from the men's bathhouses.

One's home in the medieval Islamic world served as a sanctuary or refuge from the primarily male-dominated public world of the market and the mosque. Most men who were not part of the ruling classes or military spent much of the day outside the home working, studying, or at prayer in the mosque with other men. Women (especially respectable women) spent a great deal of their time at home with their children and other women. Women generally performed their ritual prayers at home. Literate women were usually educated at home, often by their fathers, uncles, brothers, or male cousins. If their mothers or other female relatives were educated, they often studied with them as well. Women who worked for a wage generally labored at home doing piecework as seamstresses, weaver, or making other handicrafts.

In addition to serving as a refuge from the outside world, the courtyard was a common area shared by the whole family (or families) who lived around it. Among rural and nomadic populations the courtyard might also serve as a corral for livestock. Women tended to prepare hot meals over a fire in such courtyards or in common neighborhood cooking areas. Meals that required an oven were prepared at home and then taken to a local bake house to be cooked. In the residences of the wealthy and the palaces of the ruling classes, courtyards were often quite elaborate. Many were equipped with fountains, gardens, and sophisticated canopies and trellises that allowed in light, but also provided a cooling shade from the often-blistering sun.

The courtyard also served as the public space of the home where guests were welcomed and entertained. In addition to the courtyard there was often a salon that served the same purpose. In either case when male guests were involved, the courtyard or the salon became extensions of the outside world in that such gatherings generally were male only affairs, especially among the wealthy classes. Because hospitality and generosity were notable virtues throughout the Islamic world, food and beverages were served in such instances. In the medieval Islamic world, few things could ruin one's reputation more than being known as stingy or inhospitable.

Because of the strict rules pertaining to sexual segregation every dwelling had an inviolable space (harem) that was separate from the rest of the house where the women retreated when male guests were present. In palaces and the homes of the wealthy this took the form of well-appointed **women**'s quarters or harems that only women, children, male kin, and eunuchs were allowed to enter. The women of less well-to-do families would retreat to a room or an area separated from the rest of the dwelling by a curtain or some sort of partition that served as a harem only when guest were present but was generally used for other purposes such as cooking, sewing, making handicrafts, study, or sleeping.

Whether one lived in a courtyard house or in a multistory tenement, a frequent concern was how best to encourage air exchange and cooling breezes in the often-stifling summer heat and at the same time preserve the sanctity and privacy of the home's interior space. One common means of achieving ventilation and privacy is what is known as *mashrabiyya*—a wooden grill or grate that was used to cover windows or balconies. The grills or lattice work were usually made of turned wood that was joined together with carved blocks or spheres of wood to create intricate patterns. (In the homes of the very wealthy or for use in public buildings, the screen was occasionally made of metalwork.) Another means of ventilation was the wind catcher, or *malqaf*. A wind catcher functioned as a kind of reverse chimney/swamp cooler in that it was consisted of a shaft that rose above the building's roof. The opening of the shaft was positioned to catch the prevailing winds of the region and force them down into the building, often flowing over pools of water or screens that were dampened with wet fabrics.

Although furnishings in the medieval Islamic world did include chairs with legs and beds with frames, it was far more common that homes were furnished with pillows, mattresses, and sofas. That is, domestic life in the medieval Islamic world was generally conducted rather close to the ground. Families did not sit in chairs around a dining room table at mealtime. Nor did they eat from individual plates. Rather, meals were served on large serving trays that were set on the floor or on a low stand. Guests then sat on a carpet, pillow, or very low seat around the serving tray and ate directly from it. They generally ate many dishes with their hands and flat breads; however, utensils (especially knives and spoons) were used for cutting meats and for eating soups (*see* **Food**).

Woodworkers and smiths did construct benches and chairs that were comparable in height to modern chairs and benches, but these were generally for use outside the home and generally were used to indicate the higher rank and status of the person (ruler, scholar, family patriarch, other person of high status) who sat on them in relation to those who were seated below him. Sitting on sofas, large pillows, pillows stacked on one another, or anything that might elevate a person over others could just as easily serve the same purpose of reflecting the hierarchy of status and rank.

The heights and kinds of the beds people slept on as well as the kinds of material used to make beds, pillows, and sofas were indications of status and wealth also. Beds with legs and frames were sign of the highest status. Beds without them were a step down, sleeping on a mat or carpet a step further, and sleeping on the bare floor was for the poorest as well as for the mendicant Sufis, who considered themselves as God's poor ones (*fuqara' Allah*).

Further Reading

Petherbridge, Guy T. "Vernacular Architecture: The House and Society," in George Michell, ed. *Architecture of the Islamic World: Its Historical and Social Meaning*. London: Thames and Hudson, 1978.

Husayn ibn 'Ali ibn Abi Talib (d. 680)

According to Shi'i tradition, after the assassination of **'Ali ibn Abi Talib**, the imamate then passed to his eldest son, **Hasan ibn 'Ali ibn Abi Talib** (d. 669). However, Hasan abdicated his claim to the caliphate in 661 and did not oppose **Mu'awiya ibn Abi Sufyan** (r. 661–680), who established the **Umayyad caliphate** (661–750) with Damascus as its capital. Despite Hasan's abdication, there remained a faction (*shi'a*) of Muslims who continued to argue that only someone from Muhammad's house (in particular a descendant of Ali) could legitimately lead the Muslim community (*see* **Shiism**). Shortly after Yazid acceded to the caliphate (r. 680–683), Ali's younger son, Husayn ibn 'Ali ibn Abi Talib (the third imam), was persuaded to leave his home in the Hijaz and to travel to Kufa to lead a revolt and to take his rightful place at the head of the Muslim community. On 10 Muharram 61 (October 10, 680), Umayyad forces routed Husayn and seventy-two armed men (together with their **women** and **children**) at Karbala. The victors beheaded Husayn and his companions and put their heads on pikes as they marched to Kufa. The women and children were taken prisoner, including Husayn's sole surviving son, Ali, who had been too ill to participate in the battle.

As was customary, Husayn's head was sent to the caliph Yazid in Damascus as proof that Husayn was indeed dead. Some reports indicate that Yazid was saddened by the death of Muhammad's grandson. Others suggest that he treated Husayn's head with contempt as he poked at Husayn's mouth with his cane, for which he was immediately taken to task by Abu Barzah al-Aslami, a companion of Muhammad

> Are you poking the mouth of al-Husayn with your cane? Take your cane away from his mouth. How often have I seen the Apostle of God kiss it! As for you, Yazid, you will come forward on the Day of Resurrection, and Ibn Ziyad will be your advocate. But this man will come forward on the Day of Resurrection, and Muhammad will be his advocate. (al-Tabari, 174)

Husayn's head was returned to his dependants who buried it. But where? His head has a place of honor in the Umayyad Mosque in Damascus. Another tradition says that it was buried in Ashkelon where the **Fatimids** built a shrine in 1098. During the Crusader period it was disinterred and moved to Cairo (1153) where it is venerated to this day at the Husayn Mosque. There are other traditions that state that Husayn's head was interred in Medina, Kufa, Najaf, Karbala, Raqqa on the upper Euphrates, and even in distant Marv in Afghanistan.

With Husayn's martyrdom, the imamate passed to his son, Ali, and then continued to be passed on from father to son as each imam designated his successor. According to Shi'i doctrine, all of the imams except the twelfth died as martyrs. Some were slain in battle, while others were poisoned or died in prison. The most dramatic martyrdom, of course, is that of Husayn. There are reports of the faithful weeping over Husayn's grave almost immediately after his tomb was constructed. In 850, the **Abbasid** caliph al-Mutawakkil had the shrine destroyed to put an end to Shi'i pilgrimages to it. His efforts proved unsuccessful as pilgrims continued to go to Karbala even though there was no shrine. The **Buyid** ruler Adud al-Dawla restored Husayn's tomb at Karbala and Ali's tomb at Najaf in 990.

Over time, elaborate rituals developed as part of the faithful's visitation and public mourning at the imams' tombs, whether at Husayn's tomb in Karbala, Ali's tomb in Najaf, or at the tombs of the imams buried in Baghdad, Samarra, Medina, or Mashhad in Iran. According to the thirteenth-century theologian Ta'usi (d. 1266), the faithful expressed their longing for the imams and their suffering as they cried over their graves.

> Could I but be your ransom! Since the Lord of the future life takes pleasure in sorrow and since it serves to purify God's servants—behold! we therefore don mourning attire and find delight in letting tears flow. We say to the eyes: stream in uninterrupted weeping forever! (Halm, 140)

The most elaborate of the lamentations is for Husayn, and the rituals of the Ashura festival date at least to the Buyid period. Sources indicate that the oldest Ashura ritual is for pilgrims to Husayn's tomb to request a sip of water in commemoration of one of Husayn's final acts prior to his martyrdom. Near the end of the battle, as Husayn pleaded for water for his infant son (whom he held in his arms), an arrow pierced the baby's throat and killed him. Undeterred by his child's death, Husayn continued to fight until he was finally slain. The elaborate passion plays and public processions where mourners beat and cut themselves in identification with Husayn's suffering so common in modern Iran, Iraq, and Lebanon appear to date from the Safavid (1501–1722) and Qajar (1779–1925) periods in Iran, well after the period covered in this book.

Further Reading

Gordon, Matthew. *The Rise of Islam*. Westport, CT: Greenwood, 2005.

Halm, Heinz. *Shiism*. Edinburgh, Scotland: Edinburgh University Press, 1991.

Momen, Moojan. *An Introduction to Shi'i Islam*. New Haven, CT: Yale University Press, 1985.

al-Tabari. *The History of al-Tabari*. Vol. 19. *The Caliphate of Yazid b. Mu'awiyya*. Translated by I.K.A. Howard. Albany: State University of New York Press, 1990.

Ibn Battuta (1304–1368/1377)

Ibn Battuta was a Berber born and raised in Tangier in what is today Morocco. Ibn Battuta was educated in the Maliki school (madhhab) of Islamic law (*shari'a*). What began as the fulfillment of his religious obligation to undertake the pilgrimage to Mecca in 1325 turned into a nearly 30-year journey (1325–1354) throughout nearly the entire Islamic world covering some 73,000 miles (117,000 km), and even to China in the east and Constantinople, the capital of the Byzantine Empire.

Most of what we know of Ibn Battuta is from his *Rihla*, an account of his travels that he dictated to a scholar named Ibn Juzayy several years after his return. Ibn Battuta could usually draw on his training in Arabic language, Islamic law, and Sufism to gain access to the scholarly, economic, and political elites of most of the regions to which he travelled. Some of Ibn Battuta's contemporaries, including the famous north African scholar Ibn Khaldun (1332–1406), viewed him as a purveyor of fanciful tall tales and as an incompetent scholarly poseur. However, as Ross Dunn beautifully demonstrated, Ibn Battuta's detailed account of his travels is a tremendously valuable source for understanding the complex societies that comprised the Islamic world in the fourteenth century.

Further Reading

Dunn, Ross E. *The Adventures of Ibn Battuta: A Muslim Traveler of the 14th Century*. rev. ed. Berkeley and Los Angeles: University of California Press, 1989.

Gibb, H.A.R., trans. *Ibn Battuta Travels in Asia and Africa*. London: Hakluyt Society, 1958–2000.

Mackintosh-Smith, Tim. *Travels with a Tangerine: A Journey in the Footnotes of Ibn Battutah*. New York: Welcome Rain Publishers, 2002.

Ibn Jubayr (1145–1217)

Ibn Jubayr was a geographer, traveler, and poet from al-Andalus. He is most famous for his detailed account of his travels (1183–1185) that he undertook in conjunction with his performance of the obligation to perform the pilgrimage to Mecca. After booking passage on a Genoese vessel, Ibn Jubayr departed from his home in Granada in February 1183, sailed across the Mediterranean to the port of Alexandria in Egypt, and traveled down the Nile to Cairo and eventually to the Egyptian Red Sea port of Aydhab. He then crossed the Red Sea with his fellow pilgrims to the west Arabian port of Jiddah on his way to Mecca. He arrived in Mecca in September 1183, where he waited until the annual pilgrimage commenced in mid-March 1184. After undertaking the pilgrimage, Ibn Jubayr then traveled northeast across the Arabian Peninsula to Baghdad and up the Tigris to Mosul. He then traveled west to Aleppo in northern Syria and south to Damascus where he spent four months (July to October 1184).

He then traveled to the port of Acre, which he departed in October 1184, and sailed westward across the Mediterranean. After a number of detours along the way, he finally reached his home in Granada in May 1185. Although Ibn Jubayr's avoidance of Jerusalem may simply have been a case of his desire to reach home after an already long and arduous trip, it may have had more to do with the fact that in 1184, Jerusalem was still the capital of the Crusader kingdom. The invocation with which Ibn Jubayr begins his brief description of Acre leaves no doubt as to his sentiments towards the Crusaders, "May God destroy (the Christians in) it and restore it (to the Muslims)" (Broadhurst, 318). Unfortunately from Ibn Jubayr's point of view, because the Crusaders controlled every major port city along the Syrian coast at the time, he had little choice but to either depart from a Crusader port or make the long overland trek to the port of Alexandria. Ibn Jubayr travelled to the East two more times (1189–1191 and 1217). Unfortunately for us, he did not leave an account of these trips. Ibn Jubayr's account of his travels is quite detailed and was well known in the centuries after its completion. In fact, his descriptions served as the basis of some of **Ibn Battuta's** description of his travels to the same places in the fourteenth century. Ibn Jubayr died in Egypt during his final journey to the east.

Further Reading
Broadhurst, R.J.C., trans. *The Travels of Ibn Jubayr*. London: J. Cape, 1952.

Iman/Imamate. *See* Caliph and Shiism

Jihad

Jihad is an Arabic noun that conveys the idea of struggle or striving. In the Qur'an jihad is often used as part of the phrase, *jihad fi sabil Allah* (striving in the path of God). Although most Muslim scholars regarded jihad as obligatory on all able-bodied Muslims, some even referred to it as a sixth pillar of Islam. As such, jihad in its various forms is essential to understanding daily life in the medieval Islamic world. The principal textual authorities for the Islamic doctrine of jihad are the Qur'an and the hadiths, or statements attributed to Muhammad about the subject. Hence, the doctrine of jihad is rooted in the life and practice of Muhammad and the early Islamic community in Medina.

The principal Qur'anic material on jihad is in the ninth chapter, which speaks of jihad as offensive warfare against idolaters, polytheists, and infidels (Qur'an 9:5),

Muhammad riding at the head of disciples to Badr to meet pagan Meccan army, 1368. Turkish book painting. The Art Archive/Topkapi Museum Istanbul/HarperCollins Publishers.

but also as defensive warfare against those who fight against Muhammad, his followers, and right religion in general (Qur'an 9:13–14). Although Jews and Christians are lumped in the category of polytheists at times—and hence are fair game—other passages in the Qur'an speak favorably of those among the Jews and Christians who shall see paradise (Qur'an 9:29–30). Finally, the Qur'an also informs us that the rewards awaiting those who strive in the path of God include "gardens watered by running streams, in which they shall abide forever" (Qur'an 9:87–88). In addition to these and other Qur'anic passages, Muslim scholars also appealed to a host of statements attributed to Muhammad that extolled the merits of jihad against the enemies of right religion (however defined) and the rewards that awaited those engaged in it.

Because Muhammad found himself at war with the Meccans and others after his *hijra* to Medina, it is easy to see the relevance of these and other statements to his immediate situations. After Muhammad's death, his followers used these texts and others like them to form the basis for an ideology of jihad in the medieval Islamic world. They inspired many of the faithful during the Islamic conquests of the seventh century even as others were undoubtedly inspired merely by booty and glory in battle. Once the frontiers of the new Islamic empire were more or less stabilized, from Spain in the west to the Indus River in the east, the caliphs maintained an expansionist jihad ideology by leading or ordering raids along the Syrian Byzantine frontier. Many caliphs and sultans strengthened their own religious *bona fides* by leading raids themselves. The Abbasid caliph **Harun al-Rashid** (r. 786–809) is one of the most famous to have done so.

As Islamic scholars honed their understanding of right religion, they divided the world into two broad spheres—the Abode of Islam (*dar al-Islam*; literally, the Abode of Surrender or the Abode of Submission) and the Abode of War (*dar al-harb*)—in an effort to clarify the role of jihad and warfare in Islam. The Abode of Islam comprised those territories under Islamic political domination. The Abode of War was everywhere else. Now this division of the world into two spheres did not mean that all Muslims were at all times engaged in a state of open warfare against the Abode of War. Formal truces did exist. Moreover, for purely practical reasons of inertia, military capability, and political calculation, expansion of the borders of Islam waxed and waned over time.

Nevertheless, throughout the Middle Ages Muslim armies did what all armies are supposed to do—they fought. At times they engaged in jihad to expand the borders of the Islamic world in Central Asia, India, Africa, Anatolia, and Europe. At other times Muslim armies went to war against other Muslim armies within the Islamic world to implement a particular vision of proper Islamic religion and government. This was the case in the civil wars that plagued the early Muslim community during the **Rashidun** (632–661) and the **Umayyad** caliphates (661–750). We see this also in the Abbasid Revolution in the late 740s that established the **Abbasid caliphate**, which endured until the Mongols sacked Baghdad in 1258. The Almoravids (1062–1147) and the Almohads (1130–1269) represent two major revivalist movements that employed the ideologies of jihad against what they viewed as corrupt Muslim regimes in North Africa and Spain, and against the Christian monarchs in Spain as well.

Whether the motivation for the jihads fought throughout the medieval Islamic world met medieval Muslim scholars' standards for religious purity in every instance is beyond our ken. We do know, however, that some of those ostensibly engaged in jihad against the external enemies of Islam and internal schismatics and heretics (however defined) were little more than bandits, thugs, and soldiers of fortune—at least they are portrayed as such by many of the Muslim scholars and historians who wrote the extant sources.

In contrast to these modes of thought and action, some Muslims, especially followers of the mystical (Sufi) traditions and other more piety-minded scholars, argued that there were two types of jihad (*see* **Sufism**). For them, the greater jihad was that internal struggle within oneself against temptation and evil. This greater jihad is also known as the jihad of the tongue or the jihad of the pen; that is, the jihad of piety and persuasion. According to this position, military jihad was the lesser jihad, or the jihad of the sword. But it was the military vision of jihad that predominated throughout the medieval Islamic world.

Further Reading

Bonner, Michael. *Jihad in Islamic History*. Princeton, NJ: Princeton University Press, 2006.
Cook, David. *Understanding Jihad*. Berkeley and Los Angeles: University of California Press, 2005.

Kharijis

The Kharijites (also known as Kharijites) get their name from the events of the Battle of Siffin between 'Ali ibn Abi Talib and Mu'awiya ibn Abi Sufyan in 656, from which they withdrew over their interpretation of how the dispute should be resolved. Hence they are known as "seceders" or *Khawarij* (sing. *Khariji*). This group disagreed with the Sunni and the Shi'i positions on the caliphate/imamate (*see* Shiism and Sunnis). They were purists in that their principal criteria for leadership of the community was piety—unlike the Shi'i position, genealogy did not matter to them, and unlike the Sunni position, nor did the practical consideration of maintaining the unity of the community. For the Kharijis, moral purity was far more important than temporal political unity.

Further Reading

Crone, Patricia, and Martin Hinds. *God's Caliph: Religious Authority in the First Centuries of Islam*. New York: Cambridge University Press, 1986.

Madelung, Wilferd. *The Succession to Muhammad: A Study of the Early Caliphate*. New York: Cambridge University Press, 1998.

Law. *See Shari'a*

Mamluk Sultanate

The Mamluk Sultanate dates to 1250 when the Ayyubid sultan of Egypt, Turanshah, was assassinated by some of the Mamluk units loyal to his father, Salih Ayyub, who had died in 1249. Over then next decade competing factions among the various Mamluk regiments violently sorted out their differences. In 1260, the Mamluk Sultanate defeated the Mongols at Ayn Jalut in Palestine, absorbed the remaining Ayyubid holdings in Syria. Sultan Baybars (r. 1260–1277) aggressively pursued a remarkably effective, multifaceted foreign policy to achieve his goals of fending off renewed Mongol incursions and removing the Franks from Syria. He cultivated good relations with the Golden Horde branch of the Mongol empire in Russia, which controlled the reservoir for the regime's new Mamluk recruits and also served as a counter to the Mongol Il-Khans in Iraq and Iran with whom the Golden Horde and the Mamluks were frequently at war.

He concluded a commercial treaty with Genoa, whose merchants held a near monopoly on trade in the Black Sea. The treaty supplied the Mamluk Sultanate with new recruits who could no longer be transported by land through Il-Khan territory, but it had the added benefit of strengthening the Genoese in their competition with the Venetians. In addition, he established a commercial treaty with the Byzantine Empire, which controlled access from the Black Sea to Alexandria via Constantinople. It too had an added benefit for the Mamluk Sultanate in that it served as a counter to the Papacy's efforts to support the Franks in Palestine. In the end, the Mamluks were able to drive the Franks from Acre in 1291, thus ending nearly two centuries of Frankish presence in the Near East. By the end of the twelfth century the Il-Khans had converted to Islam and by the 1320s were no longer a major threat to the Mamluk regime in Syria and Egypt.

Further Reading

Humphreys, R. Stephen. "Ayyubids, Mamluks, and the Latin East in the Thirteenth Century." *Mamluk Studies Review* 2 (1998): 1–17.

Irwin, Robert. *The Middle East in the Middle Ages: The Early Mamluk Sultanate, 1250–1382*. Carbondale: Southern Illinois University Press, 1986.

al-Ma'mun ibn Harun al-Rashid (d. 833)

Al-Ma'mun (r. 813–833), the seventh **Abbasid** caliph, was a son of **Harun al-Rashid** (r. 786–809), al-Ma'mun was engaged in a 4-year civil war with his brother, al-Amin (r. 809–813). After al-Amin's murder, al-Ma'mun acceded to the caliphate. Al-Ma'mun is most famous for his contributions to learning; namely, his patronage of the translation of classical Greek scientific and philosophical texts into Arabic.

Further Reading

Gordon, Matthew. *The Rise of Islam*. Westport, CT: Greenwood, 2005.
Kennedy, Hugh N. *When Baghdad Ruled the Muslim World: The Rise and Fall of Islam's Greatest Dynasty*. Cambridge, MA: Da Capo Press, 2005.
Robinson, Chase F. *al-Ma'mun*. Oxford, UK: Oneworld, 2005.

al-Mansur (d. 775)

al-Mansur (r. 754–775) was the second **Abbasid** caliph. He is responsible for consolidating Abbasid authority in the wake of the success of the Abbasid revolution and the regime of his predecessor, Saffah (r. 749–754). al-Mansur determined that the movement's consolidation phase required the establishment of a new palace city in more stable surroundings. al-Mansur searched along the Tigris River for the ideal location, and in 762 he settled on the site of the ancient Persian village of Baghdad. Part of his effort to consolidate Abbasid authority, al-Mansur pursued a policy of integrating Muslims of Persians and other ethnic backgrounds into his regime. He was also responsible for initiating the famous translation movement of classical Greek learning: mathematics, science, medicine, philosophy, and so forth.

Further Reading

Gordon, Matthew. *The Rise of Islam*. Westport, CT: Greenwood, 2005.
Kennedy, Hugh N. *When Baghdad Ruled the Muslim World: The Rise and Fall of Islam's Greatest Dynasty*. Cambridge, MA: Da Capo Press, 2005.

Modesty. *See* **Clothing and Modesty**

Money and Coinage

Medieval Islamic rulers minted three types of coins. For the most part a gold coin was called a *dinar*, a silver coin was called a *dirham*, and a base metal coin (usually copper) was generally called a *fals*. There were other regional (even slang) names for the coins, but *dinar*, *dirham*, and *fals* were the customary terms used throughout the medieval Islamic world. Despite the common vocabulary, it would be a gross exaggeration to assert that a *dirham* minted under **Abd al-Malik** in the late seventh century had much in common with *dihrams* minted in eleventh-century Cairo, twelfth-century Damascus, or thirteenth-century Nishapur. Basically, the only thing they had in common was that they were (generally) all made from the same type of metal. However, unless one actually has the opportunity to examine a specific *dinar* (or *dirham* or *fals*), there is no way to know the quality of the metal used, the weight of the individual coin, or its value relative to other coins in circulation at the time. Because at any given time one could find merchants from Damascus, Baghdad,

Cairo, Cordoba, Isfahan, Tashkent, Bukhara, Delhi, Constantinople, and a host of other Afro-Eurasian cities in the markets of the medieval Islamic world, one of the most important men in any market was the *sayrafi*, usually translated as money-changer. But his job entailed far more than simply making change; it was also to determine the precise value of a coin, especially foreign coins that traveling merchants needed to exchange for Islamic issues.

The standard way for a *sayrafi* to determine the value of a coin was to measure its bullion content by weighing the coin itself. Because weighing individual coins was a rather tedious and time-consuming affair, it was standard practice for coins to be bought and sold in purses that were sealed by a government assaying office or a local merchant with the exact weight indicated on the outside. It should be noted that though the seal on a purse might indicate that its value was 76 dinars, it did not necessarily follow that the purse held 76 gold coins. It could very well contain 80 dinars, some of which were worn, gouged, cut, nicked, and so forth, reducing the purse's total weight (and hence its value) by four dinars.

Further Reading
Bates, Michael. *Islamic Coins.* New York: American Numismatic Society, 1982.
Schultz, Warren C. "The Monetary History of Egypt, 642–1517," in *The Cambridge History of Egypt*, vol. 1. Edited by Carl F. Petry. New York: Cambridge University Press, 1998, pp. 318–338.

Mu'awiya ibn Abi Sufyan (d. 680)

Mu'awiya ibn Abi Sufyan (r. 661–680) was the son of Abu Sufyan, the leader of the Abd Shams clan, most of which had rejected Muhammad's prophetic mission. It was only after Muhammad's conquest of Mecca in 630 that Mu'awiya, Abu Sufyan, and other members of the clan submitted to Muhammad. Mu'awiya then served as one of Muhammad's scribes. Shortly after the conquest of Syria, **Umar ibn al-Khattab** appointed Mu'awiya governor of Syria, a position he held until he consolidated his control over the lands of Islam in the wake of the assassination of the fourth **Rashidun** caliph, '**Ali ibn Abi Talib** (656–661).

Mu'awiya moved the capital of the Islamic empire to Damascus, continued raiding along the Byzantine frontier, and renewed the expansion to North Africa in the west and Iran to the east. The importance of Mu'awiya's role in holding the new Islamic empire together cannot be overstated. Near the end of his reign Mu'awiya arranged for the succession of his son, Yazid, which marked the establishment of the first hereditary dynasty in Islamic history.

Further Reading
Gordon, Matthew. *The Rise of Islam.* Westport, CT: Greenwood, 2005.
Humphreys, R. Stephen. *Mu'awiya ibn Abi Sufyan: From Arabia to Empire.* Oxford, UK: Oneworld, 2006.

al-Muqaddasi (c. 945–c. 1000)

The details of al-Muqaddasi's life are fairly sketchy. Most of what we know about him is derived from his pioneering work in the fields of physical, economic, political, and human geography: *The Best Divisions for Knowledge of the*

Regions: Ahsan al-taqasim fi ma'rifat al-aqalim. We do know that he undertook the pilgrimage in 966 and spent the next 20 years traveling. As he criss-crossed the Islamic world from Morocco to the frontiers of Sind, he made the pilgrimage two more times—in 977 and 987. He is careful to record material praising the merits (*fada'il*) of each province and is fond of detailed descriptions of their topography and climate as well as the agricultural produce, manufactured goods, and items imported to and exported from their markets. As a native of Jerusalem (*Bayt al-Muqaddas* or *Bayt al-Maqdis;* hence the *nisba* al-Muqaddasi), his descriptions of his hometown and province and the province of Syria are especially detailed. *See also* Documents 6 and 7.

Further Reading

Collins, Basil, trans. *The Best Divisions for Knowledge of the Regions: Ahsan al-taqasim fi ma'rifat al-aqalim.* Reading, UK: Garnet Publishing, 2001.

Naser-e Khosraw (fl. eleventh century)

The particulars of Naser-e Khosraw's life are fairly scanty. We do know that in the fall of 1045 he had a dream that convinced him that he was on the wrong path. He left his career as a civil administrator in Khurasan and undertook a personal quest for truth, which involved making the pilgrimage to Mecca. His conversion to Ismaili Shiism probably coincided with his desire to undertake the pilgrimage for although he eventually made it to Mecca, he took a circuitous route to the Hijaz. He avoided most of the major cities of his day (including Damascus) but visited many Ismaili outposts along his journey through Iran, Syria, Egypt and back home. Of particular concern for our purposes are his sojourns in Cairo, the capital of the Ismaili **Fatimid** caliphate, and Jerusalem, which was nominally under Fatimid control at the time of his visit. In addition, Naser-e Khosraw's civil administrator's eye for detail resulted in an account full of meticulous descriptions of the markets, civil infrastructure, and public ceremonies he observed during his seven-year trip. *See also* Document 8.

Further Reading

Thackston, Wheeler M., trans. *Naser-e Khosraw's Book of Travels (Safarnama).* Albany: State University of New York Press, 1986.

Nizam al-Mulk (d. 1092)

Nizam al-Mulk served as the chief minister for two of the greatest Seljukid Sultans, Alp Arslan (r. 1063–1073) and his son, Malikshah (r. 1073–1092). Nizam al-Mulk is probably most famous for his *Book of Government or Rules for Kings,* a lengthy treatise that is essentially a handbook for how to rule justly and to maintain order in the realm, which is a recasting of the ancient Persian theory of kingship with an Islamic veneer. Hence scholars, refer to it as Perso-Islamic kingship. Nizam al-Mulk was murdered in 1092 by the Ismaili Assassins, who were the bane of the Seljukids and many other regimes in the Middle Ages. *See also* Document 9.

Further Reading

Darke, Hubert, trans. *The Book of Government or Rules for Kings: The Siyar al-Mulk or Siyasat-nama of Nizam al-Mulk.* Richmond, UK: Curzon Press, 2002.

Rashidun Caliphs

According to the Sunni tradition, the first four caliphs or successors of Muhammad—**Abu Bakr, Umar ibn al-Khattab, Uthman ibn Affan**, and **'Ali ibn Abi Talib**—were the rightly guided (*rashidun*) caliphs. All four men belonged to the Meccan tribe of Quraysh, were early converts, and were close companions of Muhammad. The **Sunnis** consider the period of their rule (632–661) to be a golden age, when the caliphs were consciously guided by Muhammad's practices.

Further Reading

Crone, Patricia, and Martin Hinds. *God's Caliph: Religious Authority in the First Centuries of Islam*. New York: Cambridge University Press, 1986.

Gordon, Matthew. *The Rise of Islam*. Westport, CT: Greenwood, 2005.

Madelung, Wilferd. *The Succession to Muhammad: A Study of the Early Caliphate*. New York: Cambridge University Press, 1998.

Saladin (d. 1193)

In 1169, Saladin participated in the conquest of Egypt on behalf of his patron, Nur ad-Din Zengid, ruler of Syria. Two years later, Saladin was finally

able to bring an end to the **Fatimid** caliphate in Cairo. Not surprisingly, as Saladin consolidated his control over Egypt, his relations with his patron, Nur al-Din, worsened. The inevitable clash between the two men was avoided when Nur al-Din died of a heart attack while playing polo in 1174. Saladin then spent the next decade consolidating his control over Nur al-Din's former lands in Syria.

Under Saladin's leadership, Egypt and Syria were ruled as a family confederation, with members of his extended family administering various provinces throughout the realm. Saladin is most famous for having dealt the Franks a decisive defeat at the Battle of Hattin in 1187 and retaking Jerusalem shortly thereafter. Named after Saladin's father, Ayyub (Job), the Ayyubid family confederation (1174–1260) ruled Syria and Egypt from Saladin's death in 1193 until the Egyptian branch of the family was overthrown in 1250 by some of its Mamluks. Ten years later, the **Mamluk Sultanate** defeated the Mongols at Ayn Jalut in Palestine, absorbed the Ayyubid holdings in Syria.

Saladin (or Salah) al-Din al-Ayyubi (1137–93). Sultan of Egypt and Syria, leader of Muslim armies against the Crusaders. Courtesy of Dover Pictorial Archives.

Further Reading

Lyons Malcolm C., and D.E.P. Jackson. *Saladin: The Politics of the Holy War*. New York: Cambridge University Press, 1997.

Nicole, David. *Saladin and the Saracens: Armies of the Middle East, 1100–1300*. London: Osprey Publishing, 1986.

Shari'a —Islamic Law

Compared to the Torah (especially Exodus, Leviticus, Numbers, and Deuteronomy), the Qur'an contains very little legal material. Qur'anic commandments, prohibitions, and punishments are quite specific; however, they do not even come close to covering the many possibilities Muslims might encounter in seventh-century Arabia, let alone the cosmopolitan centers of the Muslim empires in the centuries to come. If the early Muslim community was to determine God's will in every aspect of life after the divine revelations ceased with Muhammad's death, it needed to find authoritative guidance outside the text of the Qur'an itself. Initially, this was found in the practice or tradition (*sunna*) of the early community. Because the early community (especially the early community in Medina) was seen to be the best community by virtue of its first-hand encounter with the messenger of God, its example could be used to answer questions that were not specifically addressed in the Qur'an.

Although assertion of Muhammad's infallibility is nowhere to be found in the Qur'an, by the late eighth century a doctrine had developed that Muhammad and all the prophets had been protected by God from gross moral error (*masum*). One of the most important early legal scholars, Muhammad ibn Idris al-Shafii (d. 820), argued that because of Muhammad's moral perfection, his sunna was the only reliable guide to right conduct apart from the Qur'an. According to al-Shafii, because Muhammad's teachings and example were necessarily preserved from error, all Muslims could confidently rely upon his sunna for guidance. Of course, this assertion only begs the question — what was Muhammad's sunna? According to al-Shafii, Muhammad's sunna could be found in those *hadith*s (reports about what Muhammad said or did) that were determined to be authentic.

Not surprisingly, as the sunna of the early community and Muhammad came to be seen as authoritative, many *hadith*s were put into circulation that purported to be the words of Muhammad but were in fact made up of whole cloth for political and sectarian purposes. In response to these fabrications, scholars devised a methodology for determining which *hadith*s were authentic and which were fabrications. Scholars began to argue that only those *hadith*s that were transmitted by an unbroken chain (*isnad*) of reliable transmitters reaching back to Muhammad himself could be deemed authentic.

Scholars were well aware that it was just as easy to fabricate an *isnad* as it was to fabricate a *hadith*. Nevertheless, by the end of the ninth century there had emerged a general consensus about which *hadith*s were authentic. By the same time, the followers of a given teacher began to refer to themselves as a *madhhab*, another Arabic word conveying the idea of pathway. *Madhhab* is generally translated as "school of law," in the sense of a "school of legal thought." By the eleventh century, there remained only four Sunni *madhhab*s to speak of (Hanafi, Hanbali, Maliki, Shafii). Each was named after the scholar whose teaching the *madhhab* ostensibly followed, though none had actually founded a formal school in his lifetime.

The science of working out the *shari'a* can be divided into two basic categories: legal theory (*usul al-fiqh*, the roots of jurisprudence) and the practical application of the theory (*furu al-fiqh*, branches of jurisprudence). Because knowledge of the Qur'an and the sunna of Muhammad were essential to the sciences of jurisprudence, and because proper jurisprudence was essential to determining what it meant to "obey God and His messenger," the entire religious educational system of the period was based on memorizing the Qur'an as well as thousands of these *hadith*s along with their *isnad*s.

Scholars employed (at least in theory) a five-step process to determine whether a given practice was acceptable.

1. If the Qur'an specifically commanded or prohibited something, there really was nothing to discuss; God had spoken.
2. If the Qur'an addressed an issue, but without specific guidance, scholars turned to the sunna of Muhammad for clarification of the Qur'anic commandment. For example, Muslims are admonished repeatedly in the Qur'an to pray; however, it is only because of the sunna of Muhammad that Muslims know that they are required to pray five times per day, to perform specific ablutions and in which order, and to perform certain prostrations and in which order.
3. Since Muhammad is understood to have been preserved from gross moral error, if an authentic *hadith* spoke specifically to an issue not addressed in the Qur'an, Muslims could be assured that if they followed the admonition of that *hadith*, they would be acting in obedience to God.
4. When neither the Qur'an nor the sunna addressed an issue, scholars argued that they had to employ their reason to extrapolate the proper response based on the principles set forth in the Qur'an and the sunna as a whole. Since most aspects of life are in this category, and since this category is most open to interpretation, it is to this category that the scholars devoted most of their energies and their arguments. In fact, they developed a range of classifications of reasoning which could be employed in this enterprise. Not surprisingly, scholars did not always agree on which methods of reasoning (if any) were legitimate.
5. Sunni scholars used the principle of consensus (*ijma*) to determine whether a doctrine or decision was legitimate in these instances. This principle of consensus is rooted in a *hadith* in which Muhammad is purported to have said that his community would never agree upon an error. In practical terms, Sunni scholars identified the community as themselves, since whenever there was no Sunni scholar of good repute holding a contrary position on a particular issue, the problem was generally considered settled.

Modern Western scholars tend to be skeptical about the authenticity of even the *hadith*s in the authoritative collections. Often, they are skeptical about when or even if the methodology described above was actually employed or whether it was simply used after the fact to legitimate practices and decisions that were really rooted in Arabian tribal custom or in the local practice of Medina, Kufa, Basra, Damascus, Baghdad, or elsewhere. In any case, it is clear that the formal positions of the *shari'a* reflect the life of the towns and cities in the medieval

Islamic world, for it is in the urban centers that the scholars were studying the religious sciences and articulating the details of the *shari'a* in response to the questions that arose in the urban environments in which they lived.

Moreover, it was in the urban centers that there were actual judges (*qadis*) and the mechanisms to enforce judges' decisions. In the countryside and among the pastoral nomadic groups, the at times arcane details of the *shari'a* tended to take a back seat to local custom. In these circumstances, a person was helpless to contest a violation of *shari'a* because there was no judge to hear his or her case nor was there anyone to enforce it. If there was an Islamic "scholar" there, he most likely was an ill-educated preacher who was not well versed in the intricate details of Islamic jurisprudence.

Whether or not the methodology of jurisprudence described here was actually employed consistently or even at all is difficult to ascertain. However, the fact that it (or some other methodology ostensibly based on the authoritative scriptures of Islam) was supposed to be employed illustrates the importance that Muslims attached to following the dictates of the Qur'an and the teachings of Muhammad in their daily lives. In short, the *shari'a* in all its manifestations gives us insight into daily life and practice in the medieval Islamic world because it was understood to comprise the entire body of duties and obligations incumbent on all believers covering every imaginable aspect of daily life. It is that straight path by which medieval Muslims believed they could (and modern Muslims believe they can) obey God and His messenger.

Further Reading

Hallaq, Wael. *Authority, Continuity, and Change in Islamic Law*. New York: Cambridge University Press, 2001.

Melchert, Christopher. *The Formation of the Sunni Schools of Law, 9th-10th Centuries* C.E. Leiden, The Netherlands: Brill, 1997.

Schacht, Joseph. *An Introduction to Islamic Law*. New York: Oxford University Press, 1964.

Shiism

There are two basic doctrines that developed among the Shi'is. First, the rightful caliph or imam had to be a lineal descendant of Muhammad, in particular through the line of '**Ali ibn Abi Talib** and Muhammad's daughter, Fatima. The second, and more controversial, is that the caliph or imam was not only the political head of the community, but an infallible religious teacher—guaranteed to be without error in matters of faith and morals. Because of this emphasis on the religious and theological role of the head of the community, Shi'i texts tend to use the title imam for this office more frequently than caliph (*Khalifa*) or commander of the believers (*Amir al-Mu'minin*). The Twelver and the Sevener Shi'is agree on these two doctrines; where they disagree is over the identity of the seventh imam.

The Shi'i doctrine of the imamate is based on the events of 18 Dhu l-Hijja A.H. 10 (March 16, 632 A.D./C.E.). According to the biographical literature, Muhammad stopped at a place called Ghadir Khumm (Pool of Khumm) on his way back to Medina after he had made his final pilgrimage to Mecca. His followers gathered in a grove of trees to escape the suffocating heat and to perform the noon prayers. At the conclusion of the prayers, Muhammad raised Ali's hand in front of the assembly and asked them if they recognized that he, Muhammad,

Shiite martyrs fallen in battle being decapitated by the enemy in the presence of their wives. Scene from the schism within Islam (7th c.). Safavid fresco, 17th century. SEF/ Art Resource.

had a claim on each of the believers that supersedes any claim they might have on themselves. They, of course, responded in the affirmative. He then took Ali's hand again and said, "Of Whomsoever I am Lord [*Mawla*], then Ali is also his Lord. O God! Be Thou the supporter of whoever supports Ali and the enemy of whoever opposes him." **Umar ibn al-Khattab** then said to Ali, "Congratulations, O son of Abu Talib! Now morning and evening [i.e., forever] you are the master of every believing man and woman" (Momen, 15).

Because the version cited above comes from Ibn Hanbal's (d. 855) *Musnad*, a Sunni hadith collection, it is clear that the Sunni tradition does not deny that the events of Ghadir Khumm actually occurred. Where they differ, and differ significantly, is on the interpretation of the event itself. According to Shi'i doctrine, the above story proves beyond a shadow of a doubt that not only had Muhammad designated 'Ali ibn Abi Talib and his descendants to succeed him upon his death (which occurred only 3 months later on 13 Rabi' al-Awal A.H. 11/8 June 632 A.D./C.E.), but also that he had bestowed his own political and religious authority on them as well. Although **Sunnis** afford Ali a tremendous amount of respect and prestige as an early convert, as Muhammad's cousin and son-in-law, and as the fourth of the **Rashidun** or rightly guided caliphs, they simply reject the Shi'i interpretation of the events of Ghadir Khumm altogether.

As things turned out, Muhammad's close companion and father-in-law, **Abu Bakr** (r. 632–634), became the first caliph. He was followed by two more companions, Umar ibn al-Khattab (r. 634–644) and **Uthman ibn Affan** (r. 644–656). After Uthman's assassination, 'Ali ibn Abi Talib (r. 656–661) became caliph/imam. However, the entirety of his caliphate/imamate was disrupted by the first civil war in Islamic history (656–661), ultimately ending in his assassination at the hands of a **Khariji** dissident. Based on the Shi'i interpretation of the events of Ghadir Khumm, Ali was the first legitimate caliph or imam; the first three caliphs—Abu Bakr, Umar, and Uthman—were usurpers.

According to Shi'i tradition, the imamate then passed to Ali's eldest son, **Hasan ibn 'Ali ibn Abi Talib** (d. 669). However, Hasan abdicated his claim to the caliphate in 661 and did not oppose **Mu'awiya ibn Abi Sufyan** (r. 661–680), who established the **Umayyad caliphate** (661–750) with Damascus as its capital. Despite Hasan's abdication, there remained a faction (*shi'a*) of Muslims who continued to argue that only someone from Muhammad's house (in particular a descendant of Ali) could legitimately lead the Muslim community. Shortly after Yazid acceded to the caliphate (r. 680–683), Ali's younger son, **Husayn ibn 'Ali ibn Abi Talib** (the third imam), was persuaded to leave his home in the Hijaz and to travel to Kufa to lead a revolt and to take his rightful place at the head of the Muslim community. On 10 Muharram 61 (October 10, 680), Umayyad forces routed Husayn and seventy-two armed men (together with their women and children) at Karbala. The victors beheaded Husayn and his companions and put their heads on pikes as they marched to Kufa. The **women** and **children** were taken prisoner, including Husayn's sole surviving son, Ali, who had been too ill to participate in the battle.

As was customary, Husayn's head was sent to the caliph Yazid in Damascus as proof that Husayn was indeed dead. Some reports indicate that Yazid was saddened by the death of Muhammad's grandson. Others suggest that he treated Husayn's head with contempt as he poked at Husayn's mouth with his cane, for which he was immediately taken to task by Abu Barzah al-Aslami, a companion of Muhammad.

> Are you poking the mouth of al-Husayn with your cane? Take your cane away from his mouth. How often have I seen the Apostle of God kiss it! As for you, Yazid, you will come forward on the Day of Resurrection, and Ibn Ziyad will be your advocate. But this man will come forward on the Day of Resurrection, and Muhammad will be his advocate. (al-Tabari, 174)

Husayn's head was returned to his dependants who buried it. But where? His head has a place of honor in the Umayyad Mosque in Damascus. Another tradition says that it was buried in Ashkelon where the Fatimids built a shrine in 1098. During the Crusader period it was disinterred and moved to Cairo (1153) where it is venerated to this day at the Husayn Mosque. There are other traditions that state that Husayn's head was interred in Medina, Kufa, Najaf, Karbala, Raqqa on the upper Euphrates, and even in distant Merv in Afghanistan.

With Husayn's martyrdom, the imamate passed to his son, Ali, and then continued to be passed on from father to son as each imam designated his successor. The most important imam after 'Ali ibn Abi Talib is Ja'far al-Sadiq (d. 765), the sixth imam. He was renowned for his piety and learning, and many of those who studied at his feet went on to be learned scholars and jurists. Ja'far designated his son, Isma'il (d. 754), to succeed him as the seventh imam upon his death. However, because Isma'il died before his father did, the question of who should succeed Ja'far was contested. One faction contended that the imamate had passed to Isma'il's son, Muhammad. This faction came to be called Seveners or Ismailis.

The other faction argued that the imamate should continue through Isma'il's brother, Musa (d. 799), whom they consider to be the seventh imam. The members of this faction (known as Twelvers or Imamis) believe that when the eleventh imam, Hasan al-Askari died in 873 or 874, he was succeeded by his son, Muhammad, as the twelfth imam. Moreover, the Twelvers believe that Muhammad did not die; rather, he went into occultation; that is, he was and still is present in some hidden form, and that at the appointed time (which of course we cannot know) he will return as the Mahdi (or Messiah). *See* "Twelver Shi'i Imams" in Appendix under Medieval Islamic Caliphs.

Further Reading

Bill, James A., and John Alden Williams. *Roman Catholics and Shi'i Muslims: Prayer, Passion and Politics*. Chapel Hill: University of North Carolina Press, 2002.

Daftary, Farhad. *The Ismailis: Their History and Doctrines*. New York: Cambridge University Press, 1990.

Halm, Heinz. *Shiism*. Edinburgh, Scotland: Edinburgh University Press, 1991.

Momen, Moojan. *An Introduction to Shi'i Islam*. New Haven, CT: Yale University Press, 1985.

al-Tabari. *The History of al-Tabari*. Vol. 19. *The Caliphate of Yazid b. Mu'awiyya*. Translated by I.K.A. Howard. Albany: State University of New York Press, 1990.

Sufism—Islamic Mysticism

Islamic mystics were called Sufis because of their habit of wearing wool (*suf*). The Arabic term for mysticism (*tasawwuf*) is derived from *suf* as well. The development of Sufism, like the development of shari'a, is rooted in the search for the proper understanding of right religion. At the risk of oversimplification, the *shari'a*-minded vision of the religious scholars and jurists described above defined Islam as a "religion of law" based on the meticulous study of the Qur'an and hadith. The Sufi-minded vision of the mystics and ascetics defined Islam as a "religion of the heart" based on the individual's direct encounter with and knowledge of God. In other words, the shari'a-minded and the Sufi-minded sought to answer the question of how knowledge is defined—knowledge about God based on what he has revealed of himself through his prophets and messengers; and knowledge of God based on one's direct mystical experience.

In his *The Sufi Orders in Islam*, J. Spencer Trimingham divided the development of Sufism into three broad periods. During the first period, what Trimingham calls the "golden age of mysticism" or *khanaqah* (lodge) period, Sufism was an intellectually and emotionally aristocratic movement. It was characterized by an ad hoc master–disciple (*murshid–murid*) relationship in which masters guided their disciples on a personal quest to experience God directly. Early Sufis often lived itinerant lives, but by the tenth century we begin to see the establishment of informal lodges (*khanaqah*s) and convents (*zawiya*s) where masters and disciples pursued mystical union (*wahda*) with God.

During the second period (c. 1100–1400) Sufi rituals and practices came to be characterized by more formal and clearly defined devotional "paths" or "ways" (*tariqas*). Consequently, the emphasis was less on the individual's surrender to God and more on his surrender to a specific rule. It was at the beginning of this "*tariqa* period" that al-Ghazali (d. 1111) composed his magnum opus, *The Revivification of the Religious Sciences*. The third period (c. 1400–1800) is beyond the chronological scope of this book. But it is worth noting that during the fifteenth century Sufism became an even more organized mass popular movement. Whatever the period or method, the goal of the Sufi remained the same — to know the ecstasy of the direct experience and knowledge of God.

There are separate Arabic words to define the types of knowledge that concern us here. The cognitive or "head" knowledge of the shari'a-minded religious scholars is known as '*ilm*. The affective or "heart" knowledge of the Sufi-minded mystics is known as *ma'rifa*, or gnosis. Hence, one who knows about God based on the study of revelation and religious texts (Qur'an, hadith, *fiqh*, etc.) is known as an '*alim* (pl. '*ulama*'). One who has direct experience or knowledge of God is known as an '*arif*. Of course, it would be incorrect to imagine that the shari'a-minded and Sufi-minded visions of Islam were mutually exclusive. Rather, they should be seen as emphases, even tendencies, along a broad spectrum of religious experience and practice in the medieval Islamic world.

Nevertheless, it should come as no surprise that extremes of the spectrum did exist. Some religious scholars condemned the more ecstatic mystical strains of Islam as departures from the true faith as defined by the commandments and prohibitions of shari'a. Some Sufis gave them reason to be suspicious by arguing that shari'a constrained, even inhibited, their superior existential knowledge of God. The most famous of these is the Sufi icon, al-Hallaj (857–922). Originally from Tus in Iran, al-Hallaj moved to Basra in his early twenties. It was in Basra and Baghdad that he made his mark as a popular ascetic and preacher.

Al-Hallaj's declarations of his burning love of and his claims of mystical union with God ignited popular passions as well as scholarly ire. He is most famous for a brief statement he made one day in Baghdad to the great Sufi master, al-Junayd (d. 910).

> It is related that Hallaj met Junayd one day, and said to him, "I am the Truth [*ana al-haqq*]." "No," Junayd answered him, "it is by means of the Truth that you are! What gibbet will you stain with your blood!" (Massignon, *The Passion of al*-Hallaj, 1:127)

By claiming one of God's titles (*al-haqq*; "The Truth" or "The Ultimate Reality") as his own, al-Hallaj was claiming to be God; that is, that he had no other "I" than God. Many of his opponents viewed his claims as blasphemous. At best, they viewed him as a vile charlatan.

Dancing dervishes. Painting from poetic anthology by Hafiz, 1320–1389, Iranian Sufi poet, 16th century manuscript. The Art Archive/National Museum Damascus Syria/Gianni Dagli Orti.

In 913, al-Hallaj was arrested. He remained in a Baghdad prison for 9 years where he preached to his fellow prisoners and is said to have healed the sick as well as performed other wonders. In the end, al-Hallaj's supporters within the Abbasid house were unable to protect him. In March 922, he was executed on charges of blasphemy. His modern biographer, Louis Massignon, described his execution before a great crowd near the Khurasan Gate in Baghdad.

> Al-Halladj, with a crown on his head was beaten, half-killed, and exposed, still alive, on a gibbet (*salib*). While rioters set fire to the shops, friends and enemies questioned him as he hung on the gibbet and traditions related some of his replies. The caliph's warrant for his decapitation did not arrive until nightfall, and in fact his final execution was postponed until the next day. During the night there spread accounts of wonders and supernatural happenings. In the morning . . . those who had signed his condemnation . . . cried out: "It is for Islam; let his blood be on our heads." Al-Halladj's head fell, his body was sprinkled with oil and burned and the ashes thrown into the Tigris from the top of a minaret (27 March 922). Witnesses reported that the last words of the tortured man were: "All that matters for the ecstatic is that the Unique should reduce him to Unity." (Massignon, "al-Halladj")

Al-Hallaj's execution may have curtailed some of the excesses of the Sufis, but his life and teachings continued to inspire Sufis for generations. Based on the teachings of al-Hallaj, al-Junayd, and many other early Sufis, Kalabadhi (d. 995) argued in the late-tenth century that Sufism conforms to the strictest standards of orthodoxy and is in no way heretical. According to Kalabadhi's translator, A. J. Arberry, Kalabadhi's *The Doctrine of the Sufis* blazed "a path which was subsequently to be followed by the Sufi who was the greatest theologian of all: Ghazali (d. 1111), whose [*The Revivification of the Religious Sciences*] finally reconciled scholastic and mystic" (Arberry, xiv). Hence, it would be a mistake to argue that Sufis were necessarily anti-intellectual or antinomian as some of their critics charged; rather, the Sufi attitude toward the intellect was that it "is an instrument of servanthood, not a means of approaching lordship" (Arberry, 51). That is, though the intellect is sufficient for determining what human beings, as God's servants, must perform in submission (*islam*) to God (for example, *shari'a*), it is insufficient as a guide to existential or mystical knowledge (*ma'rifa*) of God.

In his chapter titled "Their Doctrine of the Gnosis of God," Kalabadhi argued that "no man knows God, save he who possesses an intellect, for the intellect is the instrument by means of which man knows whatever he may know; nevertheless, he cannot know God of himself" (Arberry, 54–55). In the same chapter, Kalabadhi illustrates the inadequacies of the intellect with a poem by al-Hallaj:

> Whoso seeks God, and takes the intellect for guide,
> God drives him forth, in vain distraction to abide;
> With wild confusion He confounds his inmost heart,
> So that distraught, he cries, "I know not if Thou art." (Arberry, 52)

He appeals to al-Hallaj again as he argues that human beings can only know God if God chooses to reveal himself to them:

> God made us to know Himself through Himself, and guided us to the knowledge of Himself through Himself, so that the attestation of gnosis arose out of gnosis through gnosis, after he who possessed gnosis had been taught gnosis by Him Who is the object of gnosis. (Arberry, 54)

Of course, unless one is mystically inclined, statements such as this are impenetrably obtuse, even nonsensical. Moreover, as evidenced by al-Hallaj's fate, they were far too fuzzy and malleable for the tastes of many of the shari'a-minded religious scholars.

Further Reading

Arberry, A.J., trans. *The Doctrine of the Sufis*. New York: Cambridge University Press, 1935.

Karamustafa, Ahmet. *Sufism: The Formative Period*. Berkeley and Los Angeles: University of California Press, 2007.

Massignon, Louis. "al-Halladj," in *Encyclopaedia of Islam, New Edition*. P.J. Bearman et al., eds. Boston: Brill Academic Publishers, 2005.

Massignon, Louis. *The Passion of al-Hallaj: Mystic and Martyr of Islam*. 4 vols. Princeton, NJ: Princeton University Press, 1982.

Trimmingham, J. Spencer. *The Sufi Orders in Islam*. New York: Oxford University Press, 1998.

Watt, W.M., trans. *The Faith and Practice of al-Ghazali*. London: George Allen and Unwin, 1953.

Sunnis

The Sunnis represent the majority of Muslims in the premodern and modern worlds. The name *Sunni* is derived from the formal title of this group—*ahl al-sunna wa l-jama'a* (people of tradition and community consensus). Obviously, every faction in early Islamic history believed that it was the true representatives of the "people of tradition and community consensus." The theological and political faction called Sunni emerged in the context of the early centuries of Islamic history.

As the community sorted out what it viewed were the criteria for leadership of the community, the Sunni position became based on pragmatic considerations of leadership and accommodation to the realities of who actually held the office rather than the Shi'i position that argued for lineal descent from the line of '**Ali ibn Abi Talib** (*see* **Shiism**). At the risk of oversimplification, one of the highest values of the Sunni community was the maintenance of the broad unity of the *umma*. As such, the general position that developed among Sunni theorists was that the caliph needed only to be good enough politically to do the job and maintain the unity of the entire community. Hence, the Sunnis are often referred to as "caliphal loyalists."

Further Reading

Crone, Patricia, and Martin Hinds. *God's Caliph: Religious Authority in the First Centuries of Islam*. New York: Cambridge University Press, 1986.

Madelung, Wilferd. *The Succession to Muhammad: A Study of the Early Caliphate*. New York: Cambridge University Press, 1998.

Umar ibn al-Khattab (d. 644)

Umar ibn al-Khattab was a close confidant of Muhammad and the second of the **Rashidun caliphs** (r. 634–644) according to the **Sunni** tradition. According to the Shi'i tradition, '**Ali ibn Abi Talib** (r. 656–661) was Muhammad's rightful successor (*see* **Shiism**). The first wave of major expansion of the Islamic empire—Syria, Iraq, Iran, Egypt—occurred during his caliphate. Umar was stabbed by a disgruntled slave and on his death bed appointed a committee (*shura*) to select his successor. The committee selected **Uthman ibn Affan** (r. 644–656). *See also* Document 2.

Further Reading

Crone, Patricia, and Martin Hinds. *God's Caliph: Religious Authority in the First Centuries of Islam.* New York: Cambridge University Press, 1986.

Gordon, Matthew. *The Rise of Islam.* Westport, CT: Greenwood, 2005.

Kennedy, Hugh. *The Great Arab Conquests: How the Spread of Islam Changed the World We Live In.* Philadelphia: Da Capo, 2007.

Madelung, Wilferd. *The Succession to Muhammad: A Study of the Early Caliphate.* New York: Cambridge University Press, 1998.

Umayyad Caliphate (661–750)

The first Ummayad caliph was the third **Rashidun caliph, Uthman ibn Affan** (644–656), who was assassinated by Egyptian rebels. Uthman was succeeded by Muhammad's paternal cousin and son-in-law, **'Ali ibn Abi Talib** (656-661), who was also assassinated, this time by a **Khariji** dissident. In the wake of Ali's assassination the governor of Syria, **Mu'awiya ibn Abi Sufyan**

(a kinsman of Uthman), consolidated his control over the lands of Islam. His son Yazid's succession marks the establishment of the first hereditary dynasty: the Umayyad caliphate that ruled from Damascus. With the conclusion of the first civil war (656–661) and Mu'awiya's consolidation of his position in Syria, Islamic expansion was renewed—in Iran, Central Asia, and Sind to the east as well as in North Africa and Spain in the west.

Further Reading

Hawting, G.R. *The First Dynasty of Islam: The Umayyad Caliphate A.D. 661–750.* Carbondale: Southern Illinois University Press, 1987.

Kennedy, Hugh. *The Prophet and the Age of the Caliphates: the Islamic Near East from the Sixth to the Eleventh Century.* New York: Longman, 2004.

Courtyard of Umayyad Mosque (also known as the Great Mosque of Damascus). Built 705–715 by Umayyad Caliph al-Walid I, Damascus, Syria. Holger Mette/Shutterstock.

Uthman ibn Affan (d. 656)

Uthman ibn Affan was close confidant of Muhammad and the third of the **Rashidun caliphs** (r. 644–656) according to the **Sunni** tradition. According to the Shi'i tradition, **'Ali ibn Abi Talib** (r. 656–661) was Muhammad's rightful successor (*see* **Shiism**).

Uthman belonged to the powerful **Umayyad** clan, which had long played the leading role in Mecca and which was among Muhammad's strongest opponents. Uthman was one of the few members of this clan to embrace Muhammad's mission, one of the first converts, and after his conversion married two of Muhammad's daughters—Rukayya and Umm Kulthum. The committee that Umar appointed on his deathbed selected Uthman as his successor. The Islamic tradition records that under Uthman's leadership, the text of the Qur'an was standardized. The tradition divides Uthman's caliphate into 6 years of good rule followed by 6 years of bad rule. Many of the principal complaints were based on his appointment of fellow Umayyad clan members to high positions in his administration. In the end, a group of rebels from Egypt assassinated Uthman. 'Ali ibn Abi Talib's (r. 656–661) succession to the caliphate was fraught with discord—*fitna*—also known as the first civil war.

Further Reading

Crone, Patricia, and Martin Hinds. *God's Caliph: Religious Authority in the First Centuries of Islam.* New York: Cambridge University Press, 1986.

Gordon, Matthew. *The Rise of Islam.* Westport, CT: Greenwood, 2005.

Kennedy, Hugh. *The Great Arab Conquests: How the Spread of Islam Changed the World We Live In.* Philadelphia: Da Capo, 2007.

Madelung, Wilferd. *The Succession to Muhammad: A Study of the Early Caliphate.* New York: Cambridge University Press, 1998.

Warfare

The year after his arrival in Medina, Muhammad engaged in a number of small-scale raids (*razzia*) against Meccan caravans, most of which were unsuccessful. The purpose of these raids appears to have been to obtain booty for the emigrants to Medina, but also to annoy, even provoke a fight with, his enemies in Mecca for their rejection of him and his message. The Islamic historiographical tradition records that Muhammad participated in at least twenty-seven campaigns and deputized at least fifty-nine others during the last 10 years of his life. It is no wonder that Muhammad's earliest biographers refer to this period as "the raids" (*al-maghazi*). Obviously, his strategy was successful because by the time he died in 632 Muhammad had subjected Medina, Mecca, the Hijaz, and much of Arabia to his political and religious authority. It should be noted that women occasionally took up arms themselves in seventh-century Arabia. However, they much more often served as the moral voice of the tribe, beating tambourines and drums to incite their men to battle. We also see them serving as battlefield nurses, caring for the dead and wounded.

Whether in relatively minor raids, in pitched battles among archers, infantry, cavalry, or when one side laid siege to another, combatants generally were outfitted with similar body armor and weapons. The sources employ a range of vocabulary to describe military equipment, which included coats of mail, helmets, shields, swords, spears, lances, knives, iron maces, bows, arrows, and (after being on the receiving end of it during the naval siege of Constantinople in the 670s) Greek fire, also known as liquid fire (*naft*). Of course, because each person was expected to provision himself, only the wealthiest were outfitted completely. For example, despite its critical role as body armor, only a small percentage of soldiers could actually afford a coat of mail given the great expense and craftsmanship involved in producing one. In fact, seven decades after Muhammad's death (704), the province of Khurasan in northeastern Iran had a military force of some fifty-thousand men, but only 350 coats of mail.

Helmets were crucial for protection as well. Many were constructed with pieces of mail or other fabric that hung down from the back to protect the neck. There is even the occasional mention of helmets with nose guards. It should come as no surprise that some fought without helmets for reasons of expense. Swords were the principal weapons employed at that time. They were straight, hilted, and carried on straps around the shoulder or waist. The earliest evidence of curved swords or scimitars is from the ninth century and among the soldiers in Khurasan. A great deal is made of swords in early Arabic literature; the best swords came from India, followed by those made in Yemen and Syria after the Indian fashion. Given the number of stories of severed legs, arms, hands, and heads, these swords appear to have been put to use effectively. Very few early Islamic swords have actually survived, but those that have correspond to the descriptions in our sources as about forty inches in length, 2½ to 3 inches in width, and 3 pounds in weight.

Most battles were fought among infantry and archers, in part because of the general paucity of horses. However, it is clear that horses were critically important to those who had them. Because of their scarcity and importance, horses tended to be led to battle and only mounted when hostilities broke out. Horses were outfitted with some sort of protection as well, but it is not clear what it was at this early stage. We do know that in the **Umayyad** period (661–750) a heavy felt armor was widely used, but there is no evidence that horses were outfitted with mail or any other sort of metallic armor until the tenth century along the Byzantine frontier (by Byzantine and Muslim forces), and even then it was quite rare. Given the scarcity of coats of mail among soldiers, one can assume that it was even more expensive to outfit one's horse in such a fashion at that early date.

In the process of the early Islamic conquests, Muslim armies captured far more horses than were available to them in Arabia. They also adopted new equipment as a result of their encounters. One of the principal innovations borrowed from the Persians in the late seventh century was the iron stirrup. Leather loop stirrups were not unknown in Arabia, and mounted archers were very effective even without the benefit of stirrups at all. In any case, as Hugh N. Kennedy argued, the adoption of the iron stirrup in the late seventh century "gave the mounted warrior greater stability and encouraged the widespread use of the mounted archer and the replacement of infantry by cavalry as the dominant force on the battlefield by the early third/ninth century" (Kennedy, 173).

The early Muslim armies laid siege to cities and even took refuge behind fortifications such as the trench dug by Muhammad at Medina in 627. However, during the conquest period as well as during the Umayyad and early Abbasid caliphates, many preferred to fight in the open and found that fighting from behind walls was too restrictive. Others even deemed it dishonorable to seek refuge behind walls. When the early Muslim armies actually deployed siege engines and other techniques of siege warfare, it tended to be against non-Muslim fortresses along the frontiers, though there were two major sieges of Baghdad in the ninth century during the civil war between **Harun al-Rashid**'s (r. 786–809) two sons, al-Amin ibn Harun al-Rashid (r. 809–813) and **al-Ma'mun ibn Harun al-Rashid** (r. 813–833).

By the early ninth century, cavalry had replaced infantry as the dominant force on the battlefield in the Islamic world. Infantry units continued to be used and used effectively, but it was the mounted archer that was now and would continue to be the core of any effective fighting force. Also, by the early ninth century the Mamluk institution was established as a means of recruiting and training elite cavalry units, largely comprising mounted archers who had been enslaved as young boys and raised to the profession of arms. Although there is evidence that some Mamluks of Iranian origin were employed in the late Umayyad and early **Abbasid** periods, the Abbasid caliph al-Mu'tasim (r. 833–842) is credited with establishing the first effective Mamluk corps with the encouragement of his brother al-Ma'mun (r. 813–833). Al-Mu'tasim's predominantly Turkish Mamluk troops represent a major change in the Abbasid military structure. No longer would the military be made up largely of men who could trace their lineage to the Arabian Peninsula. Rather, it would increasingly be the preserve of ethnic minorities such as Turks, Berbers, Armenians, Daylamis, and others recruited from the fringes of the empire. Al-Mu'tasim even built a new city—Samarra—to house his new troops. Located some 80 miles north of Baghdad on the Tigris, Samarra served as the Abbasid capital to the late ninth century.

Although the preferred route for developing Mamluk regiments was to purchase boys and to train them in barracks apart from the rest of society in the sciences of horsemanship, warfare, and religion, some adults were incorporated into Mamluk regiments, especially during the early years of the institution. According to Islamic law, a free person could only be enslaved if he was a non-Muslim and resided outside the Abode of Islam; that is, in the Abode of War. Hence, military slaves were recruited from peoples who lived on the fringes of the Abode of Islam—sub-Saharan Africans, Eastern Europeans, Greeks, Armenians, Circassians, Indians, and so forth. However, the preferred practice was to purchase boys from the slave markets along the Central Asian frontier north of the Oxus River. Although these boys were generally referred to as Turks, many were not actually ethnic Turks in the modern sense of the word. Nevertheless, the term *turk* functioned as a kind of shorthand for anyone who was a pastoral nomad from the Central Asian steppe, and it was this steppe that served as a vast military reservoir for many of the regimes in the medieval Islamic world.

From the outset, purchasing Turkish boys had at least three advantages for their *ustadh*. First, given the high rates of infant mortality in the prevaccination age of the medieval Islamic world, to purchase children at a younger age was simply a bad investment. However, once a boy had reached 10 to 12 years of age, had survived his childhood diseases, and had built up considerable immunities, he was very likely to live a relatively long and healthy life. Second, because these boys were taken from their homes and families at such young ages, they were still quite amenable to the kind of training designed to produce an elite force of mounted warriors with a high level of esprit de corps and intense loyalty to their *ustadh*. Finally, it was widely believed at the time that Turks were by nature tough and loyal, but also superior horsemen and archers. Therefore, because the goal was to produce elite mounted warriors, purchasing Turkish boys who already were quite skilled in horsemanship and archery by the time they were 10 to 12 years old was a pragmatic policy and saved an *ustadh* considerable effort and expense with respect to basic training in the necessary skills.

One of the clear strengths of the Mamluk system was that it produced superb cavalry forces that were intensely loyal to one another as well as to their *ustadh*. This strength also proved to be a weakness, in large part because the loyalty that Mamluks felt toward their *ustadh* did not always transfer to their sons upon their death. Although it was the *ustadh* who made the Mamluks, in many fundamental ways it was the Mamluks who made the son. An early and dramatic example of this was when some of the Abbasid Turkish troops assassinated the Abbasid Caliph al-Mutawakkil in December 861 because they felt that their positions of privilege under al-Mutawakkil's father (al-Mu'tasim) were threatened.

The ethnic shift within the Abbasid army that began under al-Mu'tasim's largely Turkish Mamluk experiment in the early ninth century moved into high gear in the late tenth century as free Muslim Turkish pastoral nomadic warriors (Turkomans) migrated into the eastern territories of the caliphate. Some of the Turkomans migrated to the northwest and pursued their nomadic raiding practices along the Byzantine frontier. For the Byzantines, these Turkomans were nothing but bandits and genuinely threatened their territory and subjects. The Turkomans, on the other hand, legitimated their raiding and pillaging in eastern and central Anatolia as the righteous work of holy warriors (*ghazis*) engaged in jihad against the Byzantines. After all, from the Turkomans' point of view, they were merely striving in the path of God (*jihad fi sabil Allah*) against the preferred infidel enemy of Islam since the days of Mu'awiya in the midseventh century. Things came to a head in 1071 as the Byzantine emperor Romanus Diogenes (r. 1068–1071) led several Byzantine columns eastward to deal with this Turkish menace once and for all. Already on campaign in Syria, the Seljukid Sultan Alp Arslan turned his forces north to come to the aid of his fellow Turkomans and fellow Muslims. A pitched battle between the two sides took place at Manzikert, near Lake Van, in the summer of 1071. Alp Arslan's forces were victorious, and Romanus Diogenes was taken captive. He was ultimately ransomed and deposed. The Battle of Manzikert marks the beginnings of the process by which Anatolia became Turkey.

In 1095, Pope Urban II preached a sermon in Clermont, France, in which he called on the interminably feuding nobility of Western Europe to turn their energies to the cause of Christ and his Church. Urban was by no means the first to call on them to use their military skills in aide of their Byzantine Christian brothers who, since the Battle of Manzikert, were increasingly threatened by Muslim Turkish marauders in eastern and central Anatolia. In fact, Pope Gregory VII had proposed that he himself lead a force of some fifty-thousand men to liberate their Eastern brethren in 1074. More important, however, Urban called on the Frankish nobility to take up the cross of Christ and make an armed pilgrimage to Jerusalem to redeem their Lord's patrimony, which had been stolen by the infidel Saracens some four centuries earlier. By the summer of 1099, Jerusalem was in the hands of the Crusaders. Unfortunately for Pope Urban II, he died shortly after Jerusalem was taken, but before word reached Western Europe.

Although the styles of weapons varied according to region and time period, the warriors of the Crusader era generally employed many of the same types of weapons used during the first Islamic centuries: coats of mail, helmets, shields, swords, spears, lances, knives, iron maces, lassos, bows, arrows, and *naft* (or Greek fire). Although the **Fatimid** navy in Egypt was able to acquit itself fairly well in the early twelfth century, there was essentially no naval resistance to the Franks from Syria. A century later, however, Saladin's navy proved essential to his victory at Ashkelon. In the end, what distinguished the Muslim forces from the Franks during the Crusader era was the absolutely crucial role of Muslim cavalry forces (freeborn and Mamluk regiments) and the Muslims' improved techniques of siege warfare. Moreover, the changed international political realities in the wake of the establishment of the **Mamluk Sultanate** and the Mongol defeat at Ayn Jalut allowed Baybars (r. 1260–1277) and his successors to pursue a more active policy of extirpation of the Franks in contrast to the more accommodationist policies of their Ayyubid predecessors. In the end, the Mamluks were able to drive the Franks from Acre in 1291, thus ending nearly two centuries of Frankish presence in the Near East.

Further Reading

Ayalon, David. "Mamluk," in *Encyclopaedia of Islam, New Edition.* P.J. Bearman et al., eds. Boston: Brill Academic Publishers, 2005.

Elgood, Robert, ed. *Islamic Arms and Armour.* London: Scholar Press, 1979.

Gordon, Matthew. *The Breaking of a Thousand Swords: A History of the Turkish Military of Samarra,* A.H. *200–275/815–889* C.E. Albany: State University of New York Press, 2001.

Guillaume, Alfred, trans. *The Life of Muhammad: A Translation of Ibn Ishaq's Sirat Rasul Allah.* New York: Oxford University Press, 1955.

Hillenbrand, Carole. *The Crusades: Islamic Perspectives.* Edinburgh, Scotland: Edinburgh University Press, 1999.

al-Jahiz. "The Merits of the Turks and of the Imperial Army as a Whole," in Charles Pellat, trans. *The Life and Works of al-Jahiz.* Berkeley: University of California Press, 1969, pp. 91–97.

Kennedy, Hugh N. *The Armies of the Caliphs: Military and Society in the Early Islamic State.* New York: Routledge, 2001.

Nicholson, Helen, and David Nicolle. *God's Warriors: Crusaders, Saracens and the Battle for Jerusalem.* London: Osprey, 2005.

Nicolle, David. *Saladin and the Saracens: Armies of the Middle East, 1100–1300.* London: Osprey, 1986.

Women

Few themes in Islamic history cut against the grain of modern American social and cultural values than the role and status of women and men in the Qur'an. In traditional Islamic thought, concepts that modern Americans take for granted—individual liberty, individual choice, personal fulfillment—necessarily lead to moral chaos because they are not informed by the admonitions and guidance of God's revelation to mankind in the Qur'an. Although the Qur'an has very little material that may be consider legal in nature, the bulk of the legal material in the Qur'an deals with the proper role and status of women and men in the family and in society as a whole.

Although the specific status of women in pre-Islamic Arabia and early Islamic history remains a mystery, it is clear that prior to the coming of Islam patrilineal and matrilineal kinship systems did exist. It is also clear that during this transitional period some women played a variety of very important public roles including those of caravan merchants (Khadija, Muhammad's first wife), religious leaders, warriors, battlefield nurses (Fatima, Muhammad and Khadija's daughter), and even instigators of rebellions (**'Aisha bint Abi Bakr**, Muhammad's third and favorite wife).

In principle, at least, the role and status of women and men in Islamic thought are governed by three concepts that if not explicitly stated in the Qur'an, are certainly implied therein. The first principle is embodied in the *shahada*—the simple two-part creedal declaration that is at the very center of Islamic belief, ritual, and worship. "There is no god but God; Muhammad is the messenger of God (*la ilaha illa'llah; Muhammadun rasul Allah*)." Each man and each woman is personally responsible for making this declaration (*shahada*) and submitting (*islam*) to the one God and acknowledging Muhammad as His messenger.

> Those who surrender themselves to God and accept the true Faith; who are devout, sincere, patient, humble, charitable and chaste; who fast and are ever mindful of God—on these, *both men and women*, God will bestow forgiveness and a rich reward. It is not for true believers—*men or women*—to take their choice in their affairs if God and His apostle decree otherwise. He that disobeys God and His apostle strays far indeed. (Qur'an 33:35–36) (Emphasis added)

The second principle is that though the Qur'an condemns many of the practices of seventh-century Mecca and Medina including idolatry, polytheism, gambling, drinking wine, the abuse of the poor by the rich, and female infanticide, it accepts the patrilineal kinship system of Arabia and many of its values as the natural order of things. "Men have authority over women because God has made the one superior to the other" (Qur'an 4:34a). The third principle—that a man must provide for every member of his household (wives, children, servants, and slaves) from his own resources—is closely connected to the second, "because they [men] spend their wealth to maintain them [women]" (Qur'an 4:34b).

Although every man and woman is morally responsible before God for his or her beliefs and actions (and despite modern interpretations, polemics, and protestations to the contrary), medieval commentators interpreted the Qur'an as uncompromisingly patriarchal in its description of proper relations between men and women. Of course, the principle that women are subordinate to men was not unique to seventh-century Arabia. It was extremely common throughout the Ancient Near East and the Mediterranean world as a whole. Although this principle is taken for granted in the Qur'an, many of the modifications to existing practices set forth in the Qur'an do represent what we might call improvements in women's status. Nevertheless, even this improved status can be jarring to many modern Americans whose conceptions of family and individual rights differ considerably from those of the Qur'an.

One of the most important elements of the system of patrilineal kinship is paternal certainty, for without it the entire system would fall apart. According to this structure, female chastity before marriage and fidelity in marriage are essential in guaranteeing paternal certainty. Sexual activity by a woman outside of marriage was not a matter of individual choice, but a violation of family honor and the Qur'anic sexual ethic that embraced it: "The adulterer and the adulteress shall each be given a hundred lashes. Let no pity for them cause you to disobey God, if you truly believe in God and the Last Day" (Qur'an 24:2–5). In theory, the Qur'anic requirements of chastity and fidelity applied equally to men and women; however, the physical consequences of sexual activity by a man outside of marriage were less readily apparent and the punishments less strictly enforced. In short, the reason that women were the guardians of the purity and honor of a kin's lineage was related to basic biology. That is, though a child's mother's identity was known to her and the midwives who helped deliver the child, the identity of the father could rarely be attested to by outside eyewitness testimony. As shari'a developed, the Qur'anic punishment of lashing was changed to death by stoning, a punishment that parallels the Biblical practice of execution for all sorts of illicit sexual intercourse described in Leviticus 20 and Deuteronomy 22.

Related to female chastity is the issue of modesty. One practice designed to ensure female chastity was the requirement that women be segregated from men who were not part of their households. Modern Americans ordinarily distinguish between private and public space, or a person's private and his or her public life. Although this division between private and public is applicable to the medieval Islamic world, a more accurate distinction would be between appropriate behavior among one's kin and appropriate behavior among those outside of one's kin group. For example, in what we would call the private space of a home, segregation of the sexes could consist of women's actual physical separation from men when unrelated men were guests in the common area of the home. In such instances, women might be segregated in the women's quarters of a dwelling or they could be separated from men who were not their kin by appropriate female dress (*see* **Clothing and Modesty**).

However, neither type of segregation was necessary among men who were close relatives. Segregation of the sexes did not apply to prepubescent girls and boys for the simple reason that they were not considered sexual beings because they were physically unable to reproduce. Likewise, many of these restrictions on women were not applied as strictly to widows or to women whose children were adults. Such women had far greater freedom of activity, especially in the public sphere, for reasons of biology and perceived sexuality. Thus, postmenopausal women were no longer considered to be sexual beings because they could no longer bear children. As such, they were no longer viewed as sources of illicit temptation for men, nor could they produce illegitimate offspring, which would bring shame to their families.

According to the Qur'an, Muhammad's wives were specifically commanded to remain in their homes and to separate themselves from men. They were, however, given the option of divorce before they were required to accept these requirements (Qur'an 33:28–34). Although some scholars argued that seclusion should be applied to women in general on the principle that all Muslim women should follow the practice of the "Mothers of the Believers," it never became an absolute practice in Islamic history. In fact, such universal cloistering of women was nearly impossible for all but the wealthiest of families in the towns and cities. Less wealthy families as well as rural and pastoral communities generally needed the labor of their male and their female kin.

Muhammad's third and favorite wife, 'Aisha (one of the "Mothers of the Believers"), certainly did not confine herself to her house. In fact, she was a major player on the losing side in the First Civil War, especially in the Battle of the Camel (656), which is so named because of her presence there on her camel. For this reason, she has been held up as a model for those who argue that women should be able to take part in public life, but more often as an example of the disasters that will befall the community when women become involved in politics.

Nevertheless, the principle of modesty and separation of the sexes was observed in the public sphere; that is, essentially everywhere outside of the home and apart from one's kin. In the most prominent of public spaces, the market, this separation of the sexes consisted of the physical separation of women from men by means of modest dress. This practice was especially important in larger oasis settlements and towns and later in major urban centers where the residents were not all close kin and where the likelihood that women would encounter strangers was a virtual certainty.

Fundamental to family life in any society are the conditions under which new families are established in marriage, how they are dissolved in divorce, and how property should be disposed of in divorce settlements or the event of a family member's death. The Qur'an addresses each of these issues explicitly. In pre-Islamic Arabia, when a man wanted to marry, he paid a dowry, or bride price, to the father or male guardian of the girl or woman to whom he was betrothed, in part as compensation for the loss of her value as a laborer in her father's or male guardian's household.

According to the Qur'an, this bride price became her property that she would bring into the marriage, not the property of her male guardian (Qur'an 4:4; 4:20). Because a man was supposed to provide for every member of his household from his own resources, the husband was to have no recourse to this wealth. It became the wife's property solely to dispense with as she saw fit. She could, of course, give a part of it to her husband, but he could not lawfully take it away from her on his own.

Despite the fact that marriage under the Qur'anic scenario described above became a contract between a man and a woman (not between a man and a woman's male guardian), most marriages resulted from some sort of arrangement between families. After all, each family had a vested interest in the prestige and economic status of the other as well as the success of the union. Unlike in the American ideal of marital bliss, where many believe one's spouse should be one's best friend and soul mate, the purpose of marriage in the Qur'an and the medieval Islamic world was the procreation of children and the strengthening of ties between two extended families. In principle, the man or the woman was able to decline a proposed match, but rarely was there an opportunity for such an arrangement to be initiated on the basis of mutual affection or common interests and certainly not after a period of courtship as in the American ideal of the institution.

Another way in which marriage differs from the modern American model is that according to the Qur'an, a man may take up to four wives at the same time, with the proviso that he treat each wife fairly in order to avoid injustice (Qur'an 4:3). Whether a man took one wife or as many as four, it is clear from the Qur'an that in return for his protection and provision, he was owed obedience. If a wife was not obedient, her husband was allowed to chastise her and even to beat her into submission.

> Good women are obedient. They guard their unseen parts because God has guarded them. As for those from whom you fear disobedience, admonish them and send them to beds apart and beat them. Then if they obey you, take no further action against them. (Qur'an 4:35)

Not surprisingly, this passage often produces embarrassment among some modern Muslims, especially in the West, where women and men (at least according to the laws in most Western countries) are supposed to be equals in a marriage relationship. However, according to the Qur'anic worldview, "men have authority over women because God has made the one superior to the other, and because they spend their wealth to maintain them" (Qur'an 4:34)

Men of the wealthy classes were able to afford slaves as well as wives. According to shari'a, in exchange for his maintenance and support, the head of the household had the right to obedience as well as sexual relations with his female slave(s). Although a concubine was in no position to refuse her owner's advances, the possibility of winning his affection prior to the onset of a sexual relationship did exist—as many poems attest. Moreover, according to shari'a, a concubine did have certain legal protections not afforded to a wife. Once a concubine bore a child she was henceforth classified as an *umm walad* (mother of a child).

Unlike the American slave system, the child of a free Muslim man and a slave woman received the status of the father not the mother. That is, the child was a legally free Muslim and bore no stigma of illegitimacy. Initially, such offspring tended to be seen as inferior (though not illegitimate) largely because their mothers were not of Arabian stock. However, as the importance of Arabian purity began to be contested vigorously in the eighth and ninth centuries, this sense of inferiority waned considerably. In fact, the mothers of many of the caliphs and sultans in Islamic history were *umm walad*s (e.g., Khayzuran, mother of the famous **Abbasid** caliph **Harun al-Rashid** [r. 786–809]). In addition, once a slave woman had borne a child, she could not be put out of the house, she could legally expect maintenance and support, and she had to be granted her freedom upon the death of her owner. A wife on the other hand could bear her husband as many children as physically possible and he could divorce her without cause.

The Qur'anic procedures under which a man can divorce his wife are fairly simple—he merely needs to say three times that he is divorcing her and the marriage is dissolved. "Divorce may be pronounced twice, and then a woman must be retained in honour or allowed to go with kindness" (Qur'an 2:229a). The woman does, however, have certain rights and protections should her husband decide to divorce her. Because the property with which she entered the marriage was supposed to remain in her possession throughout the marriage, whatever property she had at the time of the divorce remained hers to do with as she saw fit (Qur'an 2:229b). A man also owed his wife three months' maintenance after the divorce for the purpose of determining whether she was pregnant (Qur'an 2:226–228). In general, the practice came to be that if a woman was pregnant, her husband was required to support her until the delivery of their child. In addition, he was required to support mother and child until the child was weaned (generally around age 2).

As shari'a developed, provisions were made for women to seek a divorce as well. However, it was much more difficult for a woman to divorce her husband, and the procedure required the services of a court. Legitimate causes for divorce included the husband having some sort of disgusting disease, his intolerable cruelty, and/or his abandonment—ranging from 10 to 90 years depending on which *madhhab* a woman followed. Needless to say, few women lived long enough to be granted a divorce on the grounds of abandonment in those courts where the husband had to have been gone missing for 90 years.

According to American law, one's right to dispose of one's wealth (after estate taxes and outstanding debts have been paid) is entirely discretionary. According to the Qur'an, the bulk of one's estate must go to specified heirs; only about one-third is discretionary. Moreover, the specific percentage of one's wealth owed to female heirs is less than that owed to males.

> God has thus enjoined you concerning your children: A male shall inherit twice as much as a female. If there be more than two girls, they shall have two-thirds of the inheritance; but if there be one only, she shall inherit the half. (Qur'an 4:11)

Whatever the division of wealth, the reason that females received a smaller percentage of an inheritance than did males is straightforward. Because a man was obligated to provide for every member of his household from his own re-sources, he simply needed more resources than did a woman, whose mainte-nance was the responsibility of her male guardian, whether husband, brother, uncle, or cousin.

The preceding discussion of the role and status of women and men in Is-lamic thought has focused on how things were supposed to be according to the Qur'an and its medieval interpreters. In the medieval Islamic world, as in any society, there were disparities between the ideal and the real in daily life. However, a few general comments about how this ideal was applied in nonur-ban settings are in order. In the countryside and especially among the pastoral nomadic populations, local custom usually outweighed the dictates of shari'a on these issues, even though they are set forth clearly in the Qur'an.

If a bride price was paid to a guardian or inheritance rights were withheld or divorce protections were not honored, to whom could a woman appeal? Moreover, if a woman decided to contest these issues, her brothers and other male relatives could always coerce her by refusing to find her a husband, much less a suitable one. Faced with the choice of never marrying or worse, most women in such circumstances likely chose to forgo their marriage and inheri-tance rights, if in fact they knew they had them at all.

In a major city, however, a woman—especially an educated upper-class woman—could appeal to a court and have confidence that a judge would rule in her favor. Moreover, she could trust that the judge would not only seek to, but also have the authority and means to enforce his ruling with the backing of the ruler who had appointed him judge, even in the face of possible opposi-tion from her husband or other relatives. As expected, surviving court records that include women as litigants tend to be women who lived in major cities.

One of the very important ways that we see the activities of women, espe-cially elite women, reflected in the surviving court records is as endowers of religious and educational institutions as well as charities for pilgrims and the destitute. In the eighth century, Harun al-Rashid's mother, the concubine Khayzuran, purchased Muhammad's traditional birthplace in Mecca and trans-formed it into the sacred Mosque of the Nativity. She also endowed a drinking fountain in Mecca, endowed a water pool in Ramle in Palestine, as well as a channel west of the city of Anbar in Iraq. Harun al-Rashid's wife, his cousin Zubayda, funded the renovation of Muhammad's mosque in Ta'if near Mecca. But she is most famous for her charitable concern for pilgrims' basic comforts and water needs. She endowed wells, rest areas, and caravanserais along the well-traveled pilgrimage route between Kufa and Mecca, which came to be known as the Zubayda Road. In the Hijaz, she funded the Mushshash Spring in Mecca and a water complex on the Plain of Arafat, which bears her name as well — the Spring of Zubayda. Five centuries later, Ayyubid princesses vied with their kinsmen in endowing religious architecture as part of the Ayyubid campaign of jihad against the Franks and Shi'is. During the Ayyubid period (1174–1260), some 160 mosques, *madrasas* (religious colleges; lit. place of study), and other religious monuments were established in Damascus alone, more than the combined total established during the century prior to and after their rule. Women attached to the Ayyubid house endowed twenty six of these monuments (16 percent), and half of all royal patrons were women.

Further Reading

Abbott, Nabia. *Two Queens of Baghdad: Mother and Wife of Harun al-Rashid*. Chicago: University of Chicago Press, 1946.

Ahmed, Leila. *Women and Gender in Islam: Historical Roots of a Modern Debate*. New Haven, CT: Yale University Press, 1992.

Humphreys, R. Stephen "Women as Patrons of Religious Architecture in Ayyubid Syria." *Muqarnass: An Annual on Islamic Art and Architecture* 11 (1994): 35–54.

Roded, Ruth, ed. *Women in Islam and the Middle East: A Reader*. London and New York: I.B. Tauris Publishers, 1999.

Spellberg, Denise A. *Politics, Gender, and the Islamic Past: The Legacy of 'Aisha bint Abi Bakr*. New York: Columbia University Press, 1994.

Walther, Wiebke. *Women in Islam*. Princeton, NJ: Markus Wiener, 1993.

Primary Documents

1. Excerpts from the Qur'an

The Qur'an, for the vast majority of Muslims, is the eternal uncreated speech of God flawlessly communicated to humankind through His messenger, Muhammad. The revelations Muhammad received and recited to the people of Mecca (c. 610–622) and Medina (622–632) are referred to as *al-Kitab* (The Scripture or The Book) as well as *al-Qur'an* (The Recitation). The traditional Muslim account places the compilation of the Qur'an into a single manuscript during the reign of the third caliph, or leader of the Muslim community after Muhammad, Uthman ibn Affan (r. 644–656), some two decades after Muhammad's passing. Because according to Muslim dogma, the Qur'an represents God's speech and not Muhammad's human teachings, it is believed to be without error. Therefore, for the believer, the veracity of the Qur'anic text cannot be called into question. Translations, of course, are another matter because, according to Muslim dogma, because God chose to reveal himself in Arabic, the true meaning of the Qur'an is simply untranslatable into another language. Therefore, Muslims generally refer to translations of the Qur'an as interpretations of or commentaries on the Arabic text. There are many English translations of the Qur'an, some more felicitous than others. I have chosen to use N. J. Dawood, trans., *The Koran*, fifth revised edition (New York: Penguin Books, 1995) primarily because it is affordable and available in nearly every major bookstore.

The Qur'an can be a rather difficult read for newcomers accustomed to the Hebrew Bible and the New Testament for two basic reasons. First, the Qur'an does not contain much sustained narrative material. Second, the Qur'an's 114 chapters are not arranged in chronological order; rather, they are generally arranged according to length, with the longer chapters first and the shorter chapters at the end. The principal exception to this ordering is the first chapter, which is quite short. Chapter 2 is by far the lengthiest chapter in the entire book. Each chapter (*sura*) of the Qur'an has a title that is derived from some word, phrase, or theme found in the chapter itself. Consequently, Muslims have traditionally cited the Qur'an by chapter title rather than by chapter number. Every chapter except chapter 9, begins with the same phrase, "In the name of Allah, the Merciful, the Beneficent." Below are chapters 1, 96, and 112 in their entirety; and excerpts from the much longer chapter 9.

Chapter 1. al-Fatiha (The Opening)

The first chapter of the Qur'an is called the *Fatiha* because it is the opening or the first chapter. It is recited daily as part of the five daily ritual prayers (*salat*). The final two lines are traditionally understood to refer to Jews and Christians, respectively.

> In the name of Allah, the Beneficent, the Merciful.
> Praise be to Allah, Lord of the Universe,
> The Compassionate, the Merciful,
> Sovereign of the Day of Judgment!
> You alone we worship; and to You alone we turn for help.
> Guide us the straight path,
> The path of those whom You have favored,
> Not of those who have incurred Your wrath [i.e., Jews],
> Nor of those who have gone astray [i.e., Christians].

Chapter 112. al-Ikhlas (True Belief)

In addition to reciting the *Fatiha* during ritual prayer Muslims are expected to recite additional passages as well. Although it is appropriate to recite any passage from the Qur'an, chapter 112 is a favorite because it is believed to succinctly capture the essence of Islamic monotheism and explicitly argues against the Christian doctrine of the Trinity, which the Qur'an and Islamic dogma views as polytheism. Hence its title "True Belief."

> Say: Allah is One!
> Allah is eternal!
> He begot none, nor was He begotten.
> None is equal to Him.

Chapter 96. al-Alaq (The Clot)

The verses of chapter 96 are traditionally understood to be the very first verses revealed to Muhammad in his home town of Mecca ca. 610.

> Recite in the name of your Lord who created—created man from clots of
>   blood.
> Recite! Your Lord is the Most Bountiful One, who by the pen taught man
>   what he did not know.
> Indeed, man transgresses in thinking himself his own master: for to your
>   Lord all things return.
> Observe them and who rebukes Our servant when he prays.
> Think: does he follow the right guidance or enjoin true piety?
> Think: if he denies the Truth and pays no heed, does he not realize that God
>   observes all?
> No. Let him desist, or We will drag him by the forelock, his lying, sinful forelock.
> Then let him call his helpmates. We will call the guards of Hell.
> No, never obey him! Prostrate yourself and come nearer.

Chapter 9. al-Tawba (Repentance); Verses 5–6, 29–31, 111

Chapter 9 includes the principal Qur'anic material on warfare and jihad and is the only chapter of the Qur'an's 114 chapters that does not begin with the phrase, "In the name of Allah, the Merciful, the Beneficent." Muslim commentators generally date this chapter to the end of Muhammad's career in Medina after his military conquests gave him control over Mecca, Medina, and most of Arabia.

> When the sacred months are over slay the idolaters wherever you find them. Arrest them, besiege them, and lie in ambush everywhere for them. If they repent and take to prayer and render the alms levy, allow them to go their way. Allah is forgiving and merciful . . . (9:5–6)
>
> Fight against such of those to whom the Scriptures were given [Jews and Christians] as believe in neither Allah nor the Last Day, who do not forbid what Allah and His apostle have forbidden, and do not embrace the true Faith, until they pay the *jizya* [protection money] out of hand and are utterly subdued. The Jews say Ezra is the son of Allah, while the Christians say the Messiah is the son of God. Such are their assertions, by which they imitate the infidels of old. Allah confound them! How perverse they are! They make of their clerics and their monks, and of the Messiah, the son of Mary, Lords besides Allah; though they were ordered to serve Allah only. There is no god but Him. Exalted be He above those they deify besides Him! . . . (9:29–31)
>
> Allah has purchased from the faithful their lives and worldly goods, and in return has promised them the Garden. They will fight for the cause of God, they will slay and be slain. Such is the true promise which He has made them in the Torah, the Gospel and the Qur'an. And who is more true to his pledge than God? Rejoice then in the bargain you have made. That is the supreme triumph. (9:111)

Source: Dawood, N.J., trans. *The Koran.* 5th rev. ed. New York: Penguin Books, 1995.

2. The Pact of Umar (c. 637)

According to Islamic sources, after Jerusalem fell to the Muslim forces in 636 to 637, Umar ibn al-Khattab, the second Rashidun caliph (r. 632–644), issued a guarantee of security for the conquered city and the remaining territories in Syria. There are numerous versions of this so-called Pact of Umar. The version reproduced here is preserved in al-Tabari's (d. 923) *The Chronicle of Prophets and Kings.* al-Tabari begins his account with several reports in which a Jew predicts to Umar at al-Jabiya (a town in the modern Golan Heights) that he would not return to his home country (Medina) until God had granted him victory over Jerusalem. According to al-Tabari's account, after Umar took control of Jerusalem, he issued the terms of protection. al-Tabari tells us that the letter was written and prepared in 636 to 637, and that Khalid ibn al-Walid, Amr ibn al-As, Abd al-Rahman ibn Awf, and Mu'awiya ibn Abi Sufyan—major figures in the early history of Islamic Syria—attested to it. Not surprisingly, there has been dispute among modern scholars as to whether Umar established a pact of protection as described below. However, what can be said with certainty is that by al-Tabari's day in the ninth century, it was accepted within the Islamic historiographical tradition that he had. In any case, this pact (and similar versions) along with the so-called *jizya* verse (Qur'an 9:29) served as the legal basis for relations between the Muslim ruling authorities and their non-Muslim subjects (namely Jews, Christians and Zoroastrians) in Islamic law.

In the Name of God, the Merciful, the Compassionate.

This is the assurance of safety which the servant of God, Umar, the Commander of the Faithful, has granted to the people of Jerusalem. He has given them an assurance of safety for themselves, for their property, their churches, their crosses, the sick and the healthy of the city, and for all the rituals that belong to their religion. Their churches will not be inhabited by Muslims and will not be destroyed. Neither they, nor the land on which they stand, nor their cross, nor their property will be damaged. They will not be forcibly converted. No Jew will live with them in Jerusalem. The people of Jerusalem must pay the poll tax [*jizya*] like the people of the other cities, and they must expel the Byzantines and the robbers. As for those who will leave the city, their lives and property will be safe until they reach their place of safety; and as for those who remain, they will be safe. They will have to pay the poll tax [*jizya*] like the people of Jerusalem. Those of the people of Jerusalem who want to leave with the Byzantines, take their property, and abandon their churches and their crosses will be safe until they reach their place of safety. Those villagers who were in Jerusalem before the killing of so-and-so may remain in the city if they wish, but they must pay the poll tax [*jizya*] like the people of Jerusalem. Those who wish may go with the Byzantines, and those who wish may return to their families. Nothing will be taken from them before their harvest is reaped. If they pay the poll tax [*jizya*] according to their obligations, then the contents of this letter are under the covenant of God, are the responsibility of His Prophet, of the caliphs, and of the faithful.

al-Tabari also includes the following letter that Umar ostensibly sent to Lydda (Lod in modern Israel). According to al-Tabari, Umar sent this same letter to the remaining provinces of Palestine as well.

In the Name of God, the Merciful, the Compassionate.

This is what the servant of God, Umar, the Commander of the Faithful, awarded to the people of Lydda and to all the people of Palestine who are in the same category. He gave them an assurance of safety for themselves, for their property, their churches, their crosses, their sick and their healthy and all their rites. Their churches will not be inhabited by the Muslims and will not be destroyed. Neither their churches, nor the land where they stand, nor their rituals, nor their crosses, nor their property will be damaged. They will not be forcibly converted, and none of them will be harmed. The people of Lydda and those of the people of Palestine who are in the same category must pay the poll tax [*jizya*] like the people of the Syrian cities. The same conditions, in their entirety apply to them if they leave (Lydda).

Source: al-Tabari. *The History of al-Tabari.* Vol. 12. *The Battle of al-Qadisiyyah and the Conquest of Syria and Palestine.* Translated by Yohanan Friedmann. Albany: State University of New York Press, 1992, pp. 191–192.

3. al-Ya'qubi's Ninth-Century Description of the Dome of the Rock in Jerusalem

The ninth-century historian and geographer, Yaqubi (d. 897), records that for political reasons, the Umayyad caliph Abd al-Malik (r. 685–705) prohibited the pilgrimage to Mecca, which was controlled by Abd Allah ibn Zubayr who claimed the caliphate for himself. When people protested that it was a religious duty to make the pilgrimage to Mecca, Abd al-Malik responded by citing a hadith to justify his policy. He then built the Dome of the Rock as an alternative pilgrimage site.

"Hath not Ibn Shihâb az-Zuhri told you how the Apostle of Allah did say: 'Men shall journey to but three Masjids (mosques, namely), Al Masjid Haram (at Makkah), my Masjid (at Madinah), and the Masjid of the Holy City (which is Jerusalem)?' So this last is now appointed for you (as a place of worship) in lieu of the Masjid al-Haram (of Makkah). And this Rock (the Sakhrah of Jerusalem), of which it is reported that upon it the Apostle of Allah set his foot when he ascended into heaven, shall be unto you in the place of the Ka'abah." Then Abd al-Malik built above the Sakhrah a Dome, and hung it around with curtains of brocade, and he instituted doorkeepers for the same, and the people took the custom of circumambulating the Rock (as-Sakhrah of Jerusalem), even as they had paced round the Ka'abah (at Makkah), and the usage continued thus all the days of the dynasty of the Omayyads.

Source: Le Strange, Guy, trans. *Palestine under the Moslems: A Description of Syria and the Holy Land from* A.D. *650 to 1500.* Boston: Houghton, Mifflin and Company, 1890, p. 116.

4. al-Ya'qubi's Description of Baghdad in the Ninth Century

Al-Ya'qubi was one of the most important early historians and geographers of the medieval Islamic world. He was born in Baghdad, served the Tahirid regime in Khurasan as a young man, traveled widely throughout the Islamic world, and later in his life settled in Egypt, where he composed his *Kitab al-Buldan* (*Book of Countries*), a detailed geographical work based on his travels. The excerpt below is from al-Ya'qubi's introductory comments about Baghdad (est. 762), the capital of the Abbasid caliphate. As can be seen from al-Ya'qubi's effusive description of his hometown, Baghdad was a thriving cosmopolitan center of trade, culture, religion, politics, and so forth in the ninth century.

I begin with Iraq only because it is the center of this world, the navel of the earth, and I mention Baghdad first because it is the center of Iraq, the greatest city, which has no peer in the east or the west of the world in extent, size, prosperity, abundance of water, or health of climate, and because it is inhabited by all kinds of people, town-dwellers and country-dwellers. To it they come from all countries, far and near, and people from every side have preferred Baghdad to their own homelands. There is no country, the peoples of which have not their own quarter and their own trading and financial arrangements. In it there is gathered that which does not exist in any other city in the world. On its flanks flow two great rivers, the Tigris and Euphrates, and thus goods and foodstuffs come to it by land and by water with the greatest ease, so that every kind of merchandise is completely available, from east and west, from Muslim and non-Muslim lands. Goods are brought from India, Sind, China, Tibet, the lands of the Turks, the Daylam, the Khazars, the Ethiopians, and others to such an extent that the products of the countries are more plentiful in Baghdad than in the countries from which they come. The can be procured so readily and so certainly that it is as if all the good things of the world are sent there, all the treasures of the earth assembled there, and all the blessings of creation perfected there.

Furthermore, Baghdad is the city of the Hashimites [the Abbasid caliphs], the home of their reign, the seat of their sovereignty, where no one appeared before them and no kings but they have dwelt. Also my own forbears have lived there, and one of them was governor of the city.

Its name is famous, and its fame widespread. Iraq is indeed the center of the world. . . . The weather is temperate, the soil is rich, the water is sweet, the trees are thriving, the fruit luscious, the seeds are fertile, good things are abundant, and springs are easily found. Because of the temperate weather and rich soil and sweet water, the character of the inhabitants is good, their faces bright, and their minds untrammeled. The people excel in knowledge, understanding, letters, manners, insight, discernment, skill in commerce and crafts, cleverness in every argument, proficiency in every calling, and master of every craft. There in none more learned than their scholars, better informed than their traditionists, more cogent than their theologians, more perspicuous than their grammarians, more accurate than their readers, more skillful than their physicians, more melodious than their singers, more delicate than their craftsmen, more literate than their scribes, more lucid that their logicians, more devoted than their worshippers, more pious than their ascetics, more juridical than their judges, more eloquent than their preachers, more poetic than their poets, and more reckless than their rakes.

Source: Lewis, Bernard, ed. and trans. *Islam: From the Prophet Muhammad to the Capture of Constantinople.* Vol. 2. *Religion and Society.* New York: Harper and Row, 1974, pp. 69–71.

5. al-Jahiz's Ninth-Century Essay on the Turks

In his essay on the Turks, al-Jahiz (d. 869) begins by commending the foresight of the Abbasid caliphs for establishing the Mamluk system in the early ninth century. More specifically, he extols the racial or ethnic superiority of Turks in the fields of horsemanship, warfare, archery, courage, and so forth. Although such an approach is largely rejected today, it was quite common in the medieval Islamic world to categorize various peoples according to their inherent racial qualities and talents. Al-Jahiz concludes his essay by stating that the Turks are to warfare what the Greeks are to philosophy and the Chinese to craftsmanship. Of course, al-Jahiz is engaging in a bit of hyperbole here, but his essay conveys very eloquently the dominant sentiment in his day that there is no better horseman than a Turk.

The Khariji relies upon his lances, but the Turks are as good with their lances as the Khawarij; and if a thousand Turkish horsemen charge and discharge a thousand arrows all at once, they prostrate a thousand men; and there is no other army which can charge as well. The Khawarij and Bedouins, however, are of little account, as far as the department of mounted archers goes. But the Turk can shoot beasts as far as the department of mounted archers goes. But the Turk can shoot beasts and birds, targets on spears and human beings, quarry crouching on the ground, figures set up and birds on the wing. And while he shoots, he will let his beast go at full gallop backwards or forwards, right or left, up or down hill. And he can shoot ten arrows before the Khariji can put one arrow on his bowstring. And he can ride his horse with a downward sweep from a mountain or down below inside a ravine at a greater speed than Khariji can accomplish on level ground. And the Turk has four eyes, two in front and two at the back of his head. The Khariji fails in following up a war, the Khurasani in beginning it. . . . . But if the Khawarij retreat, they retreat for good, and never think of returning to the fray after retreat, save on a very few occasions. As for the Turks, they do not wheel like the Khurasanis; and if they do turn their backs, they are to be feared as much as deadly poison and sudden death; for their arrows his the mark as much when they are retreating as when they are advancing. And one cannot be sure of not being caught by their lasso or having one's horses caught and their riders seized in the same motion . . . And sometimes they cast their lasso with some other design; and if they do not take their victim with them, he is made to think in his ignorance that it is only the stupidity of the Turk and his own sagacity. . . .

Turks are nomads, dwellers in the wilderness and owners of beasts. . . . Whereas they do not busy themselves with industry and merchandise and medicine and agriculture and engineering and forestry and architecture and irrigation and the raising of crops, but all their interest is in raids and incursions and hunting and riding and the fights of warriors and seeking for plunder and subduing countries, and their energy is turned in that direction and fitted for such exercises and limited and adapted accordingly, they have made themselves completely masters of that department, and learned all that is to be learned in it; and so it has for them taken the place of industry and merchandise and become their delight and their boast and the subject of their discourse by day and night. Accordingly they occupy in war the position that the Greeks occupy in science and Chinese in art.

Source: Pellat, Charles, trans. *The Life and Works of al-Jahiz.* Berkeley and Los Angeles: University of California Press, 1969.

6. al-Muqaddasi's Tenth-Century Description of the Aksâ Mosque in Jerusalem

Most of what we know about al-Muqaddasi is derived from his pioneering work in the fields of physical, economic, political, and human geography— *The Best Divisions for Knowledge of the Regions (Ahsan al-taqasim fi ma'rifat al-aqalim)*—based on some 20 years of travel throughout the Islamic world. As a native of Jerusalem (*Bayt al-Muqaddas* or *Bayt al-Maqdis*; hence the *nisba* al-Muqaddasi), his descriptions of his hometown and Greater Syria (*bilad al-sham*) are especially detailed. The excerpts below are descriptions of the two major examples of monumental religious architecture in his hometown: the Aksâ Mosque and the Dome of the Rock. Both buildings are situated on what Muslims refer to as the Noble Sanctuary (*al-Haram al-Sharif*). Because this is the site of the ancient Jewish temple, it is known as the Temple Mount in the Jewish and Christian traditions. Le Strange's translation of al-Muqaddasi's text was published in 1890, hence his transliteration of Arabic titles and names differs slightly from current transliteration conventions.

The Masjid al-Aksâ (the Further Mosque with the Haram Area) lies at the south-eastern corner of the Holy City. The stones of the foundations of the Haram Area wall, which were laid by David, are ten ells, or a little less, in length. They are chiseled (or *drafted*), finely faced, and jointed, and of the hardest material. On these the Khalif Abd al-Malik [r. 685–705] subsequently built, using smaller but well-shaped stones, and battlements are added above. This mosque is even more beautiful than that of Damascus, for during the building of it they had for a rival as a comparison the great Church (of the Holy Sepulchre) belonging to the Christians at Jerusalem, and they built this to be even more magnificent than that other. But in the days of the Abbasids occurred the earthquakes, which threw down most of the Main-building (*al-Mughatta,* which is the Aksâ Mosque); all, in fact except that portion which is round the Mihrâb. Now when the Khalif of that day (who was al-Mahdi [r. 775–785]) obtained news of this, he inquired and learned that the sum at that time in the treasury would in no wise suffice to restore the mosque. So he wrote to the governors of the provinces, and to all the commanders, that each should undertake the building of a colonnade. The order was carried out, and the edifice rose firmer and more substantial than ever it had been in former times. The more ancient portion remained, even like a beauty spot, in the midst of the new, and it extends as far as the limit of the marble columns; for beyond, where the columns are of concrete, the later building commences.

The Main-building of the Aksâ Mosque has twenty-six doors. The door opposite to the Mihrâb is called the Great Brazen Gate; it is plated with brass gilt, and is so heavy that only a man strong of shoulder and of arm can turn it on its hinges. To the right hand of the (great Gate) are seven large doors, the midmost covered with gilt plates; and after the same manner there are seven doors to the left. And further, on the eastern side (of the Aksâ), are eleven doors unornamented. Over the first-mentioned doors, fifteen in number, is a colonnade supported on marble pillars, lately erected by Abd Allah ibn Tahir [governor of Khurasan 828–844].

On the right-hand side of the Court (that is along the West Wall of the Haram Area) are colonnades supported by marble pillars and pilasters; and on the back (or North Wall of the Haram Area) are colonnades vaulted in stone. The centre part of the Main-building (of the Aksâ) is covered by a mighty roof, high pitched and gable-wise, over which rises a magnificent dome. The ceilings everywhere — except those of the colonnades at the back (along the North Wall of the Haram Area) — are covered with lead sheets; but in these (northern) colonnades the ceilings are made of mosaics studded-in.

On the left (or east side of the Haram Area) there are no colonnades. The Main-building of the (Aksâ) Mosque does not come up the Eastern Wall of the Haram Area, the building here, as it is said, never having been completed. Of the reason for this they give two accounts. The one is, that the Khalif 'Omar [r. 634–644] commanded the people to erect a building "in the western part of the Area, as a place of prayer for the Muslims;" and so they left this space (which is towards the south-eastern angle) unoccupied, in order not to go counter to his injunction. The other reason given is, that it was not found possible to extend the Main-building of the (Aksâ) Mosque as far as the south-east angle of the Area Wall, lest the (great) Mihrâb, in the centre-place at the end of the Mosque should not then have stood opposite the Rock under the Dome; and such a case was repugnant to them. But Allah alone knows the truth.

Source: Le Strange, Guy, trans. *Palestine under the Moslems: A Description of Syria and the Holy Land from* A.D. *650 to 1500.* Boston: Houghton, Mifflin and Company, 1890, pp. 98–99.

7. al-Muqaddasi's Tenth-Century Explanation of the Construction of Jerusalem's Dome of the Rock

Writing a century after Yaqubi (d. 897) (*see* Document 3), Al-Muqaddasi (d. c. 1000) provides a different explanation for the construction of the Dome of the Rock. He reports a conversation with his paternal uncle who told him that Abd al-Malik constructed the Dome of the Rock as an architectural expression of Muslim supremacy over the majority Christian population of Syria. Whether as an alternative pilgrimage site (al-Ya'qubi) or to demonstrate Islamic superiority (al-Muqaddasi), each explanation indicates that Abd al-Malik constructed the Dome of the Rock as an expression of his political and religious authority over Muslims and Christians alike.

Now one day I said, speaking to my father's brother, "O my uncle, verily it was not well of the Khalif al-Walîd [r. 705–715] to expend so much of the wealth of the Muslims on the Mosque at Damascus. Had he expended the same on making roads, or for caravanserais, or in the restoration of the Frontier Fortresses, it would have been more fitting and more excellent of him." But my uncle said to me in answer, "O my little son, thou hast not understanding! Verily al-Walîd was right, and he was prompted to a worthy work. For he beheld Syria to be a country that had long been occupied by the Christians, and he noted herein the beautiful churches still belonging to them, so enchantingly fair, and so renowned for their splendour, even as are the Kumâmah (the Church of the Holy Sepulchre at Jerusalem), and the churches of Lydda and Edessa. So he sought too build for the Muslims a mosque that should prevent their regarding these, and that should be unique and a wonder to the world. An in like manner is it now evident how the Khalif Abd al-Malik, noting the greatness of the Dome of the (Holy Sepulchre called) al-Kumâmah and its magnificence, was moved lest it should dazzle the minds of the Muslims, and hence erected above the Rock, the Dome which now is seen there?"

The Court (of the Haram Area) is paved in all parts; in its centre rises a Platform, like that in the Mosque at Medina, to which, from all four sides, ascend broad flights of steps. On this Platform stand four Domes. Of these, the Dome of the Chain, the Dome of the Ascension, and the Dome of the Prophet are of small size. Their domes are covered with sheet-lead, and are supported on marble pillars, being without walls.

In the centre of the Platform is the Dome of the Rock, which rises above an octagonal building having four gates, one opposite to each of the flights of steps leading up from the Court. These four are the Kiblah (or southern) Gate; the Gate of (the Angel) Israfil (to the east), the Gate al-Sûr (or of the Trumpet), to the north; and the Women's Gate (Bâb al-Nisâ), which last opens towards the west. All these are adorned with gold, and closing each of them is a beautiful door of cedar-wood finely worked in patterns. These last were sent hither by command of the mother of the Khalif al-Muqtadir-billah [r. 908–932]. Over each of the gates is a porch of marble, wrought with cedar-wood, with brass-work without; and in this porch, likewise, are doors, but these are unornamented.

Within the building are three concentric colonnades, with columns of the most beautiful marble, polished, that can be seen, and above is a low vaulting. Inside these (colonnades) is the central hall over the Rock; it is circular, not octagonal, and is surrounded by columns of polished marble supporting circular arches. Built above these, and rising high into the air, is the drum, in which are large windows; and over the drum is the Dome. The Dome, from the floor up to the pinnacle, which rises into the air, is in height 100 ells. From afar off you may perceive on the summit of the Dome the beautiful pinnacle (set thereon), the size of which is a fathom and a span. The Dome, externally, is completely covered with brass plates gilt, while the building itself, its floor, and its walls, and the drum, both within and without, are ornamented with marble and mosaics, after the manner that we shall describe when speaking of the Mosque of Damascus. The Cupola of the Dome is built in three sections; the inner is of ornamental panels. Next come iron beams interlaced, set in free, so that the wind may not cause the Cupola to shift; and the third casing is of wood, on which are fixed the outer plates. Up through the middle of the Cupola goes a passage-way, by which a workman may ascend to the pinnacle for aught that may be wanting, or in order to repair the structure. At the dawn, when the light of the sun first strikes on the Cupola, and the Drum reflects his rays, then is this edifice a marvelous sight to behold, and one such that in all Islam I have never seen the equal; neither have I heard tell of aught built in pagan times that could rival in grace the Dome of the Rock.

Source: Le Strange, Guy, trans. *Palestine under the Moslems: A Description of Syria and the Holy Land from* A.D. *650 to 1500.* Boston: Houghton, Mifflin and Company, 1890, pp. 117–118, 123–124.

8. Naser-e Khosraw's Description of the City of New Cairo in the Eleventh Century

Almost immediately after his conquest of Egypt in 969, the Fatimid general, Jawhar, began laying the foundations for the new Fatimid palace city, al-Qahira (Cairo). There are a number of legends about the founding of the city and the etymology of its name. According to one, Jawhar had staked out the perimeter of the city with wooden stakes and ropes with bells on them but wanted to wait to break ground until the astrologers determined the most propitious time. When a crow lit on one of the ropes, the workmen took the sound of the ringing bells as the signal to begin their work. Although the astrologers determined that Mars (al-Qahir, the Ruler) was in the ascendant—a bad sign—work commenced nevertheless. Another legend relates that the Fatimid Imam al-Mu'izz had instructed Jawhar before he left North Africa to build a new walled city and call it al-Qahira, for it would rule the world. According to yet another legend, the city was first called al-Mansuriyya (the Victorious; the name of the Fatimid capital in North Africa), but al-Mu'izz changed it to al-Qahira after his arrival 4 years later. Whatever the truth of these stories, Jawhar built the new Fatimid capital on a sandy plain north of Fustat [known as Old Cairo] where it was protected on the east by the Muqattam Hills and on the west by a canal (*khalij*) running along the east bank of the Nile.

Under Fatimid tutelage Egypt and its new capital became one of the wealthiest and most important cosmopolitan way stations for international trade and culture in the Mediterranean world, southwest Asia, and the Indian Ocean. The description of Cairo below is that of the Persian Ismaili traveler, Naser-e Khosraw (d. 1088). By time Naser-e Khosraw visited the city in 1047, the Fatimid capital had grown considerably since Jawhar laid its foundations some eight decades earlier. Saladin brought an end to the Fatimid caliphate in 1171, but Cairo and Egypt continued to flourish under his leadership and that of his Ayyubid successors (1171–1250) and of the Mamluk Sultans (1250–1517).

The city of New Cairo has five gates. . . . There is no wall, but the buildings are even stronger and higher than ramparts, and every house and building is itself a fortress. Most of the buildings are five stories tall, although some are six. Drinking water is from the Nile, and water carriers transport water by camel. The closer the well is to the river, the sweeter the well water; it becomes more brackish the farther you get from the Nile. Old and New Cairo are said to have fifty thousand camels belonging to water carriers. The water carriers who port water on their backs are separate: they have brass cups and jugs and go into the narrow lanes where a camel cannot pass.

In the midst of the houses in the city are gardens and orchards watered by wells. In the sultan's harem are the most beautiful gardens imaginable. Waterwheels have been constructed to irrigate these gardens. There are trees planted and pleasure parks built even on the roofs. At the time I was there, a house on a lot twenty by twelve ells was being rented for fifteen dinars a month. The house was four stories tall, three of which were rented out. The tenant wanted to take the topmost floor also for an additional five dinars, but the landlord would not give it to him, saying that he might want to go there sometimes, although, during the year we were there, he did not come twice. . . . All the houses of Cairo are built separate one from another, so that no one's trees or outbuildings are against anyone else's walls. Thus, whenever anyone needs to, he can open the walls of his house and add on, since it causes no detriment to anyone else.

Going west outside the city, you find a large canal called al-Khalij (Canal), which was built by the father of the present sultan, who has three hundred villages on his private property along the canal. The canal was cut from Old to New Cairo, where it turns and runs past the sultan's palace. Two kiosks are built at the head of the canal, one called Lulu (Pearl) and the other Jawhara (Jewel).

Cairo has four cathedral mosques where men pray on Fridays. One of these is called al-Azhar, another al-Nur, another the Mosque of al-Hakem, and the fourth the Mosque of al-Mo'ezz. This last mosque is outside the city on the banks of the Nile. When you face the *qebla* in Egypt, you have to turn toward the ascent of Aries. The distance between Old and New Cairo is less than a mile, Old Cairo being to the south and New Cairo to the north. The Nile flows through Old Cairo and reaches New Cairo, and the orchards and outbuildings of the two cities overlap. During the summer, when the plain and lowlands are inundated, only the sultan's garden, which is on a promontory and consequently not flooded, remains dry.

Source: Thackston, Wheeler M., trans. *Naser-e Khosraw's Book of Travels (Safarnama)*. Albany: State University of New York Press, 1986, pp. 46–47.

9. Excerpts from Nizam al-Mulk's *Book of Government or Rules for Kings* (Eleventh Century)

Nizam al-Mulk (d. 1092) served as the chief minister for two of the greatest Seljukid Sultans, Alp Arslan (r. 1063–1073) and his son, Malikshah (r. 1073–1092). Nizam al-Mulk was murdered in 1092 by the Ismaili Assassins who were the bane of the Seljukids and many other regimes in the middle ages. Although the Seljukids conquered the Middle East as Turkomans (that is, as free Muslim Turkish pastoral nomads), they soon sought to establish themselves as rulers of the settled agrarian world of Iran and Iraq. To do this, they adopted the trappings of Perso-Islamic kingship employed by the Abbasid caliphs in Baghdad and later by the Abbasids' Buyid overlords. Nizam al-Mulk (d. 1092), articulates this theory of kingship in his *Book of Government or Rules for Kings*. Composed at the behest of Malikshah (r. 1073–1092), the first chapter is titled "On the Turn of Fortune's Wheel and in Praise of the Master of the World—May God Confirm His Sovereignty." The opening paragraphs outline a vision of kingship in which God in His wisdom chooses the sultan to rule on His behalf. The sultan's duty is to provide justice and maintain order in society. If he does, he and his kingdom will prosper. If he does not, he will lose God's favor, be replaced by another, and the cycle begins anew.

The rest of Nizam al-Mulk's lengthy treatise is essentially a handbook for how to rule justly and to maintain order in the realm. According to Nizam al-Mulk, the upright administration of a just ruler necessarily results in prosperity among the agrarian peasants and among the traders in the towns and cities. Such prosperity also results in a full treasury with which the sultan can pay his soldiers, who are absolutely essential to protecting his throne against interlopers as well as maintaining order and economic prosperity in the realm so that his subjects "may live their lives in constant security and ever wish for his reign to continue." Although others had articulated similar theories of kingship based on the ancient Persian model, including the Abbasids and the Buyids, Nizam al-Mulk's iteration is one of the most influential and would continue to be used to legitimate regimes for centuries after its composition.

In every age and time God (be He exalted) chooses one member of the human race and, having adorned and endowed him with kingly virtues, entrusts him with the interests of the world and the well-being of His servants; He charges that person to close the doors of corruption, confusion and discord, and He imparts to him such dignity and majesty in the eyes and hearts of men, that under his just rule they may live their lives in constant security and ever wish for his reign to continue.

Whenever—God be our refuge!—there occurs any disobedience or disregard of divine laws on the part of His servants, or any failure in devotion and attention to the commands of The Truth (be He exalted), and He wishes to chasten them and make them taste the retribution for their deeds—may God not deal us such a fate, and keep us far from such a calamity!—verily the wrath of The Truth overtakes those people and He forsakes them for the vileness of their disobedience; anarchy rears its head in their midst, opposing swords are drawn, blood is shed, and whoever has the stronger hand does whatever he wishes, until those sinners are all destroyed in tumults and bloodshed, and the world becomes free and clear of them; and through the wickedness of such sinners may innocent persons too perish in the tumults; just as, by analogy, when a reed-bed catches fire every dry particle is burned also, because it is near to that which is dry.

Then by divine decree one human being acquires some prosperity and power, and according to his deserts The Truth bestows good fortune upon him and gives him wit and wisdom. . . . He selects ministers and their functionaries from among the people, and giving a rank and post to each, he relies upon them for the efficient conduct of affairs spiritual and temporal. If his subjects tread the path of obedience and busy themselves with their tasks he will keep them untroubled by hardships, so that they may pass their time at ease in the shadow of his justice. If one of his officers or ministers commits any impropriety or oppression, he will only keep him at his post provided that he responds to correction, advice or punishment, and wakes up from the sleep of negligence; if he fails to mend his ways, he will retain him no longer, but change him for someone who is deserving. . . .

Further he will bring to pass that which concerns the advance of civilization, such as constructing underground channels, digging main canals, building bridges across great waters, rehabilitating villages and farms, raising fortifications, building new towns, and erecting lofty buildings and magnificent dwellings; he will have inns built on the highways and schools for those who seek knowledge; for which things he will be renowned for ever; he will gather the fruit of this good works in the next world and blessings will be showered upon him.

Source: Darke, Hubert, trans. *The Book of Government or Rules for Kings: The Siyar al-Mulk or Siyasat-nama of Nizam al-Mulk.* Richmond, UK: Curzon Press, 2002, pp. 9–10.

10. Excerpts from al-Shayzari's *The Book of the Islamic Market Inspector* (Twelfth Century)

One of the most important officials of any Islamic administration was the *muhtasib* (public censor or market inspector) whose job it was to ensure the honesty and trustworthiness of the markets that were essential to the economic prosperity of the medieval Islamic world. Handbooks such as al-Shayzari's (d. 1193) twelfth-century *The Book of the Islamic Market Inspector* included prescriptions for the enforcement of public morality in the very public space of the marketplace as defined by Islamic law, including the moral and economic regulation of every profession one might find in a market: bakers, confectioners, sausage makers, money changers, slave traders, livestock traders, smiths, grain sellers, baths and their attendants, physicians, teachers, and so forth. The text below is excerpted from al-Shayzari's chapter titled "Supervision of the Markets and Roads."

The markets must be situated on an elevated and spacious site as they were in Ancient Rome. If the market is not paved, there should be a pavement on either side of it for the people to walk on in winter. Nobody is permitted to bring a shop bench from the roofed passageway into the main thoroughfare as this obstructs passers-by. The *muhtasib* must remove and forbid this because of the harm it may do people. The people of every trade should be allotted a special market for which their trade is known, as this is more economically sound for them and will bring them better business. The *muhtasib* should also segregate the shops of those whose trade requires the lighting of fires, like bakers and cooks, from the perfumers and cloth merchants due to their dissimilarity and the possibility of damage.

When the *muhtasib* is unable to understand the people's occupations, to each trade he may appoint an *arif* who is a virtuous fellow tradesman, is experienced in their trade, aware of their swindles and frauds, is well known for his trustworthiness and reliability and who will oversee their affairs and acquaint the *muhtasib* with what they are doing. The *arif* must inform the *muhtasib* of all the commodities and merchandise brought into their market and the current prices, as well as other matters of which the *muhtasib* ought to be aware. It is related that the Prophet said: "Over every trade seek the assistance of a virtuous fellow tradesman."

The *muhtasib* is not permitted to set the prices of merchandise over the heads of its owners nor to oblige them to sell it at a fixed price. This is because during the time of the Prophet prices rose and the people said to him: "O Prophet, set the prices for us." But the Prophet replied: "God is the one who sets prices. I wish to meet God and want nobody to demand that I commit a transgression against a person or money."

If the *muhtasib* comes across someone who is hoarding a certain foodstuff, that is, buying it when prices are low and waiting until they rise so that the food becomes more expensive, he should compel him to sell it. This is because monopolizing is unlawful and it is a duty to prevent what is unlawful. The Prophet said: "He who brings in merchandise is blessed, and he who monopolizes it is cursed."

It is not permitted to meet a caravan, that is, for people to go outside the town and meet it as it approaches, telling them that the market is slow and thus buying cheaply from them. The Prophet forbade the meeting of a caravan and forbade selling merchandise until it is taken to the market. If the *muhtasib* finds anyone intending to do this, he should chastise and prevent him.

Source: al-Shayzari, Abd al-Rahman ibn Nasr. *The Book of the Islamic Market Inspector.* Translated by R.P. Buckley. Oxford and New York: Oxford University Press, 1999, pp. 36–38.

11. Medieval Islamic Recipes

Rather than dividing meals into discrete courses as modern Americans tend to do, in the medieval Islamic world more than one dish (for example, a lamb dish and a chicken dish) would be served at the table at the same time. It was customary that a dish of dates would be present with which to begin the meal. A fruit salad of some type often was eaten to conclude the meal. I have included four recipes here—a lamb recipe (*Ibrahimiya*), a chicken recipe (*Shaljamiya*), a cold dish recipe (*Bahinjan mahshi*), and a date dish recipe (*Rutab mu'assal*). Because specific quantities are rarely given in medieval Arabic cookbooks, one must do some guessing, especially with respect to spices and condiments. Essentially, the cook is advised to season to taste, "God willing" (the formula with which many recipes conclude). The recipes below are taken from David Waines, *In a Caliph's Kitchen* (London: Riad el-Rayyes Books, 1989). As the title indicates, these are dishes that would be found in the kitchens of the caliphs and other elites of medieval Islamic society. Waines recreates the medieval recipes into specific Western measurements in quantities sufficient to feed four.

1. *Ibrahimiya* – made with lamb (named after the eight-century gourmand, Ibrahim ibn al-Mahdi, the brother of Harun al-Rashid) Cut the meat into medium sized pieces, and place in a casserole with water to cover, salt to

taste, and boil until the juices are given off. Throw in a bag of stout cotton containing coriander, ginger, pepper, all ground fine, then add some pieces of cinnamon bark and mastic. Cut up two or three onions very small and throw in. Mince red meat and make into kabobs as usual, and add. When the ingredients are cooked, remove the bag of seasonings. Add to the broth the juice of sweet old grapes or, if unprocurable, of fresh grapes, squeezing in the hand without skinning, or else distilled vinegar. The juice is strained then sweet almonds are chopped fine and moistened in water, the grape juice is poured on them, and the mixture is sweetened slightly with white sugar, so as not to be too sour. Leave over the fire an hour to settle. Wipe the sides of the casserole with a clean cloth and sprinkle with rose water. When settled, remove. (Waines, 33)

2. *Shaljamiya*—made with chicken and turnips (*shaljam*, hence the name, *shaljamiya*) Take the breasts of chicken or other fowl, cut into thin slices and place in a pot with a lot of oil adding water to cover. Remove the scum. Throw in chick peas and olive oil and the white of onion and when cooked, sprinkle on top with pepper and cumin. Next take the turnip and, boil it until cooked and then mash it so that no hard bits remain in it. Strain in a sieve and place in the pot. Then take shelled almonds and put in a stone mortar adding to it a piece of cheese and bray very fine. Break over this the whites of five eggs and pound until it becomes very soft. Put this mixture over the turnip and if there is milk in it, put in a bit of nard and leave on the fire to settle. Serve it with mustard. (Waines, 35)

3. *Badhinjan mahshi*—cold dish made with eggplant Take the eggplant and stew it. Cut it up into small pieces after stewing. Next take a serving dish and put into it vinegar, white sugar and crushed almonds, saffron, caraway and cinnamon. Then take the eggplant and the fried onion and put them in the dish. Pour oil over it and serve, God willing. (Waines, 37)

4. *Rutab mu'assal*—"Honeyed Dates" Take freshly gathered dates and lay in the shade and air for a day. Then remove the stones and stuff with peeled almonds. For every ten *ratl*s of dates take two *ratl*s of honey. Boil over the fire with two *ugiya* of rose water and half a dirham of saffron, then throw in the dates, stirring for an hour. Remove and allow to cool. When cold, sprinkle with fine-ground sugar scented with musk, camphor and hyacinth. Put into glass preserving jars, sprinkling on top some of the scented ground sugar. Cover until the weather is cold and chafing dishes are brought in (Waines, 39)

Measurements used in medieval Arabic cooking

1 *ratl* = 12 *ugiya*s = 16 ounces = 1 pint
1 *ugiya* = 10 *dirham*s
1 *dirham* = 6 *daniq*

Source: Waines, David. *In a Caliph's Kitchen.* London: Riad el-Rayyes Books, 1989, pp. 33, 35, 37, 39.

Appendix: Medieval Islamic Caliphs

Rashidun Caliphs
  Abu Bakr (632–634)
  Umar (634–644)
  Uthman (644–656)
  'Ali ibn Abi Talib (656–661)

Umayyad Caliphs (Damascus)
  Mu'awiya I (661–680)
  Yazid (680–683)
  Mu'awiya II (683)
  Marwan I (684–685)
  Abd al-Malik (685–705)
  al-Walid (705–715)
  Sulayman (715–717)
  Umar II (717–720)
  Yazid II (720–724)
  Hisham (724–743)
  al-Walid II (743–744)
  Yazid III (744)
  Ibrahim (744)
  Marwan II (744–750)

Abbasid Caliphs (Baghdad)
  al-Saffah (749–754)
  al-Nansur (754–775)
  al-Mahdi (775–785)
  al-Hadi (785–786)
  al-Rashid (786–809)
  al-Amin (809–813)
  al-Ma'mun (813–833)
  al-Mu'tasim (833–842)
  al-Wathiq (842–847)
  al-Mutawakkil (847–861)
  al-Muntasir (861–862)
  al-Musta'in (862–866)
  al-Mu'tazz (866–869)
  al-Muhtadi (869–870)

al-Mu'tamid (870–892)
al-Mu'tadid (892–902)
al-Muktafi (902–908)
al-Muqtadir (908–932)
al-Qahir (932–934)
al-Radi (934–940)
al-Muttaqi (940–944)
al-Mustakfi (944–946)
al-Muti' (946–974)
al-Ta'i' (974–991)
al-Qadir (991–1031)
al-Qa'im (1031–1075)
al-Muqtadi (1075–1094)
al-Mustazhir (1094–1118)
al-Mustarshid (1118–1135)
al-Rashid (1135–1136)
al-Muqtafi (1136–1160)
al-Mustanjid (1160–1170)
al-Mustadi' (1170–1180)
al-Nasir (1180–1225)
al-Zahir (1125–1126)
al-Mustansir (1226–1242)
al-Musta'sim (1242–1258)

Twelver Shi'i Imams
  'Ali ibn Abi Talib (d. 661)
  al-Hasan (d. 669)
  al-Husayn (d. 680)
  Ali Zayn al-Abidin (d. 713)
  Muhammad al-Baqir (d. 735)
  Ja'far al-Sadiq (d. 765)
  Musa al-Kazim (d. 799)
  Ali al-Rida (d. 818)
  Muhammad al-Jawad (d. 835)
  Ali al-Hadi (d. 868)
  al-Hasan al-Askari (d. 874)
  Muhammad al-Mahdi (in occultation, 874)

Ismaili Fatimid Caliphs (Cairo, North Africa)

Ubayd Allah al-Mahdi (909–934)
al-Qa'im (934–946)
al-Mansur (946–953)
al-Mu'izz (953–975)
al-'Aziz (975–996)
al-Hakim (996–1021)
al-Zahir (1021–1036)

al-Mustansir (1036–1094)
al-Musta'li (1094–1101)
al-Amir (1101–1130)
al-Hafiz (1130–1149)
al-Zafir (1149–1154)
al-Fa'iz (1154–1160)
al-'Adid (1160–1171)